ANGLO-
AMERICAN
LAW

A COMPARISON

ANGLO-

AMERICAN

LAW

A COMPARISON

Dr. Michael Arnheim

TALBOT
PUBLISHING
Clark, New Jersey

ISBN 978-1-61619-632-5

TALBOT PUBLISHING

AN IMPRINT OF

THE LAWBOOK EXCHANGE, LTD.

33 Terminal Avenue
Clark, New Jersey 07066-1321

*Please see our website for a selection of our other publications
and fine facsimile reprints of classic works of legal history:*
www.lawbookexchange.com

Library of Congress Cataloging-in-Publication Data

Names: Arnheim, M. T. W. (Michael T. W.), author.
Title: Anglo-American law : a comparison / Dr. Michael Arnheim, Barrister at Law, Sometime Fellow of St. John's College, Cambridge.
Description: Clark, NJ : Talbot Publishing, 2019. | Includes bibliographical references and
index. | Summary: "English and American law share a common origin. Yet the differences
between them are now greater than the similarities. Anglo-American Law: A Comparison identifies the differences between the two systems of law and their constitutions.
From Anglo-Saxon law to Brexit, from the Founders to President Trump, Arnheim
compares the English and American legal systems and shows how they differ, particularly
in matters of constitutional law, tort, civil and human rights, abortion, codification, freedom of religion, privacy, judicial review, defamation, and more"-- Provided by publisher.
Identifiers: LCCN 2019044238 | ISBN 9781616196325 (hardback)
Subjects: LCSH: Common law. | Law--Great Britain. | Constitutional law--Great Britain. |
Law--United States. | Constitutional law--United States. | Comparative law.
Classification: LCC KD671 .A975 2019 | DDC 349.41--dc23
LC record available at https://lccn.loc.gov/2019044238

Printed in the United States of America on acid-free paper

To the Sacred Memory of My Beloved Parents

Dr. Wilhelm Arnheim (1901-75),
a wise medical doctor and true polymath, with the driest sense of humor
and
Mrs. Vicky Arnheim (1905-90),
a brilliant musician, gifted teacher, dedicated social organizer,
great cook, and loving mother
and
To the sacred memory of my beloved grandmother, "Oma"
Mrs. Martha Arnheim (1875-1965),
an eternally cheerful and optimistic courageous spirit
who taught me German and whose wonderful humorous tales
of the old Germany will remain with me always.

TABLE OF CONTENTS

PREFACE

This book has had a long gestation period. At the age of 17 my entry in the Royal Commonwealth Society Essay Competition was a comparison between the British and American constitutions, for which I was awarded a special prize. As a junior barrister I wrote a fortnightly column in the *Solicitors Journal*, in which I dealt with issues of US law as well as English law. In 1994 I was invited to edit the comparative *Common Law* volume in the prestigious *International Library of Essays in Law and Legal Theory* published by Ashgate Dartmouth. As a practicing English barrister I have also collaborated with American attorneys on international cases. And most of my previous 20 published books, on both English Law and the US Constitution, have been a preparation for this book.

My classical and historical training has served me in good stead in my study and practice of law. Professor Theo Haarhoff taught me how difficult it sometimes is to differentiate between objective views and subjective views that mimic objectivity. Professor Hugo Jones, my doctoral supervisor in Cambridge, and Professor John Crook, my mentor and colleague at St. John's College, Cambridge, were two of the most tolerant minds that I have ever come across, but they never made the mistake of equating toleration with acceptance of all views as equally valid.

I owe a special debt of gratitude to my former student, colleague and longtime friend, Attorney Tom Malnati of Florida, without whose selfless assistance this book would have taken a lot longer to complete. Thanks also to my friends Jack Ward, Shola Awoderu, Brian Abramson, and special thanks to my cousin Colonel Ralph Holstein for his constant encouragement and vibrant conversation.

Not least, I must thank my editor, Valerie Horowitz, for all her hard work. And I also owe a debt of gratitude to Greg Talbot, President of the Lawbook Exchange Ltd., of which Talbot Publishing is an imprint. It is now more than 20 years since I first happened upon his bookstore, which was then in the fur district of New York City. For further information about myself, see: https://en.wikipedia.org/wiki/Michael_Arnheim.

As I don't have a cat, I can't blame it for clambering over the keyboard. The sole responsibility for any mistakes rests on me. The law as stated in the book is correct as of Labor Day, Monday, September 2, 2019.

Labor Day, 2019

STOP PRESS

On September 24, 2019, a unanimous 11-member UK Supreme Court (UKSC) decided that Prime Minister Boris Johnson's advice to the Queen to prorogue (i.e. suspend) Parliament for five weeks was unlawful and that the Queen's order of prorogation (an exercise of the royal prerogative) was accordingly also "unlawful, void and of no effect." [*R. (Miller) v. The Prime Minister* [2019] UKSC 41.] . This was based on the decision in *The Case of Proclamations* that "the King hath no prerogative but that which the law of the land allows him." [1610] EWHC KB J22. What this means is that the royal prerogative is subject to regulation by Parliament—not by the courts, as the UKSC appears to believe. The UKSC decision also does nothing to dispel the impression of the disarray of UK law. It reverses the unanimous decision of the English High Court (made up of the Chief Justice, the Master of the Rolls and the President of the Queen's Bench Division), which concluded in regard to prorogation that: "It is not a matter for the courts." Adding: "The Prime Minister's decision that Parliament should be prorogued at the time and for the duration chosen and the advice given to Her Majesty to do so in the present case were political." [2019] EWHC 2381 (QB). My own view is that this was the correct decision and should have been affirmed by the UKSC.

GLOSSARY

Jurisdictions: **The United Kingdom (UK)** has three separate jurisdictions: England & Wales, Scotland, and Northern Ireland. (The Republic of Ireland has its own separate jurisdiction.) Politically speaking, England and Scotland united in 1707 to form the United Kingdom of Great Britain, and in 1801 Ireland joined to form the United Kingdom of Great Britain and Ireland. In 1922 Southern Ireland broke away, leaving the UK as the United Kingdom of Great Britain and Northern Ireland, which remains the position today. In this book, the term "English law" is used for all law that applies only to England and Wales, and also sometimes more generally. Law that applies to the whole of the UK, like constitutional law, is referred to as "UK law" or "British law."

The United States (US) is made up of 52 separate jurisdictions: Federal, the 50 states, and the District of Columbia. When referring to Federal law I sometimes use the term "American" as synonymous with "US" law.

Courts: **UK**: The UK Supreme Court (UKSC), established in 2009, is the highest court in the UK. It replaced the Appellate Committee of the House of Lords, usually referred to simply as the "House of Lords." It is important not to confuse this with the House of Lords as a branch of the legislature, the second chamber of Parliament. The term "Supreme Court" is also confusing, as, between 1873 and 2009, it referred to the English High Court, Court of Appeal and (from 1972) the Crown Court. The High Court of England & Wales, is a court of first instance for high value cases and cases deemed to be of high importance, and also exercises a supervisory jurisdiction over most lower courts and tribunals. The High Court has three divisions: Queen's Bench (while there is a female Monarch), Chancery, and Family Division. Queen's Bench includes the Administrative Court, which may sit as a Divisional Court (two judges). Lower value claims are dealt with by County Courts.

US – Federal: The US Supreme Court is the highest court in the United States. It hears appeals from the US Courts of Appeals (the next level down), which in turn hear appeals from the US District Courts, which are general federal trial courts. However, most of the cases heard by the US Supreme Court are cases of judicial review, in which the Court decides whether a law or executive decision at federal or state level is constitutional.

US – States: Most state court systems consist of three levels: trial courts, often designated as District Courts, then Courts of Appeals, and finally State Supreme Courts. Different states use different designations for their courts. The New York Supreme Court, for example, is a trial court, and the highest court in that state is called the New York Court of Appeals, whereas in California the Supreme Court is the highest state court and trial courts are called Superior Courts.

Judicial designations: **UK**: "Halsbury J" would denote a High Court judge; "Halsbury LJ" a Lord Justice of Appeal, i.e. a judge of the Court of Appeals; and "Halsbury MR," or "Lord Halsbury MR," Master of the Rolls, the head of the Court of Appeal (Civil Division). The term "Law Lord" refers to a Lord of Appeal in Ordinary, a member of the Appellate Committee of the House of Lords, usually just referred to as the "House of Lords," which was replaced by the UKSC in 2009. Members of the UKSC are called "Justices," but are given the courtesy title of "Lord" or "Lady" without the right to sit in the House of Lords as a Parliament.

US: The US Supreme Court is made up of the Chief Justice and eight Associate Justices, usually just referred to as "Justices." All other federal judges (sometimes referred to as Article III judges) are called "Judges." In state courts practice varies, but the title "Justice" is usually reserved for the highest—and the lowest—members of the judiciary. In most states, members of the State Supreme Court are called "Justices"—and in a number of states "justices of the peace" hear minor criminal cases and sometimes small claims. In New York, uniquely as usual, the members of the Supreme Court, a trial court, are called "justices," while the members of the New York Court of Appeals, the highest court in the state, are called "Judges." In the US generally, the letter "J." after a name can mean either "Judge" or "Justice."

Plaintiff/Claimant: In 1999 the time-honored "Plaintiff," which had been in use since 1278, was replaced in English civil courts with the lame "Claimant," cutting England & Wales off from the rest of the Common Law world, which continues to use "Plaintiff." "Pursuer," the feisty Scottish designation for Plaintiff, would have been a better choice.

Damage & Damages: These are not synonyms, as is sometimes assumed, nor is the one the plural of the other. The two terms are in a sense reciprocal to each other. "Damage" refers to the injury or loss suffered by a plaintiff. "Damages" refers to compensation for damage—the money claimed by the Plaintiff or awarded by a court to compensate the Plaintiff.

Magna Carta: Latin for "Great Charter." This is a document dating back to the year 1215 containing a number of concessions made by King John of England to his rebellious barons. It was revised and reissued several times, finally by Edward I in 1297, when it was formally enrolled as a statute. Most of it has been repealed, but the most important surviving provision reads: "XXIX. No freeman shall be arrested or imprisoned, or be deprived of his rights or property, or be outlawed or exiled ... except by the lawful judgment of his peers or by the law of the land." Such is the veneration accorded Magna Carta in America that in 1957 the American Bar Association erected as memorial to it in England. And the 1297 reissue of Magna Carta (sold at auction in 2007 for $21.3 million) sits in a glass case in the National Archives rotunda in Washington DC – right beside the original texts of the Declaration of Independence and the US Constitution. Here are a few examples of ways Magna Carta may have influenced the American Founding Fathers, as evidenced in the Declaration of Independence and the US Constitution:

- Taxation without representation: Only indirectly.
- Trial by jury: The right to be tried by your "peers" is often taken to foreshadow trial by jury. The right to a jury trial is still alive and well in America and enshrined in the Sixth and Seventh Amendments of the US Constitution, In England trial by jury has largely been abolished, except in cases of serious crime or "hybrid" offenses "triable either way" (i.e. either summarily in a magistrates' court or on indictment before a judge and jury in the Crown Court.)
- Habeas Corpus: This important privilege (not a right) exists in both England and America. It is enshrined in the Habeas Corpus Act 1679 and Article I Section 9 of the US Constitution respectively. It is an application challenging unlawful detention. Magna Carta may be considered a trailblazer for this privilege.

Due Process/Rule of Law: Magna Carta's prohibition on anyone's arrest, imprisonment, or deprivation of rights or property "except by the law of the land" was glossed in a 1354

statute from the reign of Edward III (1327-77) as meaning: "No
man of what state or condition he be, shall be put out of his
lands or tenements nor taken, nor disinherited, nor put to death,
without he be brought to answer by due process of law." [28
Edw. 3, c. 3.] This is the earliest use of the phrase "due process of
law." However, the phrase gradually disappears from view in
England during the 18th century and is ultimately replaced by the
term "the rule of law," which is related but not synonymous.
"Due process" appears in both the Fifth and Fourteenth
Amendments to the US Constitution. The Fifth Amendment
version reads: "No person shall…be deprived of life, liberty, or
property, without due process of law." The meaning of this
would appear to be simply that proper legal procedure must be
observed in any trial. But its meaning has been greatly expanded
by linking it with the Fourteenth Amendment and expanding
"due process" beyond procedure to "substantive due process"
encompassing rights considered by the Court to be
"fundamental." Originalists like Justices Scalia and Thomas have
opposed the whole concept of "substantive due process," which
Antonin Scalia described as an "oxymoron" and also as a "judicial
usurpation." The term "rule of law," which is more common in
England than America, was defined by A.V. Dicey in 1885 in a
similar way to procedural due process: "No man is punishable or
can be lawfully made to suffer in body or goods except for a
distinct breach of law established in the ordinary legal manner
before the ordinary Courts of the land." [Dicey (1885).] The
recent idea that "the rule of law" is potentially in competition
with the sovereignty of Parliament is fallacious, because that
would be an attempt to demote the sovereignty of Parliament
from its time-honored role as the bedrock principle of the
British Constitution, which it is not within the power of any
court to do. [See the *Privacy International* case discussed on pages
28ff. of Chapter 1; and see also Chapters 14 and 17.]

Democracy: Democracy has two main meanings. It can *either* refer simply to a *method* of electing a government in which every citizen has a vote; *or* it can refer to a type of government based on a certain value system. Under the former definition, there is no restriction on what policies the government can implement, provided it has a popular mandate. It is in this sense that "populist" or "illiberal" democracies can still qualify as democracies. The second definition includes a variety of types of government as well, ranging from Western liberal democracies to communist "people's republics" and to fascist states, each of which believes that it alone is a true democracy.

Rights vs. Privileges: The confusion between rights and privileges is a serious fallacy. Rights are entitlements that belong equally to everyone, whereas privileges are entitlements enjoyed only by a minority of the population. For rights to be genuine they must be *equal.* The right to life, the right to freedom of speech and the right to freedom of religion are examples of rights. Discrimination by the majority against a minority group on whatever basis is a denial of equal rights. In the US, "affirmative action," or positive discrimination in favor of groups previously discriminated against, is permitted by the US Supreme Court – but quotas are not. Why not? Affirmative action is undeniably discriminatory, but quotas are a blatant example of privilege. Whenever rights are in issue, it is important to determine whether they really are rights or whether they are privileges in disguise.

Yo-yo case: This is my own made-up term for the all-too-frequent phenomenon in the UK of a case being decided one way at first instance, reversed on appeal and then reversed back again on final appeal. This encourages appeals and detracts from certainty and predictability in the law—and therefore from justice.

TABLE OF CASES
UNITED KINGDOM & EUROPEAN

TABLE OF CASES
UNITED STATES

ANGLO-
AMERICAN
LAW

A COMPARISON

PART I

SUPREME LAW

Under the US Constitution there is a separation of powers system of government, with checks and balances between the three branches of government, the legislature, the executive and the judiciary. By contrast, the bedrock principle of the British Constitution is the sovereignty of Parliament. Paradoxically, however, in practice the courts in the United Kingdom are probably even more dominant than their counterparts in the United States.

In the United Kingdom, judicial power has expanded greatly at the expense of the executive and has also eroded parliamentary sovereignty to some extent. This is largely but not entirely the product of judicial activism. But it is also partly the result of the courts' filling the vacuum left by Parliament's dereliction of duty over many years in failing to codify or even to do much in the way of consolidating, the law—or even to respond to earnest entreaties by the judiciary to pass legislation. The resulting spate of judge-made law, lacking as it almost invariably is, in principle, certainty or predictability, has left the law in a state of disarray, imperiling both justice and the rule of law.

In the United States the nuclear power of judicial review enables the courts, and especially the US Supreme Court, to strike down Acts of Congress as well as Executive acts. However, this formidable power is mostly exercised responsibly, with decisions resting on "black letter" authority. There have been some US Supreme Court decisions which have adopted strained interpretations of the Constitution or appear to have been politically motivated. But, with the possible exception of *Marbury v. Madison* (1803) itself, it would be hard to find any motivated primarily by judicial activism—a feature all too common in Britain.

It is also important to note that the dominance of the judiciary at federal level in the United States is not replicated at state level, where legislation and other forms of black-letter or pseudo-black-letter law hold sway. State courts *do* have the power of judicial review enabling them to strike down state laws, but the power of state courts over state legislatures is constrained in various ways.

1

UNITED KINGDOM
THE SOVEREIGNTY OF PARLIAMENT

In both the British and American Constitutions the power to make law is entrusted to the legislature: the UK Parliament and the US Congress respectively. But there the similarity ends.

In the United States, legislation passed by Congress and approved by the President becomes an Act of Congress or a statute and has the force of law—subject to judicial review. This nuclear power allows federal courts, and especially the US Supreme Court, to strike down or set aside Acts of Congress held to be unconstitutional.

Under the (unwritten) UK Constitution, Parliament is subject to no such control. On the contrary. Parliament is sovereign, and its sovereignty is expressed by means of Acts of Parliament, or statutes, passed by the House of Commons and the House of Lords with the assent of the Crown (that is, the King or Queen).

"The most fundamental rule"

This principle was well stated by Chief Justice Lord Thomas of Cwmgiedd delivering the judgment of the High Court (the Divisional Court of Queen's Bench) in a recent leading constitutional case:

> "It is common ground that the most fundamental rule of UK constitutional law is that the Crown in Parliament is sovereign and that legislation enacted by the Crown with the consent of both Houses of Parliament is supreme (we will use

the familiar shorthand and refer simply to Parliament).
Parliament can, by enactment of primary legislation,, change
the law of the land in any way it chooses. There is no superior
form of law than primary legislation, save only where
Parliament has itself made provision to allow that to happen.
The European Communities Act (ECA) 1972, which confers
precedence on EU law, is the sole example of this. But even
then Parliament remains sovereign and supreme, and has
continuing power to remove the authority given to other law
by earlier primary legislation. Put shortly, Parliament has
power to repeal ECA 1972 if it wishes." [*R* (*on the application of
Gina Miller & another*) *v. Secretary of State for Exiting the
European Union* [2016] EWHC 2768 (Admin).]

This was endorsed by the UK Supreme Court in the same case in
January 2017. Delivering the judgment of the 8–3 majority, Lord
Neuberger, President of the Court, held that:

"Parliamentary sovereignty is a fundamental principle of the
UK constitution, as was conclusively established in" a number
of statutes, notably the Bill of Rights 1688/89 and the Act of
Settlement 1701 in England and Wales, the Claim of Right
Act 1689 in Scotland, and the Acts of Union 1706 and 1707 in
England and Wales and in Scotland respectively. (Northern
Ireland joined the United Kingdom pursuant to the Acts of
Union 1800 in Britain and Ireland)." [*R* (*on the application of
Gina Miller & another*) *v. Secretary of State for Exiting the
European Union* [2017] UKSC 5.]

"Grotesque expression"

Lord Neuberger then went on to cite briefly Dicey's famous
summary of the same principle. Here is the full classic statement
of the principle as made by Professor A.V. Dicey (1835–1922) in
his *Introduction to the Study of the Law of the Constitution*, first
published in 1885 (with a further seven editions up to 1915):

"The sovereignty of Parliament is (from a legal point of view) the dominant characteristic of our political institutions. ... Parliament means, in the mouth of a lawyer (though the word has often a different sense in ordinary conversation), the King, the House of Lords, and the House of Commons; these three bodies acting together may be aptly described as the 'King in Parliament,' and constitute Parliament. The principle of Parliamentary sovereignty means neither more nor less than this, namely that Parliament thus defined has, under the English Constitution, the right to make or unmake any law whatever; and further, that no person or body is recognised by the law of England as having a right to override or set aside the legislation of Parliament. ... The important thing is to make clear that the doctrine of Parliamentary sovereignty is, both on its positive and on its negative side, fully recognised by the law of England."

Dicey goes on to quote a remark made by the Genevan jurist Jean Louis De Lolme (1740–1806) in his *Constitution de l'Angleterre*, published in 1771: "De Lolme has summed up the matter in a grotesque expression which has become almost proverbial. 'It is a fundamental principle with English lawyers, that Parliament can do everything but make a woman a man, and a man a woman.'" It may be said that even this limitation on the scope of parliamentary legislation fell away with the enactment of the Gender Recognition Act 2004, which allows people in certain circumstances to change their gender.

Even more authoritative than Dicey is Blackstone—Sir William Blackstone (1723–1780), a judge and first Professor of English Law at the University of Oxford, and author of the four-volume *Commentaries on the Laws of England*, first published between 1765 and 1769, which, despite its modest title, was in reality nothing less than a thoroughly researched, systematic and comprehensive exposition of the "primary rules and fundamental principles" of English law at the time.

"What they do, no authority on earth can undo"

Blackstone heartily endorsed the characterization by the famous 17th century judge and jurist Sir Edward Coke (1552–1634) of Parliament as sovereign—in Blackstone's words, "this being the place where that absolute despotic power, which must in all governments reside somewhere, is entrusted by the constitution of these kingdoms":

> The power and jurisdiction of parliament, says Sir Edward Coke, is so transcendent and absolute, that it cannot be confined, either for causes or persons, within any bounds. And of this high court he adds, it may be truly said *"si antiquitatem spectes, est vetustissima; si dignitatem, est honoratissima; si juridictionem, est capacissima."* It hath sovereign and uncontrolable authority in making, confirming, enlarging, restraining, abrogating, repealing, reviving, and expounding of laws, concerning matters of all possible denominations, ecclesiastical, or temporal, civil, military, maritime, or criminal: this being the place where that absolute despotic power, which must in all governments reside somewhere, is entrusted by the constitution of these kingdoms. All mischiefs and grievances, operations and remedies, that transcend the ordinary course of the laws, are within the reach of this extraordinary tribunal. It can regulate or new model the succession to the crown; as was done in the reign of Henry VIII and William III. It can alter the established religion of the land; as was done in a variety of instances, in the reigns of king Henry VIII and his three children. It can change and create afresh even the constitution of the kingdom and of parliaments themselves; as was done by the act of union, and the several statutes for triennial and septennial elections. It can, in short, do every thing that is not naturally impossible; and therefore some have not scrupled to call its power, by a figure rather too bold, the omnipotence of parliament. True it is, that what they do, no authority upon earth can undo. ... And, as Sir Matthew Hale observes, this being the highest and greatest court, over which none other

can have jurisdiction in the kingdom, if by any means a misgovernment should any way fall upon it, the subjects of this kingdom are left without all manner of remedy. [Blackstone (1765–1769), Vol. I, p.160ff.]

It is no accident that Blackstone refers to Parliament as a court: "this high court," "this extraordinary tribunal," "the highest and greatest court." Parliament, or, more, particularly the House of Lords (or, between 1948 and 2009, strictly speaking its Appellate Committee) was literally always the highest court in the United Kingdom until its judicial functions were transferred to a newly created "United Kingdom Supreme Court" in 2009.* But, besides this, Parliament in its capacity as a legislature had long been designated the "High Court of Parliament" to underline its superiority over any ordinary law court. The Oxford English Dictionary (under "Court IV.10.") quotes a reference to the impeachment of the Duke of Suffolk in Paston Letters No. 76, line 105, dating from the year 1450: "We … pray that this be enacte in this your High Courte of Parlement." Likewise, in Shakespeare's Henry IV Part 2, v.ii.134, dating from 1597, the "High Court of Parliament" mentioned here by King Henry V refers to parliament as a deliberative and advisory assembly rather than as a court of law: "Now call we our High Court of Parliament. And let us choose such Limbes of Noble Counsaile/ That the great body of our state may go /In equal rank with the best govern'd nation." Similarly, in the Book of Common Prayer of 1662 we find "A Prayer for the High Court of Parliament, to be read during their

---

* This designation, copied from its American counterpart, caused not a little confusion. Between 1981 and 2009 there was, under the Appellate Committee of the House of Lords. a "Supreme Court of England and Wales," made up of the Court of Appeal, the High Court and the Crown Court, but excluding all Scottish and Northern Ireland courts.

Session"—clearly a reference to parliamentary legislative sessions rather than to any judicial business.

As Parliament is the highest court in the land, no other court can strike down any Act of Parliament, and, moreover, as we shall see, Parliament can revoke any decision made by any other court—which is still the legal position today.

"Subversive of all government"

Here is Blackstone's explanation of why no court can strike down any Act of Parliament, including even one that is "unreasonable":

> Acts of parliament derogatory from the power of subsequent parliaments bind not. ... Because the legislature, being in truth the sovereign power, is always of equal, always of absolute authority: it acknowledges no superior upon earth, which the prior legislature must have been, if its ordinances could bind a subsequent parliament. ... 10. Lastly, acts of parliament that are impossible to be performed are of no validity: and if there arise out of them collaterally any absurd consequences, manifestly contradictory to common reason, they are, with regard to those collateral consequences, void. I lay down the rule with these restrictions; though I know it is generally laid down more largely, that acts of parliament contrary to reason are void. But if the parliament will positively enact a thing to be done which is unreasonable, I know of no power in the ordinary forms of the constitution, that is vested with authority to control it: and the examples usually alleged in support of this sense of the rule do none of them prove, that, where the main object of a statute is unreasonable, the judges are at liberty to reject it; for that were to set the judicial power above that of the legislature, which would be subversive of all government. But where some collateral matter arises out of the general words, and happens to be unreasonable; there the judges are in decency to conclude that this consequence was not foreseen by the parliament, and therefore they are at liberty to expound the statute by equity, and only *quoad hoc* [as to this] disregard it. Thus if an act of

parliament gives a man power to try all causes, that arise within his manor of Dale; yet, if a cause should arise in which he himself is party, the act is construed not to extend to that, because it is unreasonable that any man should determine his own quarrel. But, if we could conceive it possible for the parliament to enact, that he should try as well his own causes as those of other persons, there is no court that has power to defeat the intent of the legislature, when couched in such evident and express words, as leave no doubt whether it was the intent of the legislature or no. [Blackstone, *Commentaries on the Laws of England*, Vol. I, p. 91.]

After reiterating the principle of the sovereignty of Parliament, Blackstone here proceeds to dispose of the proposition that "acts of parliament contrary to reason are void." His objection to this proposition is a *tour de force*: if judges had the right to strike down even an unreasonable Act of Parliament, "that were to set the judicial power above that of the legislature, which would be subversive of all government." Supporters of an activist judiciary would take issue with this. Judges, they would remonstrate, are trained professionals and politically neutral. So they should be allowed wide latitude to strike down statutes that they adjudge to be unreasonable—and should also have the right to make new law when they deem it necessary.

Letters a foot high

Blackstone's answer needs to be printed in letters a foot high: *"That were to set the judicial power above that of the legislature, which would be subversive of all government."* It may appear strange that Blackstone, himself a High Court judge (1770–1780) after serving as a Member of Parliament (1761–1770), considered it "subversive of all government" for the judiciary to have any power in any circumstances whatsoever over Parliament. The reason is clearly his concern to champion the sovereignty of Parliament as the bedrock principle of the British Constitution.

Although the House of Commons of Blackstone's day was far from democratic, it was nevertheless an elected body, and in that sense representative of the nation.

The "Glorious Revolution"

Blackstone's England was the product of a century of conflict between Crown and Parliament, in which Parliament defeated one king, Charles I, in a bloody civil war and had him executed in 1649, and then deposed another king, James II, in the so-called "Glorious Revolution" of 1688/89. It was this event that permanently subordinated the Crown to Parliament and formalized Parliamentary sovereignty in legislation. But the doctrine of parliamentary sovereignty goes back a lot further.

"Transcendent and absolute"

Here is the full passage from Coke's *Institutes* to which Blackstone referred. Written in the 1630s, it describes the power of Parliament in glowing terms:

> "Of the power and jurisdiction of the Parliament for the making of laws in proceeding by bill, it is so transcendent and absolute, as it cannot be confined either for causes or persons within any bounds. Of this court it is truly said: *Si antiquitatem spectes, est vetustissima, si dignitatem, est honoratissima, si jurisdictionem, est capacissima.* ('If you look at its antiquity, it is the most venerable; if you consider its dignity, it is the most honorable; if you measure its jurisdiction, it is the most ample' —my translation)." [Co 4 Inst 36].

If ever there was a full-throated enunciation of the doctrine of the supremacy of Parliament, this is it. It is worth noting that Coke here specifically describes Parliament as a "court" imbued with legislative power and authority second to none.

"Most high and absolute power"

Coke was at this time of his life an active member of the parliamentary opposition to King Charles I. But the principle of parliamentary sovereignty long predates Coke. Here for example is what was said on the subject in the highly authoritative treatise, *De Republica Anglorum: the Manner of Gouernement or Policie of the Realme of England,* written between 1562 and 1565 by Sir Thomas Smith (1513–1577), a leading government adviser, Member of Parliament and a Cambridge academic.

> "The most high and absolute power of the realme of Englande, is in the Parliament. ... The Parliament abrogateth olde lawes, maketh newe, giveth orders for thinges past, and for thinges hereafter to be followed, changeth rightes, and possessions of private men, legittimateth bastards, establisheth formes of religion, altereth weightes and measures, giveth formes of succession to the crowne, defineth of doubtfull rightes, whereof is no lawe alreadie made, appointeth subsidies, tailes, taxes, and impositions, giveth most free pardons and absolutions, restoreth in bloud and name as the highest court, condemneth or absolveth them whom the Prince will put to that triall. ... [T]he parliament of Englande. ... representeth and hath the power of the whole realme both the head and the bodie. For everie Englishman is entended to bee there present, either in person or by procuration and attornies, of what preheminence, state, dignitie, or qualitie soever he be, from the Prince (be he King or Queene) to the lowest person of Englande. And the consent of the Parliament is taken to be everie mans consent."

Here, therefore, early in the reign of Queen Elizabeth I (1558–1603) we already have the full-blown principle of the Sovereignty of Parliament, whose power is described as "most high and absolute." Surprisingly, perhaps, Smith emphasizes Parliament's all-encompassing representative function, at a time when only a small fraction of the nation had the right to vote.

And, significantly, as in Coke's description quoted above, Parliament is described as "the highest court," leaving no room for its enactments to be set aside by the judiciary.

The Coronation Oath

A particularly telling piece of evidence is the wording of the Coronation Oath. In the Coronation Oath of William III and Mary II, taken on April 11, 1689 in the wake of the "Glorious Revolution," the joint monarchs were asked: "Will you solemnly promise and sweare to governe the people of this kingdome of England and the dominions thereto belonging according to the statutes in Parlyament agreed on and the laws and customs of the same?" The King and Queen each answered: "I solemnly promise soe to doe." [House of Commons Library (2008) "The Coronation Oath." www.parliament.uk]

This wording replaced the earlier Coronation Oath, as for example in the coronation of Charles I in 1625, in which the King was asked: "Sir, Will you grant and keep, and by your Oath confirm to the People of England, the Laws and Customs to them granted, by the Kings of England ... agreeable to the Prerogative for the Kings thereof ... and the ancient Customs of the Realm?" To which the King replied: "I Grant and Promise to keep them."

Note the specific emphasis on "the statutes of Parliament agreed on" in the 1689 oath, which was added in recognition of the final victory of Parliament over the Crown in the so-called Glorious Revolution. This formula was enshrined in a statute titled the Coronation Oath Act 1688, which is still in force unamended, although some changes have been made to the actual oath as administered since then.

At the coronation of George VI in 1937 and again at that of Elizabeth II in 1953 the phrase "according to the statutes in Parliament agreed upon" was dropped. But that in no way reflects any change in the constitutional position of Parliament in the UK Constitution. George VI and Elizabeth II were crowned as monarchs not only of the United Kingdom but also of a number of self-governing "dominions," such as Canada, Australia, New Zealand and South Africa, which since the Statute of Westminster 1931 had ceased to be under the control of the British Government and Parliament but each of which had its own completely independent government and parliament—still nominally, however, under the King or Queen as head of state. To reflect this new situation, the Coronation Oath was amended so that the Monarch promised "to govern the peoples of [*there follows a list of all the countries concerned*] according to their respective laws and customs." [Watt, Graeme (2017).]

Even though Parliament was first specifically mentioned in the Coronation Oath only in 1689, there are indirect references to it going back much further:

Here, for example, is the Coronation Oath taken by Edward IV in 1461 as quoted by Blackstone from old documents in his possession:

> "And that he will cause to be maintained the laws and customs of the kingdom, and as far as in him lies will make those be confirmed and kept which the people have made and chosen, and will abolish entirely all bad laws and customs, and will, in all respects, as far as he can, maintain a firm and established peace for the people of his kingdom." [Blackstone Bk 1, Ch. 6 "Of the King's Duties."]

The emphasis on the laws and customs "which the people have made and chosen" is worth noting, as well as the promise to "abolish entirely all bad laws and customs," for which the king would have needed the consent of Parliament.

Going back still further, even the Coronation Oath of Edward II of 1308, is redolent of popular sovereignty. Such was the potential power of Parliament even then that it was by a Parliament, summoned by two bishops and the rebel nobleman (and probable lover of the queen) Roger Mortimer, that King

Edward II was deposed in 1327—the first time that anything like that had occurred. Here is the wording of his Coronation Oath, one of the main complaints against him being that he had broken this solemn contractual promise with the people:

> "Archbishop: Sire, do you grant to be held & observed the just laws and customs that the community of your realm shall determine, and will you, so far as in you lies, defend and strengthen them to the honour of God?
> King: I grant and promise them."

Scroll forward 700 years to the present day, and the sovereignty of Parliament is still there, at the heart of the British Constitution, but badly neglected and hardly recognized even among those who ought to know better. As we have seen, the UK Supreme Court, affirming the High Court, based its decision in the important *Miller* case on the fundamental constitutional principle of the sovereignty of Parliament.

In addition, Lord Neuberger, President of the UK Supreme Court from 2012 to 2017, who delivered the majority opinion in the *Miller* case, has felt it necessary to stress the importance of the sovereignty of Parliament and the duty that this imposes on Parliament and the Government to give guidance to the judiciary. For example, on August 8, 2017, Lord Neuberger told the BBC: "If [the government] doesn't express clearly what the judges should do about decisions of the European Court of Justice (ECJ) after Brexit, or indeed any other topic after Brexit, then the judges will simply have to do their best. But to blame the judges for making the law when Parliament has failed to do so would be unfair." Adding: All judges "would hope and expect Parliament to spell out how the judges would approach that sort of issue after Brexit, and to spell it out in a statute." [www.bbc.com, August 8, 2017.]

Although Lord Neuberger was referring here specifically to problems arising as a result of "Brexit," his message is actually more general, trying to impress on Parliament its responsibility for making law and explaining that it is when a void is created by Parliament's dereliction of duty that judge-made law occurs to fill it. The last quoted sentence is particularly pointed, inviting Parliament to do its duty of leading the way by means of legislation. Needless to say, Lord Neuberger's timely and apposite warnings have gone unheeded.

Revocation

But Lord Neuberger went further. In the Neill Lecture to the Oxford Law Faculty delivered in February 2017, Lord Neuberger concluded with a tactful reminder of a nuclear weapon in Parliament's arsenal:

> "A safeguard against judicial law making which is subsequently thought to be wrong exists in the fact that, where the law has been developed by a judge through a decision which is thought to be inappropriate, Parliament can always reverse the decision by legislation. And, in a speech concerned with the role of judges under a constitutional system based on Parliamentary sovereignty, it is perhaps appropriate to end with a reminder that any judicial decision can be revoked by Parliament through a statute."

Revocation, i.e. cancellation, of any court decision by means of an Act of Parliament? Yes, indeed. The best-known use of this nuclear weapon was when the War Damage Act 1965 was passed to revoke the decision of the House of Lords (then the highest court in the land) in *Burmah Oil v. Lord Advocate* [1965] AC 75. The case arose out of a scorched earth policy implemented by the British Government in 1942 during World War II to prevent oil installations in Burma falling into the hands of the advancing Japanese forces. These oil installations belonged to a British company, which sued the Government after the war for compensation. Like so many others, this turned out to be what one might call a yo-yo case, with one decision at first instance, reversed on appeal, and then finally reversed back again. The House of Lords (then the highest court in the land) held 3–2 that, though the destruction was not unlawful, the Burmah Oil Company had to be compensated by the British Government. Parliament then passed the War Damage Act 1965 specifically to revoke this decision, so no compensation was paid. The long title of the Act reads as follows: "An Act to abolish rights at common law to compensation in respect of damage to, or destruction of, property effected by, or on the authority of, the Crown during, or in contemplation of the outbreak of war." The Act went on to order the Court in the Burmah Oil case "on the application of any party, forthwith [to] set aside or dismiss the proceedings. ..." The Act makes clear the power of statute law to override the common law. In addition, the Act had retroactive effect, or, in other words, was an *ex post facto law*, something which is expressly prohibited by the US Constitution for both federal and state laws. The fact that there is no barrier to such laws being passed by the UK Parliament is just another spin-off from the fact that Parliament is sovereign.

What was wrong with the House of Lords decision in *Burmah Oil v. Lord Advocate*? Besides the all-too-usual disagreement among the judges, *nothing at all.* The reasoning and legal arguments deployed in Lord Reid's leading opinion are still regarded as exemplary—except that the decision itself has been fed into the shredder.

Lord Neuberger's choice of the word "reminder" in connection with revocation is noteworthy. A "reminder" is needed only in regard to something important that is likely to have been forgotten or lost sight of—which is precisely the situation here. Though the *Burmah Oil* judgment itself was unexceptionable in terms of law, there is no shortage of recent court decisions that are crying out for revocation. Yet Parliament has done nothing about them.

Separation of Powers

Is Separation of Powers a feature of the British constitution? That there is a weak form of separation of powers in the British constitution is undeniable, but its importance should not be overestimated. The English philosopher John Locke (1632–1704), writing just after the so-called "Glorious Revolution" in 1690, was an advocate of separation of powers combined with legislative supremacy. [John Locke, John (1690), ed, Peter Laslett, 1988, p. 366f.] It is simply incorrect to claim, with M.J.C. Vile, that Locke cannot be regarded as a proponent of separation of powers "even in a modified form," because of his "emphatic assertion of legislative supremacy." [M.J.C. Vile,M.J.C. (1998), p. 68f.; Cf. Waldron (2013), 433 at 441.] As a friend of the new Queen Mary II, whom he actually accompanied in her return to England to claim the throne together with her husband William III, Locke evidently supported the ideals of the "Glorious Revolution," notably the Sovereignty of Parliament subordinating the power of the Crown, coupled with an independent judiciary. This still remains the constitutional position today.

"Arbitrary power if judge is legislator"

The French political philosopher Montesquieu (1689–1755), in his *De L'Esprit des Lois* (*The Spirit of the Laws*), published in 1748, greatly admired the British Constitution as an exemplification of the separation of powers, which he believed was a necessary guarantee of liberty. It is to his credit that he recognized the danger of judicial legislation: "Nor is there liberty if the power of judging is not separate from legislative power and from executive power. If it were joined to legislative power, the power over the life and liberty of the citizens would be arbitrary, for the judge would be the legislator." [Montesquieu (1748), ed. Anne M. Cohler, 1989, p. 157.]

"The British Constitution is firmly based on the separation of powers."

So much for the theory, but what is the practical situation on the ground in Britain today? Lord Diplock (Law Lord 1968–1985) is frequently quoted as saying: "[I]t cannot be too strongly emphasized that the British Constitution, though largely unwritten, is firmly based on the separation of powers: Parliament makes the laws, the judiciary interpret them...It is for Parliament, not for the judiciary, to decide whether any changes should be made to the law as stated in the Act. ..." In the same case Lord Scarman (Law Lord 1977–1986): "If Parliament says one thing but means another, it is not, under the historic principles of the common law, for the courts to correct it. ... We are to be governed not by Parliament's intentions but by Parliament's enactments. ... In this field Parliament makes, and unmakes, the law; the judge's duty is to interpret and apply the law, not to change it to meet the judge's idea of what justice requires." [*Duport Steels v. Sirs* [1980] 1 All ER 529.] The case was a sensitive trade union matter, in which Lord Denning (Master of the Rolls 1962–1982) in the Court of Appeal took it upon himself (not for the first time) to fill in the gaps as he saw fit in a defectively drafted statute. The House of Lords reversed that decision, making the point that it was not for judges to make law, only to interpret and apply it.

That was what Lord Diplock was referring to in his remark quoted above: the separation of powers between the legislature and the judiciary. He says nothing about the relationship between the judiciary and the executive, nor between the executive and the legislature. And his claim that "the British Constitution. ... is firmly based on the separation of powers" is simply untenable. Ironically, it is an example of the very thing he was warning against: judicial legislation. Because his remark was then quoted and re-quoted as if it itself had the force of law. It is a good warning against judge-made law, which, even when correct, tends to lack the clarity and precision of statutory language.

"Parliament, the executive and the courts each have their distinct and largely exclusive domain."

Lord Mustill (Law Lord 1992–1997 and a member of my Cambridge college) provided a fuller and more accurate description of the separation of powers in Britain in his dissenting opinion in *R v. Secretary of State for the Home Department, ex parte Fire Brigades Union* [1995] UKHL 3:

> "It is a feature of the peculiarly British conception of the separation of powers that Parliament, the executive and the courts, have each their distinct and largely exclusive domain. Parliament has a legally unchallengeable right to make whatever laws it thinks right. The executive carries on the administration of the country in accordance with the powers conferred on it by law. The courts interpret the laws, and see that they are obeyed."

This is an admirably clear and accurate statement of the legal position under the British Constitution. He neatly combined the sovereignty of Parliament, or parliamentary legislative supremacy, with executive independence and judicial power limited to interpreting the laws and seeing that they are obeyed. But what impelled Lord Mustill to set out the law in this area in this didactic manner lecturing his brother Law Lords in very direct terms? The clue is in the fact that this passage occurs in a dissenting judgment. The case was a claim against the Home Secretary, a government minister, for failing to bring a statutory criminal injuries compensation scheme into effect by naming a commencement date, as he was empowered to do by the relevant legislation. Instead of doing so, the minister introduced a non-statutory tariff scheme which cost less. Several trade unions and other similar organizations sued the minister claiming that in failing to set a commencement date for the statutory scheme he had acted unlawfully. The Court of Appeal by 2–1 found in favor of the trade unions. And a 3–2 majority in the House of Lords (then the highest court in the land) affirmed that decision and held that the minister had acted unlawfully. Lord Mustill, dissenting, recognized that the minister may have acted improperly as against Parliament and that Parliament's failure to keep the Government in line (more generally, not just in this case) had left a vacuum into which judicial power was drawn. But he made the point that it was not the function of judges to step into the role of Parliament. It was in that context that he carefully set out the legal relationships between the three branches of government as quoted above. The other dissenter, Lord Keith of Kinkel (1977–1996), made the same point: "*To grant [the trade unions] the relief which they seek, or any part of it, would represent an unwarrantable intrusion by the court into the political field and a usurpation of the function of Parliament.*" This is strong language indeed—but warranted by justifiable concerns.

"The court shall not grant an injunction" against the Crown

This case is by no means a unique example of "intrusion" or "usurpation" on the part of the judiciary. On the contrary, it has become all too common. A particularly egregious example is *M. v. Home Office* [1992] QB 270 (Court of Appeal); [1994] 1 AC 377 (House of Lords), in which a specific prohibition in an Act of Parliament was flouted. The case concerned a failed asylum seeker, known only as "M.", whose application for permission to apply for judicial review of the Home Secretary's decision was refused by the High Court and also by the Court of Appeal, to which he had applied "at the fifty-ninth minute of the eleventh hour" on the very day when he was due to be repatriated to the country then known as Zaire. Yet another application was made on his behalf to the High Court, which adjourned it to the next day on the understanding (which was later disputed) that the Home Secretary had undertaken not to deport him in the meantime. M. was nevertheless removed from the United Kingdom at the time originally notified to him. When this was brought to the judge's attention late that night, he immediately ordered the Home Secretary to bring M. back to Britain. But the Home Secretary maintained, on legal advice, that the judge's order "was made without jurisdiction." Even though M. was never located, the case trundled on all the way up to the House of Lords.

Who was right? Could a court issue an injunction against the Home Office or the Home Secretary? The correct answer, as given at first instance, is a simple "No", as is clear from the wording of section 21(1)(a) of the Crown Proceedings Act 1947, which states quite categorically that "the court shall not grant an injunction" against the Crown. The Court of Appeal, which was now revisited, also rejected the possibility of an injunction against the Home Office, but instead issued a *personal* injunction and contempt finding against Kenneth Baker, the then Home Secretary. This conclusion was reached on the basis that "neither the Crown nor the Home Office has any legal personality", or, to put it more simply, that "in law they are non-persons." [1992] QB 270. [1992] 2 WLR 73, 94, 101. The fact that every criminal prosecution is brought by the Crown shows just how implausible this argument is. And, as Blackstone was well aware, the Crown most certainly has a legal personality—as a *corporation sole*, which is still the position today.

A more egregious error was the purported relationship between the executive and the judiciary as expounded by Nolan LJ : "The proper constitutional relationship of the executive with the courts is that the courts will respect all acts of the executive within its lawful province, and that the executive will respect all decisions of the courts as to what its lawful province is." According to this formulation, the scope and extent of the "lawful province" of the executive is determined by the judiciary. But determining the "lawful province" of the executive is *legislation*—which is the exclusive "lawful province" of *Parliament*. There is no indication where this purported explanation comes from. Not only is the bedrock principle of the Sovereignty of Parliament completely ignored, but Parliament does not figure here at all. Which is not perhaps particularly surprising in view of the fact that Parliament's right to legislate is here usurped (to use Lord Keith's term) by the judiciary in this formulation. Even a quick comparison of this formulation with that of Lords Keith and Mustill in the *Fire Brigades Union* case reveals that Nolan LJ's formulation is far from being a description of the "proper constitutional" relationship of the two branches, as it purports to be.

Except for the mistake about the "legal personality" of the Crown (which was corrected in the House of Lords), the mistakes made in M's case by the Court of Appeal were compounded by the House of Lords, which substituted "the Secretary of State for Home Affairs" for "Kenneth Baker" as the party guilty of contempt of court for allegedly disobeying an injunction. However, section 21 of the Crown Proceedings Act disallows court injunctions not only against the Crown but also against "an officer of the Crown" "which could not have been obtained in proceedings against the Crown". The House of Lords was therefore effectively rewriting a statute—something that unelected judges have no authority to do.

"Constitutional imperative of judicial self-restraint"

In the late 20th century some judges took it upon themselves to rewrite some key constitutional principles. Here for example is Lord Woolf threatening in 1995 to retaliate if Parliament enacted an "unthinkable" law. The courts, he said, would be very reluctant to declare any Act of Parliament invalid, but then went on: "However, if Parliament did the unthinkable, then I would say that the courts would also be required to act in a manner which would be wihout precedent. ... Ultimately there are even limits on the supremacy of Parliament, which it is the courts' inalienable responsibility to identify and uphold. They are limits of the most modest dimensions, which I believe any democrat would accept. They are no more than are necessary to enable the rule of law to be preserved." [Woolf, Harry (1995). *Public Law* p. 57, 68–69.]

What exactly did Woolf mean by an "unthinkable" Act of Parliament? Chiefly, it seems, an Act removing or reducing the courts' power of judicial review. But it could presumably be extended to *any* law that the judiciary did not happen to like.

"The democratic imperative"

In a speech given to the Administrative Law Bar Association in 1995, Lord Irvine of Lairg (Lord Chancellor 1997–2003) tore into Lord Woolf's exorbitant claims together with similar claims made by two High Court judges, stressing that there was a "Constitutional imperative of judicial self-restraint," for which he gave three reasons, the most important of which being "the democratic imperative," under which judges, who are unelected, unaccountable and cannot be dismissed, must respect the democratic mandate of the other two branches of government.

Lord Irvine was simply reasserting the classic constitutional position as set out, for example, by Lord Reid in *Madzimbamuto v. Lardner-Burke* [1969] 1 AC 645 at 723: "It is often said that it would be unconstitutional for the United Kingdom Parliament to do certain things, meaning that the moral, political and other reasons against doing them are so strong that most people would regard it as highly improper if Parliament did these things. But that does not mean that it is beyond the power of Parliament to do such things. If Parliament chose to do any of them the courts would not hold the Act of Parliament invalid."

"Shall not be called into question in any court of law"

There have, however, been a few attempts to circumvent parliamentary sovereignty, especially in regard to judicial review. The best known of these occurred in *Anisminic v. Foreign Compensation Commission* [1968] UKHL 6. The case concerned eligibility for British companies to receive compensation from the Egyptian government for UK-owned property that had been nationalized by that government. The Foreign Compensation Act 1950 set up a tribunal, known as the Foreign Compensation Commission to determine applications for compensation. Section 4(4)contained an "ouster" clause (a clause ousting the jurisdiction of the court) reading as follows: *"The determination by the Commission of any application made to them under this Act shall not be called into question in any court of law."* In this particular case, the Commission decided that Anisminic Ltd. was not eligible for compensation because its "successor in title," a company called The Economic Development Organization (TEDO), an Egyptian-owned entity, did not have British nationality as was required. Anisminic's challenge to this decision in court went all the way up to the House of Lords (the highest court in the land). The whole case turned on the validity of the ouster clause. As so often, this became a yo-yo case—my term for a case that is decided one way, reversed on appeal and then reversed back again. At first instance, in the English High Court, the ouster clause was declared to be invalid. This was reversed by a unanimous Court of Appeal, and, by a 3–2 majority, the House of Lords restored the first instance judge's order. They held that the Commission had come to the wrong decision by misunderstanding the term "successor in title." According to the majority, this meant that the Commission's decision was a nullity, just as though it had made no determination at all, so the ouster clause did not apply. The result was that Anisminic won and were entitled to compensation from the Egyptian government.

The significance of this decision lies in the court's nullification of a clear provision of an Act of Parliament, thus flying in the face of the whole principle of parliamentary sovereignty. The court's argument will simply not stand up to scrutiny. What it says essentially is:

- The Commission's determination was wrong.
- Which amounts to there being no determination at all.
- So the ouster clause preventing the court from challenging any determination of the Commission just falls away.
- And, as the Commission's determination was wrong to begin with, the court simply reverses it.

The logic of this argument is wrong for the following reasons:

- An Act of Parliament cannot be overridden by the court in any circumstances.
- The ouster clause is clear and quite definite.
- The Act prohibits the court from challenging the Commission's determination.
- So the court does not even have the right to examine that determination to decide whether it was right or wrong.
- And, as it happens, of the nine judges involved in this case—one at first instance, 3 in the Court of Appeal, and 5 in the House of Lords—only 4 agreed with the final decision (the first instance judge plus three in the House of Lords), as against 5 (all three members of the Court of Appeal plus two dissenters in the House of Lords) who disagreed.
- In any event, that the Commission's determination was wrong is by no means certain. For example, Lord Pearson, dissenting in the House of Lords, reached a conclusion diametrically opposed to that of the majority. He concluded: "I would say therefore that the commission construed the article correctly and did not ask themselves any wrong question or exceed

their jurisdiction in any way. ... The decision ...
whether right or wrong, was plainly within their
jurisdiction, and therefore by virtue of section 4(4) of
the Foreign Compensation Act 1950 it cannot be
called in question in any court."

• The bottom line is that invalidating a clause in an
Act of Parliament is *legislation*, which is a no-no for
a court—and all the more so when, in so doing, the
court was simply giving itself more power.

Flouting the Sovereignty of Parliament

We turn now to a more recent assault on an ouster clause in
an Act of Parliament. On May 15, 2019, a majority on the UK
Supreme Court invalidated a clearly worded ouster clause in an
Act of Parliament. [*R. (Privacy International) v. Investigatory
Powers Tribunal* [2019] UKSC 22.] The ouster clause, which
occurs in section 67(8) of the Regulation of Investigatory Powers
Act 2000 ("RIPA"), provides as follows: *"Except to such extent as the
Secretary of State may by order otherwise provide, determinations,
awards, orders and other decisions of the [Investigatory Powers]
Tribunal (including decisions as to whether they have jurisdiction)
shall not be subject to appeal or be liable to be questioned in any court."*

What this ouster clause means is that the courts cannot
interfere with a decision of the tribunal in question. In the words
of Lord Sumption (dissenting), The main functions of the
tribunal "are to determine proceedings against the intelligence
services in respect of breaches of human rights and complaints
about the interception of communications, in a way which
enables these claims to be examined judicially without the risk of
disclosure of secret matters." [para 169.] However, the practical
effect of the majority ruling is minimal, because the tribunal in
question is made up entirely of judges and senior barristers
anyway, who are probably just as unlikely to find in favor of the
government in any dispute as the courts are.

The majority on the Court seems to have based their decision to invalidate the ouster clause on the submission made by the claimants that "a clause purporting to 'oust' the supervisory role of the High Court to correct errors of law cannot properly be upheld because it would conflict with the 'rule of law,' a principle which is as fundamental to our constitution as the principle of Parliamentary sovereignty." [para 114.]

The logic of this argument is less than persuasive. Even if we accept for argument's sake that the "rule of law" is as fundamental a principle of the British constitution by the court as parliamentary sovereignty, how is any clash between these principles to be resolved? It seems that the "rule of law" is being promoted by the court as superior to parliamentary sovereignty. And above all, what does the "rule of law" actually mean? It is interesting that in the quoted extract it was placed in inverted commas (in the official court record), indicating just how vague a concept it is. [See the section in Chapter 17 on The Rule of Law: or of Lawyers?]

This very clearly worded ouster clause in an Act of Parliament, under parliamentary sovereignty, should have been conclusive—as indeed was found to be the case by the Divisional Court and a unanimous Court of Appeal. In addition to these five judges, three members of the UK Supreme Court dissented, making a total of eight judges against only four in the Supreme Court majority. This fact alone, showing just how uncertain English law is in this area (among many), is enough in itself to cast doubt that the majority were upholding the "rule of law."

By contrast with this, the ruling doctrine in the US is "*Chevron* deference," about which more will be said in the next chapter.

2

UNITED STATES
"A DESPOTIC BRANCH"

Separation of Powers

The Framers of the US Constitution considered separation of powers essential in order to avoid "tyranny"—but the phrase "separation of powers" does not figure anywhere in the text of the document itself.

It was justified by James Madison, the "Father of the Constitution" and future fourth American President, in these terms: "The accumulation of all powers, legislative, executive, and judiciary, in the same hands, whether of one, a few, or many, and whether hereditary, self-appointed or elective, may justly be pronounced the very definition of tyranny." [*The Federalist Papers* No. 47, 1788.]

The wording of the Constitution was intended to achieve this objective:

Here are the relevant references:

• Art 1, Section 1 gives Congress "all legislative powers" under the Constitution. This means the other two branches of government are not allowed to be involved in law-making. (In reality, they both are involved—as we shall see.)

• Article II, Section 1 declares: "The executive Power shall be vested in a President of the United States."

• Art III, Section 1 similarly reads: "The judicial power of the United States, shall be vested in one supreme Court, and in such inferior Courts as the

Congress may from time to time ordain and establish."
Although this section does not say "All judicial power,"
the phrase "the judicial power" makes it clear that the
courts are to have a monopoly of judicial power,
excluding the other two branches from judicial
activities.

The concept of the separation of powers in a "mixed" form
of government goes back to ancient times, exemplified by the
Roman Republic (as described in somewhat exaggerated terms
by the Greek historian Polybius (c. 208–c.125 BCE)). But the
chief influence on the American Founding Fathers in this
respect was exerted by the British Constitution as seen through
the rather inexact prism of *De L'Esprit des Lois* (*The Spirit of the
Laws*) published in 1748 by the French political philosopher
Montesquieu (1689–1755).

Montesquieu had a rather simplistic view of the British
Constitution, which he used as a stick to beat the French
government of his day. Madison was not entirely taken in by
this, commenting: "On the slightest view of the British
Constitution, we must perceive that the legislative, executive,
and judiciary departments are by no means totally separate and
distinct from each other." [James Madison, *The Federalist Papers*,
No. 47, February 1, 1788.]

Madison recognized that a complete separation of powers
was impractical and had to be supplemented by a system of
checks and balances between the three branches of government.
In the next *Federalist Paper*, number 48, Madison accordingly
undertook "to show that unless these departments be so far
connected and blended as to give to each a constitutional control
over the others, the degree of separation which the maxim
requires, as essential to a free government, can never in practice
be duly maintained." [James Madison, *The Federalist Papers*, No.
48, February 1, 1788.]

Three Coequal Branches?

This plan is reflected in the text of the US Constitution, which establishes an elaborate system of checks and balances.

Checks by the Executive on the Legislature

- **Veto:** The President has the power to veto any bill passed by both houses of Congress. To override the veto there has to be a two-thirds majority in both houses.
- **Vice President:** The Vice President is automatically President of the Senate, but he is not a member of that body, does not have the right to speak, and cannot even vote except to break a tie. In practice, most Vice Presidents have more important things to do than to preside over the deliberations of the Senate.

Checks by the Legislature on the President

- **Impeachment:** This is the most serious potential check on the President, because it can result in his removal from office. The power to impeach belongs to the House of Representatives, which acts as prosecutor in a trial before the Senate, which sits as a jury and decides the case, a two thirds majority being needed for conviction and removal from office. The judiciary has a role to play here as well, as the Chief Justice presides over the trial of a president. So far only two presidents have been impeached—Andrew Johnson and Bill Clinton—but neither was convicted. Richard Nixon, who is commonly assumed to have been impeached, resigned before he could be impeached.
- **"Advice and Consent":** The president's power of appointment of senior office-holders such as federal judges, Cabinet secretaries and ambassadors, as well as the president's power to make Treaties, is subject to the "advice and consent" of the Senate. Treaties need a two-thirds majority in the Senate for confirmation, but since 2013 appointments to federal courts (since

2017 including US Supreme Court appointments) and executive appointments need only a simple Senate majority for confirmation.

- **Commander in Chief** : Article II, Section 2 of the Constitution makes the President Commander in Chief of the armed forces. But under Article I, Section 8, Congress has the power to "declare war." The precise relationship between the President and Congress in regard to war remains the subject of intense debate. [See Arnheim (2018), page 153ff.]
- **Choosing the President:** Article II, Section 1, Clause 3 provides that if no presidential candidate obtains more than 50% of the electoral votes, the election is thrown into the House of Representatives, with every state having one vote.

Checks on the Judiciary

- **Appointment**: Federal judges, including Supreme Court justices, are appointed by the President, subject to confirmation by the Senate.
- **Impeachment:** This is the only way in which federal judges can be removed from office, as they are appointed for life. The rules are the same as for presidential impeachment, except that these trials are not presided over by the Chief Justice. Samuel Chase is the only Supreme Court justice to have been impeached, in 1804, and he was acquitted. Fourteen other federal judges have been impeached, eight of whom were convicted by the Senate and removed from office.
- **Pardons**: Article II, Section 2 gives the President the "Power to grant Reprieves and Pardons for Offences against the United States, except in Cases of Impeachment." Is this power a check on the judiciary? Yes, in a sense, because a pardon cancels the sentence without cancelling the conviction.

It is important to stress that these instances of checks and balances are all mentioned in the text of the US Constitution. The resulting picture is one that could possibly be reconciled with the popular image of three "coequal branches," although the Constitution carefully eschews any attempt to weigh up the relative strength or power of the three branches against one another.

Madison himself believed that "In republican government, the legislative authority necessarily predominates." [James Madison, *The Federalist Papers*, No. 51, February 1, 1788.] He considered this a danger, and suggested that "The remedy for this inconveniency is to divide the legislature into different branches" with "different modes of election and different principles of action. ... As the weight of legislative authority requires that it should be thus divided, the weakness of the executive may require, on the other hand, that it should be fortified" [James Madison, *The Federalist Papers*, No. 51, February 1, 1788.] This reads strangely in the wake of the rise of the so-called "Imperial Presidency" from the time of President Franklin Roosevelt (in office 1933–1945). However, in the decades after the Civil War, several weak presidents tended to kowtow to Congress—though not quite enough to the liking of a young politics professor who in 1885 published a book titled *Congressional Government* in which he criticized Congress for not being powerful enough to "decide at once and with conclusive authority what shall be done." That young professor was none other than Thomas Woodrow Wilson, who would become, if not an "imperial" president, certainly one who greatly enhanced executive power.

"The weakest of the three departments of power"

Alexander Hamilton's underestimate of the likely power of the judiciary has become notorious. In *The Federalist Papers*, Number 78, he predicted that, in a separation of powers system, "the judiciary, from the nature of its functions, will always be the least dangerous to the political rights of the Constitution. ... The Executive not only dispenses the honors, but holds the sword of the community. The legislature not only commands the purse, but prescribes the rules by which the duties and rights of every citizen are to be regulated. The judiciary, on the contrary, has no influence over either the sword or the purse; no direction either of the strength or of the wealth of the society; and can take no active resolution whatever. It may truly be said to have neither FORCE nor WILL, but merely judgment; and must ultimately depend upon the aid of the executive arm even for the efficacy of its judgments. This simple view of the matter ... proves incontestably, that the judiciary is beyond comparison the weakest of the three departments of power; that it can never attack with success either of the other two; and that all possible care is requisite to enable it to defend itself against their attacks."

> "Some perplexity respecting the rights of the courts to pronounce legislative acts void, because contrary to the Constitution, has arisen from an imagination that the doctrine would imply a superiority of the judiciary to the legislative power. It is urged that the authority which can declare the acts of another void, must necessarily be superior to the one whose acts may be declared void. ...
>
> It can be of no weight to say that the courts, on the pretense of a repugnancy, may substitute their own pleasure to the constitutional intentions of the legislature. [Alexander Hamilton, *The Federalist Papers*, No. 78, May 1788.]

"Bound down by strict rules and precedents"

This kind of naïvety is perhaps not surprising in someone who recklessly lost his life in a needless and illegal duel with an experienced duelist—three years after his son was killed in a similarly senseless duel. But, it is worth noting that Hamilton goes on, sensibly, to recommend codification and *stare decisis*:

> "It has been frequently remarked, with great propriety, that a voluminous code of laws is one of the inconveniences necessarily connected with the advantages of a free govern-

ment. To avoid an arbitrary discretion in the courts, it is indispensable that they should be bound down by strict rules and precedents, which serve to define and point out their duty in every particular case that comes before them."

John Marshall's "Twistifications"

Even on the basis of the text of the US Constitution, the judiciary has fewer checks on its power than either of the other two branches, because, once appointed, a federal judge is there for life unless he or she really steps out of line sufficiently to be impeached. The judiciary also exercises more power over the other two branches than either of those branches has over the judiciary.

But, besides all this, the judiciary has in its power the ultimate nuclear weapon against both the President and Congress—and the individual States as well. This of course is the power of judicial review, which does not figure anywhere in the text of the US Constitution.

This formidable power is commonly believed to have been conjured into existence by Chief Justice John Marshall in *Marbury v. Madison*. However, there were some tentative earlier precedents. For example, in *Hylton v. United States*, 3 US (3 Dall.) 171 (1796), the US Supreme Court was confronted with the question whether a law placing an annual tax on carriages was a "direct" tax , which would have needed to be apportioned among the states under Article I of the Constitution. The Court decided that the tax in question was not a direct tax and so was a valid use of the power of Congress. But what would have happened had the Court come to the opposite conclusion? Would the offending Act of Congress have been declared void? The justices were themselves in a quandary about this. Justice Samuel Chase put it like this: "As I do not think the tax on carriages is a direct tax, it is unnecessary, at this time, for me to determine, whether this court, constitutionally possesses the power to declare an act of Congress void, on the ground of its being made contrary to, and in violation of, the Constitution; but if the court have such power, I am free to declare, that I will never exercise it, but in a very clear case."

Marbury v. Madison

John Marshall had no such qualms, although he should have recused himself from sitting on *Marbury v. Madison* because of a serious conflict of interest, and the legal reasoning that he used was well described by the term "twistifications" applied to it by his distant cousin and personal foe, Thomas Jefferson. The case arose out of lame-duck President John Adams's last-minute attempt to appoint a whole raft of "midnight judges" the very day before his term was due to end. These were all political appointees. It rankled Adams, a Federalist, that he had been deprived of a second term by defeat in the 1800 election at the hands of his own Vice President, Thomas Jefferson of the Democratic Republican party. Adams decided to take his revenge by ensuring that the judiciary remained Federalist dominated well beyond his presidency.

All these "midnight" appointments were rushed through the Senate. But the commissions, or official letters of appointment, still had to be delivered to each of the new appointees. Time ran out on Adams's presidency before all the commissions had been delivered—and without an official commission an appointment could not take effect.

William Marbury was one of Adams's "midnight" justices of the peace whose commission was not delivered in time. Thomas Jefferson, who was now president, ordered the new Secretary of State, James Madison, to withhold the commissions that had not been delivered, including Marbury's. So Marbury petitioned the US Supreme Court to order Madison to deliver his commission to him.

Madison was the named defendant because delivering commissions to new appointees was one of the duties of the

Secretary of State. But the person who really let Marbury down was not Madison—it was Madison's predecessor as Secretary of State, none other than one John Marshall—yes, the very same John Marshall who was presiding over the case as Chief Justice! If ever there was a blatant case of a conflict of interest, this had to be it.

But that did not deter Marshall from going on to expand the power of the Supreme Court—and of himself as Chief Justice—by what Jefferson called "the cunning and sophistry within which he is able to enshroud himself."

Writing for the Court, Chief Justice Marshall held that:

- *Madison's refusal to deliver the commission to Marbury was unlawful.* This was undoubtedly correct.
- *But the Supreme Court did not have the power to order him to do so.* This was not actually correct.
- *Because the law that purportedly gave the Supreme Court this power was itself unconstitutional.* This was also probably wrong.
- *And the Supreme Court had the power to strike down unconstitutional laws.* The Constitution certainly does not say so.

This last assertion is the most important of all, and forms the basis of judicial review. But where does it come from? Marshall offered this curiously worded "explanation":

> *"Certainly all those who have framed written Constitutions contemplate them as forming the fundamental and paramount law of the nation, and consequently the theory of every such government must be that an act of the Legislature repugnant to the Constitution is void. This theory is essentially attached to a written Constitution, and is consequently to be considered by this Court as one of the fundamental principles of our society. It is not, therefore to be lost sight of in the further consideration of this subject."* The vague and oblique language of this "explanation" is hard to miss. Why does Marshall not come out directly and say: "The

Constitution is the paramount law of the land, so any law repugnant to it is void"? Because the Constitution itself does not make this claim: it only asserts the superiority of federal over state law. So Marshall resorted to vague talk about "theory"—a good example of a "twistification." But, having purportedly now established the paramountcy of the Constitution, he is ready to take the next step.

"It is emphatically the province and duty of the Judicial Department to say what the law is." Here we do at least have a direct statement—but why "emphatically"? That word gives the game away. It is a sign of special pleading—"Methinks the lady doth protest too much!" Because, once again, the Constitution does not give the judiciary this power. This "emphatic" but baseless assertion enables Marshall finally to square the circle:

"So, if a law be in opposition to the Constitution...the Court must determine which of these conflicting rules governs the case. This is of the very essence of judicial duty. If, then, the Courts are to regard the Constitution, and the Constitution is superior to any ordinary act of the Legislature, the Constitution, and not such ordinary act, must govern the case to which they both apply." Q.E.D.! [*Marbury v. Madison*, 5 US (1 Cranch) 137 (1803).]

"A despotic branch"

Marbury v. Madison is terribly worrying in regard to the doctrine of the separation of powers:

- Not only did it give the judiciary the right to strike down Acts of Congress held to be unconstitutional;
- It also gave them the exclusive right to interpret the Constitution, a power that the Constitution itself does not confer on it. Such was Marshall's skill that his "twistifications of the law", as Jefferson put it, have become accepted as valid constitutional law.
- It gave the judiciary the ability to add to its own power simply by means of a Supreme Court decision—which is also nowhere to be found in the Constitution; and is in

any case contrary to the whole principle of the separation of powers.

Jefferson's own take was quite different. This is what he said about Marbury's case:

> "If this opinion be sound, then indeed is our Constitution a complete felo de se. (act of suicide). ... The Constitution, on this hypothesis, is a mere thing of wax in the hands of the judiciary, which they may twist, and shape into any form they please. It should be remembered, as an axiom of eternal truth in politics, that whatever power in any government is independent, is absolute also; in theory only, at first, while the spirit of the people is up, but in practice, as fast as that relaxes. Independence can be trusted nowhere but with the people in mass. They are inherently independent of all but moral law. My construction of the Constitution is ... that each dept [or branch of government] is truly independent of the others and has an equal right to decide for itself what is the meaning of the Constitution in the cases submitted to its action; and especially where it is to act ultimately and without appeal. ... In the case of Marbury and Madison, the federal judges declared that commissions, signed and sealed by the President were valid, although not delivered. I deemed delivery essential to complete a deed, which, as long as it remains in the hands of the party, is as yet no deed., it is in *posse* only, but not in *esse*, and I withheld delivery of the commissions. They cannot issue a mandamus to the President or legislature, or to any of their officers." [Thomas Jefferson to Spencer Roane, 6 Sept 1819 – Works 12:135–138.]

Above all, the effect of *Marbury* is to give a group of unelected justices the power to strike down as unconstitutional any laws passed by a democratically elected Congress that the unelected justices deem unconstitutional.

Here is what Jefferson wrote to Abigail Adams, John Adams's wife, who agreed with her husband and with John Marshall:

> "You seem to think it devolved on the judges to decide on the validity of the sedition law, but nothing in the Constitution has given them a right to decide for the Executive, more than to the Exec to decide for them. Both magistracies are equally independent in the sphere of action assigned to them. ...
>
> That instrument [the Constitution] meant that its coordinate branches should be checks on each other. But the opinion which gives to the judges the right to decide what laws are constitutional and what not, not only for themselves in their own sphere of action but for the Legislature and Executive also in their spheres, would make the judiciary a despotic branch." [Thomas Jefferson to Abigail Adams, Sept 11, 1804.]

Despite Jefferson's visceral antipathy towards his cousin, he never felt able to take any action against him. It appears that he was hoping to have Marshall impeached, but after the failure of the impeachment of Justice Samuel Chase in 1804, he gave up that idea, remarking: "Impeachment is a farce which will not be tried again." Nevertheless, he did not hold back from attacking Marshall in his correspondence. Here is what Jefferson wrote about him in a letter to his friend and successor as president, James Madison:

> "[A]nd infinitely the more from the want of any counterpoise to the rancorous hatred which Marshall bears to the government of his country, and from the cunning and sophistry within which he is able to enshroud himself. ... His twistifications in the case of Marbury, in that of Burr, and the late Yazoo case, shew how dexterously he can reconcile law to his personal biases." [Jefferson to James Madison, May 25, 1810.]

Conservative judicial activism

Present-day supporters of judicial activism are commonly assumed by their detractors to be left-leaning, "liberal," or "progressive" in their politics. However, some of the leading exemplars of judicial activism, or even judicial supremacism, were actually activated by conservative political views. Most notably among these were John Marshall himself, his successor, Chief Justice Roger Taney (in office 1836–1864), and the so-called "Four Horsemen," conservative members of the US Supreme Court between 1932 and 1937 who did their best to block the New Deal legislative program of President Franklin Roosevelt.

After *Marbury*, no Act of Congress was declared void by the Supreme Court for another 54 years, the next one being Taney's striking of the Missouri Compromise in the so-called "Dred Scott" case of 1857. [*Scott v. Sandford*, 60 US (19 How.) 393 (1857.] These were the only two Acts of Congress struck down by the Court before the Civil War.

180 Acts of Congress declared unconstitutional

Since then there have been another 180 Acts of Congress held by the US Supreme Court to be unconstitutional in whole or part. But this figure gives an exaggerated impression of the extent of the Court's activism. For one thing, in some of these cases only a small part of the statute concerned was struck down. In others, what was objected to by the court was the breadth of the statute, which just had to be amended in order to pass muster. Others again, like the Rehnquist Court's attack on the scope of the congressional exercise of the Commerce Clause, were part of the so-called "new federalism," which was intended to redress the balance between federal and state power in the interests of the states.

"Depictions of animal cruelty"

In *United States v. Stevens*, 559 US 460 (2010) an Act of Congress that criminalized trafficking in "depictions of animal cruelty" was struck down by an 8–1 majority on the US Supreme Court. The case was brought by a film producer who had been sentenced to a 37-month prison sentence for videotapes depicting dogfights. Even more surprisingly, perhaps, the majority opinion was written by Chief Justice John Roberts himself. The basis of the decision was that the statute was "overbroad" and therefore violated the First Amendment's protection of freedom of speech. Congress immediately passed a new bill restricting the ban to "crush videos" depicting the crushing of small animals for perverted sexual gratification. This bill was signed into law by President Obama some seven months later.

Flag-burning protected as symbolic speech

The decision in *Stevens* is not really as surprising as it may at first appear. It belongs to a long tradition of Supreme Court decisions upholding freedom of speech, sometimes probably excessively, such as *Texas v. Johnson*, 491 US 397 (1989) and *US v. Eichman*, 496 US 310 (1990), which struck down state laws against flag-burning, which was deemed by the court to be "symbolic speech" protected under the First Amendment. A heart-rending case which did not involve the striking of any statutory law, was *Snyder v. Phelps*, 562 US 443 (2011), in which the Supreme Court again ruled 8–1 in favor of what they deemed to be protection of freedom of speech. The case involved the hostile picketing of the funeral of a US Marine, Matthew Snyder, killed at the age of 20 in the line of duty in Iraq.

"Funeral turned into a media circus"

The picketers, who were on public property (which was a strong point in their favor), displayed anti-gay placards reading

"God hates you," "Fag troops," and "Thank God for dead soldiers." In fact, Matthew Snyder was not gay, but the picketers believed that the deaths of American service personnel was God's punishment for the country's toleration of homosexuality. Albert Snyder, the dead marine's father, testified: "They turned this funeral into a media circus, and they wanted to hurt my family. They wanted their message heard, and they didn't care who they stepped over. My son should have been buried with dignity, not with a bunch of clowns outside."

A Maryland jury found in favor of Albert Snyder and awarded him a total of $10.9 million including punitive damages for suffering intentional emotional distress. This was reduced to $5 million on appeal, but was set aside altogether by the Supreme Court. Once again, the majority opinion was delivered by Chief Justice Roberts and the sole dissenter was Justice Alito, who wrote: "Our profound national commitment to free and open debate is not a license for the vicious verbal assault that occurred in this case. In order to have a society in which public issues can be openly and vigorously debated, it is not necessary to allow the brutalization of innocent victims." Retired Justice John Paul Stevens was reported (by Justice Ruth Bader Ginsburg) as telling the Federal Bar Council that, had he still been on the court, he would have joined Alito's "powerful dissent"—an interesting alliance between a staunch conservative and a justice who is generally regarded as a liberal. [Ginsburg speech, July 27, 2011, www.supremecourt.gov.]

The significance of "the"

My own view is that the Supreme Court's interpretation of the First Amendment's protection of freedom of speech has tended to be too broad, and that *Snyder* and the flag-burning cases were wrongly decided. The relevant wording reads as follows: *"Congress shall make no law ... abridging the freedom of speech, or of the press."* What exactly is meant by *"the* freedom of speech"? It can only be a reference to *already existing* freedom of speech, in other words freedom of speech as recognized under English law in 1791—which most certainly would not have extended to flag-burning. In fact, even at the time of this writing, although there is no UK law against flag burning or desecration, burning the "Union flag" or "Union Jack," as it is commonly known, can result in a conviction for causing a breach of the peace, as indeed occurred in 1999 when two self-styled "committed socialists" threw a burning Union flag in the direction of the Queen's motor car in Edinburgh, Scotland, and were fined £450. [*Edinburgh Evening News*, October 13, 1999.]

Chevron deference

The approach of the US Supreme Court to decisions of government agencies stands in stark contrast to the approach of the British courts as discussed in the previous chapter. In *Chevron USA Inc. v. Natural Resources Defense Council Inc.*, 467 US 837 (1984), one of the most important Supreme Court decisions, it was held essentially that, when a law is ambiguous, the court should defer to the interpretation adopted by the government agency which administers that statute, provided the agency's decision is reasonable. This has come to be known as "*Chevron* deference." In the words of Justice John Paul Stevens, writing for a unanimous (albeit depleted) Court: "First, always, is the question whether Congress has directly spoken to the precise question at issue. If the intent of Congress is clear, that is the end of the matter, for the court, as well as the agency, must give effect to the unambiguous intent of Congress. If, however, the court determines Congress has not directly addressed the precise question at issue, the court does not simply impose its own construction on the statute. ... Rather, if the statute is silent or ambiguous with respect to the specific issue, the question for the court is whether the agency's answer is based on a permissible construction of the statute." [*Chevron USA Inc. v. Natural Resources Defense Council Inc.*, 467 US 837, 842–843 (1984).]

In *City of Arlington, Texas v. Federal Communications Commission,* 133 S. Ct. 1863 (2013) the question before the Supreme Court was whether *Chevron* deference would apply even where the issue concerned the nature or scope of the jurisdiction of the agency concerned itself. Writing for the 6–3 majority, Justice Scalia held that *Chevron* deference applied just as much to "jurisdictional" interpretations as to any others: "Those who assert that applying Chevron to 'jurisdictional' interpretations 'leaves the fox in charge of the henhouse' overlook the reality that a separate category of 'jurisdictional' interpretations does not exist. ... Where Congress has established a clear line, the agency cannot go beyond it, and where Congress has established an ambiguous line, the agency can go no further than the ambiguity will fairly allow. But in rigorously applying the latter rule, a court need not pause to puzzle over whether the interpretive question presented is 'jurisdictional.' If 'the agency's answer is based on a permissible construction of the statute,' that is the end of the matter." [The last quotation is from *Chevron* itself.]

Interestingly, in *Arlington* it was a conservative alliance of Chief Justice Roberts with Justices Kennedy and Alito who dissented, objecting to excessive *Chevron* deference. In the words of Chief Justice Roberts: "My disagreement with the Court is fundamental. It is also easily expressed. A court should not defer to an agency until the court decides, on its own, that the agency is entitled to deference. Courts defer to an agency's interpretation of law when and because Congress has conferred on the agency interpretive authority over the issue at issue. An agency cannot exercise interpretive authority until it has it; the question whether an agency enjoys that authority must be decided by a court without deference to the agency."

Roberts then quoted from the *Federalist* No. 47 written by Madison that the "accumulation of all powers, legislative, executive, and judiciary, in the same hands ... may justly be pronounced the very definition of tyranny." He pointed out that, though modern administrative agencies "fit most comfortably within the Executive Branch," in practice they exercise legislative, executive and judicial power. [This is arguably something of an exaggeration.] "The accumulation of these powers in the same hands is not an occasional or isolated exception to the constitutional plan; it is a central feature of modern American government."

Despite the Chief Justice's description of his disagreement with the majority as "fundamental," he did not reject *Chevron* deference as such, but essentially only deference in regard to "jurisdictional" interpretations. And of course he was in the minority!

CONCLUSION

In America, no judge likes to be accused of "activism," "legislating from the bench" or creating "judge-made law." Justice Stephen Breyer, who interprets legislation according to its "purpose" and likely "consequences," has sometimes been described as an activist, but, in a tally done in July 2005, it turned out that he had voted less frequently than any other member of the US Supreme Court to strike down Acts of Congress. Other "liberal" Justices Ruth Bader Ginsburg, David Souter and John Paul Stevens were next, while Justice Clarence Thomas was most inclined to vote to invalidate Acts of Congress, followed by other "conservative" justices. [Gewirtz, Paul (2005).] As far as the justices' attitudes to executive decisions are concerned, a tally of cases between 1989 and 2005 showed that: "The conservative members of the Court have been the most likely to vote to strike down executive branch decisions, and the liberal members of the Court have been the least likely to do so. The voting patterns of the justices are significantly affected by whether the executive's decision is liberal or conservative. But even here, there is a kicker: Liberal justices vote to uphold conservative decisions more often than conservative justices vote to uphold liberal decisions." [Miles, Thomas J. & Sunstein, Cass R. (2006).]

The different schools of thought among the justices have different criteria for interpreting the Constitution and other legislation, but it would be hard to find an example where a member of the US Supreme Court wrote an entirely arbitrary opinion.

In the UK, by contrast, for the past half century or more, judicial activism has been rife. Judge-made law has been drawn into the vacuum left as a result of Parliament's dereliction of duty. But, besides that, the judiciary has itself developed an appetite for making law and expanding its own power, with decisions that have hamstrung government policy, especially in

49

regard to terrorism, and even flouted Acts of Parliament. A comparison between the UK decisions in *Anisminic* and *Privacy International* on the one hand, and, on the other, the doctrine of *Chevron* deference in the US (all discussed above) is instructive.

SEPARATION OF POWERS
AND CHECKS AND BALANCES
A CHECKLIST

Relationship between Legislature and Executive

- **Membership – US:** *Strict separation.* Neither the President nor any member of the Cabinet or Administration is allowed to serve at the same time as a member of the House of Representatives or the Senate. And *vice versa:* No sitting member of either house of Congress is allowed to hold a position in the Administration at the same time. There is of course no objection to transitioning from one branch to the other. For example, having been President from 1825 to 1829, John Quincy Adams served as a member of the House of Representatives from 1831 until his death in 1848.

- **Membership – UK:** *Overlap.* The Prime Minister, Cabinet ministers and junior ministers have by convention to be either Members of Parliament or members of the House of Lords. Those few ministers who have been appointed without being in Parliament scrambled to obtain a seat in Parliament or resigned their government post. (The best-known examples are Frank Cousins and Patrick Gordon Walker, both appointed by Harold Wilson in 1964.)

- **Function – US:** *Co-operation.* For a Bill to become an Act of Congress it needs to be passed by a simple majority in both houses of Congress and then signed into law by the President. The President's veto can be overridden by a two-thirds majority in both houses of Congress. The Legislature has no executive or administrative functions.

- **Function – UK:** *Fusion.* For a Bill to become an Act of Parliament it needs (with a few exceptions) to be passed by a simple majority in both Houses of Parliament before becoming law by obtaining the Royal Assent, which is automatic. Most successful Bills are introduced by a Government Minister, and most Government Bills become law. The situation today is still much the same in this respect as described by Bagehot in his *English Constitution* of 1867, namely that there is a "close union and an almost complete fusion of legislative and executive power."

Relationship between Legislature and Judiciary

- **Membership – US**: *Strict separation.* A position in one branch cannot be combined with a position in the other, but transitioning from one to the other is permissible. A curious example is Alcee Hastings, who, after being impeached and removed from office as a federal judge in 1988, has served as a Member of the House of Representatives since 1993.

- **Membership – UK**: *Strict separation.* Sitting Members of Parliament and of the House of Lords cannot serve as judges at the same time. Until 2009, Lords of Appeal in Ordinary, members of the Judicial Committee of the House of Lords, or "Law Lords," as they were commonly known, combined membership of the House of Lords as the highest court in the land with membership of the House of Lords as a legislature. There was a convention, which was not always observed, that they would not speak or vote on controversial matters in the House of Lords as a branch of the legislature. With the establishment of a new UK Supreme Court in 2009, the Law Lords ceased to sit in the House of Lords.

- **Function – US**: *Critical.* The greatest power in the hands of federal courts, and particularly the US Supreme Court, is judicial review, meaning that they can strike down any Act of Congress that they consider to be unconstitutional. Although very great, this power does not figure in the text of the US Constitution. The only power that Congress has in relation to the judiciary is the right of the Senate to confirm or reject a presidential nomination to the US Supreme Court.

- **Function – U.K**: *Dereliction of Duty.* The Sovereignty of Parliament is the bedrock principle of the UK Constitution, which means not only that Parliament can pass any law that it likes but also that it can revoke, or cancel, any decision of any court for any reason, or none at all. But, Parliament has long been guilty of dereliction of duty over many years, in regard to both legislation and revocation. The resulting vacuum has been filled by judicial lawmaking, including unjustifiably effectively rewriting statutes and handing down rulings crying out for revocation, while Parliament has stood idly by. Because of the principle of the sovereignty of Parliament, the courts are not allowed to set aside Acts of Parliament. While the UK remained part of the European Union, there was one apparent exception to this rule, which is discussed later in this chapter under the heading "The non-exception exception."

Relationship between Executive and Judiciary

- **Membership – US**: *Strict separation.* No President or member of the Administration may serve as a judge at the same time. Of course, there is no barrier to transitioning between the two branches. John Marshall, for example, (ominously) served as Secretary of State before being appointed Chief Justice. And William Howard Taft, President from 1909 to 1913, served as Chief Justice from 1921 until his death in 1930. He is the only person to have held both these offices.

- **Membership – UK**: *Strict separation.* Neither a sitting Prime Minister nor any other minister may serve as a judge at the same time. And no judge may moonlight as a member of the Government. This has been the position since the passing of the Constitutional Reform Act 2005. Until then, the Lord Chancellor was both a senior Government minister and head of the judiciary with the right to sit as a law lord.

- **Function – US**: *Critical.* The power of judicial review exercised by federal courts, and particularly the US Supreme Court, extends to a review of executive decisions as well, though this is regulated to some extent by legislation known as the Administrative Procedure Act of 1946. An example of this kind of judicial review is *Nielsen v. Preap* (2019) in which the US Supreme Court ruled 5–4 that the US Government's policy in regard to the detention of legal immigrants was in conformity with the Illegal Immigration Reform and Immigrant Responsibility Act of 1996 [8 USC. § 1226.]

- **Function** – **UK**: *Dereliction of Duty*. The Sovereignty of Parliament can be exercised only by passing legislation, which in practice depends on the Government. The majority party (if there is one) in the House of Commons is automatically asked by the Crown to form a Government, and in practice most legislation that reaches the statute book is Government-sponsored. The Sovereignty of Parliament gives Parliament the *right* to pass any laws it likes, but it also imposes on Parliament the *duty* to legislate, which means that the Government has a duty to co-ordinate legislation and see it passed through Parliament—which it has not done for many years. There certainly is no shortage of legislation, but it is like isolated little beads on a string, with very little consolidation and no codification. This leaves a vacuum that is filled by judge-made law, which, not surprisingly, is in a state of disarray. The Sovereignty of Parliament means not only that Parliament can pass any legislation it likes, but also that it can revoke, i.e. cancel, any court decision for any reason—or none at all.

PART II

FROM ETHELBERT
TO THE SNAIL IN THE BOTTLE

3

FROM CODIFIED STATUTES TO COMMON LAW

"The English and the Americans are two peoples divided by a common language." This mock-serious remark attributed to the famous comic dramatist George Bernard Shaw (1856–1950) is even more applicable to law than it is to language.

The United Kingdom and the United States both claim to be democracies, both purport to be based on "the rule of law," both claim to protect civil rights or human rights, and both are said to be "common law" systems. How true are these claims and how significant are they? And then, what are the problems of both systems, and how can they be improved?

This Part covers a long sweep of thirteen hundred years, starting with the earliest Anglo-Saxon Code of King Ethelbert dating from about the year 600 and ending with the famous 1932 House of Lords decision in the case of the snail in the bottle, *Donoghue v. Stevenson.* The case was decided by a 3–2 majority, the leading opinion being delivered by Lord Atkin with his purported "neighbor principle," a form of judge-made law. Lord Buckmaster, in a strenuous dissent, did not hide his contempt for Atkin's "neighbor principle," and hectored Lord Atkin on the basics of the Common Law:

> "The law applicable is the common law, and, though its principles are capable of application to meet new conditions not contemplated when the law was laid down, these principles cannot be changed nor can additions be made to them because any particular meritorious case seems outside their ambit." [*Donoghue v. Stevenson* [1932] UKHL 100.]

The main point that Lord Buckmaster was trying to hammer home was that the common law was based on principles that could not be changed by judges.

In the present chapter I trace the priority of legislation to the common law in time and status alike for about 700 years down to about the year 1300. And in the next two chapters I propose to carry the story forward another 600 years, down to 1932, showing that in that long period too, contrary to common belief, judge-made law was not the driving force behind the development of the common law. I intersperse this development with some modern comparisons.

As far as English common law is concerned, since 1932 judicial dominance has been the order of the day. But, in America, particularly at state level, there is much less judicial dominance over the other two branches of government.

"Nobody ever went to a ball game to see the umpire."

Americans of all political stripes, lawyers and lay people alike, are very concerned about any perceived judicial activism. Judges at all levels are labeled as either "conservative" or "liberal," or are accorded other choice epithets (some of their own choosing and some not), such as "strict constructionists," "originalists," "textualists," "loose constructionists," "pragmatists," or proponents of a "living constitution." "Legislating from the bench" is generally seen as a bad thing, and it is a reckless judge who would ever admit to indulging in that sport. Instead, judges more often claim to be neutral umpires, as in Chief Justice John Roberts's oft-quoted remark during his nomination hearing in 2005: "Judges and justices are servants of the law, not the other way around. Judges are like umpires. Umpires don't make the rules; they apply them. The role of an umpire and a judge is critical. They make sure everybody plays by the rules. But it is a limited role. Nobody ever went to a ball game to see the umpire."

Priority in Status

Which takes priority, common law or statute law? The unequivocal answer, under English law and US law (both federal and state) alike, is that statute law is superior to common law. Why does this matter? It is important because judge-made law tends to be less certain and less predictable than legislation.

In the US, where there is much more concern in the public at large about judges who "legislate from the bench," that tendency is much less prevalent—especially among American state court judges, many of whom are democratically elected—than it is in Britain, where all judges are appointed.

Common Law: Some Serious Fallacies

Ask any British or American lawyer or law student to define "common law" and you will probably be told that it is "judge-made law." This definition is largely, and increasingly, true of English common law, but is far less applicable to American state-based common law, much of which is codified. Nevertheless, many American lawyers still persist in defining common law as "judge-made law." Even the widely respected *Black's Law Dictionary*, an American publication, defines "Common Law" as: "The body of law derived from judicial decisions, rather than from statutes or constitutions." This view is inculcated into the minds of law students by a mistaken understanding of legal history found in textbooks and reference works, like this bald statement in the Wikipedia article on "Common Law":

> "Judge-made common law operated as the primary source of law for several hundred years, before Parliament acquired legislative powers to create statutory law. It is important to understand that common law is the older and more traditional source of law, and legislative power is simply a layer applied on top of the older common law foundation. Since the 12th century, courts have had parallel and co-equal

authority to make law*—'legislating from the bench' is a traditional and essential function of courts, which was carried over into the US system as an essential component of the 'judicial power' specified by Article III of the US Constitution."

This is the exact opposite of the truth in all respects. The true legal position is as follows:

- The English common law started out as statutory codes, with case-law developing much later on. This is discussed below.
- In Britain to the present day, Acts of Parliament trump common law rulings.
- The English courts do not and have never had "parallel and co-equal authority" to Parliament to make law.
- US state law is chiefly based on statute law, statutory codes and Restatements published by the American Law Institute (ALI).
- "Legislating from the bench" is *not* authorized by the US Constitution.

First reason: Wishful thinking

How and why, then, has the fallacy of the priority of the common law, and even of judge-made law, taken hold, including among those who should know better? One reason is wishful thinking. "What," you may well ask, "could possibly be wrong with judges making law? Isn't it a good thing to have a judiciary that is professional, politically neutral, and independent of the government?"

The trouble with this is that the decisions of idiosyncratic or doctrinaire judges tend to result in disarray, leading to uncertainty and unpredictability , especially in a jurisdiction like

---

* William Burnham (2006), p. 42.

England, where most civil lawsuits are decided by a single unelected judge sitting without a jury. We are reminded here of Justice Oliver Wendell Holmes's definition of law as "systematized prediction". The connection between predictability, justice and the rule of law is discussed in Chapter 17 in the section on The Rule of Law: or of Lawyers?

Two types of judicial activism

Judicial activism can go in any direction. Chief Justice John Marshall got the activist ball rolling early on in the history of the US Supreme Court with his "twistifications" (Jefferson's term)—in a "conservative" direction. His successor, Chief Justice Roger Taney, is now excoriated for his decision in the *Dred Scott* case in 1857, only the second time that an Act of Congress was struck down by the Supreme Court—in a conservative, or indeed even a reactionary direction. The "Four Horsemen" (of the Apocalypse) were conservative activist judges who did their best to block President Franklin Roosevelt's "New Deal" legislative program in the 1930s. It was really only with the Warren Court—under Chief Justice Earl Warren (1953–1969)—that the Supreme Court took a sharp turn to the left. And since then it has been divided between a "liberal" wing and a "conservative" wing, although membership of these two wings has not been unwavering.

In Britain, similarly, judicial activism has been practiced by some essentially "conservative" judges, like Lord Denning (Law Lord 1957–1962, Master of the Rolls 1962–1982), as well as by a clutch of "liberal" or more "politically correct" judges.

In his influential book, *The Politics of the Judiciary* (which went into five editions between 1977 and 2010), the socialist law academic, Professor J.A.G. Griffith (1918–2010), attacked the senior judiciary of the 1970s and 1980s for their conservative activism. He quoted the "conservative" Lord Donaldson (Master of the Rolls 1982–1992) as saying, "In relation to statutes, the only duty of the judiciary is to interpret and apply them." But Griffith went on to argue that this was not a true reflection of what the conservative judiciary actually did. "Innumerable cases ... show how easily the courts can subvert the intentions of Parliament when they think it appropriate to do so." [4th ed, p. 298]. As a true believer in Parliamentary democracy, Griffith was equally critical of judicial activism in a "politically correct" direction, which he identified as a danger in the early 2000s. Hence some long hard-hitting articles, such as "The Brave New World of Sir John Laws," [*Modern Law Review*, Vol 63, Issue 2, March 2000] and "The common law and the political constitution," [*Law Quarterly Review*, 2001].

In general, Griffith believed that judicial discretion in judicial review cases was too wide and should be strictly confined to cases where public authorities had clearly exceeded their statutory powers (*ultra vires* in its literal sense, meaning "beyond their powers"). He strongly opposed the broad "principles of administrative law," which he saw as essentially "invented" by the judiciary. Griffith offered two main reasons why judges tended to exceed their powers and become involved in politics: "First, statute law does not seek with any precision to indicate where, between Ministers and judges, final decision making should be. Secondly, judges themselves, in the common law tradition of judicial creativity, frequently invent or re-discover rules of law which enable them to intervene and to exercise political judgment in areas that hitherto had been understood to be outside their province. In the event, for these two reasons, legislators and Ministers and public authorities are continuously being surprised to discover that, in the view of the judges, they do not have the powers they thought they had." [J.A.G. Griffith (1983). p. 55.] Griffith believed that extending the idea of "the rule of law" beyond the need to ensure that government operated in accordance with the law, was "a fantasy invented by the Liberals of the old school in the late-19th century and patented by the Tories to throw a protective sanctity around certain legal and political institutions and principles which they wish to preserve at any cost."

Second reason: Indoctrination

Besides wishful thinking, the second reason for the prevalence of the fallacious belief in the priority of the common law over statute is indoctrination, or the way law tends to be taught by "liberal," or, to be more precise, left-leaning or "politically correct" academics—a phenomenon which is highly prevalent in British universities.

This kind of thinking was identified and scotched by Lord Reid (Law Lord 1948–1975) alas early as 1969: "It is often said that it would be unconstitutional for ... Parliament to do certain things, meaning that the moral, political or other reasons against doing them are so strong that most people would regard it as highly improper. ... But that does not mean that it is beyond the power of Parliament to do such things. If Parliament chose to do any of them, the courts would not hold the Act of Parliament invalid." [*Madzimbamuto v. Lardner-Burke* [1969] 1 AC 645 at 723.]

The only thing wrong with this remark is that the courts not only *would* not invalidate the statute concerned; they *could* not do so, because they lack the power to do so.

Priority in Time

There is a widely held myth that the common law just started growing naturally as judge-made law on a case by case basis before the existence of statute law. This myth must be scotched, as it is totally false. By the early middle ages, law as experienced for centuries throughout Europe was codified. The magnificent codified system of Roman law was imitated by the various Germanic successor states in the West, giving rise to a number of law codes, notably the various Visigothic Codes, the Burgundian Code, the Lombard Code, and the Code of Salic Law.

Anglo-Saxon Codes

There was also a whole succession of Anglo-Saxon codes,
significantly written in the Old English vernacular and
therefore accessible to the populace, starting soon after the
Christianization of the Anglo-Saxon kingdoms. [See Wormald,
Patrick (2005); Oliver, Lisi (2002).] Among the earliest of these
is the code (or *dom*, meaning "law" or "edict") of Anglo-Saxon
king Aethelberht (or Ethelbert) of Kent, dating from around
the year 600. The Venerable Bede tells us in his *Ecclesiastical
History of the English People*, that Aethelberht established these
laws "with the advice of his counselors," namely the Anglo-
Saxon *witan* or *witenagemot* (literally, "meeting of wise men"), a
forerunner of Parliament. [Bede, *Ecclesiastical History*, ii.5]. The
code contains an elaborate series of penalties and fines,
depending on the deed and the status of the person concerned.
As keeping the peace was the King's prime concern, many of
the provisions of the code concerned criminal offences. The
whole scheme was clearly intended to provide a peaceful
alternative to blood feuds, where the victim or the victim's
family would pursue the perpetrator and either kill him or
injure him to compensate for the harm that he had inflicted.
The code substituted monetary compensation in the form of
wergild or *wergeld* (literally "man-price") or some multiple or
fraction of that, plus a fine which went to the Crown. As far as
personal injury was concerned, serious damage to the penis
carries the highest compensation. Striking off a foot or gouging
out an eye comes next, whereas ear-piercing comes right at the
bottom of the list, valued at only 3 shillings. Not all the laws
are criminal. Clause 31 reads: "If a freeman lies with a free
man's wife, let him pay recompense [with] his/her *wergild* and
obtain another wife [for the husband] [with] his own money
and bring her to the other man at home." This is evidently a
reference to consensual adultery rather than to rape.

"Six shillings for defamation"

Another early Anglo-Saxon compilation of laws comes down to us under the joint names of Hlothhere and his nephew Eadric, who ruled Kent jointly between 679 and 685. An interesting provision of this code occurs at §4: "If a freeman should die with a living wife and child, it is right that it, that child, should be under the protection of the mother, and one should give for him one among his father's kin who willingly gives surety to maintain his property, until he should be 10 years old." This code contains an interesting provision relating to defamation at §7: "If a person in another's house calls a person a perjurer or accosts him shamefully with mocking words, let him pay a shilling to him who owns that house, and 6 shillings to him to whom he spoke that utterance, and let him pay 12 shillings to the king." So, a verbal attack on somebody is actionable only if made in the presence of a third party—similar to the modern requirement for defamatory words to be "published" to a third party in order to be actionable. Keeping the peace without violence is the subject of §9: "If a person should draw a weapon where men are drinking and no harm is done there, a shilling to him who owns that house, and 12 shillings to the king." If there is bloodshed, the penalty is increased, as provided at §9.1: "If that house becomes bloodied, let him pay the man [the price for violation of] his protection and 50 shillings to the king."

"Oath supporters"

The laws of Hlothhere & Eadric introduce a new feature, oath supporters, who, for example, could vouch for the lawfulness of a sale as a defence against an accusation of theft. This is a predecessor of the jury, which was originally made up of local men who could swear to the true circumstances of an alleged crime. It was only much later on that a jury had to be

made up of men who did *not* have any first-hand knowledge of
an alleged crime.

"English law the instrument and expression of the power of the Government"

Referring to the period from Alfred the Great (reigned 871–
899) onward, Patrick Wormald concluded: "England's law is
distinctive because it is as old as the English kingdom. What
above all distinguishes the history of England from that of its
neighbours and counterparts is that the power of government
has been longer and more consistently felt throughout the area it
has claimed to rule. English law has been the instrument and
expression of that power ever since it was exercised by King
Alfred (871–899) and his heirs. Henry II (r. 1154–1189) made
law like no other twelfth-century king, because he inherited a
system of royal justice that was already uniquely old and active."
[Patrick Wormald (1999), p, xi.] After Alfred's so-called *Domboc*,
Wormald identified no fewer than eleven pre-Conquest codes of
law produced by Anglo-Saxon kings. He tentatively suggested
that in these codes could be glimpsed "green shoots of the
Common Law." (p. xii). An interesting provision from chapter
36 of Alfred's *Domboc* prefigures the tort of negligence:
"Moreover, it is established: If anyone has a spear over his
shoulder, and a man is transfixed on it, the *wergild* is to be paid
without the fine." [Translated by Carole Hough [2014.] A
distinction is drawn here between a deliberate killing and an
accidental death. If you negligently drape a spear over your
shoulder, which accidentally kills somebody, then you have to
pay the victim's *wergild*. But a fine, which goes to the Crown, is
added only if the killing was deliberate—a neat distinction
between criminal conduct and negligence. As the king is
concerned to keep the peace and to punish crime, he gets his
share of the action when a crime has been committed, but not if
the conduct concerned is just negligent.

700 Years of codified statute law

The numerous Anglo-Saxon codes were succeeded by codified statute law promulgated in the two centuries after the Norman Conquest of 1066, giving us a period of some seven hundred years of statute law before the Common Law came into existence—a period as long as the whole length of time that elapsed from the earliest days of the common law until today!

Statutes of Westminster 1275, 1285 & 1290

It is important to note that statute law pre-existed not only the common law but also the existence of Parliament. Statutory codes are found from the very earliest days of the English Parliament. A notable example is the Statute of Gloucester of 1278 in the reign of Edward I, the first statute recorded in a Statute Roll. This important enactment gave jurisdiction to the king's courts over actions concerning property damage worth more than 40 shillings, and "maims," beatings and wounds. The passing of the Statute of Gloucester gave rise to writs (i.e. claims) of trespass alleging physical or property damage *vi et armis* ("by force and arms") and *contra pacem* ("against the king's peace"), which led in due course to claims for negligence. The three Statutes of Westminster of 1275, 1285 and 1290, are also really important pieces of legislation, the second of which Bishop William Stubbs (1825–1901), the great Victorian constitutional historian, described as, "like the first Statute of Westminster, ... a code in itself." [*The Constitutional History of England*, 3 vols, 1874–1878].

The Development of Case-Law

So, far from predating statutory legislation, case-law took a long time to develop—and even when it did it remained subordinate to statute law, which is still the position in English law today. In the words of Sir Percy Winfield (1878–1953), a member of my Cambridge College and a noted authority on legal history: "The principle that counsel may and must cite previous cases to the judges, who must adopt them as the bases of their judgments, is practically non-existent in the Year Books." [Winfield, *The Chief Sources of English Legal History*, p. 149]. The Year Books were reports of "pleas," or cases, heard before the Court of Common Pleas between 1268 and 1535. In the view of Frederic Maitland (1850–1906) and other leading legal historians, the Year Books lacked any official status but were compilations made by law students. Not surprisingly, case-law did not develop during the Year Book period.

Case-law essentially depends on the doctrine of *stare decisis*, or binding precedent, which in turn depends on accurate law reports, the dissemination of which in turn depends on printing, which was only introduced into England by William Caxton in 1476. The earliest printed Year-Books appeared in 1481–1482.

[Winfield, *op. cit.*, p. 183f.]. Winfield identified three stages of law reports:

(a) 1537–1765
(b) 1765–1865, when the "Law Reports" series began.
(c) 1865 onwards.

The law reports in the first period are described as "named reports," so called because they were unofficial reports compiled by individual lawyers and judges, often of cases in which they themselves had participated—which sometimes resulted in less than accurate accounts.

"In the second period," Winfield explains, "reports acquired the accuracy and completeness which we have come to regard as commonplace in the third period; but in the first period, they varied infinitely in value. At the top of the list stand great lawyers like Plowden, Coke, and Saunders; at the bottom are incompetents like Barnardiston, who is said to have fallen asleep over his note-book in court, and to have had nonsense scribbled in it by wags who leaned over from the seat behind." (Winfield, *op. cit.,* p.184)

The third period was ushered in by the establishment in 1865 of the non-profit Incorporated Council of Law Reporting (ICLR) for England and Wales, which not only publishes reports of leading contemporary cases but also, in a series titled the *English Reports*, reprinted "named" or "nominate" reports going back to the year 1220.

This brings us to a major paradox. After almost 700 years of codified law, the rise of Parliament—potentially the most obvious dispenser of codification—saw the end of codification in English law. [Of course, the American story is very different, as we shall see in due course]. The reason for this was evidently the Government's confidence that law was now on a firm footing.

Forms of Action

With the establishment of the centralized courts of the Exchequer of Pleas, King's Bench and Common Pleas, all sitting in Westminster Hall (Common Pleas, as stipulated in Magna Carta in1215, and King's Bench from 1318), a formal system of civil litigation came into existence based on the so-called Forms of Action. In order to bring a claim, a plaintiff would purchase a standardized "writ" from the Chancery office (not to be confused with the Court of Chancery), or, less commonly, file a "bill," which gave him slightly more flexibility. The writs were couched in formulaic language, and a plaintiff had to bring his case within the rigid wording, which was not always easy, or even possible.

Trials of different forms of action were conducted by different procedures. Trial by battle or ordeal, formally abolished in 1819 although it had long fallen out of use, was applicable to certain writs. "Compurgation," or "wager of law," was used in trials for Debt or Detinue, for example. The defendant would swear under oath that he was not guilty or not liable. If he could find the requisite number of "compurgators" (usually twelve) to swear that they believed him, he would be acquitted.

Compurgation can be traced back to Anglo-Saxon times, and it
survived as a defense to Debt and Detinue until 1833.

Jury Trials

Jury trial clearly owes something to compurgation. The
Assize of Clarendon, an Act promulgated by Henry II in 1166,
set up a system that was a precursor of the grand jury, which
continued to exercise its pre-trial function in England until 1933
(as of course it still does in the US today).

The petit jury (literally, "little jury"), or trial jury, grew out
of the grand jury, and trial by jury was standard in cases of
trespass, which is one of the reasons why that form of action
became so popular.

Trespass

The writ of trespass, which arose out of the Statute of
Gloucester, enacted in 1278 during the reign of Edward I, is the
origin of the tort of negligence. The word "trespass" originally
referred to wrongdoing of any kind, as in the traditional
translation of the Lord's Prayer: "Forgive us our trespasses, as we
forgive those who trespass against us." In the original Greek text
the word translated here as "trespasses" is *opheilemata*, which
literally means "debts," and this is how it is translated in some
versions of the passage in Matthew 6:12. The modern use of
"trespass" in the specific sense of trespass to land is just one of
three types of trespass, the others being trespass to goods and
trespass to the person. However, in the early days "trespass"
covered all three of these.

Vi et Armis

But, as we saw in regard to the Anglo-Saxon codes, the
Crown was primarily interested in keeping the peace. So the
standard wording of the writ alleged trespass *vi et armis* (by force

and arms"), often combined with *contra pacem* (against [the king's] peace"). But, so popular did the writ of trespass become that before long victims of tort, crime or even breach of contract started using it even when there was no force or violence involved at all. The fictitious nature of the allegation *vi et armis* or *contra pacem* was sometimes simply ignored by the court.

For example, in an Anonymous case of 1304 (Baker & Milsom (B&M) (1986), p. 297) the plaintiff claimed that the defendants had come "wrongfully *vi et armis* and cut and carried away wood" belonging to the plaintiff. It turned out that the defendants had indeed removed the wood, but not by force of arms. Judge William Bereford, the future Chief Justice of Common Pleas, "adjudged that [the plaintiff] should recover his damages etc., and that the defendant should be taken [and imprisoned] notwithstanding that they did not come *vi et armis*."

Fictitious allegations of violence

In *Petstede v. Marreys* [1310—B, p. 298], a case alleging the theft of a large number of deer, counsel for the plaintiff actually admitted that the allegation of violence was fictitious. Sir Roger Brabazon, Chief Justice of King's Bench, "adjudged the writ good."

In *Rattlesdene v. Gruneston* (1317—B&M, p. 300) the purchaser of a tun (vat or cask) of wine claimed that the seller had, "with swords, bows and arrows", adulterated much of the wine with salt water. Neither of the allegations makes sense. A merchant wishing to dilute the wine that he was selling would be unlikely to add *salt* water to the product—and to do so by force of arms! The allegation of violence was almost certainly fictitious—and the adulteration with salt water was probably accidental rather than deliberate. As suggested by Mark Lunney and Ken Oliphant, the incursion of salt water was probably the result of a shipping accident. [Lunney, M. & K. Oliphant (2013), p. 5]. This case is therefore an early example of negligence.

Humber Ferryman's Case

In *Bukton v. Tounesende,* or *The Humber Ferryman's case* (1348–B&M 358) a ferryman, appropriately described as Nicholas Tounesende of Helle, undertook to carry John Bukton's mare across the River Humber, but so overloaded the boat with horses that Bukton's mare fell overboard and was drowned. The claim was brought by bill alleging trespass, but without *vi et armis* or *contra pacem.* The defendant argued that the claim should have been brought as a breach of covenant, and that it should fail, as there was no contract under seal. The judge, however, upheld the claim as lodged: "It seems that you did him a trespass when you overloaded his boat so that his mare perished." So the case was treated as one of negligence rather than as a breach of contract.

Edward I (1272–1307): a period of statutory activity"

These cases show just how wrong it is to dismiss the forms of action as being fixated on form at the expense of the merits of the case. But it should always be remembered that the whole system was driven by *legislation.* Professor Frederic Maitland (1850–1906), the famous legal historian, characterized the reign of Edward I (1272–1307) as "a period of statutory activity. Statutes made by the king and Parliament now interfere with many details both of substantive law and of procedure. ... The whole system stiffens. Men have learnt that a power to invent new remedies is a power to create new rights and duties, and it is no longer to be suffered that the chancellor or the judges should wield this power." The Statute of Westminster (at §11) allows Chancery to "vary the old writs—but it is not to invent new rights or new remedies." And, if no suitable writ exists for a particular case, the Statute stipulates that it may be necessary for the plaintiff concerned to wait for the next Parliament." [Maitland, Frederic (1909), p. 344f.].

[Note: The Chancellor, Lord Chancellor or Lord High Chancellor, was until the early 18th century the chief minister of the English Crown. His office, staffed by clerks known as cursitors (literally, "runners"), was called the Chancery, which was responsible for issuing official documents, including the writs for use in lawsuits. The word chancellor had humble origins, coming as it does from the late Latin word *cancella*, meaning a screen of the kind seen in medieval churches, behind which a clerk would sit making records. Edward I gave the chancellor increased responsibilities, which before long turned his office into the Court of Chancery, dispensing equity rather than law. The Court of Chancery was headed up by the Chancellor, who often heard cases himself. The Court of Chancery ceased to exist in 1875, when it was converted into the Chancery Division of the High Court, which still exists, now dispensing both equity and law].

Conclusion

Trespass was not the only Form of Action, but it was the most popular, because trials were by jury, and the writ itself, contrary to a common assumption, was actually quite flexible. In the standard form writ, obtainable from the Chancery office for a fee, the plaintiff claimed that he had been injured by the defendant in his person, goods or land, *vi et armis* ("by force and arms"), and also sometimes *contra pacem* ("against the king's peace")—wording showing its statutory origin, because the government was not interested in becoming involved in private disputes, but was only concerned to keep the peace. But this apparently inflexible wording was soon circumvented, and it seems to have been well understood that the allegations of violence, sometimes coupled with an elaborate description of the weapons purportedly employed by the wicked defendant against the innocent plaintiff, were fictitious. The outcome of the case did not depend on these fictions but on the true facts underlying the writ—how the plaintiff's mare drowned, for example, or how the plaintiff's wine came to be contaminated with seawater. To say, with academics who should know better, that fault and the general merits counted for nothing in these trespass cases, is clearly wrong. And it is equally wrong to see any major role in these cases for judges.

The rise of "trespass on the case" or "action on the case," as a writ separate from trespass, complicated the system and gave judges more power. But the idea that the common law grew simply at the whim of individual judges is not true. On the contrary, the next period was one governed by principles based on Maxims of the Law, whose influence was as great then as their oblivion is now.

THE ERA OF PRINCIPLE
IN ENGLISH LAW

From Trespass to Assumpsit

I fully agree with the view expressed by Professor David Ibbetson of Cambridge University that judge-made law was not much in evidence in the period up to the mid-14th century while the dominant form of action was trespass:

> "The general action of trespass gave little scope for judicial control, and ... it seems that in practice it would normally be for the jury to determine whether the circumstances were such that liability might be imposed. In anachronistically modern terms, that is to say, the jury would have decided both whether a duty was owed and whether that duty had been breached." [David & D.J. Ibbetson,(2001), p. 63.]

How, if at all, did the situation change in the following centuries, when fuller pleadings in trespass on the case and generally in actions brought by bill, which necessitated more detailed pleadings, allowed greater judicial input?

The fourteenth and fifteenth centuries saw the convergence of four major developments in English law:

- The development of trespass on the case or action on the case;
- The development of assumpsit;
- The rise of maxims;
- The rise of the Court of Chancery.

In Consimili Casu

The codified Second Statute of Westminster of 1285 allowed
the expansion of forms of action *in consimili casu* ("in a similar
case"), meaning that new writs could be created to cater for cases
similar to existing ones. The relevant wording in Westminster II
is as follows: "That as often as it shall happen in the Chancery, that
in one case a writ is found, and in a like case (*in consimili casu*)
falling under the same right, and requiring like remedy, no writ is
to be found, the clerks of the Chancery shall agree in making a
writ, or adjourn the complaint till the next parliament, and write
the cases in which they cannot agree, and refer them to the next
parliament." Inclusion of the mention here of Parliament, which is
usually omitted in the extract from the statute quoted in modern
books, is of particular importance, showing the legislative basis of
the whole system of forms of action.

Writs were issued by Chancery, the department of state
headed up by the Chancellor, or Lord Chancellor, the chief
minister of the Crown, which was staffed by clerks. Of all the
forms of action initially created, trespass was by far the most
popular, one of the chief reasons for this being that writs of
trespass were decided by jury trial, as distinct from wager of law
or compurgation employed by certain other forms of action.
Compurgation (literally, "cleansing, exonerating"), or wager of
law, gave the defendant an opportunity to have the claim against
him dismissed if he could find twelve neighbors who could
swear to his innocence. As we saw in the previous chapter, writs
of trespass, originating from the Crown's concern to keep order,
initially claimed that the defendant had caused the plaintiff
injury, loss or damage *vi et armis* ("by force and arms"), often
combined with *contra pacem* ("against the king's peace"), though
these descriptions were often fictitious, and recognized as such
by all concerned, and were added purely for form's sake.

The popularity of writs of trespass led to their use spreading
from claims for direct to indirect damage. So many and varied

were the uses to which the writ of Trespass was applied that by the mid-14th century writs claiming for indirect damage needed to specify the facts on which the claim was based, and so came to be called "Action on the Case," "Trespass on the Case," or just simply "Case." The classic statement of the difference between trespass and case is that someone struck by a log thrown on to the street would bring trespass against the thrower, but someone tripping over that log would have to bring an action on the case. Case had a number of ramifications, one of the most important of which was *assumpsit* ("he undertook, promised"), or *indebitatus assumpsit* ("being indebted, he promised or undertook"). Both these forms were used for breach of contract, the latter starting in the mid-16th century, but the pleading was not exactly the same.

"The Legislative Impulse"

In his detailed study of English law in the wake of the Black Death of 1348, which wiped out probably over 40% of the population of England, Professor Robert C. Palmer rejected the accepted orthodoxy of Professor S.F.C. ("Toby") Milsom and concluded: "The government initiated and directed change, making the law an affirmative instrument of social control." [Palmer, Robert C.(1993), p. 149] "This study thus proposes the approach Milsom was most ardent to disprove: the presence of a legislative impulse in the beginnings of case and assumpsit." [Ibid., p. 150] And again: "Milsom talks about chancery provision of a writ, but his assumption for the 14th century is always that the justices made the law. That assumption contains the anachronistic assertion of separation of powers. Jettisoning that assumption collapses the whole framework of Milsom's argument."

Palmer explains the litigation process as follows: "Chancery issued the writs; the writs constituted the causes of action and were the primary source of law. The justices had no authority to go beyond the 'four corners of the writ' and create a wholly new cause of action. Certainly they could and did allow the manipulation of old writs, much as courts today allow manipulation of statute. But just as common law construction of a statute is far different from the common law, so was medieval construction and manipulation of the given writs different from a common law solely or primarily judge-made." [Ibid., p. 297] And: "Instead of operating solely by internal decisions, Chancery preferred to act primarily in reinforcement of parliamentary statute."

Palmer's (unfashionable) approach to the period after the Black Death rings true and ties in with the situation in the pre-plague period considered in the previous chapter. It is also supported by legislation enacted by Edward III (reigned 1337–1377). A Proclamation of 1349, for example, directed anyone who had a problem with the common law to petition the Chancellor— foreshadowing the development of Chancery into a separate Court of Equity. [Calendar of Close Rolls Preserved in the Public Record Office: Ed III, 14 vols, (London, 1896–1913) 1346-1349, p. 615.] In the same year the King issued the Ordinance of Labourers, confirmed by Parliament as the Statute of Labourers 1351, which introduced stringent control of the labor market and wages. The Statute of Treasons 1351 was another important piece of legislation, which is still on the UK statute book and also forms the basis of the US law of Treason as incorporated into Article III, Section 3 of the US Constitution.

The "fashionable" view

The "fashionable" view of Medieval law is essentially that it was primitive and largely judge-made. This is simply not borne out by the evidence. Theodore Plucknett (1897–1965), author of a book titled the *Concise History of the Common Law*, is quoted as saying: "It is still too often said that English law can only be understood historically. Now English law may be bad, but is it really as bad as that?" [S.F.C. Milsom, (2010).] Since Plucknett's death English law has undoubtedly fallen into a state of disarray and lack of principle far worse than during his lifetime, but for the six centuries up until 1932, English law was stable and principled, contrary to the currently fashionable view.

Here is an example of this "fashionable" view, as expressed by A.W.B. Simpson in his *History of the Common Law of Contract*: "It is now no longer believed that the appearance of the action on the case has anything to do with c. 24 (*consimili casu*) of the Statute of Westminster." [Simpson, A.W.B. (1987), p. 202n., citing Plucknett and Miss E.J. Dix]. Where then did action on the case come from? Are we to believe, without any real evidence, that action on the case was judge-made law? It is important to stress that action on the case started as *trespass* on the case, and actually continued to be referred to as such side by side with "action on the case," or simply "case." The form of action of trespass was itself infinitely adaptable to many different circumstances, as we have seen. The stock wording of *vi et armis* or *contra pacem* was early on recognized in many cases as fictitious—until these stereotyped phrases were dropped, leaving the way open to even greater flexibility by adding details of the actual case in question. Hence the designation of the claim as "trespass on the case," "action on the case," or simply "case." It is a natural extension of "trespass," which in turn can certainly be traced back to the Statute of Westminster II of 1285.

Action on the case

We have an example of an action on the case from as early as 1329: *The Oculist's Case* [B&M, p. 340.] A man sued an oculist by bill alleging trespass on the case in that the oculist had undertaken to heal his eye, but that as a result of the treatment he lost his eye. The defendant submitted that the action sounded in covenant rather than in trespass, but an action of covenant required a deed, which the plaintiff obviously did not have. Justice Denum of King's Bench, drawing parallels from a physician whose patient had died and a farrier who had injured a horse with a nail, causing its death, concluded that the oculist, as a professional, had done the best he could. Not surprisingly, the plaintiff then decided to discontinue his action.

Assumpsit

This case shows how trespass on the case could cover not only negligence but also breach of contract—which explains how it extended into assumpsit, as can be seen from *Stratton v. Swanlond* (1374) [B&M p. 360]. A woman sued her surgeon, who had undertaken to heal her injured hand but whose treatment was so negligent that her hand was now badly disfigured. The writ contained no claim of *vi et armis* or *contra pacem*. Although the case is brought by writ of trespass, it is really an early example of trespass on the case, and, in particular, assumpsit, as the basis of the claim was that the surgeon *undertook* to heal the injured hand. It is sometimes cited as the earliest medical malpractice case. The claim itself was dismissed on a technicality. But its importance lies in the clear summary by King's Bench Chief Justice Sir John Cavendish of the basic principles of professional negligence generally, again using the example of a farrier: a farrier who undertook to heal a horse but negligently made the horse worse should be held liable. But there is no liability if the farrier conscientiously tries his best but the horse still dies. Why can the farrier not be held liable if he tries his best? The answer appears to lie in the concept of negligence. A farrier, or any other professional person or skilled tradesman, is judged in terms of the standards of that profession or trade. If the professional person or skilled tradesman acts conscientiously in accordance with those standards, even if unsuccessfully, then no negligence and no liability will be found.

Quid pro quo

The overlap between contract and negligence is well illustrated by a case of trespass on the case of a century later concerning hiring a carpenter to build a house: Anon 1440 [B&M p. 389.] Justice William Ayscough drew the then standard contrast between the carpenter doing a bad job, which was misfeasance (i.e. negligence—sometimes also called malfeasance), where trespass on the case would lie, and nonfeasance (i.e. non-performance), where the remedy would depend on having a contract under seal. But Thomas Browne, the second prothonotary, is then recorded as adding a rider that if the carpenter was paid some money (probably only a deposit or first instalment) to build a house but did not do the work, then action on the case would lie, "because the defendant has *quid pro quo* and the plaintiff has suffered a loss"—foreshadowing the development of trespass on the case into assumpsit. This is particularly noteworthy in being in the Court of Common Pleas, which was generally disinclined to allow assumpsit to replace the older contractual writ of debt, on which that court had a monopoly.

[Note: A prothonotary was essentially a junior judge. The post continued until 1837, when it was renamed "Master," which still survives today.]

Certainly by 1532 we find this same view strongly held in a King's Bench case brought on an assumpsit concerning the non-delivery of malt, which had been paid for in cash: *Pykeryng v. Thurgoode* (1532) [B&M, p. 411.] The defendant pleaded "Non assumpsit," adding that the case ought to have been brought by writ of debt. Justice John Spelman firmly rejected this submission, emphasizing that it made no sense to distinguish between malfeasance (or misfeasance) and nonfeasance.

"Ridiculous conclusion"?

Another less than persuasive remark of Simpson's is relevant here:

"[T]o a modern English lawyer a 'contract' means an agreement supported by consideration, the notion of

agreement being analysed in terms of the doctrine of offer and
acceptance. Medieval lawyers had never heard of either the
doctrine of consideration (which evolved in the 16th century)
or the doctrine of offer and acceptance (which evolved in the
19th), and to make matters more complicated, their general
term for 'agreement' was 'covenant' and not 'contract'.
Consequently any attempt to investigate the medieval law of
contract in terms of modern legal theory would be perfectly
futile, for it could only lead to the ridiculous conclusion that
no law of contract then existed."

Practically everything in this passage is questionable at best.
The remark about the terminology is particularly puzzling. In
fact, besides "covenant," for which there was a distinct writ
(applicable to "specialty" contracts, being contracts under seal, or
deeds), there was also "debt *sur contract*," (debt on contract),
which could be used to claim payment from the defendant for
goods already delivered or services rendered by the plaintiff. A
defence to a claim for debt could be that the claim should have
been brought by covenant—with the support of a contract under
seal. But we have an example of a claim for work done from as
early as 1338, in which Judge Sharshulle held: "If one were to
count simply of a grant of a debt, he would not be received
without a specialty; but here you have his service for his
allowance, of which knowledge may be had, and you have *quid
pro quo*." [Anon (1338) Year Book 11–12 Edw. III (R.S.) 587.]
Not only, therefore, do we have here an action on a "contract,"
but also *quid pro quo*, which of course is a recognition of offer
and acceptance and consideration—both of which Simpson
claimed were unknown until much later. In the action of debt
sur contract great emphasis was placed on the mutuality or
reciprocity of the agreement. So, in a 1473 case, Chief Justice
Brian held: "I bring cloth to a tailor to have a cloak made; if the
price be not determined beforehand that I shall pay for the
making, he shall have no action of debt against me." [Anon.
(1473) Y.B. 12 Edw. IV, East, fol. 9, pl. 22.]

As we have seen, just as trespass on the case was an extension of the original writ of trespass (with or without *vi et armis*), so assumpsit started out as a variant of trespass on the case. As even Simpson admits, "we can now trace the history of assumpsit back into the 14th century," [p. 199]. *Stratton v. Swanlond* (discussed above) of 1374 is an example of this, but *Slade's Case* of 1602 marks the triumph of assumpsit over debt for contractual claims: *Slade's Case* or *Slade v. Morley* [4 Co. Rep. 91 (1602).]

Slade's Case (1602)

Commonly described as a "watershed decision," *Slade's Case* is also often wrongly regarded as an example of judicial legislation. The facts of the case are quite straightforward. In 1596 John Slade, a grain merchant, brought a bill claiming that Humphrey Morley agreed or undertook (*assumpsit*) to buy a crop of wheat and rye from him for £16, but that Morley reneged on the agreement. Morley pleaded *Non assumpsit* ("He did not undertake, promise"). A jury returned a verdict for Slade in the amount of £16. The case had been brought before the Assizes (an itinerant court), where it was heard by two judges, one of King's Bench and one of the Court of Common Pleas. As a result of this unusual arrangement, judgment was not entered for Slade right away, as would normally have occurred if he had brought the case directly in Queen's Bench, which would have been the end of the matter. Instead of that, however, Queen's Bench Chief Justice John Popham transferred the case to an informal Court of Exchequer Chamber made up of all eleven justices of England drawn from the Court of Common Pleas, Exchequer and Queen's Bench. The resulting deadlock caused the case to drag on for five years, but Slade was eventually awarded his £16, plus costs. In delivering what purported to be the majority decision, Chief Justice Popham held: "It was resolved, that every contract executory imports in itself an assumpsit, for when one agrees to pay money, or to deliver anything, thereby he promises to pay, or deliver it; and therefore when one sells any goods to another, and agrees to deliver them at a day to come, and the other in consideration thereof promises to pay so much money to the other, in this case both parties may have an action of debt, or an action on the case on assumpsit, for the mutual executory agreement of both parties imports in itself reciprocal action upon the case, as well as action of debt, and therewith agrees the judgment in *Reade and Norwoods Case.*" [1 Plowden 180, 75 ER 277 (1558).]

This reliance on a case of nearly half a century earlier detracts from the novelty and celebrity normally accorded *Slade* in modern writings. *Norwood v. Read* (1558) was not nearly as straightforward as *Slade's Case* itself, yet the use of assumpsit for breach of contract was upheld there in King's Bench* without much trouble. The plaintiff was suing the executors of a deceased estate. The claim was that the testator, in consideration of 40 shillings paid to him by the plaintiff, promised to deliver a consignment of wheat to the plaintiff, for which the plaintiff was to pay on delivery. Although the plaintiff was waiting at the agreed time to take delivery and though the testator was still alive at that time, he never delivered any wheat to the plaintiff, and the deceased testator's executors likewise refused to deliver any wheat to the plaintiff. The "consideration" of 40 shillings purportedly paid in advance by the plaintiff purchaser may possibly have been fictitious—an interesting example perhaps of

---

* An interesting sidelight on Plowden's report of this case is the fact that, though this case was heard during the reign of Queen Mary I (Tudor) (reigned 1553-58), the court is referred to as King's Bench rather than Queen's Bench, which would be normal during a female reign. The reason is that Mary's husband, King Philip II of Spain, was also recognized as King (consort) of England, so that his portrait appeared on the coins together with Mary and all statutes and official documents were dated "in the xth year of the reign of King Philip and Queen Mary."

the need felt to insist on some concrete consideration as validation of the contract.

The adulation accorded *Slade* is excessive. Here is an example:

> "[T]he burning questions in the minds of those who awaited the final pronouncement in *Slade's Case* were not Year Book questions or ancient moot points, but new questions which had only come to the fore in the preceding ten or fifteen years." [Baker, J.H. [1971], pp 213–236.]

In fact, however, by 1602 assumpsit had been successfully pleaded in contract cases for well over two hundred years—in King's Bench. The main issue in *Slade* was whether the Court of Common Pleas could be persuaded to accept assumpsit as a substitute for the writ of debt—the point being that, while assumpsit could be brought in either court, the Court of Common Pleas had a monopoly on actions for debt. That was why Popham referred the case to an informal Court of Exchequer Chamber including judges from Queen's Bench and Common Pleas alike.

But why has so much printer's ink been expended on *Slade's Case?* One reason is that it was a titanic battle between two legal superstars, two showmen who also happened to be political rivals and personal enemies: Coke and Bacon. But probably the main reason is because of the way Coke took ownership of the case.

Sir Edward Coke (1552–1634) not only represented Slade but also in 1604 published a detailed account of the case in his *Reports*, in which he gave the impression that the eventual decision by the assembled justices was based on his arguments and that the decision was unanimous—which, like so much else that flowed from Coke's pen, is almost certainly untrue. (Perhaps it is no accident that his name, though spelled Coke, is pronounced "Cook," as he certainly knew how to cook the books!)

"The Forms of Action We Have Buried...."

Frederic Maitland (1850–1906) famously remarked: "The forms of action we have buried, but they still rule us from their graves." [Maitland, Frederic (1909), p. 2.] The forms of action, with certain variations, survived until the Judicature Acts of 1873 and 1875, which introduced some major structural and procedural reforms but did nothing to make up for the period of close on six centuries during which Parliament had neglected its duty to place the substantive law on a codified or even a consolidated legislative footing. But there is a justification for this, which is that for that long period the forms of action— together with legal maxims and equity—provided English law with a stable set of principles.

"Due care and skill"

Here is an example of a case from 1862, which, except for one statutory aspect, could have been brought in 1362. [*Hammack v. White* 11 C.B. N.S. 588. (1862).]

This one exceptional feature is the fact that the case was brought under the Fatal Accidents Act 1846, commonly known as Lord Campbell's Act, which for the first time allowed compensation to family members for deaths caused by actionable wrongs such as negligence. With this exception, the claim was essentially the same as a trespass on the case for negligence. The facts of the case are quite simple. William Hammack was walking on the sidewalk in Finsbury Circus in Central London "when he was knocked down and kicked by a horse on which the defendant was riding. " He died from his injuries eleven days later. The question was whether the defendant, White, had "used due care and skill," failing which he would have been negligent. In the words of Chief Justice Erle of the Common Pleas: "The sort of negligence imputed here is, either that the defendant was unskilful in the management of the horse, or imprudent in taking a vicious animal (or one with whose propensities or temper he was not sufficiently acquainted) into a populous neighbourhood. The evidence is: that the defendant was seen riding the horse at a slow pace, that the horse seemed restless and the defendant was holding the reins tightly, omitting nothing he could do to avoid the accident; but that the horse swerved from the roadway on to the pavement, where the deceased was walking and knocked him down and injured him fatally. I can see nothing in this evidence to shew that the defendant was unskillful as a rider or in the management of a horse." It turned out, surprisingly, that the defendant had only bought the horse the day before the accident, and was trying it out in a busy public place. But neither these facts, nor the fact that the defendant was riding on the sidewalk was enough to persuade any of the three judges to decide that the case ought to have been left to the jury. Keating J. summed up the case like this: "It is equally probable that there was not as that there was negligence on the part of the defendant. The plaintiff, therefore, fails to sustain the issue the affirmative of which the law casts upon her."

This is a harsh decision indeed. But it was decided on the basis of principle—the same principle that we have seen at work in a number of medieval cases. Though being a horserider was not a trade or profession, it is treated in very much the same way. Did the defendant exercise "due care and skill"? In the absence of what Erle C.J. elsewhere termed "affirmative proof of negligence," the claim must be dismissed.

Henry John Stephen's Treatise on Pleading in Civil Actions, 1824

The pleadings in this magnificent compilation published by Henry John Stephen (1787–1864—a member of St John's College, Cambridge) in 1824 and in subsequent editions in both England and America until 1859, look not very different from pleadings of several centuries earlier—except that until 1731 they would have been in Latin instead of English. Here is Stephen's comment on assumpsit in the original 1824 edition:

> "The action of *assumpsit* lies where a party claims damages for breach of a simple contract, i.e. a promise not under seal. Such promises may be express or implied; and the law always implies a promise to do that which a party is legally liable to perform. This remedy is consequently of very large and extensive application." [Stephen, Henry John (1824), p. 16.]

Nothing in that description would have been out of place had it been written in 1624 or even in 1524. And here is the actual form of the pleading as it appears in Stephen's book:

WRIT OF TRESPASS ON THE CASE

In Assumpsit

For goods sold and delivered

A.B. before that time sold and delivered to the said C.D., at his special instance and request; and being so indebted, he, the said C.D., in consideration thereof afterwards. ... undertook and faithfully promised the said A.B. to pay him the said sum of money.

The following features are worth noting:

- That in 1824 the heading is still "Trespass on the Case," with "In Assumpsit" as a sub-heading.
- The strong emphasis on the reciprocity of the arrangement with the words "at his special instance and request"—offer and acceptance.
- The claim of indebtedness *before* the promise to pay (which, as Stephen pointed out, may actually have been implied).
- The specific mention of "consideration."
- The undertaking and faithful promise to pay.

Deeds under Seal

It could be argued that at least some of the forms of action are still alive. For example, the action of covenant, which was created in the 13th century to cover breaches of contract under seal, or deeds, also known as "specialty" contracts. To this day, in both English and American law, a deed, also termed a contract under seal, or a specialty contract, does not require consideration for validity.

A Shocking Case

The medieval rule which we have come across repeatedly in this chapter, that professionals or skilled tradesmen cannot be held liable for negligence if they act conscientiously despite inflicting injury or loss, still forms the basis of the so-called *Bolam* test for clinical negligence, medical malpractice or indeed any kind of professional negligence in English law to this day. Based on the verdict in the case of *Bolam v. Friern Hospital Management Committee* [1957] 1 WLR 582, the test sets the standard of reasonable care in cases of medical negligence. The test was put like this by McNair J in the *Bolam* case itself: A doctor "is not guilty of negligence if he has acted in accordance with a practice accepted as proper by a responsible body of medical men skilled in that particular art." However, the term "responsible body of medical men" is not defined and can end up, as it unfortunately did in *Bolam*, with a negligent doctor winning a case with the evidence of a few other equally negligent doctors accepted by the court as "a responsible body of medical men." Though the *Bolam* test is a survival from the days of trespass on the case, judicial intervention in that case itself turned a perfectly good test into a disaster. Mr. Bolam, who was suffering from depression, was a voluntary patient in a mental hospital. Without being told the risks involved, he agreed to undergo electro-convulsive therapy, or shock treatment. The treatment was performed without Mr. Bolam being given any relaxant drugs (which subsequently became standard practice) or even being held down on the bed. As a result, when he went into convulsions (which is expected in this kind of treatment) he suffered serious injuries including a bilateral fracture of the pelvis, and he arrived in court in a pitiful state. The jury was virtually directed by the judge to return a verdict for the defendant hospital on the basis of the supposed "responsible body of medical men". Had the jury been left to their own devices, it is quite likely that they would have found the hospital negligent. This highly unsatisfactory outcome was the result of the superimposition of post-1932 judicial activism on a perfectly sound ancient principle. *Bolam* is no isolated case. To adapt a remark of Mark Twain's, reports of the death of the *Bolam* test have been greatly exaggerated. *Montgomery v. Lanarkshire Health Board* [2015] UKSC has overruled only one aspect of *Bolam* by requiring a patient's "informed consent" to risks, but *Bolam's* "responsible body of medical men" test for the standard of treatment itself remains in force.

Concurrent Liability

Trespass on the case, as we have seen, includes early examples of concurrent liability—liability in both contract and tort—an area of the law that remains in disarray in English law to the present day. The exponential growth of tort liability in the wake of *Donoghue's* case decided in 1932 reached fever pitch in the House of Lords decision in *Junior Book v. Veitchi* [1983] 1 AC 520, which was welcomed by some as presaging the fusion of contract and tort into a united "law of obligations." The case involved defective flooring laid by a subcontractor. As the customer had no contract with the subcontractor, they sued the subcontractor in tort. A 4–1 majority in the House of Lords held the subcontractor liable, even though this was a case of pure economic loss, as the defective floor damaged only itself—and even though the customer had a contract with the main contractor, who could presumably have been sued in contract. This case proved the high watermark of tort liability, and, though it has never been overruled, it is routinely distinguished as turning on its own unique facts. As a result, it has jokingly been referred to as "a very distinguished case."

Another very different type of concurrent liability is found in cases of clients suing their lawyers , where it turns out that a client who was given free advice is likely to be able to recover the higher tortious level of damages, while a paying client would be restricted to claiming the lower level of contractual damages: [See: *Wellesley Partners LLP v. Withers* [2015]. and *AIB Group v. Mark Redler & Co. Solicitors* [2014] UKSC 58.]

Economic Loss Rule and Source of Duty Rule

US law is not quite immune from problems arising out of concurrent liability either, but the Economic Loss Rule (ELR) and the Source of Duty Rule (SDR), as applied by some states, have successfully tackled the problem. As so often in US law, there is a pseudo-black letter basis here. The ELR is enunciated in the Restatement, (Third) Torts: Liability for Physical and Emotional Harm § 6, in the following terms: "*A plaintiff cannot recover in tort for pure economic loss caused by negligence in the negotiation or performance of a contract between the parties.*" [See: Farnsworth, Ward (2016).] The goal of ELR is to prevent contract from "drowning in a sea of tort." [See: *Tiara Condominium v. Marsh & McLennan Companies*, 607 F.3d 742 (11th Cir. 2010); 110 So. 3d 399 (Fla. 2013).] SDR is related to the so-called Independent Tort Duty Rule, which states essentially that: "You cannot commit a tort without breaching a duty imposed by tort law;" and: "If the duty flows only from contract, you cannot be liable in tort. There is no such thing as 'negligent breach.'" ["Avoiding Tort Liability in Breach of Contract Actions," mediastraffordpub.com, October 31, 2013.] Also: "Where damages sought in tort are the same as those for breach of contract a plaintiff may not circumvent the contractual relationship by bringing an action in tort." [*Ginsberg v. Lennor Fla. Holdings, Inc.*, 645 So. 2d 490, 494 (Fla 3d DCA 1994).] This principle was applied in: *AFM Corp. v. Southern Bell Telephone & Telegraph Co.*, 515 So.2d 180 (Fla. 1987). AFM contracted with Bell to advertise in the yellow pages. AFM's entry listed an incorrect phone number. AFM's claim against Bell solely in negligence failed because they had not proved that Bell committed a tort independent of the breach of contract.

5

MAXIMS OR MINIMS?

In the previous chapter we found that in the 600 years before 1932 English common law was on a stable basis of principle resting on a substratum of legislation. The common law in day-to-day practice was expressed in terms of writs of forms of action, notably trespass, trespass on the case, and assumpsit, covering a variety of claims, notably negligence and breach of contract.

But bolstering up this array of writs and pleadings there was an impressive collection of principles in the form of legal maxims. It is to this important, and much underestimated, aspect of the law that I now turn, followed by yet another important stabilizing feature of English law prior to 1932, namely Equity.

It must never be forgotten that throughout this period the bedrock principle of the English (and later, the United Kingdom) Constitution was the sovereignty of Parliament.

Maxims: Pro and Con

Maxims, or pithy expressions of legal principle, were in constant use by English judges and lawyers for at least five hundred years before 1932—the "Year of the Snail"—and they were also exported across the Atlantic. They can be divided into two types, maxims of the common law and maxims of equity. Most of them have been forgotten, resulting in the loss of principles to which the courts can turn for guidance.

Where did these maxims come from, and what role did they play? "Maxims," opined Sir James Mackintosh (1765–1832), "are the condensed Good Sense of Nations." Sir Edward Coke, about whom more will be said anon, described "A maxime in law" as "a proposition to be of all men confessed and granted without proofe, argument, or discourse." [Co. Litt. 67a]. And again: "Maxime, i.e. a sure foundation or ground of art, and a conclusion of reason, so called quia maxima est ejus dignitas et certissima auctoritas, atque quod maxime omnibus probetur, ["so called because it enjoys the greatest prestige and most certain authority, and because it is approved by everyone"], so sure and uncontrollable as that they ought not to be questioned." [Co. Litt. 10b–11a]. From this it can be seen that maxims got their name, not from a noun but from a Latin adjective, meaning "the greatest".

In the late 19th century, however, the authority of maxims started to be questioned. Sir James Fitzjames Stephen (1829–1894) in his *History of the Criminal Law of England,* tore mercilessly into the authority enjoyed by maxims: "It seems to me that legal maxims in general are little more than pert headings of chapters. They are rather minims than maxims, for they give not a particularly great but a particularly small amount of information. As often as not, the exceptions and qualifications to them are more important than the so-called rules." [vol 2, 94 n.1]. Stephen's remark cannot be taken as a criticism of principle. Quite the opposite, in fact, as he was a great believer in codification, and, though he made no headway in England, he was responsible for the codification of Indian Contract and Evidence law, and his Criminal Law codes were adopted by Canada, New Zealand and several Australian colonies.

A sharp criticism of maxims was voiced by John Townshend in *A Treatise on the Wrongs Called Slander and Libel*: "We believe that not a single law maxim can be pointed out which is not obnoxious to objection." [4th ed, s. 88, p. 71 n.1]. Also: Jeremiah Smith (1837–1921), a Justice of the Supreme Court of New

Hampshire and a Harvard Law professor: "The Use of Maxims in Jurisprudence," *Harvard Law Review* (1895) vol 9, No. 1, 13–26]: "The truth is, that there are maxims and maxims; some of great value, and some worse than worthless. And the really valuable maxims are peculiarly liable to be put to a wrong use. A proposition, in order to gain currency as a maxim, must be tersely expressed. But the very brevity which gives it currency, also, in many instances, gives rise to misconception as to its meaning and application. ... How common it is to meet with decisions on important points, where the only hint at an expression of the *ratio decidendi* consists in the quotation, without comment, of a legal maxim!"

Even those, like Jeremiah Smith, who disparaged the use of maxims, were forced to recognize just how much reliance was placed on them by the courts. So important were they in practice that 100 maxims are even appended to Walter Shirley's *Selection of Leading Cases in the Common Law*, which went through eight editions between 1883 and 1908.

In reply to Jeremiah Smith and other critics, it has to be stressed that published collections of maxims generally contained full commentaries on each maxim, including a discussion of correct—and incorrect—translations and interpretations of the maxim concerned, and how it could be applied in practice.

"It is the duty of a judge to extend justice"

So, for example, in his magnificent compilation of maxims, Dr. Herbert Broom (see below) did not hesitate to point out the error in the way that an important maxim had been transmitted and understood: "Boni judicis est ampliare jurisdictionem," meaning "It is the duty of a judge to extend his jurisdiction"—a clarion call for judge-made law. But Broom is quick to correct this false impression. "This maxim, as above worded and literally rendered, is erroneous. Lord Mansfield suggested that for the word *jurisdictionem*, *justitiam* should be substituted." The corrected maxim therefore reads: "It is the duty of a judge to extend justice"—a completely unexceptionable principle. Broom then also cites another maxim of similar import, which he attributes to Sir Francis Bacon: optima est lex quae minimum relinquit arbitrio judicis, optimus judex qui minimum sibi.— "That system of law is best, which leaves least to the discretion of the judge—that judge the best, who relies least on his own opinion." [Broom, p. 66, citing Bacon Aphorisms 46.]

The Doctor and Student

An early reference to maxims occurs in a charming dialogue known as *The Doctor and Student*, published by Christopher St. Germain (1460–1540) during the reign of Henry VIII, first in Latin in 1528 and then in an English translation in 1530 or 1531. It is a dialogue between a doctor of divinity and a student of law. In Chapter 7 we read: "And of these general customs, and of certain principles that be called maxims, which also take effect by the old custom of the realm, depends most part of the law of this realm. And therefore our sovereign lord the king, at his coronation, among other things, takes a solemn oath that he shall cause all the customs of his realm faithfully to be observed. ... [A]nd first, I shall show you how the custom of the realm is the very ground of diverse courts in the realm, that is to say, of the chancery, of the king's bench, of the common pleas, and the exchequer, the which be courts of record. ... [A]ll the ground and beginning of the said courts depend upon the custom of the realm; the which custom is of so high authority, that the said courts ne their authorities, may not be altered. Ne their names changed, without parliament." "And they (viz, maxims) be of the same strength and effect in the law as statutes be." (Ch 8) And so many times the old maxims of the law be changed by statutes.

Several points are worth noting:
- The identification here of the maxims with principles;
- The connection between maxims and custom;

- The connection between maxims and "most part of the law of this realm";
- The statement that maxims have the same strength and effect as statutes;
- The statement that maxims have been changed by statute;
- Recognition of the supremacy of Parliament.

Francis Bacon, *The Maximes of the Law*, 1636

Francis Bacon (1561–1626), the great thinker, statesman and jurist, wrote extensively on the law and other subjects. It is worth noting that, unlike his nemesis, Sir Edward Coke, who was a judicial activist, Bacon was very much the opposite. Here are some relevant remarks of his.

Essay LVI: Of Judicature (ebooks.adelaide.edu.au) 1612:

"Judges ought to remember, that their office is *jus dicere*, and not *jus dare*; to interpret law, and not to make law, or give law."

"Let judges also remember, that Solomon's throne was supported by lions on both sides: let them be lions, but yet lions under the throne; being circumspect that they do not check or oppose any points of sovereignty."

His collection of maxims is disappointingly brief, but it was intended to be the beginning of a grand design of producing an accessible summary of English law. To this end he collected 300 maxims, of which he published a selection of 25 with a commentary on each. Here is the introduction to his published maxims:

"[H]aving collected 300 of them, I thought good before I brought them all into forme to publish some few"—no more than 25, as it happens. Bacon never got around to publishing the remaining 275 maxims, but the importance that he attached to maxims is clear from the title page of his selection: A Collection of some principall Rules and Maximes of the Common Lawes of England, with their latitude and extent,

explicated for the more facile introduction of such as are
studiously addicted to that noble Profession."

Here are a few samples of Bacon's maxims, or "rules," as he
called them:

> *Regula 1: In jure non remota causa sed proxima spectatur.*

> "Rule 1: In law, the immediate, not the remote, cause of any
> event is regarded."

> "It were infinite for the law to judge the causes of causes, and
> their impulsions one of another, therefore it contenteth itselfe
> with the immediate cause, and judgeth of acts by that, without
> looking to any further degree."

In his extensive commentary on this maxim, Dr. Herbert Broom
cites, among many other instances, the case of *Hadley v.
Baxendale* [EWHC J70 (1854), which is still authoritative today
in both English and American law. It is in fact incorporated into
§ 351 of the Restatement (Second) of Contracts. The general rule
as laid down by the Court of Exchequer in that case is as follows:
"Where two parties have made a contract which one of them has
broken, the damages which the other party ought to receive in
respect of such breach of contract should be such as may fairly
and reasonably be considered either arising naturally, i.e.
according to the usual course of things, from such breach of
contract itself, or such as may reasonably be supposed to have
been in the contemplation of both parties at the time they made
the contract as the probable result of the breach of it." What if
there were special circumstances? "[H]ad the special
circumstances been known, the parties might have specially
provided for the breach of contract by special terms as to the
damages in that case; and of this advantage it would be very
unjust to deprive them." As Broom mentions, the maxim and the
principle of proximate cause applies to tort as well as to contract.

[*Broom's Legal Maxims*, 5ed, 1874, p. 226.] See the discussion on "proximate cause" in Chapter 5: "United States: The Exploding Parcel."

> *Regula 3: Verba fortius accipiuntur contra proferentem*

> "... [A] man's deeds and his words shall be taken strongliest against himselfe."

This is particularly relevant to contracts. Where there is a disagreement about the meaning of a word or clause, the interpretation favored by the drafting party should be subordinated to the opposing interpretation.

> *p. 15: Verba ita sunt intelligenda, ut res magis valeat quam pereat.*

> "So it is a rule, that words are so to be understood, that they worke somewhat, and be not idle and frivolous."

Or: "Words should be understood, so that the objective should be valid rather than perish." So, for example, if a document is intended to be a contract, it should be held to be valid rather than void.

> *Regula 5: Necessitas inducit privilegium quoad jura privata.*

> "The law chargeth no man with default where the act is compulsory, and not voluntary, and where there is not a consent and election; and therefore if either there bee an impossibility for a man to doe otherwise, or so great a perturbation of the judgment and reason as in presumption of law man's nature cannot overcome, such necessity carrieth a privilege in itselfe. Necessity is of three sorts, necessity of conservation of life, necessity of obedience, and necessity of the act of God or of a stranger."

E.g. "First of conservation of life, If a man steale viands to satisfie his present hunger, this is no felony nor larceny."

But this privilege does not extend to "private rights: "for death is the last and farthest point of particular necessity, and the law imposeth it upon every subject, that he preferred the urgent service of his Prince and Country before the safety of his life."

> *Regula 15: In criminalibus sufficit generalis malitia intentione cum facto paris gradus.*
>
> "Therefore if an impoisoned apple be laid in a place to poison I.S. and I.D. commeth by chance and eateth it, this is murther in the principall that is actor, and yet the malice *in individuo* was not against I.D."

Broom's Legal Maxims

The brevity of Bacon's selection of maxims was in due course supplemented by other writers, notably Dr. Herbert Broom (1815–1882), a practicing barrister whose impressive compilation of maxims, running to some 800 pages, first appeared in 1845 and went through seven editions , the last of which was published in 1900.

Here is an extract from the Preface to the original edition:

> "The frequency with which Maxims are not only referred to by the Bench, but cited and relied upon by Counsel in their arguments; the importance which has, in many decided cases, been attached to them; the caution which is always exercised in applying, and the subtlety and ingenuity which have been displayed in distinguishing between them, seem to afford reasonable grounds for hoping that the mere Selection of Maxims here given may prove useful to the Profession. ..." [*A Selection of Legal Maxims,* Preface to 1st edition, 1845].

The maxims encapsulated the principles of English law for at least 500 years before the "year of the snail," 1932. But a number of them have survived to the present day, on both sides of the

Atlantic. However, as English law since 1932 has been largely judge-made law, the maxims have also fallen under judicial control. In America, by contrast, the surviving maxims are more likely to be applied in their original sense. Here are examples of a few leading maxims that still survive.

Volenti non fit iniuria

"That to which a person assents
is not esteemed in law an injury."

Broom explains the maxim as follows: "It is a general rule of the English law that no one can maintain an action for a wrong where he has consented to the act which occasions his loss; and this principle has often been applied under states of facts, showing that though the defendant was in the wrong, the plaintiff's negligence had contributed to produce the damage consequential on the act complained of." [Ibid., p. 267.]

This important principle, which still forms part of both English and American law—in the latter under the title of "assumption of risk"—is sometimes, unfortunately, wrongly ignored or sidelined as a result of judicial intervention, which tends to occur more often in England than America.

"Flopper"

In America, Benjamin Cardozo's classic opinion in the so-called "Flopper" case still holds the field, based squarely on *volenti*, which he cited: *James Murphy v. Steeplechase Amusement Co., Inc.* 250 N.Y. 479, 166 N.E. 173 (1929).

The facts of the case are quite simple. James Murphy, described by Cardozo as "a vigorous young man," suffered a fractured knee-cap when, while riding "the Flopper," a moving belt in an amusement park at Coney Island, New York, he felt a "a sharp and sudden jerk" and was thrown to the ground. "A fall was foreseen as one of the risks of the adventure. There would have been no point to the whole thing, no adventure about it, if the risk had not been there. The very name above the gate, the Flopper, was warning to the timid. If the name was not enough, there was waning more distinct in the experience of others." There was no evidence that the "Flopper" was defective or had malfunctioned in any way. Cardozo concluded: "One who takes part in a sport accepts the dangers that inhere in it so far as they are obvious and necessary, just as a fencer accepts the risk of a thrust by his antagonist or a spectator at a ball game the chance of contact with the ball. … The plaintiff was not seeking a retreat for meditation. Visitors were tumbling about the belt to the merriment of onlookers when he made his choice to join them. He took the chance of a like fate, with whatever damage to his body might ensue from such a fall. The timorous may stay at home." The judgment of the (intermediate) Appellate Division entered on a jury verdict for the plaintiff was reversed and a new trial ordered.

[Cf. Stephen Sugarman (1996), 833, who presents a lengthy, convoluted and unpersuasive argument that Cardozo and many other judges have got it wrong because they have failed to distinguish between assumption of the physical risk and assumption of the legal risk.]

"Hot Coffee" Case

In the well-known "Hot Coffee" case, *Stella Liebeck v. McDonald's Restaurants* [US District Court for the District of New Mexico, 1994], concerning a 79-year-old grandmother who suffered third-degree burns to her legs and groin area, requiring extensive surgery, as a result of spilling a cup of coffee held between her knees (her grandson's car had no cup-holders). The case caused an international sensation when Mrs Liebeck was awarded $2.9 million, mostly in punitive damages (which was subsequently reduced by the court to $640,000). Had Mrs

Liebeck assumed the risk of injury, as she must have known that
the coffee was hot and that lifting the lid off was quite likely to
cause the cup to tip over, scalding her? She accepted that she was
at least partly to blame, and her contributory negligence was in
fact assessed at 20%. But she blamed McDonald's for serving
unduly hot coffee—between 180 and 190 degrees Fahrenheit,
near boiling point—without adequate warning. It is perhaps
worth noting that Mrs Liebeck was initially asking only for
$20,000, essentially to cover her medical bills, and it was only
when McDonald's offered her a derisory $800 that she decided to
file suit against them. The case was eventually settled for less
than $600,000. Had it not been for McDonald's intransigence
and Mrs Liebeck's hotshot Texas attorney, S. Reed Morgan, the
numbers in the case would not have been quite so stratospheric.
[*Liebeck v. McDonald's Restaurants*, 1994 Lexis 23 (Bernalillo
County, New Mexico District Court 1994).]

The question remains: Should Mrs Liebeck's case have been
dismissed on the basis that she had voluntarily assumed the risk
of scalding when she bought that 49 cent cup of coffee? My own
view is that, regardless of the figures involved, Mrs Liebeck was
rightly held not to have voluntarily assumed the risk of injury.
How does this compare with the opposite determination in the
"Flopper" case? My opinion is that Cardozo CJ's straight
application of *volenti* was the correct decision. Unlike the "Hot
Coffee" case, in "Flopper" the risk of injury was not only obvious,
but was the basis of the thrill and excitement of going on the ride
in the first place.

Tetraplegic Diver

The English cases on *volenti* are not quite so satisfactory. A
House of Lords decision of 2003 concerned an 18-year-old boy
who became paralyzed as a tetraplegic after diving into an
artificial lake and hitting his head on the sandy bottom, breaking
the fifth vertebra in his neck: *John Tomlinson v. Congleton Borough*

Council [2003] UKHL 47. The lake formed part of a country park
in Cheshire, England, owned by a local authority. As the area
concerned was out of bounds to him, John Tomlinson was
technically a trespasser, but as such was still owed a duty by the
local authority under the Occupiers' Liability Act 1984 "to take
such care as is reasonable in all the circumstances of the case to
see that he does not suffer injury on the premises by reason of
the danger concerned." Though there were notices reading
"Dangerous Water. No Swimming," there were evidently no
specific warnings against diving. Tomlinson 's case was that the
council was in breach of their duty to him under the 1984 Act ,
particularly because there had not been adequate warning of the
dangers of diving into the lake. However, a unanimous House of
Lords found in favor of the council: "Mr. Tomlinson suffered his
injury because he chose to indulge in an activity which had
inherent dangers, not because the premises were in a dangerous
state." This is a slightly puzzling remark. Diving is not in itself an
"inherently dangerous" activity. It was so on this occasion only
because of the "dangerous state" of the lake, which had shallow
water. Tomlinson only "chose" to dive in because he had not
been made aware of the danger. To regard Tomlinson as having
voluntarily assumed the risk of serious and life-changing injury
is hard to justify. And an even more worrying dimension of the
case is revealed by this remark by Lord Hobhouse: "The pursuit
of an unrestrained culture of blame and compensation has many
evil consequences and one is certainly the interference with the
liberty of the citizen. Of course there is some risk of accidents
arising out of the *joie de vivre* of the young, but that is no reason
for imposing a grey and dull safety regime on everyone." The
case was heard at a time when there was concern about what
was seen as a growing "compensation culture," but there is no
reason to regard John Tomlinson's claim as part of an
"unrestrained culture of blame and compensation."

It is instructive to compare this case with the two American
lawsuits, the "Flopper" case and the "Hot Coffee" case. In

"Flopper" the risk of injury, which was unlikely to be serious or life-threatening in any event, was clear to all concerned—and part of the attraction of the ride. In Tomlinson's case, by contrast, there was no suggestion that he would have dived into that shallow lake had he been aware of the magnitude of the risk—any more than Mrs Liebeck would have been likely to attempt to drink her coffee in the car had she been properly warned of its temperature. The difference between the English and American cases is that the two American cases faithfully applied the time-honored principle of the *volenti* maxim, leading to a just result in both, while in the English case judicial intervention resulted in the principle being thwarted, with resulting injustice.

Ex turpi causa non oritur actio

("No right of action can be based on a dishonorable cause.")

This well-known and oft-cited maxim, one of several related maxims, expresses an important and very ancient principle, enabling what is sometimes called the "illegality defense." It is best known from Lord Chief Justice Mansfield's 1775 judgment in the case of *Holman v. Johnson* 1 Cowp. 341 (1775).

Holman v. Johnson (1775)

Holman, based in Dunkirk, in France, sold a consignment of tea to Johnson which was intended to be smuggled into England to avoid customs duties. But, though the plaintiff was aware of the smuggling scheme, he was not a party to it. To the claim for non-payment, the defendant, relying on the principle of *ex turpi causa*, pleaded that the contract was illegal and therefore unenforceable. Lord Mansfield held that, as the tea was to be delivered to Dunkirk and not to England, there was no illegality under English law. So the defendant could not get out of paying. Here is the relevant part of the judgment:

"The objection, that a contract is immoral or illegal as
between plaintiff and defendant, sounds at all times very ill in
the mouth of the defendant. It is not for his sake, however,
that the objection is ever allowed; but it is founded in general
principles of policy, which the defendant has the advantage of,
contrary to the real justice, as between him and the plaintiff,
by accident, if I may so say ... No Court will lend its aid to a
man who founds his cause of action upon an immoral or an
illegal act."

"The Highwayman's Case"

Though *Holman v. Johnson* of 1775 is the classic statement
of the maxim, it was already well established by that time and
can be traced back to Roman law. Its earliest known
application in an English case occurred some 50 years before
Holman, in the entertaining case of *Everett v Williams*,
commonly dubbed "The Highwayman's Case," of 1725, but only
reported in English in 1893. ["The Highwayman's Case," *Law
Quarterly Review 9:* 197 (1893).] The case concerned two
highwaymen who had an agreement to share their ill-gotten
gains equally. Believing that he was being cheated out of his
fair share by his partner, Everett took the matter to court. The
pleadings set out a thinly veiled description of the partnership
business, claiming, for example, "dealings with good success on
Hounslow Heath, where they dealt with a gentleman for a gold
watch." The court was not deceived by this language, dismissed
the claim as "both scandalous and impertinent," and issued a
warrant for the arrest of the solicitors involved, who were
fined £50 each, with the originating attorney being ordered to
pay the costs. Both Everet and Williams were subsequently
rounded up and hanged, and, some years later, one of the
solicitors was convicted of robbery and sentenced to death, but
had his sentence commuted to transportation!

The Unrepentant Killer

In the three centuries since "The Highwayman's Case," there has certainly been no shortage of English cases where the maxim has been invoked, but the application of the principle has been inconsistent. A particularly satisfying example occurred, albeit only on appeal, in a strange case involving a convicted killer. Christopher Clunis, a former mental patient, launched a sudden and unprovoked fatal attack on a stranger, Jonathan Zito, who was waiting on a London Underground platform to join his new wife for their first Christmas together. Clunis lunged at his unsuspecting victim from behind, stabbing him three times in the face and piercing his brain. Jonathan Zito died in hospital two hours later. After being taken into custody, Clunis mindlessly remarked to a police officer: "I've murdered someone, haven't I?" Charged with murder, Clunis's defense of diminished responsibility was accepted, so he was convicted only of manslaughter and ordered to be confined indefinitely in a secure psychiatric hospital.

Clunis blamed his killing of Jonathan Zito on his local health authority's failure to recognize how dangerous he was! He sued the health authority in negligence. They sought to have his claim struck out, on the basis of *ex turpi causa*, as disclosing no cause of action. This defense failed at first instance but, sensibly, succeeded on appeal. Did it matter whether Clunis was aware that he was committing an illegal and immoral act when he was stabbing Jonathan Zito? Yes, but the Court of Appeal drew a distinction between diminished responsibility and insanity. [*Clunis v. Camden & Islington Health Authority* [1998] 3 All ER 180.]

A Tall Tale

Another straightforward application of the principle occurred in *Joyce v. O'Brien* [2013] EWCA Civ 546. Joyce was seriously injured when he fell out of the back of as van being driven by

O'Brien, who happened to be not only his uncle but also his partner in crime. The two men had just stolen several long ladders, which were hastily loaded into the van but which protruded through the open door. While O'Brien was driving recklessly in order to get away from the scene of the crime as quickly as possible, Joyce was holding on to the ladders for dear life until a sharp turn dislodged him from the van and he hit his head on the ground, suffering a serious head injury. He sued his uncle in negligence, but his claim was dismissed on the basis of the principle of *ex turpi causa*. This decision was affirmed on appeal.

"Converting a legal principle into an exercise of judicial discretion"

Regrettably, the simplicity of the principle has not prevented it from becoming "encrusted with an incoherent mass of incoherent authority" in English law. [Per Lord Sumption in *Jetivia S.A. v. Bilta (UK) Ltd (in liquidation)* [2015] UKSC 23.] However, this area of English law is still far from settled.

In *Patel v. Mirza*, decided soon after Jetivia, Lord Sumption commented wryly: "The present appeal exposes, not for the first time, a long-standing schism between those judges and writers who regard the law of illegality as calling for the application of clear rules, and those who would wish to address the equities of each case as it arises. ... The common law is not an uninhabited island on which judges are at liberty to plant whatever suits their personal tastes. It is a body of instincts and principles which, barring some radical change in the values of our society, is developed organically, building on what was there before. It has a greater inherent flexibility and capacity to develop independently of legislation than codified systems do. But there is a price to be paid for this advantage in terms of certainty and accessibility to those who are not professional lawyers. The equities of a particular case are important. But there are pragmatic limits to what law can achieve without becoming arbitrary, incoherent and unpredictable even to the best advised citizen, and without inviting unforeseen and undesirable collateral consequences." Lord Sumption concluded disagreeing with Lord Toulson's conclusion "that the application of the illegality principle should depend on 'the policy factors involved and...the nature and circumstances of the illegal conduct, in determining whether the public interest in preserving the integrity of the justice system should result in the denial of the relief claimed.' (para 109). In my opinion, this is far too vague and potentially far too wide to serve as the basis on which a person may be denied his legal rights. It converts a legal principle into an exercise of judicial discretion, in the process exhibiting all the vices of 'complexity, uncertainty, arbitrariness and lack of transparency' which Lord Toulson attributes to the present law. I would not deny that in the past the law of illegality has been a mess. The proper response of this court is not to leave the problem to case by case evaluation by the lower courts by reference to a potentially unlimited range of factors, but to address the problem by supplying a framework of principle which accommodates legitimace concerns about the present laws. We would be doing no service to the coherent development of the law if we simply substituted a new mess for the old one." [*Patel v. Mirza* [2016] UKSC 42. para 265.]

Despite this fundamental schism among the justices, the UK Supreme Court unanimously ruled that in this case the illegality of a failed scheme involving insider trading should be ignored. The claimant, Patel, paid the defendant, Mirza, £620,000 under an illegal agreement to use insider information (which Mirza claimed to be expecting to obtain} to bet on the price of certain bank shares. In the event, the insider information was not forthcoming and the bet was not placed. The UK Supreme Court (UKSC) held that, as there had been a failure of consideration, Patel was entitled to recover the money as restitution of unjust enrichment, in spite of his own illegality.

The UKSC overruled the House of Lords decision in *Tinsley v. Milligan* [1993] UKHL 3, which held that you could not normally base a claim or defense on your own illegality. In that case the parties had bought a house together. Title was registered in Tinsley's name alone and held in trust for Milligan and herself.

Lord Sumption's bold attack on the approach adopted by the majority of his colleagues is worth noting. It is arguable, however, that he did not go far enough. He claims that its "flexibility" is an advantage that English common law has over codified systems of law, but he admits that "there is a price to be paid for this advantage in terms of certainty and accessibility to those who are not professional lawyers." Yet, he does not stop to consider whether this price is worth paying. For, are certainty and accessibility not the very essence of justice? Trading them for "flexibility,"—essentially meaning judicial power—amounts to trading justice for injustice.

The *ex turpi* principle is alive and well in the US as well as in the UK And, though the American cases also show some inconsistencies, on the whole, they tend, in keeping with a general tendency in American law, to be more faithful to principle and to form a more orderly and organized body of law.

Classic US Supreme Court Case

The *ex turpi* principle has been applied in a number of American state lawsuits, but the classic federal US case on it is still the US Supreme Court decision in *McMullen v. Hoffman* (1899), concerning a contract for the construction of the "Bull Run Pipe Line" in Portland, Oregon. The plaintiff and the defendant put in competing bids for the works to the city of Portland. The defendant's bid being the lowest of all the bids submitted, he was awarded the contract, the work was duly completed and he was paid the agreed contract price. But the purported competition between the two parties was merely a front, because there was also a contract between the two of them agreeing to share the profits of the contract with Portland. It was on that contract that the present lawsuit was brought. But the court would have none of it. "Being of the opinion that the contract proved in this case was illegal, in the sense that it was fraudulent, and entered into for improper purposes, the law will leave the parties as it finds them."

Laughed out of Court

Thomas v. UBS AG 706 F.3d 846 (2013) US Court of Appeals, seventh Circuit, is a highly entertaining case in which the principle was squarely applied, a class action suit against UBS, the biggest Swiss bank, brought by thousands of Americans with UBS accounts seeking damages from UBS to recover the penalties, interest, and costs that they had had to disgorge to the IRS after their previously secret accounts were disclosed by UBS, who paid $780 million in fines and cooperated with Uncle Sam. Their lawsuit was almost literally laughed out of court by the ebullient Judge Richard Posner delivering the unanimous opinion of the Seventh Circuit: "The plaintiffs are tax cheats. ... [I]n 2009 UBS admitted having helped tens of thousands of its clients to evade US income taxes, and paid a $789 million fine." The plaintiffs argue "that the bank should have prevented them from violating the law. This is like suing one's parents to recover tax penalties one has paid, on the ground that the parents had failed to bring one up to be an honest person who would not evade taxes and so would not subject himself to penalties. There is in general no common law duty to prevent another person from violating the law. At worst, UBS ... violated an agreement with the IRS designed to prevent the kind of evasion that the plaintiffs engaged in. That might conceivably make UBS an aider or abettor of the plaintiffs' tax evasion and so make this case a distant relative to *Everet v. Williams*, better known as The Highwayman's Case. ... Minus the hanging and with certain exceptions (such as contribution and indemnity) irrelevant to this case, the principle enunciated in The Highwayman's Case applies to accomplices in civil wrongdoing. ... In The Highwayman's Case one accomplice was seeking a larger share of the profit from the crime from the other one; here one accomplice is seeking a smaller share of the costs of the crime from the other one. The principle is the same; the law leaves the quarreling accomplices where it finds them." Judge Posner concluded: "This lawsuit, including the appeal, is a travesty. We are surprised that UBS hasn't asked for the imposition of sanctions on the plaintiffs and class counsel."

The Chancellor's Foot

Until the early 18th century the Chancellor, or Lord Chancellor, was essentially the first minister of the Crown. He headed up a huge department known as the Chancery staffed by a number of clerks, or cursitors (literally, "runners"). The Chancery issued all writs for use in lawsuits, which were authenticated by the king's great seal. By the reign of Edward I (1272–1307) disappointed plaintiffs started petitioning the Crown by "bill" lodged with the Chancery, which before long came to be recognized as a Court in its own right, the Court of Chancery, which dispensed, not the common law, but "equity", based on "conscience," initially in three specific types of case, as memorialized in an old rhyme: "These three give place in court of conscience, Fraud, accident, and breach of confidence." [Maitland, p. 7n]. It was said by critics, like John Selden (1584–1654), that the decisions of the Court of Chancery were arbitrary, based on the length of the Chancellor's foot—which of course varied from one Chancellor to the next. In fact, however, the Court of Chancery developed "rules of equity and good conscience," which formed a set of maxims parallel to those of the common law.

Equity regards as done what should have been done.

So, for example, the purchaser of real property becomes the equitable owner of the property as soon as the sale contract has been executed, but the vendor retains legal title until the date of conveyance. If the vendor refuses to convey title, the purchaser can ask the court for specific performance, ordering title to be transferred to the purchaser.

He who comes to equity must come with clean hands.

In other words, equity will not allow a party to profit by his own wrong. But equity does not go to extremes. So, in the words of Justice Brandeis, "Equity does not demand that its suitors shall have led blameless lives." [*Loughran v. Loughran* 293 US 216, 229 (1934)].

Equity will not assist a volunteer.

This means that equity will not allow someone to benefit without any legal claim, e.g. a so-called "officious intermeddler." So, if, without A's knowledge, B constructs a swimming pool in A's garden while A is on vacation, B cannot demand that A pay for it. This maxim is particularly relevant in restitution, an area of the law which is well developed in the US but which was only explicitly recognized in English law in 1991 [in *Lipkin Gorman v. Karpnale* [1988] UKHL 12] and still remains a highly unsettled area of English law. [See *Bank of Cyprus v. Melissa Menelaus* [2015] UKSC 66].

Equity abhors a forfeiture.

Graf v. Hope Building Corp. [254 N.Y. 1 (1930)]. Hope Building Corp had a mortgage loan with Graf. Because of a miscalculation of the interest owed, the "acceleration clause" in the mortgage kicked in, requiring the borrower to pay the entire debt within 20 days. The lender waited until the 21st day of default to commence a foreclosure action in court. Although the president of Hope immediately offered to cure the default, the lender refused to back down from their demand for payment of the entire balance. At trial the foreclosure application was dismissed as being contrary to equity. The Appellate Division affirmed this decision, but by a 4–3 majority the New York Court of Appeals reversed and allowed the lender to foreclose. Among the dissenters was Chief Judge Benjamin Cardozo (1870–1938), who would later be appointed to the US Supreme Court. Cardozo, citing *Console v. Torchinsky*, [97 Conn 353, 357 (1922)], based his dissent on equity, the purpose of which, he held was "to prevent [a] creditor from taking an unconscionable advantage of" the debtor (at 11–12). "In this case," held Cardozo, "the hardship [was] so flagrant, the misadventure so undoubted, the oppression so apparent, as to justify holding that only through acceptance of the tender will equity be done." (at 14). More recent American case-law has largely followed Cardozo in his reasoning, based on equity, that "foreclosure may be denied in the case of an inadvertent, inconsequential default in order to prevent unconscionably overreaching conduct by a mortgagee": *Karas v. Wasserman*, 91 A.D. 2d 812 (App. Div. 1982).

By contrast with this beautifully principled approach which retains the meaning and principled purpose of the original maxim, English law is in disarray here as in so many other areas of the law. What follows is a particularly shocking, but by no means unique, example of the complete disregard of this valuable equitable principle.

Unwelcome Improvements

UK statute law is so diffuse that it is difficult for courts to interpret and apply it. A terrible, but not unique, case involved the forfeiture of a property worth £600,000 by a long leaseholder who breached his lease—essentially only because he upgraded his property without permission from the freeholder! [*Malik v. McCadden*, Claim No. E00W1513.] In 2016 Charles McCadden, who suffered from chronic illness, purchased a maisonette with a 99-year lease, the freehold of which belonged to the owner of the only other apartment in the building. Without consulting the freeholder, McCadden redecorated his home and had a new kitchen and bathroom and new central heating installed. Leaseholders are treated considerably more severely in forfeiture cases than fraudsters in the criminal courts. In *R v. Waya* [2012] UKSC 51, for example, the UK Supreme Court was scrupulous in returning the seed capital to a convicted mortgage fraudster!

According to the First-Tier property Tribunal, to which the freeholder complained, McCadden had "carried out major refurbishment works," including removing fixtures and fittings belonging to the freeholder: "The breaches which we have found are of the utmost seriousness. The next step will be for the Applicant to apply to the County Court to forfeit his lease." And sure enough, some nine months later, on 22 August 2018, a Deputy District Judge sitting in a County Court ordered Charles McCadden to give up possession of his £600,000 maisonette to the freeholder. [*Malik v. McCadden*, Claim No. E00W1513] He was given fourteen days to move out of his home. Not surprisingly, the evicted homeowner said he had been left destitute and feeling suicidal after the ruling. Sebastian O'Kelly, from the charity Leasehold Knowledge Partnership (LKP), commented: "Mr. McCadden has been found to be an inconsiderate neighbour. But the loss of a £600,000 asset is out of proportion to the dispute." [*The Times*, September 15, 2018]. McCadden did not apply for relief from forfeiture, as he should have done, but the court could still have offered it to him of its own motion instead of just going for the jugular as it did. Relief from forfeiture would mean that McCadden could keep his home provided he remedied his breaches of the lease. He could have been asked to restore the maisonette to the state it was in before he started his refurbishment—which would have made no sense, as his breaches generally amounted to improvements. More sensibly, he could have been ordered simply to fill the few holes in the walls that were left by his (unfinished) works. The trouble is that the law gives no guidance to the court on what to do. Most leases contain a forfeiture clause allowing the landlord to "re-enter" the property if the tenant is in breach of the lease. A landlord can sometimes exercise the right of "peaceable re-entry" without going to court—and, in the case of a really serious breach, even in the absence of a forfeiture clause. In 1925 a whole raft of statutes relating to real estate was passed by Parliament, but the only provision relating to forfeiture is section 146 of the Law of Property Act 1925, which stipulates that forfeiture of a lease cannot take place unless the landlord has served a notice on the leaseholder specifying the breaches and requiring the leaseholder to remedy the breach and pay the landlord compensation. But there is nothing about what breaches qualify for forfeiture. The only statutory provision referred to in the McCadden tribunal case was Section 168(4) of the Commonhold and Leasehold Reform Act 2002, which provides that: "A landlord under a long lease of a dwelling may make an application to the appropriate tribunal for a determination that a breach of a covenant or condition in the lease has occurred." Again, no indication whatsoever on what level of breach is needed to trigger forfeiture.

Charles McCadden's sad case aroused a flurry of sympathy in the media, but the question is: How could this have happened in the first place and how can a repetition be avoided? As long ago as 1985 the Law Commission published a 195-page report on "Forfeiture of Tenancies" [Law Com. No. 142], which concluded: "The law of forfeiture has become unnecessarily complicated, is no longer coherent and gives rise to injustices. The report recommends its replacement by a new system." However, this suggested "new system" was in some ways even harsher than the existing one. For example, the report recommended abolition of the requirement for a landlord to give notice to the tenant before starting forfeiture proceedings against the tenant! Needless to say, the recommendations of this report were never implemented. In

2006 the Law Commission published a related report, titled "Termination of Tenancies for Tenant Default" [Law Com. No. 303], which, while proposing abolition of forfeiture, recommended a new scheme making it even easier than before for landlords to terminate a tenancy—including long leaseholds! The 1985 report was produced under the laughable general heading, "Codification of the Law of Landlord and Tenant"—which had been dropped by 2006 presumably because codification of this area of the law was no longer even touted as a goal.

Amazingly, however, on 10 December 2018 the Law Commission announced that it was proposing "reforms that would support the expansion of commonhold as an alternative to leasehold." These proposals were published in the form of a Consultation Paper titled "Reinvigorating commonhold, the alternative to leasehold ownership." At last the Law Commission seemed to have identified a deep-seated cause of the problems with long leaseholds. Commonhold ownership is similar to the familiar American condominium and certainly marks a great improvement on leasehold. Under commonhold each unit is owned outright, with no term date. The unit owners collectively own the common parts. There is no landlord—and no risk of forfeiture. However, commonhold has been available in England and Wales since 2002, but, as the Law Commission admits, "take-up has been poor: fewer than 20 commonhold developments have been built." [www.lawcom.gov.uk]. Without abolishing long leasehold tenure altogether and replacing it with commonhold it is hard to see how commonhold is ever going to take off. It would need to be done by Act of Parliament, but at the time of this writing there does not appear to be any appetite for it.

The central question as far as the whole sorry *McCadden* saga itself is concerned is: how could this brutal forfeiture have occurred in the first place? What about the equitable principle against forfeiture? Needless to say, it was not even mentioned, and might as well have been consigned to the rings of the planet Saturn.

PART III

PRINCIPLE OR DISARRAY?

6

UNITED KINGDOM
THE SNAIL IN THE BOTTLE

British law students and even qualified lawyers are generally under the impression that the Tort of Negligence began with the memorable and faintly comical case of the snail in the bottle, *Donoghue v. Stevenson* [1932] AC 562. In August 1928 Mrs May Donoghue was treated by an unnamed female friend to a ginger beer "ice cream float" at Francis Minghella's Wellmeadow café in Paisley, Scotland. Minghella prised open the metal lid of the opaque "stone" ginger beer bottle and poured some of the liquid into a tumbler containing a scoop of ice cream. Mrs Donoghue drank a little of the mixture. Her anonymous friend then proceeded to pour the rest of the ginger beer into the tumbler for her, when a semi-decomposed snail floated into view. Mrs Donoghue claimed that, as a result, she experienced shock and contracted severe gastroenteritis.

At first sight, this is a fairly straightforward case. But there was one small legal problem: Mrs Donoghue had not bought the ginger beer herself, so could not sue in contract, as she did not have a contractual relationship with either Minghella or David Stevenson, the manufacturer of the ginger beer. And her friend, who *did* have a contract with Minghella, had no case because she had not suffered any loss or injury. Donoghue's lawyers decided to adopt a daring approach, although it had failed in a very similar case involving a mouse in a ginger beer bottle less than three weeks earlier. Donoghue's claim, based on the tort of negligence, alleged that Stevenson owed her a duty of care as the end user of his product, that he was in breach of that duty, and that this breach had caused May Donoghue's illness. Stevenson

121

rejected all these allegations, denying that there had been any snails in any of his bottles of ginger beer, that any illness suffered by Donoghue "was due to the bad condition of her health at the time," and that the claim had no legal basis.

At first instance, before the Outer House of the Scottish Court of Session, Donoghue won, but she lost 3–1 before the Inner House, made up of the same four judges who had decided the mouse case. The case finally came before the House of Lords, which was then the highest court in the United Kingdom. Here, as every British law student knows, Mrs Donoghue won a famous victory, albeit only by a majority of three to two. Lord Atkin, an Australian Welshman, delivered the majority opinion, with concurring opinions by two Scottish law lords, while the two English judges, Lord Buckmaster and Lord Tomlin, registered a strenuous dissent.

Lord Atkin's "Neighbour Principle"

Lord Atkin's opinion in favour of Mrs Donoghue centered on his so-called "neighbour principle," which has generally been assumed to be the *ratio decidendi*, or the reasoned legal basis of the decision, and has accordingly been followed as a precedent ever since. It is actually open to doubt whether the "neighbour principle" really was the *ratio* of the case, as neither of the two Scottish wingmen, Lords Thankerton and Macmillan, even so much as mentioned it. Their two speeches were really, therefore, only concurring opinions, agreeing with the decision in favor of Mrs Donoghue, but not entirely on the same basis as Lord Atkin. Of course, only the *ratio decidendi* of a case has binding, precedential force.

Lord Atkin expounded his "neighbour principle" in characteristically long-winded language:

> "The rule that you are to love your neighbour becomes in law
> you must not injure your neighbour; and the lawyer's

question 'Who is my neighbour?' receives a restricted reply. You must take reasonable care to avoid acts or omissions which you can reasonably foresee would be likely to injure your neighbour. Who then in law is my neighbour? The answer seems to be persons who are so closely and directly affected by my act that I ought reasonably to have them in contemplation as being so affected when I am directing my mind to the acts or omissions which are called in question."

From this Lord Atkin derived the "proposition" that:

"A manufacturer of products which he sells in such a form as to show that he intends them to reach the ultimate consumer in the form in which they left him with no reasonable possibility of intermediate examination, and with the knowledge that the absence of reasonable care in the preparation or putting up of the products is likely to result in injury to the consumer's life or property owes a duty to the consumer to take that reasonable care."

Whew! What all this verbiage boiled down to in *Donoghue v. Stevenson* itself was the conclusion that Stevenson owed Mrs Donoghue a duty of care. But this is not of course enough to establish liability. To fix Stevenson with liability, Mrs Donoghue would have had to show not only that Stevenson owed her a duty of care but also that he was in breach of that duty, and, moreover that that breach of duty caused her injury, loss or damage. However, Lord Atkin quickly waved "breach" aside:

"In the present case we are not concerned with the breach of the duty; if a duty exists that would be a question of fact which is sufficiently averred and for present purposes must be assumed. We are solely concerned with the question whether as a matter of law in the circumstances alleged the defender [Scots for "defendant"] owed any duty to the pursuer [Scots for "plaintiff"] to take care."

"Common law principles cannot be changed"

So incensed was Lord Buckmaster (a former Lord Chancellor) by Lord Atkin's opinion that he deliberately stayed away from the traditional ceremony at which the law lords read out their "speeches" (i.e. their opinions) in the House of Lords chamber. Instead, he handed his speech to his co-dissenter, Lord Tomlin, a distinguished Chancery judge, to read out. Lord Tomlin's own short speech cut quickly to the chase:

> "Upon the view which I take of the matter, the reported cases, some directly, others impliedly, negative the existence as part of the Common Law of England of any principle affording support to the appellant's [viz. Mrs Donoghue's] claim, and therefore there is, in my opinion, no material from which it is legitimate for your Lordships' House to deduce such a principle."

Here we have no ducking and diving, no polite pussyfooting, but a root-and-branch rejection of the "neighbour principle" as "illegitimate." In his speech Lord Buckmaster adopted the didactic tone of a schoolmaster admonishing a particularly ignorant student:

> The law applicable is the common law, and, though its principles are capable of application to meet new conditions not contemplated when the law was laid down, these principles cannot be changed nor can additions be made to them because any particular meritorious case seems outside their ambit.

As the law stood, in the absence of contract a manufacturer owed no duty to anyone, except:

(1) In the case of an article dangerous in itself and

(2) where the article not in itself dangerous is in fact dangerous due to some defect or for any other reason, and this is known to the manufacturer.

As no one could suppose that ginger beer was an article dangerous in itself, Lord Buckmaster concluded that Stevenson did not owe Mrs Donoghue any duty.

It is worth mentioning that to this day it is still not known whether there actually was a snail in that bottle or not. Lord Atkin mentioned that breach of duty was assumed, but the very existence of the duty was also based on assumed facts. The House of Lords remitted the case back to the Scottish Court of Session for May Donoghue to prove the factual basis of her claim, namely that there had been a snail in the bottle, that its presence there was the result of Stevenson's negligence, and that this had been the cause of her illness. But the hearing never took place, because David Stevenson died before the date listed for the hearing. [See Chapman, Matthew (2010).]

"The categories of negligence are never closed"

Lord Buckmaster concluded his opinion by summing up the "neighbour principle" much more succinctly than Lord Atkin, and in so doing brought out just how uncontrolled it was:

> "The principle contended for must be this: that the manufacturer or indeed the repairer of any article, apart entirely from contract, owes a duty to any person by whom the article is lawfully used to see that it has been carefully constructed. ... This conception is simply to misapply to tort doctrines applicable to sale and purchase."

As Lord Buckmaster predicted, this kind of judicial activism has prevailed ever since over a centuries-old principle-based approach to the common law. Ironically, Lord Macmillan, one of Lord Atkin's Scottish wingmen, also foresaw a widening of the whole concept of negligence and even the possibility of "diversity of view", although, as mentioned above but which is hardly ever noticed, neither he nor Lord Thankerton, who together gave Lord Atkin his majority, expressly endorsed the "neighbour principle." However, unlike Lord Buckmaster, Lord Macmillan welcomed the opening of the floodgates:

> "The categories of negligence are never closed. The cardinal principle of liability is that the party complained of should owe to the party complaining a duty of care, and that the party complaining should be able to prove that he has suffered damage in consequence of a breach of that duty. Where there is room for diversity of view, it is in determining what circumstances will establish such a relationship as to give rise, on the one side, to a duty to take care, and on the other side to a right to have care taken."

"A notable degree of disarray and a marked lack of reliable principle"

Since *Donoghue v. Stevenson*, UK tort law has certainly burgeoned, though it has attracted a good deal of criticism on the way. In a speech delivered in 2017, Lord Neuberger, the retiring President of the UK Supreme Court (UKSC), remarked: "Analysis of tort cases appears to demonstrate a notable degree of disarray and a marked lack of reliable principle. Thus, what appears to be principle turns out, on examination, to be policy." [Neuberger, David (2017).]

Lord Neuberger also quoted similar opinions expressed by others:

> "In the *Fairchild* case, which I shall discuss later, Lord Nicholls of Birkenhead described legal concepts determining the appropriate scope of liability in tort, including duty of care, causation, proximity, and remoteness as 'afflicted with linguistic ambiguity.' And, as the equally formidable Professor Jane Stapleton has written, 'the legal reasoning in judgments in tort cases is often obscure, so that it is difficult to distil a coherent body of principles'."

Lord Neuberger's explanation for this situation is that "almost all aspects of tort law, above all negligence, are based on policy." Adding: "Of course, almost all legal principles can be said to be ultimately based on policy, but, given the very broad area which tort (in particular negligence) covers, and given the infinite variety of human life, any attempt to identify or distil clear principles in such an area is fraught with problems."

Policy an "unruly horse"

This last remark is somewhat puzzling, to say the least. What exactly is meant by "policy"? It is important to realize that, even when the term used is "public policy," we are not talking about government policy or that of any executive agency, but about judge-made law purportedly based on what is in the public interest. Hence such high-handed remarks as this by Chief Justice Tindal in *Horner v. Graves* (1831) 7 Bing. 743: "Whatever is injurious to the interests of the public is void, on the grounds of public policy." But how can an unelected judge be expected to gauge what is in the public interest? And, more particularly, what right do they have to presume to do so? Is that not a function of the legislature? Sir George Jessel, Master of the Rolls , adopted a more realistic position when he commented: "It is impossible to say what the opinion of a man or a judge might be as to what public policy is." [*Besant v. Wood* (1879) L.R. 12 C.D. 620.]

However, a long line of judges has issued stern warnings against the judicial use of arguments from public policy. Here are a few relevant citations: "I, for one, protest ... against arguing too strongly upon public policy;—it is a very unruly horse, and when once you get astride it you never know where it will carry you." [Burrough J. in *Richardson v. Mellish* (1824) 2 Bing 252.]

According to Lord Bramwell, who cites this remark with approval in *Mogul Steamship v. McGregor, Gow & Co.* [1892] AC 25, it goes back to Chief Justice Hobart (c. 1560–1625), who may possibly have been reacting to his predecessor as Chief Justice of Common Pleas, Sir Edward Coke, a master of policy decisions.

Also from Burrough J. in *Richardson v. Mellish*: "The argument of public policy leads you from sound law, and is never argued but when all other points fail."

And: "Public policy is a high horse to mount, and is difficult to ride when you have mounted it." (A. L. Smith M.R., *Driefontein Consolidated Mines v. Janson* (1901) Times LR vol xvii, 605.]

In short, policy or public policy, when used in reference to a judicial decision, means no more and no less than the personal opinion of the judge concerned—or judge-made law. The suggestion that "almost all legal principles" are "ultimately based on policy" makes no sense, and it is significant that no examples are given. Groucho Marx's famous line, "Those are my principles, and if you don't like them I have others," is funny precisely because principles do not change, whereas policy, being the personal opinion of one individual at one particular time, is subject to constant flux. How, for example, could these fundamental principles possibly have been "based" on policy?

- *Nemo debet esse judex in causa sua* ("Nobody ought to be a judge in his own case.")—The fundamental principle against bias.
- *Audi alteram partem ("Hear the other side too.")*—The fundamental principle of fairness.
- *Ei qui affirmat, non ei qui negat, incumbit probatio."* "The burden of proof lies upon him who asserts, not on him who denies."—The burden of proof is on the party making an allegation or a claim, not on the party denying it, who would have to prove a negative.
- *Ex dolo malo non oritur actio* ("A lawsuit cannot be based on fraud.")

Can it be believed that any of these principles was the product of judge-made law? They are all fundamental principles that go back to ancient times and reflect basic values of justice and honesty.

"Fair, just and reasonable"

In his speech Lord Neuberger examines a number of UK tort decisions, starting with *Caparo plc v. Dickman* [1990] 2 AC 605, which, in Lord Neuberger's words, "was, and in some quarters still is, regarded by many as finally laying down the test for determining whether a duty of care exists." He quotes from the leading speech in that case by Lord Bridge what he calls "that famous three-fold test:" foreseeability of damage, proximity and "that the situation should be one in which the court considers it fair, just and reasonable that the law should impose a duty of a given scope upon the one party for the benefit of the other." Lord Neuberger comments on this test: "The first aspect of that famous three-fold test, foreseeability of damage, involves a principle, and the second aspect, proximity, could, I suppose, just about be said to do so, although it involves a heavy dollop of policy; but the third aspect, fairness justness and reasonableness, it seems to me, is pure policy; and it may be said to subsume the first two ingredients in any event." [See my article on the 500th anniversary of my college, St John's, Cambridge: Arnheim (2011).]

"The road to hell is paved with good intentions"

In his 2017 speech Lord Neuberger quoted with approval an academic description of the *Fairchild* case as a "good example of the maxim 'the road to hell is paved with good intentions.'" [Neuberger (2017) citing McBride & Bagshaw (2012).] The case in question is *Fairchild v. Glenhaven Funeral Services* [2003] 1 AC 32. Arthur Fairchild, a construction worker, died of malignant pleural mesothelioma, which he had contracted as a result of inhaling asbestos fibers at work. He had done the same job for two different employers in succession, both of whom were in breach of duty to him by causing him to be exposed to asbestos. Inhaling a single asbestos fiber was enough to trigger the disease, but there was a long latency period, anything from 25 to 50 years, before the disease manifested itself. It was not known under which employer he had inhaled the "guilty" fiber. At first instance and in the Court of Appeal the claim failed, on the basis of the "but for" (or *sine qua non)* test, as it was not possible to say that the disease would not have occurred "but for" the wrongful conduct of Employer A (or, alternatively, of Employer B). This result was rejected by a unanimous House of Lords. The decision below was reversed and the defendant employers held jointly and severally liable to the claimant. But there was no intention to jettison the "but for" test generally and replace it with some laxer new test—except in specific cases. Lord Hoffmann even proposed a special "five-factor" test to govern such specific cases. *Fairchild* was decided on the same basis as the House of Lords decision in *McGhee v. National Coal Board* [1972] 3 All ER 1008, which, though never overruled, was disapproved of and sidelined in later House of Lords decisions such as *Hotson v. East Berkshire Health Authority* [1987] AC 750 and *Wilsher v. Essex Area Health Authority* [1988] AC 1074.

"Materially increased the risk"

In the *McGhee* case, James McGhee worked in brick kilns for the National Coal Board. After a day's work his skin would be caked in coal dust, grime and sweat. His employer did not provide showers, so he could not wash off the coal dust until he had cycled home every evening. He contracted dermatitis, but would the provision of showers at the workplace have prevented him from developing a rash? In other words, would he not have contracted dermatitis "but for" the lack of showers? It could not be said that it was more likely than not that the absence of showers gave him dermatitis. So, discarding the "but for" test, the House of Lords found in McGhee's favor on the basis of the much laxer "rule" that to establish liability it was enough that the defendant's negligence had "materially increased the risk" of the plaintiff's contracting dermatitis. It was this doctrine that was dredged up and applied again in *Fairchild*.

"No rational, factual or legal justification"

In the words of Lord Bingham: "If the mechanical application of generally accepted rules leads to such a result [as the decision of the Court of Appeal in *Fairchild*], there must be room to question the appropriateness of such an approach in such a case." Lord Neuberger comments: "[T]here is a powerful case for saying that the House should have left it to Parliament to change the law." Adding: "Indeed, Lord Hoffmann, who was party to the decision and justified it in his judgment by reference to material increase in risk, has subsequently suggested, reflecting many academic critics, that the House in *Fairchild* created a special exception to the 'but for' principle which could not be justified by reference to any general principle and depended on a distinction which had no rational, factual or legal justification."

"Stage set for confusion"

But worse was to come. The "principle" of *Fairchild* was "refined" by the House of Lords four years later in *Barker v. Corus* [2006] 2 AC 572, which in turn was reversed less than three months later by section 3 of the Compensation Act 2006, which provided that *all* defendants who had caused or "materially increased a risk" of a claimant's contracting mesothelioma should be held jointly and severally liable. Lord Neuberger comments: "The courts having taken what may be unkindly characterised as an intellectually dubious wrong turning in *Fairchild* and Parliament having legislated on a rushed piecemeal basis in the 2006 Act, you might have thought that the stage was set for confusion, and so it proved."

"The *Fairchild* enclave"

He traces the sorry saga of subsequent cases leading to the necessity for the courts to develop special rules of causation for what Lord Hodge judicially described as "[t]he *Fairchild* enclave." Lord Neuberger continued: "We were effectively forced to go on developing new rules to deal with this situation. ... As Lord Reed and I said in our (minority) judgment [in *Zurich v. IEG* [2016] AC 509], 'there can be no real doubt but if Fairchild had been decided the other way, in accordance with normal common law principles, Parliament would have intervened very promptly. That may very well have been a better solution, but it can fairly be said that that observation is made with the wisdom of hindsight.'"

Causation yields to policy

If *Fairchild* represented an extension of *McGhee*, which in turn was an extension of the normal rule, the case of *Chester v. Afshar* [2004] UKHL 41 went further still. Lord Neuberger remarked that it "has been seen by many as a more revolutionary departure from the principle of causation." Carole Chester had surgery for her lower back pain. The operation was evidently performed competently, but she was left with a condition known as cauda equina (literally, horse's tail) syndrome. She had not been warned that there was a 1–2% risk of the operation going wrong. Although she sued her surgeon for negligence, she did not claim that she would have refused consent for the surgery if she had been duly warned, only that she would not have consented to have the operation *on that particular day*—three days after her initial consultation with the surgeon—and that she would have taken a second (and possibly a third) opinion before undergoing the surgery.

A 3–2 majority in the House of Lords, affirming the decisions of the courts below, found in favor of the claimant.

Lord Steyn, speaking for the majority, held that "but for the surgeon's negligent failure to warn the claimant of the small risk of serious injury the actual injury would not have occurred when it did and the chance of it occurring on a subsequent occasion was very small. It could therefore be said that the breach of the surgeon resulted in the very injury about which the claimant was entitled to be warned." He described the majority decision in favor of the claimant as entailing only "a narrow and modest departure from traditional causation principles. ... This result is in accord with one of the most basic aspirations of the law, namely to right wrongs. Moreover, the decision ... reflects the reasonable expectations of the public in contemporary society."

"A substantial and unjustified departure from sound and established principle"

Lords Bingham and Hoffmann registered a strong dissent. Lord Bingham characterized the majority decision as "a substantial and unjustified departure from sound and established principle. It is trite law that damage is the gist of the action in the tort of negligence. ... A claimant is entitled to be compensated for the damage which the negligence of another has caused to him or her. ... But the corollaries are also true: a claimant is not entitled to be compensated, and a defendant is not bound to compensate the claimant, for damage not caused by the negligence complained of."

Lord Hoffmann's dissent was even more strident: "The purpose of a duty to warn someone against the risk involved in what he proposes to do, or allow to be done to him, is to give him the opportunity to avoid or reduce that risk. ... In the context of the present case, that means proving that she [viz. the claimant] would not have had the operation. The judge made no finding that she would not have had the operation. He was not invited by the claimant to make such a finding. The claimant argued that as a matter of law it was sufficient that she would not have had the operation at that time or by that surgeon, even though the evidence was that the risk could have been precisely the same if she had it at another time or by another surgeon. ... In my opinion this argument is about as logical as saying that if one had been told, on entering a casino, that the odds on No. 7 coming up at roulette were only 1 in 37, one would have gone away and come back next week or gone to a different casino. ... The judge found as a fact that the risk would have been precisely the same whether it was done then or later or by that competent surgeon or by another. It follows that the claimant failed to prove that the defendant's breach of duty caused her loss. On ordinary principles of tort law, the defendant is not liable."

"Causation no longer an absolute principle"

Lord Neuberger (who was not himself involved in *Chester*) comments: "One does not need to read the brief, almost contemptuous, dissenting judgments of Lord Bingham and Lord Hoffmann (both of whom, it is to be noted, were prepared to depart from the normal principle in *Fairchild*) to see that there is no getting away from the fact that one of the most fundamental principles of tort law, causation, is now no longer an absolute principle at all, but must yield to policy."

More helpful to abandon principle and to take a stand on policy?

All these strictures passed by Lord Neuberger and others on some of the most important tort cases in the past twenty years may appear to amount to a damning indictment. But Lord Neuberger shrugs them off, remarking: "The cases I have so far referred to tend to suggest that principle rather than policy may be a dangerous guide to those analysing, advising on, debating, or deciding cases involving claims in tort." He then makes an apparent concession: "However, clarity and predictability are vitally important ingredients of the rule of law. Accordingly, it can be said with considerable force that it is quite right for the judges to be striving to identify principles in the field of tort law. Even if a particular principle cannot always apply, it may prove reliable in the great majority of cases." He then returns to the fray: "But there is no getting away from the fact that there are real risks in developing principles in the field of torts, as they may not infrequently operate to mislead rather than to help. There is a strong argument that, in some areas at least, it may be more helpful to abandon principle and to take a stand on policy."

Not a single example is cited in support of this sweeping assertion. Lord Neuberger then sets up another straw man just to knock it down: "There are of course arguments, well summarized by Professor Stevens, as to why judges should leave policy alone: judges are unelected, judges lack the technical competence, and policy leads to less certain outcomes." [Stevens, Robert (2012), pp. 308–310]. "It is often said that judges are often neither informed or experienced enough to make the economic and social assessments which questions of policy in the field of torts so often involve. I wonder. Many of the most important judicial decisions in the field of torts seem to me to involve those sort of assessments [*sic*]. *Donoghue v. Stevenson* is a prime example: it involved a considerable extension of product liability; *Hedley Byrne* involved extending liability for negligent misstatements to consequential economic loss; the same is true of *SAAMCo*, the surveyor's negligence 'cap' case considered in *BPE Solicitors* ..." [He then goes on to make a similar claim in regard to domestic judicial review, an area that I discuss in Chapter 8.]

Lord Neuberger finally gives the names of three cases to illustrate the importance of policy in tort decisions. In fact, however, all they show is how greatly policy decisions have extended the scope of tort. They certainly do not answer the allegations summarized by Professor Stevens, particularly the allegation that "policy leads to less certain outcomes."

After taking a look at the three cases mentioned by Lord Neuberger, namely *Donoghue v. Stevenson, Hedley Byrne* and *SAAMCo*, I shall sum up the pros and cons of his claims for the superiority of judicial policy over principle.

"If one step, why not fifty?"

That *Donoghue v. Stevenson* "involved a considerable extension of product liability," as Lord Neuberger put it, cannot be doubted. But was that really such a good thing? Lord Buckmaster in his strenuous dissent foresaw that Lord Atkin's non-principle would open the floodgates and correctly warned that it would not be a pretty sight. The legacy of *Donoghue v. Stevenson* was uncertainty, unnecessary appeals and injustice—with a tendency towards what might be called "yo-yo cases," with one decision at first instance, reversed on appeal, and reversed back again on a final appeal. The semi-decomposed snail started spreading its baneful influence very early on. A good example of this was the Australian case of *Grant v. Australian Knitting Mills* [1935] UKPC, heard finally by the Privy Council in London, which at the time was the final court of appeal for all "imperial" cases and carried persuasive, but not binding, authority in English law.

The Unhygienic Doctor

Dr. Richard Thorold Grant, a medical practitioner from Adelaide, South Australia, bought some woollen underpants (or "long johns," covering the legs) manufactured by Australian Knitting Mills. He continued to wear the same pair of underpants for a week, even though he had started feeling itchy on the ankles after the first day! He was diagnosed with acute dermatitis and stopped wearing the underpants. But the rash continued to get worse and spread throughout his body. He was confined to bed for 17 weeks, and, after some improvement, had a relapse and was hospitalized for three months. It appears that Dr. Grant was allergic to some free sulphites used in the manufacturing process which were trapped in the cuffs of the underpants.

This turned out to be a yo-yo case. Basing his decision on the recently decided *Donoghue v. Stevenson,* Chief Justice Murray sitting in the Supreme Court of South Australia, gave judgment in favor of Dr. Grant and awarded him £2,450 in damages. The High Court of Australia reversed this decision by a 3–1 majority, among other reasons because the manufacturer had evidently adopted a process that was both prudent and reasonable.

The Privy Council, which always just delivered a single undifferentiated "Advice" to the Crown, restored the Chief Justice's original decision in favor of Dr. Grant—even though the manufacturer adduced evidence that they had made no fewer than 4,737,600 of the same articles over the previous six years, without any complaints.

The Privy Council does not appear to have attached any weight to this remarkable fact, but they also failed to suggest any basis on which it could be ignored—such as, perhaps, the "eggshell skull" rule. They also did not consider any way of gauging the degree of care a manufacturer was expected to take, nor the possibility that there should be strict liability for any defect.

"Without responsibility on the part of this Bank"

The second of the three cases singled out by Lord Neuberger for special praise was *Hedley Byrne v. Heller Partners Ltd* [1964] AC 465, which Lord Neuberger praised for "extending liability for negligent misstatements to consequential economic loss." This case marks another departure from principle, again on the basis of policy. With this House of Lords decision Lord Buckmaster's prognostication of the uncontrolled expansion of liability under Lord Atkin's neighbour "principle" took a leap forward with a vengeance by extending liability in two respects:

to.cover negligent words as well as negligent deeds, and to cover pure economic loss as well as physical injury.

A company called Easipower ordered an advertising campaign with Hedley Byrne, who were advertising agents. To check Easipower's creditworthiness, Hedley Byrne asked their bank to ask Easipower's bank for a report. The report, which was provided without charge, came in under a heading: "CONFIDENTIAL. For your private use and without responsibility on the part of this Bank or its officials." The body of the letter said: that Easipower was "considered good for its ordinary business engagements." But it then added, ominously: "Your figures are larger than we are accustomed to see." Ignoring both this warning and the disclaimer, Hedley Byrne went ahead with the advertising campaign. Easipower went into liquidation, leaving Hedley Byrne with a big debt. Hedley Byrne sued Heller (with whom they did not have a contractual relationship) in negligence, but lost because of the disclaimer. In the words of Lord Devlin: "A man cannot be said voluntarily to be undertaking a responsibility if at the very moment when he is said to be accepting it he declares that in fact he is not." Recognition of this down-to-earth truth should have knocked the case on the head long before it reached the House of Lords. If the law had been clearer, it should not have gone to court at all.

But would liability have been found had there been no disclaimer? Evidently, yes. Lord Morris of Borth-y-Gest put it like this: "I consider that it follows and that it should now be regarded as settled that if someone possessing special skill undertakes, quite irrespective of contract, to apply that skill for the assistance of another person who relies upon such skill, a duty of care will arise." This was the exact opposite of the law prevailing up to that point, as decided in a long line of cases culminating in *Candler v. Crane, Christmas & Co.* [1951] 2 KB 164. In that case an investor in a company lost his money after being induced to invest by misleading draft company accounts. His claim against the auditors failed by 2–1 in the Court of Appeal as there was no contractual or fiduciary relationship with them. The sole dissenter, Denning LJ, as he then was, based his opinion on *Donoghue v. Stevenson's* sidestepping the absence of a contractual relationship between Mrs Donoghue and Stevenson. It was Denning's dissenting judgment in *Candler* that formed the basis of the House of Lords decision in *Hedley Byrne.*

"Fair, just and reasonable"

But the snail's mischief was not yet done. In a leading case with similar facts to *Candler,* the House of Lords in a yo-yo case backtracked to *Candler.* The case is called *Caparo Industries plc v. Dickman* [1990] UKHL 2. Caparo held shares in a company called Fidelity plc, which Caparo was interested in taking over, even though Fidelity was not doing too well. When Caparo gained control of Fidelity, they found that Fidelity's financial state was even more parlous than the company's accounts had led them to believe. So Caparo sued the accountant who had prepared the accounts. This is one of the many yo-yo cases littering the English law reports—in other words, a case decided one way at first instance, reversed on appeal, and then finally reversed back again. Here the plaintiff lost at first instance, won a 2–1 victory in the Court of Appeal and then lost again before a unanimous House of Lords.

The judges were flailing around for some basis of principle. Lord Oliver said: "[F]or my part, I think that it has to be recognised that a search for any single formula which will serve as a general test of liability is to pursue a will-o'-the wisp." It was Lord Bridge who proposed a new threefold test of "foreseeability of damage," "a relationship characterised by the law as one of 'proximity' or 'neighbourhood' and that the situation should be one in which the court considers it fair, just and reasonable that that the law should impose a duty of given scope upon the one party for the benefit of the other." However, he endorsed "the wisdom of the words of Brennan J. in the High Court of Australia in *Sutherland Shire Council v. Heyman* (1985) 60 ALR 1, 43–44, where he said: "It is preferable, in my view, that the law should develop novel categories of negligence incrementally and by analogy with established categories, rather than by a massive extension of a prima facie duty of care restrained only by indefinable considerations which ought to negative, or to reduce or limit the scope of the duty or the class of person to whom it is owed."

The new threefold test is anything but clear cut or certain. And the final result in *Caparo* was essentially a return to the decision in *Candler* taken by the two members of that court who stuck to precedent and were resistant to the influence of *Donoghue* (or Denning).

'Their shoulders are broad enough to bear the loss"

In his dissenting speech in *Donoghue*, Lord Buckmaster correctly sounded a mock-comical warning that the Atkin approach could throw open the floodgates even to cover the negligent construction of a house:

> "If such a duty [as the Atkin "neighbour principle"] exists, it seems to me it must cover the construction of every article, and I cannot see any reason why it should not apply to the construction of a house. If one step, why not fifty? Yet if a house be, as it sometimes is, negligently built, and in consequence of that negligence the ceiling falls and injures the occupier or anyone else, no action against the builder exists according to English law, although I believe such a right did exist according to the laws of Babylon."

[Note: This snide remark about Babylon is a reference to the Code of Hammurabi, dating from about 1754 BCE, which provided that if a house collapsed killing the owner, then the architect was to be killed; and if it collapsed killing the owner's son, then the architect's son would suffer the same fate.]

Sure enough, in *Anns v. Merton London Borough Council* [1978] AC 728, a unanimous House of Lords did indeed extend the "neighbour principle" to cover the negligent construction of a house (blamed on the relevant local authority), and it was followed by a number of subsequent decisions. This turned out to be the high-water mark of the extension of tort liability in this type of negligence. Some thirteen years later a seven-judge panel of the House of Lords was specially assembled in *Murphy v. Brentwood District Council* [1991] 1 AC 398 to overrule those decisions. In overruling *Anns* and its progeny, Lord Bridge pilloried Lord Denning's judgment in *Dutton v. Bognor Regis* [1972] 1 QB 373, a precursor of *Anns*, in which he had said, in characteristically robust style:

"Mrs Dutton has suffered a grievous loss. The house fell down without any fault of hers. She is in no position herself to bear the loss. Who ought in justice to bear it? Who are they?" After blaming, first, the builder and, secondly, the council's inspector, he continued: "In the third place, the council should answer for his failure. They were entrusted by Parliament with the task of seeing that houses were properly built. They received public funds. The very object was to protect purchasers and occupiers of houses. Yet they failed to protect them. Their shoulders are broad enough to bear the loss."

Lord Bridge then made a revealing remark:

"These may be cogent reasons of social policy for imposing liability on the authority. But the shoulders of a public authority are only "broad enough to bear the loss" because they are financed by the public at large. It is pre-eminently for the legislature to decide whether these policy reasons should be accepted as sufficient for imposing on the public the burden of providing compensation for private financial losses. If they do so decide, it is not difficult for them to say so."

This is essentially an admission that the judiciary had overstepped the mark with policy decisions in cases like *Anns* and *Dutton*—coupled with recognition of the sovereignty of Parliament, which, needless to say, failed to rise to the occasion.

In *Anns v. Merton London Borough Council* [1977] UKHL 4, building plans for a block of maisonettes were approved by the local council, which had a right but not an obligation to inspect the foundations. The council did not take the trouble to do so, and, as the building was constructed on inadequate foundations, it developed cracks, sloping floors and other structural defects. The lessees of the maisonettes, who had purchased 999-year leases, sued the local authority in negligence. A unanimous House of Lords upheld the lessees' claim against the council. Lord Wilberforce, who gave the leading speech, took the opportunity to widen the "neighbour principle" by suggesting a two-stage test for duty of care:

(a) *"A sufficient relationship of proximity or neighbourhood" based on foreseeability; and*

(b) *"Any considerations which ought to negative, or to reduce or limit the scope of the duty."*

This test, the second part of which is a matter of pure policy, did not last long, after *Anns v. Merton* was overruled by the House of Lords (using a power it had arrogated to itself in 1966) in *Murphy v. Brentwood District Council* [1991] UKHL 2. Here again there was a house without proper foundations and a local authority which negligently approved them. Overruling *Anns*, the House of Lords held that the council could not be held liable for pure economic loss. In the words of Lord Keith of Kinkel: "In my opinion there can be no doubt that Anns has for long been widely regarded as an unsatisfactory decision. ... I think it must now be recognized that it did not proceed on any basis of principle at all, but constituted a remarkable example of judicial legislation." The phrase "a remarkable example of judicial legislation," or judge-made law, is clearly not meant as praise— and it is contrasted with principle.

"I find this reasoning unsatisfactory"

The last of the three cases singled out for praise by Lord Neuberger was *South Australia Asset Management Corp v. York Montague Ltd* (SAAMCo) [1997] AC 191 as considered in *BPE Solicitors v. Hughes-Holland* [2017] 2 WLR 1029. *SAAMCo*, yet another yo-yo case, was about the measure of damages where a surveyor negligently over-valued a property at a time when the property market was falling. Was the surveyor liable only for the difference between his negligent valuation and the true value of the property or should he also be liable for losses occasioned by the fall in the property market? Phillips J., at first instance in *Banque Bruxelles Lambert v. Eagle Star* [1995] QB 375 (which, combined with other cases, became known as *SAAMCo*) held that the negligent surveyor was not liable for losses resulting from market fluctuations. This was reversed on appeal by a unanimous Court of Appeal, and then reversed back again by a unanimous House of Lords—yet another yo-yo case. Lord Hoffman, who delivered the only substantive opinion, curtly dismissed the Court of Appeal's approach, with the words: "I find this reasoning unsatisfactory." [para 21.]

This only shows that what really is unsatisfactory is the state of the law, when there is no agreement even on the basic parameters on how to value damages in not entirely unprecedented circumstances.

A sad case

A sad case illustrating the quandary in which the English courts find themselves in regard to negligence is *Pickford v. Imperial Chemical Industries plc* [1998] UKHL 25, concerning a secretary suffering from cramp in her hands, a condition classified as PDA4 (related to what in layman's terms is referred to as repetitive strain injury). This was yet another yo-yo case, with the plaintiff's case being dismissed at first instance, winning

2–1 in the Court of Appeal and then losing 4–1 in the House of Lords. In reversing the trial judge's decision, the majority in the Court of Appeal reversed his findings on causation, foreseeability and negligence! Lord Steyn, sounded the only dissent in the House of Lords, was contemptuous of the judge, never naming him but repeatedly stressing that he was only a Deputy High Court Judge. Lord Steyn gleefully picked on the judge's "conceptual difficulties," exemplified by the judge's finding on causation, when he had said: "... I am disposed to find that she had a cramp of the hand, but I am not satisfied that it was due to the repetitive movements of typing in the sense that such movements were an effective cause of the cramp, as opposed to being merely the *causa sine qua non* ..." (It is clear from this that the judge did not have a clear understanding of the term *causa sine qua non,* which of course means the opposite of what he thought it meant). Lord Steyn's comment was scathing: "The judge concluded that the cramp in Miss Pickford's hand was associated with her work but not caused by it. He said that the typing was 'only a causa sine qua non.' This is not the first time that a judge has been led astray by a Latin tag. Plainly the judge thought that the typing contributed to Miss Pickford's cramp and it was therefore even on his own findings in causative terms a sufficient contributory cause." Lord Steyn was for dismissing the employer's appeal and reinstating the Court of Appeal's decision in favor of Miss Pickford, but of course that did not happen as the four other law lords were against him.

Was it really necessary for this case to go all the way to the House of Lords? It is true that there was a major conflict over the factual evidence, but the main reason for the divided opinions among the judges was the absence of agreed principles governing this whole area of English law—among others.

Policy or Principle?

"Analysis of tort cases appears to demonstrate a notable degree of disarray and a marked lack of reliable principle." Thus Lord Neuberger in a 2017 speech discussed above. [Neuberger, David (2017).] Lord Neuberger also cited remarks to similar effect made by others. This characterization reads like a damning indictment of UK tort law. But it turns out that Neuberger is actually setting up these criticisms only in order to shrug them off.

- The message of the talk is evidently encapsulated in this sentence: *"There is a strong argument that, in some areas at least, it may be more helpful to abandon principle and to take a stand on policy."* (para 21.) There are two serious problems with this remark. First, on the fundamental principle of the sovereignty of Parliament (which Lord Neuberger has repeatedly and correctly championed, both on and off the bench) it is not for judges to legislate. That is reserved to Parliament. Yet "policy" is just another term for judge-made law. So, how can judges decide not only to "legislate from the bench" but to "abandon principle" to do so. If there is an applicable principle in place, the courts simply cannot decide to "abandon" it. Secondly, Neuberger says there is a "strong argument" in favor of his proposition, yet no argument is provided.

- The closest we get to an argument is this remark in the previous paragraph: *"The cases I have so far referred to tend to suggest that principle rather than policy may be a dangerous guide to those analysing, advising on, debating, or deciding cases involving claims in tort."* So let us go back to those cases to see whether they do in fact suggest anything like this:

  - In *Fairchild v. Glenhaven Funeral Services* [2003] 1 AC 32, a unanimous House of Lords reversed a unanimous Court of Appeal upholding he first instance judge in departing even further from the established principles of causation than had been done in *McGhee v. National Coal Board* [1973] 1 WLR 1. So it was a victory of five judges over four—and over principle. Lord Hoffmann, who was party to the House of Lords decision, later remarked that the decision *"depended on a distinction which had no rational, factual or legal justification."* And Lord Neuberger (who was not himself involved in the case) commented: *"The courts having taken what may be unkindly characterised as an intellectually dubious wrong turning in Fairchild and Parliament having legislated on a rushed piecemeal basis in the 2006 Act, you might have thought that the stage was set for confusion, and so it proved."* [para 10.] "Dubious wrong turning" and "no rational, factual or legal justification"—Does this commend policy over principle?

- In *Chester v. Afshar* [2004] UKSC 41, Lord Hoffmann decided not to go any further down the unprincipled policy line of *Fairchild,* and was joined in his dissent by Lord Bingham, who characterized the majority decision as *"a substantial and unjustified departure from sound and established principle."* How does this prove Lord Neuberger's point that principle may be more dangerous than policy? What it shows is exactly the opposite.

- In *SAAMCo.,* one of the many yo-yo cases, which I discussed above, Lord Hoffmann's comment on the Court of Appeal decision says it all: *"I find this reasoning unsatisfactory."* The different approaches adopted by the two courts was a policy difference—pointing again to the unreliability of policy in judicial decision-making.

- Lord Neuberger recognizes in his talk that principle embodies *"predictability and logical cohesion"* [para 27] and also *"clarity and predictability," which "are vitally important ingredients of the rule of law."* [para 20.] This is a major concession, but one needs to go further and recognize that there can be no rule of law without logical cohesion, clarity and predictability, which together combine to create certainty and justice.

- At the end of his talk, Lord Neuberger stresses an extremely important principle, namely that *"if a judge makes a policy based decision with which the legislature is not happy, the remedy in a system with parliamentary supremacy, such as we enjoy in the UK, lies with Parliament. Any decision made by a court can always be reversed by the legislature."* Adding: *"On the other hand, the notion that Parliament can be reliably expected to step in is often little more than a pious hope, given the enormous pressure on legislative time and the understandably slender political importance which some may think is attributed to most legal issues (as is apparent from Parliament's failure to take up judicial invitations, indeed judicial pleas, to enact a law on illegality, leading the courts to do so, in Patel v. Mirza)."* One might add privacy, another area where, despite judicial entreaties, Parliament has steadfastly refused to act, leaving that area in serious disarray. [See Chapter 9.] Parliament's dereliction of duty goes back centuries. It can be traced as far back as to the 14th century, when, with the law on an even keel of forms of action, maxims and equity, Parliament essentially abdicated its role of controlling the common law by means of legislation and turned its attention elsewhere: to the Hundred Years' War, the War of the Roses, war with Spain, Civil War leading to the execution of a king, a bloodless "Glorious Revolution," the American Revolutionary War, the

Napoleonic War, wars of imperial expansion, and two World Wars. Parliament's dereliction of duty created a vacuum, which, once Lord Atkin showed the way, came increasingly to be filled by judge-made law, with all the uncertainty and unpredictability that that naturally entails, detracting at once from justice and democracy. However, it is clear from the cases that we have examined that Parliament's torpor is not in itself a sufficient explanation of the rise of judicial policy at the expense of principle.

7

UNITED STATES
THE EXPLODING PARCEL

Although in *Donoghue v. Stevenson* Lords Buckmaster and Tomlin registered their total rejection of Lord Atkin's whole approach to the law of negligence, there was surprisingly little criticism of the "neighbour principle" in the years following 1932. On the contrary, that "principle" was not only accepted by the English courts but extended further and further until it became necessary to rein it in. By contrast, Benjamin Cardozo's much less radical approach in *Palsgraf v. Long Island Railroad Co.* 248 N.Y. 339, 162 N.E. 99 (1928) aroused a great deal of controversy and was never universally accepted by the different American state jurisdictions.

MacPherson v. Buick Motor Co.

Before turning to *Palsgraf,* it may be worth taking a look at another milestone opinion by Judge Benjamin Cardozo, which was actually cited with approval in *Donoghue* by both Lord Atkin and his nemesis, Lord Buckmaster. The case in question is *MacPherson v. Buick Motor Co.,* 111 N.E. 1050, 217 N.Y. 382, decided by the New York Court of Appeals in 1916. Donald MacPherson was thrown out of the car and injured when one of the wooden wheels on his Buick Runabout collapsed while he was driving prudently at eight miles an hour. The car was manufactured by Buick, but the wheel, though fitted by Buick, was made by another company. The plaintiff did not have a contract with Buick, because he bought the car from a dealer.

149

According to the evidence, the defect could have been discovered by reasonable inspection, but as Cardozo put it, "that inspection was omitted."

In *Donoghue v. Stevenson*, Lord Atkin enthusiastically latched on to what he called "the illuminating judgment of Cardozo J. in *MacPherson v. Buick Motor Co. ...* in which he states the principles of the law as I should desire to state them." This is somewhat disingenuous. The law both in England and America was that, in the absence of a contractual relationship, a manufacturer was liable to the end user only if the product was either dangerous in itself or dangerous by reason of some defect or for any other reason, and this is known to the manufacturer. Cardozo was well aware of this and brought the MacPherson case within this rule:

> "If the nature of a thing is such that it is reasonably certain to place life and limb in peril when negligently made, it is then a thing of danger. Its nature gives warning of the consequences to be expected. If to the element of danger there is added knowledge that the thing will be used by persons other than the purchaser, and used without new tests, then, irrespective of contract, the manufacturer of this thing of danger is under a duty to make it carefully. That is as far as we are required to go for the decision of this case. There must be knowledge of a danger, not merely possible, but probable. ... Beyond all question, the nature of an automobile gives warning of probable danger if its construction is defective. This automobile was designed to go fifty miles an hour. Unless its wheels were sound and strong, injury was almost certain. ... The defendant knew the danger. It knew also that the car would be used by persons other than the buyer."

Not surprisingly, in citing MacPherson's case with approval, Lord Atkin made no mention of the crucial "dangerous" test. Lord Buckmaster's reference to the New York case was more accurate: "In ... *MacPherson v. Buick Motor Co.*, where a manufacturer of a defective motor-car was held liable for damages at the instance of a third party, the learned judge appears to base his judgment on the view that a motor-car might reasonably be regarded as a dangerous article."

In *MacPherson*, therefore, Cardozo's judgment was in keeping with the principles of the tort of negligence as recognized at the time. In *Palsgraf*, however, he was a little more adventurous.

Palsgraf v. Long Island Railroad Co.

In August 1924 Helen Palsgraf was waiting on a Brooklyn railroad station platform to board a train with her two teenage daughters when she was injured. Two men came rushing on to the platform to board an earlier train, which was already pulling out of the station. One managed to clamber aboard unaided. The other, who was carrying a package, was assisted by two railroad employees, a platform guard pushing him from behind and a train crew member holding the door open and pulling him into the moving train. But in his haste he dropped the package, which contained fireworks. It exploded crashing into a weighing machine, which fell on Mrs Palsgraf, who was shaken up and bruised and developed a bad stammer a few days later.

Helen Palsgraf sued the railroad company for negligence. At first instance in the Supreme Court of New York, Kings County, the jury found the railroad company liable to Mrs Palsgraf and awarded her $6,000 in damages. The jury verdict was affirmed by a 3–2 decision of the Appellate Division of the New York Supreme Court for the Second Department. [*Palsgraf v. Long Island Railroad Co.* 248 N.Y. 339, 162 N.E. 99 (1928).]

By a 4–3 majority the New York Court of Appeals (the state's highest court) reversed the lower courts' decision and dismissed Mrs Palsgraf's suit with costs. The majority opinion was delivered by Chief Judge Benjamin Cardozo, who would be elevated to the U.S. Supreme Court in 1932. His statement of the facts was characterized by Judge Richard Posner as "elliptical and slanted." [Posner (1993) p. 38.] Describing Mrs Palsgraf as "standing far away," Cardozo waved aside the allegation of negligence on the part of the railroad guard, who, he claimed, owed Mrs Palsgraf no duty: "Relative to her, it was not negligence at all."

Judge William Andrews and two other judges dissented. Andrews's opinion became almost as well-known as Cardozo's. Here is how he explained his agreement with the lower courts' decision in favor of Mrs Palsgraf:

> "Except for the explosion, she would not have been injured. We are told by the appellant [viz. the railroad company] in his brief 'it cannot be denied that the explosion was the direct cause of the plaintiff's injuries. ... The only intervening cause was that instead of blowing her to the ground the concussion smashed the weighing machine which in turn fell upon her. There was no remoteness in time, little in space. And surely, given such an explosion as here it needed no great foresight to predict that the natural result would be to injure one on the platform at no greater distance from its scene than was the plaintiff. Just how no one might be able to predict. Whether by flying fragments, by broken glass, by wreckage of machines or structures no one could say. But injury in some form was most probable." [at 356]

Because of Cardozo's mistake in describing Mrs Palsgraf as "standing far away," her lawyer asked the court to allow the case to be reargued. This motion was curtly denied: "If we assume that the plaintiff was nearer the scene of the explosion than the prevailing opinion would suggest, she was not so near that injury from a falling package, not known to contain explosives, would be within the range of reasonable prevision." This rebuff was probably written by Cardozo—the flowery phrase "within the range of reasonable prevision," instead of the simple "reasonably foreseeable", is a dead giveaway. It is factually incorrect—Cardozo had apparently confused Helen Palsgraf's position in relation to the explosion with that of her daughter. And its tone may possibly be a sign of Cardozo's bias against Mrs Palsgraf. It is also a poor logical argument, which is answered by Andrews in the passage quoted above: It was foreseeable that anyone standing as close to the explosion as Mrs Palsgraf was would be injured by it in some way.

The essential difference between the two judges was that for Cardozo liability for negligence could arise only when the defendant owed a duty of care specifically to the plaintiff, whereas for Andrews this was "too narrow a conception." Another important difference is that Andrews held that foreseeability was an issue to be left to the jury, while Cardozo decided it himself, and his ruling also reversed the $6,000 jury verdict for Mrs Palsgraf.

Andrews explained the difference between them in clear terms. What is the nature of negligence? he asks. "Is it a relative concept—the breach of some duty owing to a particular person or to particular persons? Or where there is an act which unreasonably threatens the safety of others, is the doer liable for all its proximate consequences, even where they result in injury to one who would generally be thought to be outside the radius of danger?"

Andrews then sets out his own view:

"The proposition is this. Every one owes to the world at large the duty of refraining from those acts that may unreasonably threaten the safety of others. Such an act occurs. Not only is he wronged to whom harm might reasonably be expected to result, but he also who is in fact injured, even if he be outside what would generally be thought the danger zone. There needs [to] be duty due the one complaining, but this is not a duty to a particular individual, because as to him harm might be expected. Harm to some one being the natural result of the act, not only that one alone, but all those in fact injured may complain. We have never, I think, held otherwise."

Andrews goes on to deal with damages.

> "The right to recover damages rests on additional
> considerations. The plaintiff's rights must be injured, and this
> injury must be caused by the negligence. ... The damages must
> be so connected with the negligence that the latter may be
> said to be the proximate cause of the former."

The "Squib" case

If Cardozo's view of negligence in *Palsgraf* is too narrow,
Andrews's is arguably too wide. The best approach was probably
that of Justice Albert Seeger in the Appellate Division (New
York's intermediate appeal court), who, writing for the 3–2
majority in that court, upholding the jury verdict for Mrs
Palsgraf in the court below, suggested that helping a passenger to
board a moving train might be considered negligent. He prayed
in aid the old English "Squib case," *Scott v. Shepherd* 96 ER 525
(1773) based on the principle of *novus actus interveniens* (literally,
"new act intervening") concerning breaking the chain of
causation. What this means is that a negligent defendant will not
be held liable if some new intervening event breaks the chain of
causation between the defendant's negligence and the plaintiff's
injury, loss or damage. In the Squib case itself, the defendant
Shepherd threw a lighted squib (a hissing exploding firework)
into a crowded market. It landed on the stall of a gingerbread
merchant named Yates. To protect Yates and himself a bystander
called Willis quickly tossed the squib away. It landed in Ryal's
stall, and he again tossed it away. The squib exploded in the face
of the fifth participant, the plaintiff Scott, putting out his eye.

Was Shepherd liable to Scott, or did each of the subsequent
events amount to a *novus actus interveniens*? By a 3–1 majority the
Court of King's Bench found Shepherd fully liable to Scott for
his injury. Chief Justice de Grey explained the ruling quite
simply: "I do not consider [the intermediaries] as free agents in

the present case, but acting under a compulsive necessity for their own safety and self-preservation."

The one dissenting voice was that of Sir William Blackstone, best known for his *Commentaries on the Law of England*, who argued quite persuasively that each of the intermediate actions did amount to a *novus actus interveniens* and that Shepherd should not therefore be held liable. "Both [Ryal] and Willis have exceeded the bounds of self-defence and not used sufficient circumspection in removing the danger from themselves. The throwing it across the market-house instead of brushing it down, or throwing it out of the open sides into the street (...) was at least an unnecessary and incautious act."

In my opinion, in the Squib case itself the arguments are equally balanced. But *Palsgraf* is more clear-cut in this respect. There certainly were several intermediate events between the dropping of the parcel and Mrs Palsgrafd's injury, but none of the events could have been prevented as none of them was an act of will by a human agent. The whole episode was so-to-speak a chain reaction. It is strange, therefore, that, though the Squib case had been at the heart of the opinion of Justice Albert Seeger, neither Cardozo nor Andrews even alluded to it.

Palsgraf: Summary

One of the key questions in *Palsgraf* was: Was the defendant railroad company or its servants negligent? Four different answers were given, two in the intermediate Appellate Division and two in the final appeal, namely Cardozo's and Andrews's. Let us take a look at them one by one.

- First, Justice Seeger, as we have seen, considered that even helping a passenger to board a moving train was probably negligent, and that, as there was nothing to break the chain of causation, the railroad company was liable to Mrs Palsgraf.

- Secondly, two dissenting justices in the intermediate appellate court, while agreeing with the jury's finding of negligence on the part of the railroad company, considered that a passenger's bringing a potentially explosive package into a crowded railroad station constituted a separate act of negligence—*a novus actus interveniens*—breaking the chain of causation and therefore reversing the jury verdict for Mrs Palsgraf.

- Thirdly, we have Cardozo's answer, which I find the least persuasive of all: "The conduct of the defendant's guard, if a wrong in relation to the holder of the package, was not a wrong in its relation to the plaintiff, standing far away." This makes very little sense, for three reasons. First, as already discussed, Mrs Palsgraf was not "standing far away." Secondly, even if she had been, that does not automatically negative the possibility that the guard's conduct was not negligent toward her. And thirdly, the suggestion that the guard was negligent toward the holder of the package will simply not stand up to scrutiny. For that to be the case, the guard would have had to owe the package holder a duty to help him to board a moving train—instead of that being, as it probably was, something actually prohibited by his terms of employment.

- Finally, there is Andrews's quite straightforward position on the defendant's negligence: "The act upon which the defendant's liability rests is knocking an apparently harmless package on to the platform. The act was negligent. For its proximate consequences the defendant is liable." And one of its proximate consequences was Mrs Palsgraf's injury.

Summing up his position on negligence, Andrews remarked, "We have never, I think, held otherwise." This is an important remark. What Andrews is saying is that his view is in keeping with precedent. But none of the other three positions marked a radical departure from principle either. All four were based on the same principles, differing only in the way those principles were applied to the facts of the case. This is the crucial difference between *Palsgraf* and *Donoghue v. Stevenson*, where Lord Atkin's "neighbour principle" marked a complete departure from the settled principles of the law.

Palsgraf: Conclusion

It is therefore surprising that the aftermath of *Palsgraf* in America was so very different from the reaction in Britain to the decision in *Donoghue v. Stevenson*. Though clearly wrong in law, as Lords Buckmaster and Tomlin strenuously insisted, the Atkin "neighbour principle" of *Donoghue v. Stevenson* has not been seriously challenged since it was first enunciated in 1932 but has remained the basis of the English tort of negligence to this day—despite resulting in precisely the serious problems predicted by Lord Buckmaster at the time. See Chapter 6, "United Kingdom: The Snail in the Bottle," for the sorry saga of the vicissitudes of the English law of negligence in the wake of *Donoghue v. Stevenson*.

But the aftermath of *Palsgraf* in America was very different. The case quickly became the subject of articles in law reviews around the country and before long figured in standard student casebooks, where it is still to be found. In some law schools there is even a celebration of "Palsgraf Day," including mock debates between Judges Cardozo and Andrews. [Cardi (2011) p. 1874.]

The point is that all the interest aroused by *Palsgraf* was far from being one-sided. Cardozo's approach was adopted by some state courts and rejected by others, mostly on the basis that foreseeability was an issue that should be left to the jury. And Cardozo's position that a defendant cannot be held liable to an unforeseeable plaintiff, though followed by New York, has found favor in only a minority of states, the majority preferring Andrews's "proximate cause" approach. [Posner (1993) p. 41]

Contract and tort remain outside the codified laws of most states—and every state has codified law, with Pennsylvania still completing the process. In California, Montana, North Dakota, South Dakota, and Georgia, contract and tort *are* incorporated into the codified laws of the state, and in Idaho, contract but not tort is so incorporated. The states where contract and tort are not codified tend to use the *Restatements of the Law* published by the American Law Institute (ALI), an organization whose membership includes judges, lawyers in practice, and legal academics. Described by Benjamin Cardozo, a founding member of the ALI, as "something less than a code and something more than a treatise," they are followed by many state courts, and, while they do not constitute binding authority, they are generally regarded as highly authoritative, though they have been not been immune from criticism. [Adams, Kristen David (2007).] "In essence," writes Catherine Biondo of the Harvard Law School Library, the *Restatements* "restate existing common law into a series of principles or rules."

Here is an extract from the *Restatement (Third) of Torts* (2009) on Negligence:

> A person acts negligently if the person does not exercise reasonable care under all the circumstances. Primary factors to consider in ascertaining whether the person's conduct lacks reasonable care are the foreseeable likelihood that the person's conduct will result in harm, the foreseeable severity of any harm that may ensue, and the burden of precautions to eliminate or reduce the risk of harm.

David Owen comments:

> "By stripping duty of foreseeability, one of duty's key features, the Restatement (Third) discards Judge Cardozo's elemental work in Palsgraf so long ago. And by harnessing juries to a sterile yoke of scope of risk for proximate-cause decision making, the draft Restatement (Third) also rejects

Judge Andrews's valuable insight that juries should be offered a wide range of fairness factors, beginning with foreseeability, in figuring how far responsibility should extend. Be that as it may, foreseeability was the moral glue of negligence before tort law was first restated many years ago, and, regardless of its reconfiguration in the Restatement (Third), foreseeability will continue, at least on earth, to ground and bind the elements of negligence law together." [Owen, David (2009), p. 1307.]

The approach adopted in the Restatement is similar to that of Judge Andrews in concentrating on the defendant's conduct: did it pose a risk to others, and not just to the plaintiff? And did the defendant exercise reasonable care? But the principles are open to more than one interpretation. In particular, what exactly is meant by "reasonable care under all the circumstances" and how is "the foreseeable likelihood" to be measured?

Let us examine how these principles have been applied in practice.

It is this emphasis on principles and rules that differentiates American state law generally from English law, which has been sorely lacking in principles or rules for nearly 90 years now.

Sports Injuries

In the chapter titled "Maxims or Minims?" we had occasion to examine the Cardozo opinion in the "Flopper" case, in which a young man was injured while on a jerky ride in Coney Island: *James Murphy v. Steeplechase Amusement Co., Inc.* 250 N.Y. 479, 166 N.E. 173 (1929). Five judges sitting in the New York Court of Appeals agreed with Cardozo, who wrote the majority opinion that this was a case of *volenti non fit injuria*, meaning that there was a voluntary assumption of risk on the part of the plaintiff, which therefore negated his claim.

The sole dissent was registered by Judge O'Brien, on the basis of an earlier case, in which he had delivered the unanimous decision of the court: *Tantillo v. Goldstein Brothers Amusement Co.,*

248 N.Y. 286 (1928). In this rather unusual case, the plaintiff, a 14-year-old boy, together with two friends, went to see a vaudeville show. After paying for their tickets in the ordinary way they unexpectedly had their money refunded and were induced to form part of the show, essentially as a butt of humor for the audience. After being catapulted from a treadmill, the plaintiff's arm was broken. Not surprisingly, the jury found the act inherently dangerous, and, as the plaintiff had no prior warning of what he was letting himself in for, the defendant was held liable in negligence. The judgment, on the basis of the jury verdict, was unanimously affirmed.

This decision was undoubtedly correct as far as *Tantillo* was concerned, but has no bearing on the "Flopper" case. The difference is quite clear cut. In "Flopper" there was ample evidence pointing to a voluntary assumption of risk by the plaintiff, whereas in *Tantillo* the young plaintiff's intention was to watch the show, not to be part of it, let alone to become a human projectile.

By contrast with the "Flopper" case, in a 2015 lawsuit also involving Coney Island, Paula Noone not only won her case after being injured in a roller coaster ride but was actually awarded $1.5 million by a Brooklyn jury after four days of deliberation, though the jury also found her 60% responsible for her own injuries, thus reducing the payout to about $600,000. Her injuries, suffered in 2008, consisted of two herniated discs in her neck and a concussion. Her lawsuit alleged that the "serious, severe, and permanent injuries" requiring emergency surgery, were caused by "inadequate restraints and excessive acceleration, which resulted in her head and neck being violently flung back and forth." [*Noone v. City of New York, Astroland Kiddie Park Inc. and Cyclone Coasters Inc.* www.lawyersandsettlements.com.] Paula Noone rode the "Cyclone" roller coaster of her own free will, despite a sign warning people not to ride if they had a neck injury. Ms. Noone had suffered a neck injury in 2003, but claimed she had not been riding the roller coaster while injured.

In the "Flopper" case, volenti lost the plaintiff the case. Should Paula Noone have suffered the same fate? It was certainly a possibility, as she could not claim to have been unaware of the risk. But, fortunately for her, back in 1975 New York had enacted the Comparative Negligence Statute (New York Civil Practice Law & Rules 1411) replacing the traditional contributory negligence rule. Under the old rule, any negligence on the part of Mrs Noone, no matter how slight, would have deprived her of any recovery. But, with the comparative negligence rule not even negligence in excess of 50% on the part of the plaintiff has that effect. The jury in this case found Paula Noone 60% negligent, which cost her 60% of her damages, but no more than that.

So far, although there have been some differences of opinion among the judges, all of them were based on the same principles. Let us see whether the same applies when we turn from participants in leisure activities to spectators.

The Foul Ball Injury

In *Robin Akins v. Glens Falls City School District,* [53 N.Y. 2d 325, 424 N.E. 2d 531 (1981)], a spectator at a baseball game was struck in the eye and seriously and permanently injured by a foul ball while standing in an unscreened section of the field, though there was protective screening behind the home plate. The jury at first instance and the New York Appellate Division found the proprietor of the ball park liable in negligence to the injured spectator. But on appeal, a majority on the New York Court of Appeals reversed this decision and dismissed the spectator's complaint. "We hold," wrote Judge Jassen for the 4–3 majority, "that, in the exercise of reasonable care, the proprietor of a ball park need only provide screening for the area of the field behind home plate where the danger of being struck by a ball is the greatest." However, Chief Judge Lawrence Cooke sounded a vigorous dissent: "The majority today engages in an unfortunate exercise in judicial rule making in an area that should be left to the jury. This attempt to precisely prescribe what steps the proprietor of a baseball field must take to fulfill its duty of reasonable care is unwarranted and unwise. ... I therefore dissent and vote to affirm."

Chief Judge Cooke here accuses the majority on the court of legislating from the bench and of usurping the role of the jury. This latter stricture is serious, but the accusation of "judicial rule making" really boils down to the fact that the majority adopted a different standard of "reasonable care" from his own—without attempting to change the rule or to legislate from the bench.

Two high-profile English cases involving the game of cricket present us with a very different spectacle.

Stoned by a Bolt out of the Blue

In *Bolton v. Stone* [1951] AC 850, Miss Stone was standing outside her house when she was injured by a cricket ball hit out of the cricket ground about 100 yards away, which was surrounded by a 12-foot fence. At first instance, Oliver J. sitting without a jury in the High Court dismissed all three causes of action advanced by the plaintiff:

- Negligence—Not applicable as there was no evidence of any injury occurring in the previous 38 years;
- Nuisance—A single incident cannot constitute a nuisance;
- *Rylands v. Fletcher* [1868] UKHL 1—This cause of action is an early example of judge-made law to cover damage (but not personal injury) resulting from a landowner's "ultra-hazardous" activities. The plaintiff claimed that the cricket ball was a dangerous article that had "escaped" from the cricket ground—which clearly made no sense. [[1949] 1 All ER 237.]

The Court of Appeal reversed this decision by a 2–1 majority as far as negligence was concerned, on the basis of the principle *res ipsa loquitur* ("the facts speak for themselves"), the classic statement of which was made by Lord Chief Justice Erle in *Scott v. London & St. Katherine Docks Co.* 159 E.R. 665 (1865): "where the thing is shown to be under the management of the defendant or his servants, and the accident is such as in the ordinary course of things does not happen if those who have the management use proper care, it affords reasonable evidence, in the absence of explanation by the defendants, that the accident arose from want of care." A common example of this sort of situation is where a shopper slips and falls in some spilled liquid on the floor of a supermarket or food store, as in *Ward v. Tesco Stores Ltd.* [1976] 1 All ER 219, in which the defendants were unable to provide evidence showing that they had taken "all reasonable care," so negligence was inferred. However, *res ipsa loquitur* should have been found inapplicable in *Bolton v. Stone,* because, far from being an unexplained event, the flying cricket ball that injured Miss Stone was admitted to have been hit out of the ground by a batsman in the course of a cricket match.

The House of Lords unanimously reversed the decision back to that of the first instance judge, finding that there was no negligence. Lord Porter made the apt observation that a road traffic accident or airplane crash are events which a driver or pilot "desires to do everything possible to avoid, whereas the hitting of the ball out of the ground is an incident in the game and, indeed, one which the batsman would wish to bring about." Lord Radcliffe said:

> "A breach of duty has taken place if [the facts] show the Appellants (i.e. the cricket club) guilty of a failure to take reasonable care to prevent the accident...Unless there has been something which a reasonable man would blame as falling beneath the standard of conduct that he would set for himself and require of his neighbour, there has been no breach of legal duty. And here, I think, the [plaintiff's] case breaks down. It seems to me that a reasonable man, taking account of the chances against an accident happening, would

not have felt himself called upon either to abandon the use of the ground for cricket or to increase the height of his surrounding fences. He would have done what the [cricket club] did: in other words, he would have done nothing."

Why was it necessary for this case to go all the way to the very top of the English judicial hierarchy—ending up as a "yo-yo" case to boot (my own term for a case with one result at first instance, which is reversed on appeal and then reversed back again on final appeal)? The reason is the formless and rudderless state of English law, resulting in the parties and the courts flailing around trying out four different causes of action without any guiding principles.

Res ipsa loquitur, which was wrongly found by the Court of Appeal in *Bolton v. Stone*, is an ancient principle with its roots in Roman law. But, unlike in English law, in America it has been incorporated into pseudo-black letter law in the shape of the Restatement (Second) of Torts, § 328D (1965), which provides:

(1) It may be inferred that harm suffered by the plaintiff is caused by negligence of the defendant when: (a) the event is of a kind which ordinarily does not occur in the absence of negligence; (b) other responsible causes, including the conduct of the plaintiff and third persons, are sufficiently eliminated by the evidence; and (c) the indicated negligence is within the scope of the defendant's duty to the plaintiff.

(2) It is the function of the court to determine whether the inference may reasonably be drawn by the jury, or whether it must necessarily be drawn.

(3) It is the function of the jury to determine whether the inference is to be drawn in any case where different conclusions may reasonably be reached.

This test was modified in the Restatement (Third) of Torts, § 17 (2005), reading as follows:

The factfinder may infer that the defendant has been negligent when the accident causing the plaintiff's physical harm is a type of accident that ordinarily happens as a result of the negligence of a class of actors of which the defendant is the relevant member.

Comparisons have been drawn between the two versions, Professor Aaron Twerski, for example, praising the newer version as "a vast improvement" over the earlier formulation:

"The doctrine implies that the court does not know, and cannot find out, what actually happened in the individual case. ... Put simply, res ipsa relies on a generalization that negligence is the best explanation for a given category of events. ... Almost the only way for a defendant to defeat a res-ipsa case is to provide some evidence that the generalization was not operative at the time the accident took place....[T]he law of negligence abhors generalizations. It is fact sensitive...The tension between the generalization and fact specificity is real and tangible. That is the dynamic that drives the case law in both negligence per se and res ipsa loquitur. The two concepts may not be twins, but they are kissing cousins." [Twerski, Aaron D. (2009).]

Would the majority on the Court of Appeal in *Bolton v. Stone* have been spared an embarrassing legal blunder if there had been an explicit formulation of this ancient principle? We can but speculate.

"Village cricket is the delight of everyone"

"In summertime village cricket is the delight of everyone." This was the opening salvo of Lord Denning's dissenting opinion in *Miller v. Jackson* [1977] QB 966. Though couched in uncontroversial language, it was far from being a statement of fact. Indeed, the case was brought by a couple, the Millers, complaining of broken roof tiles and other minor damage to their property caused by cricket balls hit out of a neighboring cricket ground. To minimize such occurrences, the cricket club had erected a fence 8 ft 9 inches in height on top of a 6-ft high boundary wall, but a few errant balls continued to land outside the cricket ground. At first instance in the High Court, the Millers were granted the injunction that they sought together with damages for negligence and nuisance. The Court of Appeal, in a 2–1 decision, held that the club was guilty of negligence "on each occasion when a ball comes over the fence and causes damage to the plaintiffs." Nuisance was also found, though when the Millers bought their house the cricket club had been going for 70 years, as Lord Denning pointed out in his strong dissenting opinion. He deplored the grant of an injunction by the High Court "at the instance of a newcomer who is no lover of cricket. This newcomer has built … a house on the edge of the cricket ground which four years ago was a field where cattle grazed. The animals did not mind the cricket." He went on to paint a dismal picture of the future after the injunction: "The cricket ground will be turned to some other use. I expect for more houses or a factory. The young men will turn to other things instead of cricket. The whole village will be much the poorer. And all this because of a newcomer who has just bought a house there next to the cricket ground." His conclusion was that "the public interest should prevail over the private interest." Unused to being outvoted in his own court, Lord Denning, Master of the Rolls, nevertheless concurred in the award to the plaintiffs of £400 to cover any past or future damage. But even this evidently did not satisfy the Millers, who moved house soon after.

In *Miller*, Lord Denning's impassioned plea on behalf of the joys of cricket was given short shrift and his oblique invocation of the old defense of "coming to the nuisance" was completely ignored. That defense is rooted in the important ancient principle of *volenti non fit injuria*: a plaintiff who buys a house near an already existing longstanding known nuisance has "come to the nuisance," and in that sense has voluntarily assumed risk. It would only be fair to take that into account if the "newcomer," as Lord Denning rather disparagingly called him, then seeks damages, or an injunction to shut down or limit the offending activity.

The area of private nuisance in English law is one of the most confused of any. As Professor Maria Lee pointed out in 2003, the idea of "reasonableness," which is central to this cause of action, is frequently bandied about but "rarely examined in detail, and it would be a brave person who would attempt to draw out a definition." [Lee, Maria (2003).] Similarly, Allan Beever's comment that reasonableness "is presented as an explanation of the operation of the law, but it does not, cannot, explain anything." [Beever, Allan (2013) p. 9ff.]

Coventry v. Lawrence

The UK Supreme Court decision in *Coventry v. Lawrence* [2014] UKSC 13*—another yo-yo case—has not helped to clarify this area of the law. In 1984 the defendants started operating speedway racing and later also motocross, for both of which they had planning permission. In 2006 the claimants bought and occupied a bungalow near the stadium and race-track. In 2011 they were awarded damages and granted an injunction by the High Court to restrict the defendants' activities to a certain maximum noise-level. In 2012 the Court of Appeal reversed this decision and held that the defendant's racing activities did not constitute a nuisance. In 2014, a unanimous UK Supreme Court reversed the decision back again (though the injunction was stayed pending the rebuilding of the claimants' fire-damaged bungalow.)

---

* This decision is sometimes referred to as *Coventry v. Lawrence* (*No. 1*), as the case returned twice more to the UKSC on other issues.

Blackstone

The ancient defense of "coming to the nuisance" was rejected. Here is how Blackstone explains that defense in his inimitable personalized style:

"If I have an ancient window overlooking my neighbor's ground, he may not erect any blind to obstruct the light: but if I build my house close to his wall, which darkens it, I cannot compel him to demolish his wall; for there the first occupancy is rather in him, than in me. If my neighbor makes a tan-yard, so as to annoy and render less salubrious the air of my house or gardens, the law will furnish me with a remedy; but if he is first in possession of the air, and I fix my habitation near him, the nuisance is of my own seeking, and must continue."
[Blackstone (1765–1769). Book 2, Ch 26.]

The example of the tan-yard is particularly relevant, and Blackstone makes it clear that priority in time is crucial—but no particular number of years is specified. If the tan-yard was already there when the complainant moved in nearby, then the nuisance is effectively of his own making, as he has essentially accepted the risk, of which he must have been aware from the outset. Blackstone's hypothetical tan-yard is a close parallel to the motor-racing in the *Coventry* case and the confectioner's clattering away with his mortar and pestle in *Sturges v. Bridgman* (discussed below), but to no avail.

Though the plaintiff only bought the bungalow in 2006, it had been built as a dwelling house in the 1950s, and so actually predated the motor-racing. Therefore, instead of dismissing the defendants' argument that the plaintiffs had "come to the nuisance" as an invalid defense in terms of law, the court could have adopted a much neater approach by accepting the "coming to the nuisance" argument as a potential defense but could then simply have dismissed it as factually incorrect, because the motor-racing had not yet begun when the bungalow was built in the 1950s.

Easement—the wrong prescription

However, instead of that, the whole defense of "coming to the nuisance" was waved aside as wrong in law, and great emphasis was placed by Lord Neuberger on the question of "The extent, if any, to which it is open to a defendant to contend that he has established a prescriptive right to commit what would otherwise be a nuisance by means of noise." [para 6.] The relevance of this, according to Lord Neuberger, was "the somewhat arbitrary, but at least clear, proposition that, where the use or activity in question has been carried on as of right for 20 years or more, then, absent special facts, the dominant owner gets a right to carry on the use or activity."

Lord Neuberger adopted the conventional definition of prescription: "The essential feature of prescription for present purposes is that, in order to establish a right by prescription, a person must show at least 20 years uninterrupted enjoyment as of right, that is *nec vi, nec clam, nec precario* ("not by force, nor stealth, nor with the license of the owner) ... of that which he now claims to be entitled to enjoy by right." [para 31.]

A prescriptive right is relevant chiefly to acquiring an *easement*, which is a landowner's right over the land of another, notably a right of way. But, can the right to create a noise nuisance possibly be an easement? Neuberger thought that it could: "I am of the view that the right to carry on an activity which results in noise, or the right to emit a noise, which would otherwise cause an actionable nuisance, is capable of being an easement." [para 33.]

Sturges v. Bridgman

In reaching that conclusion, Lord Neuberger prayed in aid the case of *Sturges v. Bridgman* (1879) 11 Ch D 852. A physician bought a house next door to the long-established premises of a confectioner. The newly arrived physician complained that the noise of the confectioner's grinding his industrial mortar and pestle disturbed him in the shed which he had just built on the border of the confectioner's property to use as a consulting room. The confectioner's defense was that he had been conducting the same business in the same way for well over 20 years, but he was unable to prove this to the satisfaction of the Court of Appeal, where the main, rather muddled, judgment, delivered by Lord Justice Alfred Thesiger (1838–1880), went way beyond the first instance decision by the Master of the Rolls, Sir George Jessel. Here are some of the anomalies in Thesiger's opinion:

- Thesiger treated the confectioner's right to carry on making noise as an "easement" obtainable by prescriptive right *nec vi, nec clam, nec precario. Nec precario* indicates that to obtain this prescriptive right the confectioner would have had to have created the noise for 20 years *without* the permission of the physician or any of his predecessors in title.

- Yet Thesiger specifically states that "consent or acquiescence of the owner of the servient tenement [i.e. the physician] lies at the root of prescription."

- While rejecting the old defense of "coming to the nuisance," Thesiger gives a couple of hypothetical examples that one could be forgiven for seeing as arguments in favor of that defense. One such example is of someone building a private residence on a vacant piece of land in the midst of the tanneries of Bermondsey (then an industrial part of London but subsequently "gentrified".) This ties in with Thesiger's comment that "what would be a nuisance in Belgrave

Square would not necessarily be so in Bermondsey." In his less than pellucid style, what Thesiger is suggesting is presumably that a newcomer to a locality "devoted to a particular trade or manufacture of a noisy or unsavoury character" should accept the character of that locality. How does this apply to the locality where the parties in Sturges were situated? Thesiger does not say. The confectioner's business was in Wigmore Street and the physician's in the neighboring Wimpole Street, both being in an upscale part of West London. Wimpole Street is famous as the home of "The Barretts of Wimpole Street" in the 1840s, while Wigmore Street was predominantly commercial. However, Frederick Bridgman was no ordinary tradesman, but confectioner by appointment to Queen Victoria and the Prince of Wales, in a business inherited from his father and operated in the same premises for over 60 years. Although this was a much more upmarket area, there is a clear parallel here with the tanneries of Bermondsey.

- Thesiger stressed that a prescriptive right could be claimed either under common law or under the Prescription Act 1832 (a short part of which is still in force), which makes it clear that it relates to easements such as rights of way and other similar rights. There is certainly no indication that it could refer to nuisance.

Following *Sturges*, the main reason for the majority decision in *Coventry* to restore the first instance judge's order was, in Lord Neuberger's words, the defendant's failure "to establish a prescriptive right to create what would otherwise be a nuisance," because "they did not show that their activities during a period of 20 years amounted to a nuisance....[I]n order to justify the establishment of a right to create a noise by prescription, it is not enough to show that the activity which now creates the noise has been carried on for 20 years. It is not even enough to show that the activity has created a noise for 20 years. What has to be established is that the activity has (or a combination of activities have) created a nuisance over 20 years. Otherwise, it could not be said that the putative servient owner [i.e. the owner of the bungalow] had the opportunity to object to the nuisance, or could be said notionally to have agreed to it." [para 143.]

Dennis v. Ministry of Defence

The whole idea of trying to identify nuisance with an easement was smartly knocked on the head by Mr. Justice Buckley in the English High Court in *Dennis v. Ministry of Defence* [2003] EWHC 793 (QB). The case concerned a complaint about noise produced by Harrier jet fighters near a stately home known as Walcot Hall, built in 1678, and subsequently developed into a "traditional residential, sporting and agricultural estate of some 1,387 acres," owned by the claimants. The Ministry of Defence (MOD) "sensibly conceded that the Harrier is a noisy aircraft. Indeed no one convincingly suggested that there was a noisier one..." The judge continued: "In view of the findings I have made in respect of the nature and extent of the noise disturbance, it seems plain to me that the noise is, on the face it, a nuisance." [para 34.]

Buckley J. then deftly disposed of the whole "prescription" idea. Defense counsel raised a plea that the MOD had acquired by prescription the right to fly the Harriers over the claimants' property. Claimants' counsel then submitted, and the judge agreed, that "that must mean the MOD had acquired the right to commit a nuisance." It was agreed by the parties "that the alleged right would have to amount to an easement and that it would therefore need to be capable of forming the subject matter of a grant. Further, that the 'user' must have been 'as of right.'" Buckley J's comment is blunt: "In my judgment the plea fails on both grounds. As to certainty, ... could a conveyancer draft it? I cannot see how." Defense counsel "did not identify what level of decibels he would put in the imaginary grant nor how the flying circuit could be defined. An open-ended right to commit any noise nuisance might be capable of arising, but surely only by express grant. ... As to use 'as of right,' ... It seems clear to me that Mr. Dennis [the claimant] has neither consented, tacitly or otherwise, nor acquiesced in the nuisance. He has complained strongly, even to the point of involving his Member of Parliament. ... In all, I find that the continued flying was not 'as of right.' It was contentious and imposed on Mr. Dennis who could do no more." After conclusively demonstrating the absurdity of the whole concept of a "prescriptive right" to commit a nuisance, Buckley J. found in favor of the claimants and awarded damages of £950,000.

Coventry: Roundup

Although *Dennis v. MOD* was only a first-instance decision, it took place a decade prior to the UKSC decision in *Coventry*. Why, then, did the UKSC in *Coventry* fail to take on board the powerful arguments advanced by Buckley J. in *Dennis* against the whole concept of a "prescriptive right" to commit a nuisance? In fact, these compelling arguments were not even referred to in *Coventry*.

Instead, the UKSC went on a wild goose chase following Thesiger L.J.'s muddled and illogical opinion in *Sturges*. Although Thesiger's decision affirmed the first-instance decision of Jessel M.R. in favor of the physician, in fact his reasoning was not the same. Jessel treated the matter as a completely open-and-shut case, remarking that "the evidence is all one way," and concluding that the fact that a noise which has not previously "injured me or interfered with my comfort or enjoyment in any way, cannot deprive me of my right. ... to come to the Court when it does seriously interfere with my comfortable enjoyment." Jessel therefore simply waved aside the whole question of "coming to" the nuisance, but did not replace it with any notion of "prescriptive right." He granted the physician an injunction, but there was no suggestion that the confectioner's business had to be closed down or relocated. The injunction was stayed over the busy London "season" and Mr. Bridgman was given time "to make the necessary alterations to his premises; and no doubt he would find some skilful mechanic in London who would tell him how to work these machines without making any noise at all."

In the whole 600-year "era of principle" of English law, as I have labeled it, from about 1300 until 1932, the "year of the snail," it is decidedly unusual to come across blatant judge-made law. Why, then, do we find here in the 19th century not only the rejection of the traditional "coming to the nuisance" defense but also the supposed principle of a "prescriptive right" of nuisance? The first of these is particularly puzzling, because, as explained by Blackstone (cited above) the defense of "coming to the nuisance" makes eminently good sense. The same cannot be said about the "prescriptive rights" idea as applied to nuisance. The connection of prescriptive rights for easements and also for adverse possession, or "squatter's rights," was far from new in 1879, but Thesiger just misapplied it to nuisance, where its completely undeserved iconic status has led to the UKSC decision in *Coventry,* leaving the law of nuisance in a state of limbo.

American Private Nuisance Law

By contrast with English law, in America the "coming to the nuisance" defense is still available, though it is not an absolute bar to a successful nuisance claim. The Restatement (Second) of Torts § 840D (1979) says that, where the plaintiff has "come to the nuisance", this is "not in itself sufficient to bar his action, but it is a factor to be considered in determining whether the nuisance is actionable." See for example the important Arizona case of *Spur Industries, Inc. v. Del E. Webb Development Co.,* 494 P.2d 700 (Ariz. 1972), in which a developer was granted injunctive relief against a long established cattle-feeding operation (or "feedlot"), but, to balance this relief, was required to indemnify the feedlot for the cost of moving or shutting down. [See Reynolds, Osborne M., Jr. (1992).] Some states, such as Iowa and Nebraska, have enacted statutes to deal with specific types of nuisance, such as odors emanating from feedlots.

However, the law of nuisance in the U.S. has not been free of problems of its own. It has been variously described as a "wilderness of law," an impenetrable jungle," a "mongrel" doctrine, a "mystery smothered in verbiage," and "a sort of legal garbage can". [See texasbusinesslaw.org Vol. 47, No. 2, 2018.] In *Crosstex North Texas Pipeline v. Gardiner* 505 S.W. 3d 580 (2016), Justice Boyd, writing for the Court, remarked that in a previous case the court had observed "that nuisance law was such a morass that although half of the precedents had to be wrongly decided, we could not say which half that was."

Crosstex has clarified the law of nuisance in Texas in a 54-page unanimous opinion of the Texas Supreme Court. While not binding in other jurisdictions, it may well serve as guidance, especially in other oil and gas producing states. In *Crosstex* itself the plaintiff Gardiner couple brought a nuisance claim involving noise from a gas pipeline compressor station located across the road from their ranch. The Court defined nuisance as "a condition that substantially interferes with the use and enjoyment of land by causing unreasonable discomfort or annoyance to persons of ordinary sensibilities attempting to use and enjoy it." Determining what is "substantial," "unreasonable," and "ordinary," is to be left to the jury to decide. The Court made it clear that the interference to justify a nuisance claim had to be "substantial"—excluding "petty annoyances and disturbances of everyday life"—and that the standard of "substantial" is to be an objective one based on a person of ordinary sensibilities.

Crosstex is a bold attempt to lay down guidelines in the field of Texas private nuisance law, which will blaze a trail for other states, but it is not judge-made law. It is firmly based on the Restatement (Second) of Torts (1979) § 822ff., which has been adopted by Texas and a number of other states, including Pennsylvania, Colorado, West Virginia, North Dakota, Ohio and New York.

Legislating from the Bench in U.S. State Courts?

Have there been no activist American judges? There is certainly no shortage of U.S. Supreme Court justices who have been accused of being activists. But what about state court judges? The liberal majority on the California Supreme Court in the 1960s, for example, notably including Justice Roger J. Traynor (1900–1983), who served on the Court from 1940 to 1970, the last five of those years as Chief Justice, and Justice Mathew Tobriner (1904–1982), who was a member of the court from 1962 to 1982, earned both praise and blame for their sometimes daring opinions. Nevertheless, on examination, they turn out to have far more respect for principle, statute and pseudo-black letter law than their English counterparts in the post-snail era.

Escola v. Coca-Cola Bottling Co.

One of the best known examples of supposed judicial activism was Justice Roger Traynor's concurring opinion in *Escola v. Coca-Cola Bottling Co.*, 24 Cal. 2d 453, 150 P.2d 436 (1944). Gladys Escola, a waitress, was placing a bottle of Coca-Cola in a refrigerator when it exploded, inflicting a deep cut in her hand and severing blood vessels, nerves and muscles. She filed suit against Coca-Cola in negligence and relied on the old English doctrine of *res ipsa loquitur* (literally, "the thing speaks for itself"), discussed above, which applies when an accident occurs that calls for an explanation at a time when the defendant is in exclusive control of the instrumentality causing the injury. The burden of proof then shifts to the defendant to show how the accident could have occurred without negligence on their part. Coca-Cola claimed that *res ipsa loquitur* did not apply because they were not in control of the bottle when it exploded and because they took precautions and kept a regular check on the pressure in their bottles. However, one of Coca-Cola's own drivers, called as a witness by the plaintiff, testified "that he had seen other bottles of Coca-Cola in the past explode and had found broken bottles in the warehouse when he took the cases out." The jury returned a verdict for the plaintiff.

On appeal, the Supreme Court of California sitting *en banc* (or "in bank," as they prefer to say in California, meaning before all the judges of the court) unanimously affirmed the judgment of the court below in favor of the plaintiff. In the words of Chief Justice Gibson:

> "Although it is not clear in this case whether the explosion was caused by an excessive charge or a defect in the glass, there is a sufficient showing that neither cause would ordinarily have been present if due care had been used. Further, defendant had exclusive control over both the charging and inspection of the bottles. Accordingly, all the requirements necessary to entitle plaintiff to rely on the doctrine of res ipsa loquitur to supply an inference of negligence are present." Then, after briefly summarizing the defendant's rebuttal evidence: "It is well settled, however, that when a defendant produces evidence to rebut the inference of negligence that arises upon application of the doctrine of res ipsa loquitur, it is ordinarily a question of fact for the jury to determine whether the inference has been dispelled."

Four justices concurred, and Justice Roger Traynor, wrote a separate concurring opinion, which became famous: "I concur in the judgment, but I believe the manufacturer's negligence should no longer be singled out as the plaintiff's right to recover in cases like the present one. In my opinion it should now be recognized that a manufacturer incurs an absolute liability when an article that he has placed on the market, knowing that it is to be used without inspection, proves to have a defect that causes injury to human beings."

So far, Traynor's opinion is simply off the wall. But then comes his justification for adopting this stance: First, a criminal statute: section 26510 of the Health and Safety Code, which prohibited the sale of "any adulterated food." Traynor continued:

> "The statute imposes criminal liability not only if the food is adulterated, but if its container, which may be a bottle, has any deleterious substance, or renders the product injurious to health. The criminal liability under the statute attached without proof of fault, so that the manufacturer is under the duty of ascertaining whether an article manufactured by him is safe. Statutes of this kind result in a strict liability of the manufacturer in tort to the member of the public injured. The statute may well be applicable to a bottle whose defects cause it to explode. ... The liability of the manufacturer to an immediate buyer injured by a defective product follows without proof of negligence from the implied warranty of safety attending the sale. Ordinarily, however, the immediate buyer is a dealer who does not intend to use the product himself, and if the warranty of safety is to serve the purpose of protecting health and safety it must give rights to others than the dealer. In the words of Judge Cardozo in the MacPherson case: 'The dealer was indeed the one person of whom it might be said with some approach to certainty that by him the car would not be used. Yet, the defendant would have us say that he was the one person whom it was under a legal duty to protect. The law does not lead us to so inconsequent a solution.' ... Judge Cardozo's reasoning ... paves the way for a standard of liability that would make the manufacturer guarantee the safety of his product even when there is no negligence. ... Warranties are not necessarily rights arising under a contract. An action on a warranty 'was in its origin, a pure action of tort,' and only late in the historical development of warranties was an action in assumpsit allowed. (Ames, "The History of Assumpsit," 2 *Harv L. Rev.* 1, 8; 4 Williston on Contracts (1936) 970.) ... Certainly there is

greater reason to impose liability on the manufacturer than on the retailer, who is but a conduit of a product that he is not himself able to test."

Traynor's reasoning is essentially a pincer movement, reaching his desired conclusion of strict liability by four different routes:

- Section 26510 of the Health and Safety Code, which, though a criminal statute, gives Traynor's conclusion respectable legislative underpinning, coupled with the fact that the section itself arguably covers similar ground to the *Escola* case itself.

- The argument that a manufacturer's warranty is not necessarily purely contractual and was originally tortious. This gives the argument historical underpinning.

- Cardozo's slightly humorous pooh-poohing of the conventional view that an implied warranty protects only the immediate buyer, who, as is generally the case, is a dealer.

- As an extra bonus, Traynor argued that *res ipsa loquitur*, on which the decision was ostensibly based, was itself really a form of strict liability. So why not throw off the pretense?

"A booby-trap for the unwary"

Nearly 20 years later, in *Greenman v. Yuba Power Products Inc.* (1963) 59 C2d 57, Justice Roger Traynor finally managed to persuade all six of his fellow judges, again sitting "in bank," as a full bench of the California Supreme Court, to concur that it was time to introduce strict products liability in that state. The facts of the case were fairly straightforward. William Greenman's wife bought him a multi-purpose power tool called the Shopsmith and he subsequently bought some additional attachments for it, including one to turn it into a lathe. But, after using it on several occasions for that purpose without incident, he was struck on the forehead by a piece of wood and was seriously injured and sued both the retailer and the manufacturer for breach of warranty and negligence. He introduced substantial evidence to show that his injuries were caused by defective design and construction of the Shopsmith. The trial jury returned a verdict for the retailer against Mr. Greenman, but awarded him damages of $65,000 against the manufacturer. The manufacturer appealed on the basis of the plaintiff's failure to comply with § 1769 of the California Civil Code, which required notice of breach of warranty to be given "within a reasonable time after the buyer knows, or ought to know, of such a breach." Judge Traynor held that the notice requirement of § 1769 "is not an appropriate one for the courts to adopt in actions by injured consumers against manufacturers with whom they have not dealt. "As between the immediate parties to the sale [the notice requirement] is a sound commercial rule, designed to protect the seller against unduly delayed claims for damages. As applied to personal injuries, and notice to a remote seller, it becomes a booby-trap for the unwary." He summed up his conclusion in these words: "To establish the manufacturer's liability it was sufficient that plaintiff proved that he was injured while using the Shopsmith in a way it was intended to be used as a result of a defect in design and manufacture of which plaintiff was not aware that made the Shopsmith unsafe for its intended use." The first instance judgment for the plaintiff was accordingly affirmed.

Was Justice Traynor not skating on thin ice by simply waving aside as "a booby-trap for the unwary" the notice requirement in § 1769 of the California Civil Code? No, because he was able to trump this statutory provision with another. He started out from where he had left off in *Escola,* with the *MacPherson* concept of implied warranties protecting consumers whether they had a contract with the manufacturer or not.

Greenman was therefore protected by just such an implied warranty. On this basis, Traynor pointed out that § 1769 was actually a provision of the Uniform Sales Act (modeled on the British Sale of Goods Act 1893, one of the few U.K. consolidation acts), which, like other provisions of that instrument, did not require notice to be given of a breach of warranty arising independently of a contract of sale between the parties. "Such warranties are not imposed by the sales act, but are the product of common-law decisions that have recognized them in a variety of situations." [Note: The *Greenman* case was decided at the time when California was replacing the Uniform Sales Act with a Commercial Code, which is a slightly varied version of the Uniform Commercial Code, (UCC) which has since been adopted, with variations, by all 50 states. The UCC similarly does not require any notice to be given of a breach of an extra-contractual implied warranty.]

Greenman, coupled with Justice Traynor's dissent in *Escola*, has established strict products liability in California, which has been followed by some other states. Under strict liability, the focus is on the product itself, rather than (as in negligence) on the behavior of the manufacturer. But strict liability is not the same as absolute liability, especially when a product is used in conjunction with the product(s) of another manufacturer. This is made clear in the Judicial Council of California Civil Jury Instructions (CACI) (2017) Series 1200. See for example the California Appellate Court decision in *Sanchez v. Hitachi Koki Co.* (2013) 217 Cal App 4th, 956, 158 Cal. Rptr. 3d. 907: "Strict liability has never been, and is not now, absolute liability. ... [U]nder strict liability the manufacturer does not thereby become the insurer of the product's user."]

The Hazardous Marshmallow

Another state that has adopted a strict liability regime for products liability is Montana. This was introduced by the

Montana Supreme Court in *Brandenburger v. Toyota Motor Sales* 513 P.2d 268 (1973*)*, in which the court applied the Restatement (Second) of Torts § 402A. [See Daniel Jones, "An Economic Analysis of Montana Products Liability," 71 *Montana Law Review* 157 (2010).] A good example of a case decided under these rules is the sad tale of the Montana toddler who was seriously brain-damaged after choking on marshmallows that he had gulped down rather too quickly: *Chad Emery v. Federated Foods* 863 P2d 426 (1993). A Montana District Court granted summary judgment to the defendant manufacturer of the offending marshmallows. The court based its decision on Restatement (Second) of Torts § 402 (1965), which provides: "(1) One who sells any product in a defective condition unreasonably dangerous to the user or consumer or to his property is subject to liability for physical harm thereby caused to the ultimate user or consumer, or to his property. ... (2) The rule stated in Subsection (1) applies although (a) the seller has exercised all possible care in the preparation and sale of his product, and (b) the user or consumer has not bought the product from or entered into any contractual relation with the seller." "Relying on comment (j) of § 402A, the court concluded that a seller is not required to warn with respect to products which are only dangerous when consumed in excessive quantities if that danger is generally known and recognized." The holding of the District Court was as follows: "The evidence in the record clearly supports a finding that the manner in which Chad consumed the marshmallows caused his damage[s]. Under these circumstances, and for the reasons stated, the Court finds that the Defendants were not under any duty as a matter of law to warn the Plaintiffs that infants and toddlers can choke on large quantities of marshmallows eaten all at one time." The District Court concluded that "no genuine issues of material fact existed."

This decision was reversed on appeal by a 5–2 majority in the Supreme Court of Montana:

"After careful review of the record in this case, we conclude that the District Court erroneously resolved disputed issues of material fact and, therefore, exceeded the scope of its role at the summary judgment stage of this case." The court held that there had been a failure to warn of "an injury-causing risk," rendering even "a technically pure and fit product. ... unreasonably dangerous"—which made the product "automatically defective." There was medical evidence showing that "A marshmallow is a particularly hazardous confection as a risk of aspiration under the age of three." And: "An aspirated piece of marshmallow can be very difficult to dislodge." In an affidavit the injured child's mother swore that, "if I had been warned of the risk of small children choking on marshmallows, I would not have purchased them at all." The Supreme Court concluded: "We hold that the District Court erred in granting summary judgment for Federated Foods on Emery's failure-to-warn claim."

Chief Justice Turnage and Justice Harrison voiced a strong dissent:

"In the real world of life as it is, the marshmallows in this case were not a product in a defective condition and thereby unreasonably dangerous to the user or consumer. If marshmallows are unreasonably dangerous to eat without a warning, then so would be nearly every conceivable food item that a two-and-one-half year-old child would try to eat; and I submit that children of that age will try to eat anything and everything. ... The net result of the majority opinion may well be that warnings must be placed on nearly every food item available to the public if the provider is to avoid litigation for a claim of products liability—an interesting challenge for the providers of edible items. ... In this case as a matter of law, however, the essential element of a products liability claim is missing—the marshmallow was not in a defective condition and unreasonably dangerous."

These cases show just how difficult it can be to apply principles and rules to the facts of a case. The first question is: What principle or rule is applicable to this case? In the "Marshmallow" case there was some doubt whether the rule requiring a warning was relevant. This legal question could only be resolved by answering the question: Were the marshmallows in question "in a defective condition unreasonably dangerous to the user or consumer"? Though this looks like a straightforward factual question, the majority on the Montana Supreme Court accepted expert opinion evidence on this point to the effect that the marshmallows were indeed defective and unreasonably dangerous, though this conclusion could only be reached by reinterpreting the meaning of the terms "defective" and "unreasonably dangerous." But even this was not enough to dispose of the case, because, however defective or dangerous the marshmallows may have been, the ultimate question was how the injured toddler's mother would have reacted to a warning. She claimed that she would not have bought the marshmallows at all, which clinched the case for the majority. The dissent by Chief Justice Turnage and Justice Harrison certainly makes a lot of sense, and avoids the strained interpretation of "defective" and "unreasonably dangerous" adopted by the majority. But the outcome of the case was crucial to the future of the injured toddler, who was left in a vegetative state.

Contributory Negligence

The British law of Contributory Negligence stands as a little oasis of (comparative) certitude amidst the shifting sands of judge-made law—an actual statute, no less, which means that in this area at least American law lagged behind English law. But, alas, this does not of course mean that this area of the law is free from any of the other multifarious problems besetting English law.

In 1945, just after the end of World War II, the British Parliament brought in as a separate stand-alone piece of legislation the Law Reform (Contributory Negligence) Act 1945, which, couched in the usual convoluted British statutory language, made a significant change to the law by introducing apportionment of liability in tort negligence cases, which is still in force. It is worth noting that this statutory rule does not apply to contract.

So unusual is it in Britain to have an actual statute laying down a principle of the common law, that the games played with judge-made law before 1945 have not been entirely eliminated. For example, courts still sometimes find it necessary to reiterate that it is for the defendant to prove the existence of contributory negligence; and that a finding of contributory negligence does not require the claimant (plaintiff) to owe any duty to the defendant. [See *Lewis v. Denye* [1939] 1 KB 540]. Here are a few examples of the way the 1945 Contributory Negligence statute works in practice. It is important to note that in English law the term "contributory negligence" always means "comparative negligence" in terms of the 1945 statute, whereas in America it refers to the old "all or nothing" rule, now abolished in most states, under which even the slightest degree of negligence on the part of a plaintiff loses them the case. [For more on that see below.]

In a recent case, *Rickson v. Bhakra* [2017] EWHC 264 (QB), a cyclist engaged in a time trial was severely injured and left paralysed when hit by a negligent van driver. The van driver was held to have been 80% liable, with the cyclist responsible for the remaining 20%. In the words of the judge:

> "The only reasonable inference to be drawn on the balance of probabilities from the failure to brake was that the claimant was not keeping a sufficient look-out at the road for one reason or another." He added: "In the absence of any evidence about how the claimant was riding at the time....it is not possible to reach any conclusion as to whether he let his head down or became too absorbed in reading his time computer or the position of fellow competitors. Despite his evidence of best practice, I conclude that none of these options can be discounted as possibilities."

One of the commonest reasons for a finding of contributory negligence is the failure of the plaintiff to wear a seatbelt. The leading English case on this is still *Froom v. Butcher* [1975] 3 All ER 520, which was decided at a time when it was obligatory in the U.K. for seatbelts to be fitted to the front seats of motor cars, though it was not obligatory to wear them until 1983 for front seats and 1991 for back seats. Lord Denning's judgment in the Court of Appeal, which is still cited as authoritative, was as follows: "Sometimes the evidence will show that the failure made no difference. The damage would have been the same, even if a seatbelt had been worn. In such cases, the damages should not be reduced at all. At other times the evidence will show that the failure made all the difference. The damage would have been prevented altogether if a seat belt had been worn. In such cases I would suggest that the damages should be reduced by 25%. But often enough the evidence will only show that the failure made a considerable difference." In which case, Lord Denning suggested, a reduction of 15% would be appropriate.

In *Smith v. Finch* [2009] EW Ch 53 (QB) a cyclist, Robert Smith, who was not wearing a helmet, was hit by a motorcyclist, Michael Finch, and suffered severe head injuries leading to post-traumatic epilepsy. The defendant, Finch, contended that Smith's injuries were wholly or partly the result of Smith's failure to wear a safety helmet as recommended by the Highway Code, though there is no legal obligation for a cyclist to do so. The judge held that "the burden is on the Defendant to prove (i) that the Claimant failed to take ordinary care of himself, or in other words, to take such care as a reasonable man would take for his own safety by not wearing as helmet and (ii) that his failure was a contributory cause of the damage." He concluded: "The Defendant has not discharged the burden of proving contributory negligence on the part of the Claimant" as he "has failed to persuade me that an approved helmet would have prevented or made less severe the head injuries sustained by the Claimant." No finding of contributory negligence was therefore made.

USA: Contributory or Comparative Negligence?

Now let me direct your gaze toward the American law of contributory negligence. As I said, in this area of the law, England stole a march on America. The pre-1945 English law of contributory negligence persisted quite a bit longer in America. The law was extremely simple but very unjust: if the plaintiff was responsible for his own injury, loss or damage to even the slightest degree, his suit was dismissed and he got nothing. So, yes, even if his share of responsibility for his own injury was just 1%, he lost his case.

Where did this crazy rule come from? It is usually traced back to an old English case called *Butterfield v. Forrester* ER 926 (King's Bench 1809). One evening while Butterfield was riding his horse at speed along the road where Forrester lived, he collided with a pole blocking part of the roadway which Forrester had placed there in the course of repairs. Butterfield failed to notice the pole, which he crashed into with his horse, and he was badly injured. According to the report, the judge, Sir John Bayley (1763–1841), ruled that: "The plaintiff was proved to be riding as fast as his horse could go, and this was through the streets of Derby. If he had used ordinary care he must have seen the obstruction; so that the accident appeared to happen entirely from his own fault."

Chief Justice Lord Ellenborough added: "Two things must concur to support this action: an obstruction in the road by the fault of the defendant; and no want of ordinary care to avoid it on the part of the plaintiff."

Was the court here really trying to lay down the ludicrous and totally unjust rule that the slightest degree of negligence on the part of the plaintiff deprives him of any recovery? The case was decided during the long period of about 600 years (c. 1300–1932) that I call "the era of principle," when the English common law was governed by maxims, or settled principles, of both law and equity—a period that was brought to an abrupt end by the snail in the bottle. The question of contributory negligence was apparently novel, which is why the court found itself making up a "rule" on the trot—something that was surprisingly rarely done throughout the era of principle. It is not even clear whether the court was actually trying to lay down a rule at all, and, if so, exactly what that rule was. In any event, it is a good example of the dangers of judge-made law.

Li v. Yellow Cab Co. of California

The pre-1945 English contributory negligence rule was exported to America as part of the "reception" of the common law, and became automatically embedded in codes of law, such as that of California. But, the incubus of the ludicrous rule was finally thrown off in the landmark case of *Li v. Yellow Cab Co. of California* 13 Cal. 3d 808 (1975) before the Supreme Court of California sitting in bank. Justice Sullivan, for the majority, opened his opinion in somber tones:

> "In this case we address the grave and recurrent question whether we should judicially declare no longer applicable in California courts the doctrine of contributory negligence, which bars all recovery when the plaintiff's negligent conduct has contributed as a legal cause in any degree to the harm suffered by him, and hold that it must give way to a system of comparative negligence, which assesses liability in direct proportion to fault."

This somber tone is all the more noteworthy in view of the fact that Justice Raymond Sullivan (1907–1999) belonged to the cohort of "liberal" justices appointed to the California Supreme Court in the 1960s. His characterization of the question of setting aside the contributory negligence rule as "grave" reflects the respect that even a liberal California judge had for a rule that, albeit ludicrous, was not only time-honored but also formed part of the California Civil Code as well as the Restatement (Second) of Torts, § 463ff., the relevant section of which reads as follows: "Except where the defendant has the last clear chance, the plaintiff's contributory negligence bars recovery against a defendant whose negligent conduct would otherwise make him liable to the plaintiff for the harm sustained by him." [Restatement (Second) of Torts, § 467.]

[Note: The "last clear chance" doctrine applies where a negligent plaintiff can show that the defendant had the last opportunity to avoid the accident.]

Sullivan made a point of stressing that 25 states had already abrogated the "all-or-nothing" rule and "enacted" in its place "general apportionment statutes"—both the word "enact" and the word "statute" of course denote *legislation*. This brought him face to face with the main arguments against setting the all-or-nothing rule aside. (a) "It is urged that any change in the law of contributory negligence must be made by the Legislature, not by this court." (b) The all-or-nothing rule had been enacted as § 1714 of the California Civil Code since its promulgation in 1872. (c) Its incorporation into the Civil Code "rendered it invulnerable to attack in the courts except on constitutional grounds." (d) "Subsequent cases of this court, it is pointed out, have unanimously affirmed that—barring the appearance of some constitutional infirmity—the 'all-or-nothing' rule is the law of this state and shall remain so until the Legislature directs otherwise." (e) "The fundamental constitutional doctrine of separation of powers ... requires judicial abstention."

While admitting that the foregoing arguments have a "superficial appeal," Justice Sullivan dismisses them as "fundamentally misguided," chiefly for the following reasons. (*My comments are in italics.*):

- The Legislature never intended to "insulate" § 1714 "from further judicial development; rather it was the intention of the Legislature to announce and formulate existing common law principles and definitions ... with

a distinct view toward continuing judicial evolution."
M.A. *There is, however, no evidence of this.*

- The 1872 Civil Code itself declared that its provisions
  were "to be liberally construed with a view to effect its
  objects and to promote justice." [Civ. Code (1872) § 4.]
  M.A. *This is plainly irrelevant as far as contributory
  negligence is concerned, because, as was said In re Jessup
  (1889) 81 Cal. 408, 419 (which is quoted by Sullivan with
  approval): "If a provision of the Code is plain and
  unambiguous, it is the duty of the court to enforce it as it is
  written." Regardless of its unfairness, the contributory
  negligence rule is undeniably "plain and unambiguous."*
- Sullivan concludes that "the intention of the Legislature
  in enacting § 1714 of the Civil Code was to state the
  basic rule of negligence together with the defense of
  contributory negligence modified by the emerging
  doctrine of last clear chance." *M.A. There is no mention of
  "last clear chance in § 1714.*

The fact that Justice Sullivan went to such great lengths to
justify setting aside the "all-or-nothing" rule is evidence in itself
that he really believed that judicial tampering with the Civil
Code could not be embarked upon lightly. He expressed the view
that in enacting the Civil Code in 1872 the state Legislature
envisioned the "continuing judicial evolution of existing
common law principles," but, even if this was true, it is still a far
cry from simply legislating from the bench.

- And Justice Clark's powerful dissenting opinion, with
  which Justice McComb concurred, made some
  trenchant points:
- The majority's decision refuses to honor the intention of
  the Legislature, "violating established principle."
- The majority encroached on the powers constitutionally
  entrusted to the Legislature. "The majority's altering the
  meaning of § 1714, notwithstanding the original intent
  of the framers and the century-old judicial

interpretation of the statute, represents no less than amendment by judicial fiat." "This court may not usurp the legislative function to change the statutory law which has been uniformly construed by a long line of judicial decisions." [Estate of Calhoun (1955) 44 Cal. 2d 378, 387.]

- "I dispute the need for judicial—instead of legislative—action in this area." "[O]ur society has changed significantly" since 1872,. "But this social change has been neither recent nor traumatic. ... I cannot conclude our society's evolution has now rendered the normal legislative process inadequate."
- "[T]he Legislature is the branch best able to effect transition from contributory to comparative or some other doctrine of negligence."
- "The courts of other states—with near unanimity—have conceded their inability to determine the best system for replacing contributory negligence, concluding instead that the legislative branch is best able to resolve the issue." The "all-or-nothing" rule has now been abolished in 45 states.
- "By abolishing this century old doctrine today, the majority seriously erodes our constitutional function. We are again guilty of judicial chauvinism."

Despite the unfairness of the "all-or-nothing" rule, the powerful arguments advanced by the two dissenting Justices Clark and McComb reflect a commonly held view that it is simply wrong for judges to make law. Perhaps it is no accident that these two judges were conservatives. Yet, as we have seen, even the liberal majority clearly had qualms about setting aside a long established rule of law which was incorporated into the Civil Code. It is worth comparing this attitude with that of British judges, who since 1932 have been less inhibited about "legislating from the bench."

8

UNITED KINGDOM
"THE CONSTITUTIONAL IMPERATIVE
OF JUDICIAL SELF-RESTRAINT"

"The Constitutional imperative of judicial self-restraint."
Lord Irvine of Lairg (1996)

Judicial review is an important branch of law in both England and America, and judge-made law is prominent in both. But the differences outweigh the similarities. Its earliest manifestation in England was in 1233, but it has changed out of all recognition since then, particularly in the past half century. It would be no exaggeration to say that of all the areas of English law none has expanded more rapidly or more extensively than judicial review—and none owes more to judge-made law. In a speech delivered in 2017, Lord Neuberger, then president of the UK Supreme Court, made no secret of his pride in this development:

> "[P]erhaps the most marked development in the common law in the past fifty years has been the very substantial growth in domestic judicial review: nobody can deny that it is a development for which the judges are responsible, or that it is a development with substantial macro-social and economic implications." [Neuberger, David (2017).]

This is refreshingly frank, but it lacks the names of any decided cases or the benefits that have supposedly flowed from them. There is also no hint of any qualms about whether this kind of judicial activism is in keeping with Parliamentary sovereignty, which Lord Neuberger himself has emphasized, "is a fundamental principle of the UK constitution." [See for example: *R. (Miller) v. Secretary of State for Exiting the European Union* [2017] UKSC 5.]

UK: "The Constitutional imperative of judicial self restraint."

In keeping with the fundamental principle, of the sovereignty of Parliament, Lord Irvine of Lairg (Lord Chancellor 1997–2003) has emphasized that "judicial review should never be an appellate process, that the court should adjudicate only upon the legality of a decision and not upon its merits." Lord Irvine then identifies the "substantive principles of judicial review. ... These principles rest upon the constitutional imperative of judicial self-restraint. There are at least three bases for this imperative:"

- "First, *a constitutional imperative*: public authorities receive their powers from Parliament, which intends, for good reason, that a power be exercised by the authority to which it is entrusted."
- "Secondly, *lack of judicial expertise*: it follows that the courts are, in relative terms, ill-equipped to take decisions in place of the designated authority."
- "Thirdly, *the democratic imperative*: it has long been recognized that elected pubic authorities, and particularly local authorities, derive their authority in part from their electoral mandate." [Irvine, Derry (2003), p.137.]

These principles are in keeping with the time-honored principles expounded by Lorde Greene in the *Wednesbury* case in 1947, and a warning against the judicial activism that has become so prevalent in this area of the law in recent years. Legislating from the bench not only flies in the face of parliamentary sovereignty, but is also undemocratic, or even anti-democratic. It encroaches on the preserve of the executive as well, which again is undemocratic, because in the UK the executive government emerges out of the elected House of Commons. And when judges announce new "rules" or "tests" for any legal issue, the wording tends to be woolly and imprecise. As an example I examine the use of the term "irrationality" in the next section. The law in this area (among others) tends to be unclear, uncertain and unpredictable—with frequent "yo-yo" cases, where the first instance result is reversed on appeal and then reversed back again. This is a serious problem in regard to the rule of law as well. [See the section in Chapter 17 on The Rule of Law: or of Lawyers?]

How does this differ from judicial review as dispensed by the US Supreme Court? Here too, as mentioned above, there is a good deal of judge-made law. But there the similarity ends. Judicial self-restraint, though not touted as much as it once was, is still alive and well, coupled with a healthy respect for precedent. The fact that the US has a written constitution while the UK does not is actually a less important distinguishing feature than might have been expected. For the past 20 years the UK has had a Human Rights Act incorporating most of the European Convention of Human Rights (ECHR), the interpretation and application of which is not a totally dissimilar task to the constitutional interpretation that engages so much of the time of the US Supreme Court. In its current incarnation, the Supreme Court is essentially divided into two ideological camps, usually labeled "conservative" and "liberal," which actually makes it easier, not harder, to predict the outcome of a particular case. Each school of constitutional thought has a fairly consistent set of interpretative principles, while English judges are rudderless except when following the "politically correct" drift of the European Court of Human Rights.

In this Part I compare English and American law in regard to judicial review and human or civil rights law more generally.

The Four Corners in English Law

There is an apocryphal old anecdote about two nineteenth century English High Court judges being entertained at a formal banquet while on circuit. When the loyal toast is proposed, the one judge jumps to his feet. "Sit down, you fool," chides his colleague: "We <u>are</u> the Queen." This brings out the traditional close tie between the judiciary and the government.

Certiorari, Mandamus and Prohibition

The possibility of a court finding fault with the government was almost as unthinkable back then as a judicial challenge to Parliament. Judicial review arose out of three ancient English prerogative writs: *certiorari, mandamus* and prohibition.

- *Certiorari,* so called from the opening words of the writ, *"certiorari volumus,"* meaning "we (viz, the king) wish to be informed," was an order to a lower court to deliver up the record of a particular decision to be scrutinized by the high court. The order was nominally made by the monarch at the instance of some third party, who was the real plaintiff. If the decision of the lower court did not pass muster, it would be set aside, or quashed, which is why this order was renamed in 2004 as a *quashing order.* But the character of the order has undergone drastic change over the years. Now the main butt of attack is the government, central as well as local, though the quaint anomaly of the Crown as the nominal plaintiff has survived.

- *Mandamus,* literally, "we order," was a command, again in the name of the monarch, addressed by the high court

to a lower court or local authority to do something that
it was obliged by law to do. Though less common than
certiorari, a *mandatory order*, as it is now called, can also
be used against government at any level.

- Prohibition, now called a prohibiting order, commands
a lower court or authority not to act on a decision to do
something which has not yet been implemented.

Although the three prerogative writs go back hundreds of
years, modern judicial review in English law is commonly
thought to originate with the famous *Wednesbury* case of 1947,
in which Lord Greene set out the narrow parameters within
which judicial review had traditionally operated. But the courts'
appetite for judicial review grew apace, vastly expanding those
traditional parameters and leading to the establishment of a
separate Administrative Court as part of the Queen's Bench
Division in 1977, a new set of procedural rules, Order 53 in the
Rules of the Supreme Court (the "White Book") and the
exponential growth of judicial review especially after the passing
of the Human Rights Act 1998. If there is any area of English law
that is almost completely judge-made, this is it. So, besides being
an important area of law in terms of its subject-matter, it is a
useful testing-ground for the advantages and disadvantages of
judge-made law.

Wednesbury unreasonableness

Every British law student has heard of "Wednesbury
unreasonableness," and far too many trial lawyers invoke it as
one of the (usually far too numerous) strands in their judicial
review applications. That is because the whole concept tends to
be so badly misunderstood. Unfortunately, the courts are not
immune from this problem either.

The *Wednesbury* case, *Associated Provincial Picture Houses v.
Wednesbury Corporation* [1948] 1 KB 223, is generally considered

to be the archetype of judicial review cases. In fact, it was not really a judicial review case at all. The plaintiff proprietors of a movie theater had been granted a license by the defendant local authority for Sunday performances, but the license was subject to a condition that "no children under the age of fifteen years shall be admitted to any entertainment, whether accompanied by an adult or not." The plaintiffs filed suit for a declaration that the condition was *ultra vires* ("beyond the powers" of the local authority) and unreasonable. At first instance the application was dismissed, and this decision was affirmed by a unanimous Court of Appeal.

Lord Greene, Master of the Rolls, delivered the judgment of the court. In a classic opinion, he summarized the principle applicable in cases of this kind, including judicial review claims properly so called:

> "The court is entitled to investigate the action of the local authority with a view to seeing whether they have taken into account matters which they ought not to take into account, or, conversely, have refused to take into account or neglected to take into account matters which they ought to take into account. Once that question is answered in favour of the local authority, it may still be possible to say that, although the local authority have kept within the four corners of the matters which they ought to consider, they have nevertheless come to a conclusion so unreasonable that no reasonable authority could ever have come to it. In such a case, again, I think the court can interfere. The power of the court to interfere in each case is not as an appellate authority to override the decision of the local authority, but as a judicial authority which is concerned, and concerned only, so see whether the local authority have contravened the law by acting in excess of the powers which Parliament has confided in them."

It is worth noting that Lord Greene refers to the contents of this whole passage as a "principle," in the singular, though it may look as though what he has set out is actually made up of several principles. The time-honored principle in question views the scope of authority of a decision-maker that is under scrutiny as a square. The question then is whether the decision-maker has kept within the four corners of that square. If he has not done so, then he has exceeded the jurisdiction granted to him and has acted *ultra vires*, or "beyond his powers," and his decision can be quashed by the court.

Who decided the size and shape of this square? It was, in the words of Lord Greene, an "executive discretion," entrusted to the local authority by Parliament under the Sunday Entertainments Act 1932, which gave any local authority the power to grant licenses for Sunday movie performances "subject to such conditions as the authority think fit to impose." The question in this case was whether the local authority was acting within the four corners of its jurisdiction in imposing a ban on children under 15. As the wording of the executive discretion granted to local authorities under the Act was extremely wide, it is not surprising that the local authority was found not to have exceeded its powers. Lord Greene: "[O]nce it is conceded, as it must be conceded in this case, that the particular subject-matter dealt with by this condition was one which it was competent for the authority to consider, there, in my opinion, is an end of the case."

In other words, the *ultra vires* question is conclusive. Nevertheless, Lord Greene went on to consider something else, namely "unreasonableness"—but only because plaintiff's counsel had couched his claim in terms both of *ultra vires* and "unreasonableness." Lord Greene would not have considered it otherwise. But he made it clear that "unreasonableness" was highly exceptional:

"It is true to say that, if a decision on a competent matter is so unreasonable that no reasonable authority could ever have come to it, then the courts can interfere. That, I think, is quite right; but to prove a case of that kind would require something overwhelming, and, in this case, the facts do not come anywhere near anything of that kind." He stressed: "It is not what the court considers unreasonable, a different thing altogether. If it is what the court considers unreasonable, the court may very well have different views to that of a local authority on matters of high policy of this kind. Some courts might think that no children ought to be admitted on Sundays at all, some courts might think the reverse, and all over the country I have no doubt on a thing of that sort honest and sincere people hold different views. The effect of the legislation is not to set up the court as an arbiter of the correctness of one view over another. It is the local authority that are set in that position and, provided they act, as they have acted, within the four corners of their jurisdiction, this court, in my opinion, cannot interfere."

Lord Greene gave the example of a "red-haired teacher, dismissed because she had red hair. That is unreasonable in one sense. In another sense it is taking into consideration extraneous matters. It is so unreasonable that it might almost be described as being done in bad faith; and, in fact, all these things run into one another." So, explains Lord Greene, though firing the teacher because of the color of her hair is unreasonable, there is no need for the court to resort to that exceptional category, because the same decision is also plainly *ultra vires*.

The plaintiff lost the case, because the restriction on children under 15 was not *ultra vires* and also not unreasonable. <u>So, it is important to note, there was no *Wednesbury* unreasonableness in *Wednesbury*.</u> The trouble is that, once Lord Greene had, against his better judgment, let the "unreasonableness" cat out of the bag, generations of law students and practitioners started imagining seeing it lurking around every corner.

"Irrationality" and "unreasonableness": the same or different?

In 1984 the courts arrogated to themselves for the first time the right to set aside government decisions made under the royal prerogative—one of the few legislative powers left to the Crown after the "Glorious Revolution" of 1689 but in practice exercised not by the monarch but by the Prime Minister and Government. The relevant case, commonly known as the "GCHQ case", arose out of Prime Minister Margaret Thatcher's ban on trade union membership for employees at GCHQ (Government Communications Headquarters), a government agency concerned with high-level intelligence gathering. Thatcher's order, made in her capacity as Minister for the Civil Service, was made in the wake of the threat of strikes. In the interests of national security, she wanted to be able to prevent strikes at this sensitive agency. [*Council of Civil Service Unions v. Minister for the Civil Service* [1984] UKHL 9.]

The House of Lords, affirming the decision of the Court of Appeal, which had reversed the first instance decision, found, in favor of the government, that issues of national security were a no-go area for the courts. In the words of Lord Diplock: "The reason why the Minister for the Civil Service decided on 22 December 1983 to withdraw this benefit was in the interests of national security. National security is the responsibility of the executive government; what action is needed to protect its interests is ... as common sense itself dictates, a matter upon which those upon whom the responsibility rests, and not the courts of justice, must have the last word. It is par excellence a non-justiciable question. The judicial process is totally inept to deal with the sort of problems which it involves."

Lord Diplock took it upon himself to rename and redefine the grounds for judicial review as "illegality," "irrationality," and "procedural impropriety." Adding: "That is not to say that further development on a case by case basis may not in course of time add further grounds … particularly, the possible adoption in the future of the principle of 'proportionality,' … but to dispose of the instant case the three already well-established heads that I have mentioned will suffice."

Can judges simply add grounds for a lawsuit at will? Is that not just blatant legislation from the bench? It most certainly is, which is a usurpation of the sovereignty of Parliament. And it is perhaps worth noting that no other member of the five-judge panel in this case besides Lord Diplock even mentioned "proportionality," which, *did* subsequently join the three "well-established heads"—followed by an innumerable host of other "grounds."

And what was the effect, if any, of Lord Diplock's revamping of the three original grounds? His definition of "illegality" is less clear than Lord Greene's traditional explanation of *ultra vires* in the *Wednesbury* case, but essentially the same. As for "procedural impropriety," Diplock explains that this is wider than "failure to observe basic rules of natural justice." This ground was not mentioned by Lord Greene at all, though natural justice certainly is an important ancient basis for challenging decisions, especially judicial decisions. Its two chief components are the rule of fairness, *audi alteram partem* (literally, "hear the other side"), and the rule against bias, *nemo debet judex in causa sua* (literally, "nobody ought to be a judge in his own case").

Diplock's third category, "irrationality," is the tricky one. He explained it like this: "By 'irrationality' I mean what can by now be succinctly referred to as 'Wednesbury unreasonableness.' It applies to a decision which is so outrageous in its defiance of logic or of accepted moral standards that no sensible person who had applied his mind to the question to be decided could have arrived at it." This raises a number of issues:

- Diplock first identifies his "irrationality" with Wednesbury unreasonableness but then proceeds to define it less clearly, less succinctly and far less memorably than Lord Greene's formulation, "So unreasonable that no reasonable authority could ever have come to it"—an almost poetic formula that trips off the tongue.

- Etymologically speaking, "irrationality" and "unreasonableness" are closely related. Both are derived from the Latin word *ratio*, meaning "reason," though the word "reason" and of course "reasonable," "unreasonable," and "unreasonableness" have undergone some changes in form through coming to us, not directly from the Latin, but via French.

- Why did Lord Diplock omit the word "ever" from his formulation? This word is crucial to Lord Greene's original wording, emphasizing just how exceptional an "unreasonable" decision would be likely to be.

- Lord Greene, quite appropriately, views "unreasonableness" entirely from the vantage point of the decision-maker. The test is what a "reasonable authority" would consider unreasonable. It is a practical test, whereas Diplock's is arguably more esoteric.

- The use of two different terms for what Lord Diplock himself claimed to be synonyms has only caused confusion. As there *are* two different terms, there is pressure to find some distinguishing features between them. Here is Lord Sumption in a 2013 case: "Rationality is not the same as reasonableness. Reasonableness is an external, objective standard applied to the outcome of a person's thoughts or intentions. ... A test of rationality, by comparison, applies a minimum objective standard to the relevant person's mental processes. It imports a requirement of good faith, a requirement that there should be some logical connection between the evidence and the ostensible reasons for the decision, and (which will usually amount to the same thing) an absence of arbitrariness, of

capriciousness or of reasoning so outrageous in its
defiance of logic as to be perverse." [*Hayes v. Willoughby*
[2013] UKSC 17, para 14.]

- In a 2015 case Lady Hale commented that Lord
  Sumption's formulation was "not a precise rendition of
  the test of reasonableness" in *Wednesbury*. [*Braganza v.
  BP Shipping Ltd*, [2015] UKSC 17, para 23.] One could
  go further and wonder where the material for this
  lengthy disquisition had come from. But then Lady Hale
  herself drifts into error by claiming that Lord Greene's
  test of reasonableness had "two limbs"—the first being
  whether a decision-maker had "taken into account
  matters which they ought not to take into account," and
  the second being the famous "unreasonableness"
  formulation. Lady Hale is wrong in lumping these two
  tests together as part of "reasonableness." What she
  identifies as the "first limb" of Lord Greene's test of
  reasonableness is not that at all, but the test for *ultra
  vires*, which for Lord Greene was far more important.

- As I have already mentioned, Lord Greene did not really
  consider "unreasonableness" to be a regular ground for
  striking down an administrative decision. Once it was
  conceded that the decision in question was not *ultra
  vires*, because it was within the four corners of the
  decision-maker's jurisdiction, "there, in my opinion," as
  he put it, " is an end of the case."

- <u>Note</u>: *It is not at all clear why Lord Diplock took it upon
  himself to rename "unreasonableness" as "irrationality" and to
  define it differently while claiming it was the same. But it is a
  good example of the water-muddying effect that judge-made
  law tends to have.*

" ... **as well as others** ... "

Another Law Lord in the same case proceeded to offer an
even more blatant example of judge-made law. Prime Minister

Thatcher's order to GCHQ employees was issued not by statute but under the royal prerogative. The House of Lords ruled, for the first time in history, that such decisions were subject to judicial review. Lord Roskill took it upon himself to list the prerogative powers that were immune from judicial challenge. On what authority did he have the right to do so? None at all. He just arrogated it to himself of his own volition, and, as with Lord Diplock's revamped grounds for judicial review, he was the only Law Lord to compile this particular list, though Lord Diplock alluded to some of the same areas, notably the prerogative of mercy and the defense of the realm. Here is Lord Roskill's unabashed contribution to judge-made law:

> "I do not think that that right of challenge can be unqualified. It must, I think, depend upon the subject matter of the prerogative power which is exercised. Many examples were given during the argument of prerogative powers which as at present advised I do not think could properly be made the subject of judicial review. Prerogative powers such as those relating to the making of treaties, the defence of the realm, the prerogative of mercy, the grant of honours, the dissolution of Parliament and the appointment of ministers *as well as others* are not, I think, susceptible to judicial review because their nature and subject matter is such as not to be amenable to the judicial process. The courts are not the place wherein to determine whether a treaty should be concluded or the armed forces disposed in a particular manner or Parliament dissolved on one date rather than another." (Emphasis added)

What a wonderfully circular argument this is! The listed prerogative powers "are not, I think, *susceptible* to judicial review because their nature and subject matter is not such as not to be *amenable* to the judicial process" (emphasis added). In this context, the words "susceptible" and "amenable" are practically synonymous. So, what Roskill is really saying here is that the listed prerogative powers are not *suitable* for judicial review because they are not *suitable* for judicial review. The words in the extract that I have italicised provide yet further amusement. After reeling off a detailed list of prerogative powers that are not suitable for judicial review, Roskill then adds "as well as others". Who is to decide what these "others" are—and, for that matter, what right do the judges have to decide which rights are and are not "amenable" to judicial review in the first place? Until 1984 the judges had not dared to try to arrogate this power to themselves. What gave them the right to change the law in their own interests in this way? And that is an important point: subjecting prerogative decisions to judicial challenge increased the power of the judiciary. It was judges giving themselves more power. Any change in the law should have required *legislation*—which the principle of the sovereignty of Parliament—and the doctrine of the separation of powers—reserved to Parliament.

"Let him have it, Chris!"

Among the list of prerogative powers ring-fenced, according to Lord Roskill, against judicial challenge was the royal prerogative of mercy. This power, exercised by heads of state from time immemorial, can be used either to reduce a convicted person's sentence or to pardon them altogether. Though it does not actually overturn the conviction, it was in a sense a counterblast by the Crown against the judiciary. It was carried over to America, where it is still exercised with great regularity by the US President and also by state governors. In Britain, together with most other prerogative powers, it was delegated by the Crown to government ministers, in this case the Home Secretary. However, it is no longer entirely immune from judicial challenge, as was shown in the case about Derek Bentley, who had been hanged for murder in 1953. Bentley, aged 19, and a confederate called Christopher Craig, who was 16, were involved in a shootout with police. When Craig was asked by a police officer to hand over his gun, Bentley called out to him: "Let him have it, Craig"—an ambiguous instruction. Craig shot the police officer, injuring him in the shoulder, and then fatally wounded another who had come after him. At the time murder carried the death penalty under English law. Both Craig and Bentley were convicted of murder, with a plea by the jury for mercy for Bentley, who had not fired a shot and was known to be of low intelligence. As a minor, Craig could not be executed, and was only sentenced to be detained "during Her Majesty's pleasure." But Bentley was sentenced to death, and, after the Home Secretary declined an application for a reprieve, was duly executed by hanging. Bentley's sister then began a long campaign for a posthumous pardon for Bentley, which was declined by the Home Secretary in 1992. An application was then made to the Divisional Court of Queen's Bench for a declaration that the Home Secretary had erred in law in declining to recommend a posthumous free pardon for her brother. The Court decided that "some aspects" of the royal prerogative of mercy were reviewable by the court, including the Home Secretary's failure to consider the appropriate form of pardon in this case. The court stopped short of making a formal order, but invited the Home Secretary to reconsider his decision, and Bentley was then granted a posthumous pardon. [*R. (Bentley) v. Secretary of State for the Home Department*, July 7, 1993.]

Like so many others, this area of the law is currently in an uncertain state. But one area of the prerogative that we would expect to be absolutely immune from judicial review is national defense, one of the most important functions of the central government. It appears in Lord Roskill's list of no-go areas, and it was also mentioned by Lord Diplock together with what he refers to as "matters so vital to the survival and welfare of the nation as the conduct of relations with foreign states." That was in 1985, but the judicial juggernaut has moved on since then. Foreign relations and defense policy are no longer respected as out of bounds to judicial interference, as can be seen from a 2019 case involving the sale of arms to Saudi Arabia, which also fortuitously happens to tie in with our discussion of "irrationality."

Politics by other means?

In 2016 an organization calling itself Campaign Against Arms Trade (CAAT) took the UK Government to court for licensing the export of arms to Saudi Arabia for use in Yemen. [*R. (CAAT) v. Secretary of State for International Trade* [2017] EWHC 1726 (QB).] The claim challenged the lawfulness of the grant by the UK Government of export licenses for the sale of arms to Saudi Arabia for possible use in Yemen. The main issue was described by the Divisional Court as "whether the Secretary of State [for International Trade] was entitled to conclude on the evidence and advice available to him, both open and closed, that there was 'no clear risk that the [UK licensed] items might be used in the commission of a serious violation of international humanitarian law' in Yemen." A unanimous Divisional Court dismissed the claim on the ground that "the Secretary of State was rationally entitled to conclude, among other things, "that there was no 'clear risk' that there might be 'serious violations' of International Humanitarian Law (in its various manifestations) such that UK arms sales to Saudi Arabia should be suspended or cancelled." [para 210] The "International Humanitarian Law" referred to here was the "Consolidated EU and National Arms Export Licensing Criteria" announced to Parliament in October 2000, reflecting a *voluntary* EU Code of Conduct on Arms Exports agreed in 1998.

The Divisional Court's unanimous decision dismissing the claim was reversed in part on appeal by a unanimous Court of Appeal: "We emphasize that we have borne fully in mind the complex and difficult nature of the decisions in question, the fact that this is an area particularly far within the responsibility and expertise of the executive branch and that, as a consequence, rationality alone can properly found interference by way of judicial review. We agree with the Divisional Court (...) that in such a case as this, the courts must accord considerable respect to the decision-maker. It is in the application of that test that we have concluded it was irrational and therefore unlawful for the Secretary of State to proceed as he did. [*R. (CAAT) v. Secretary of State for International Affairs* [2019] EWCA Civ. 1020, para 145.]

This is a worrying decision. On what basis could the Government be said to have acted "irrationally"? The Court of Appeal, citing another decision by the Divisional Court, conceded that: "Judicial review is not an appeal against government decisions on their merits. The wisdom of governmental policy is not a matter for the courts and, in a democratic society, must be a matter for the elected government alone. ... Judicial review is not, and should not be regarded as, politics by another (sic) means." [para 54.]

On what basis could three unelected judges who are not answerable to anyone possibly decide that the Government had acted irrationally by allowing arms sales to a particular country? Especially when a panel of two judges in the Divisional Court had decided that the Government's decision was *not* irrational. The standard of rationality applied was "the duty which falls upon a decision-maker to 'take reasonable steps to acquaint himself with the relevant information,'" in this case concerned with the "assessment of risk" in regard to "International Humanitarian Law." [Quoting Lord Diplock in *Secretary of State for Education v. Tameside MBC* [1977] AC 1014 at 1065.]

CAAT is a political pressure group, which is described on its own website as "a UK-based organization working to end the international arms trade." The Court of Appeal decision is summarized on the CAAT website in these words: "The Court of Appeal concluded that it was 'irrational and therefore unlawful' for the Secretary of State for International Trade to have granted licences without making any assessment as to whether violations of international humanitarian law had taken place." "It should not take a group of campaigners taking the Govt to court to force it to apply its own rules." Referring to the civil war in Yemen, the CAAT website continues: "It shouldn't take four years of schools, hospitals, weddings, and funerals being bombed. It should not take tens of thousands of deaths and the worst humanitarian crisis in the world."

Was it "irrational," as the Court of Appeal held, for the British Government to allow arms to be sold to Saudi Arabia that would likely be used in Yemen—because the Government had not "made any assessments whether violations of International Humanitarian Law had taken place"? Even if this was true, which the Divisional Court had *not* found to be the case, it certainly did not mean that the Government had acted illegally—and the Court of Appeal was careful not to claim that the Government *had* acted illegally. Instead, the Court rested its conclusion on the vague concept of "irrationality." But, if it was not illegal for the Government to allow arms sales to Saudi Arabia, then why was it "irrational" to do so? So-called International Humanitarian Law is not really law at all but, as mentioned above, is based on a *voluntary* EU Code of Conduct on Arms Exports. CAAT's claim on their website that their court action force the Government " to apply its own rules" is mistaken. So-called International Humanitarian Law is *not* the Government's "own rules," and the Government is *not* bound by it. So, in what sense could it be regarded as "irrational" to ignore it? The recent carnage in Yemen has undoubtedly been catastrophic. But the idea that stopping British arms sales to one side or the other will end the bloodshed there is simply naïve— or even irrational. How can one court characterize the Government decision as "irrational" another finds that it was not? Which court was more rational? On June 26, 2019, British Prime Minister Theresa May explained in the House of Commons that the Government was working toward a negotiated settlement of the war in Yemen. She also pointed out that the side supported by Saudi Arabia is the legitimate government of Yemen recognized by the United Nations, and that the war there was the result of the overthrow of this legitimate government by "rebels." I would endorse Yossi Nehushtan's comment: "The decision to grant licenses could have been irrational only if the means (granting licenses) had no causal or logical connection to the Government's end (whatever that end might be). This question, however, was not discussed in *CAAT.*" [Nehushtan, Yossi (2019). "The Unreasonable Perception of Rationality and Reasonableness in UK Public Law," UK Const. Law Blog, https://ukconstitutionallaw.org/.] The Court of Appeal went out of its way to stress that they were not judging the Government's policy decision on its merits or trying to substitute their own decision on arms sales for that of the Government. But, if the Government's policy was "irrational," as the court decided, that effectively paralyzed the Government until it came up with a less "irrational" policy. For the courts to get involved in such issues is indeed "politics by other means" and a usurpation of the executive function.

Parliament's nuclear option

The Government's characteristically lame response to this worrying decision was that they would be seeking permission to appeal to the UK Supreme Court. This feeble response has only subordinated the Government even more to the judiciary. The correct response, for which judicial decisions like this are crying out, is to resort to the largely forgotten but extremely important nuclear option of *revocation*—the power of Parliament to reverse any court decision for any reason, or none. It is a natural concomitant of the fundamental constitutional principle of the sovereignty of Parliament. Of course, this crucial power belongs not to the Government but to Parliament. But in normal times the British Government will have a built-in majority in the House of Commons. [I discuss this in more detail in Chapter 1, "United Kingdom: The Sovereignty of Parliament."]

Human Rights Cases

Human rights cases chiefly account for the exponential growth of judicial review in the past twenty years. The Human Rights Act (HRA) 1998, which came into force in 2000, was passed to incorporate (most of) the European Convention on Human Rights (ECHR) into UK law. The UK ratified the Convention in 1951, but it could not be invoked in the UK courts until incorporation in the HRA. A few points need to be stressed:

- The ECHR and its supervising court, the European Court of Human Rights, which sits in Strasbourg, France, have nothing whatsoever to do with the European Union, but were set up under a completely separate organization known as the Council of Europe. So, "Brexit," the UK's departure from the EU, does not affect the HRA or the validity of the ECHR in the UK.

- Since the year 2000 all UK courts have had jurisdiction to hear cases brought under the HRA and the ECHR. It is only after exhausting all domestic remedies that a party can take their case to the European Court of Human Rights in Strasbourg.

- If a UK court "is satisfied" that any UK Act of Parliament is "incompatible" with a Convention right, the court "may make a declaration of that incompatibility." [HRA § 4(2).] *Note: This is **all** that a UK court can do in these circumstances. It has no right to declare any UK statute void or to set it aside for any reason.*

- In deciding human rights cases, according to HRA s 2(1), the UK courts "must take into account any judgment, decision, declaration or advisory opinion" of the European Court of Human Rights." *Note: "Take into account" is not the same as "follow."*

A surprisingly large number of human rights cases are brought under ECHR Article 3: "No one shall be subjected to torture or to inhuman or degrading treatment or punishment."

The commonest claims brought under this article are what are known as "Third party" cases, in which the courts have prevented the government from deporting convicted criminals or terror suspects to their home countries on the ground that they may be subjected to torture there.

"Third party" cases typically go through the following stages:

a) A convicted criminal or terror suspect is notified that the Home Secretary "deems his deportation to be conducive to the public good".

b) The person concerned is then detained pending his deportation.

c) The person concerned takes the matter to court claiming that if deported to his home country he will be likely to be tortured, in violation of his rights under ECHR Article 3.

d) The UK government obtains assurances from the person's home country that the person concerned will not be tortured if he is deported to that country.

e) Ignoring or rejecting such assurances, the court finds in favor of the applicant, preventing the UK government from deporting him.

f) In addition, as the person concerned cannot now be deported, he also cannot be detained as his detention was only meant to be "pending deportation".

g) So the person concerned wins and is allowed to remain in the UK.

h) The UK government loses and has egg all over its face.

i) But the real losers are justice and ordinary law-abiding UK citizens and other inhabitants, whose security is endangered by this decision and who as taxpayers will generally have to foot the bill for the legal to-ings and fro-ings and probably also for maintenance of the person concerned for an indefinite period.

Soering v. UK

This wrong approach to ECHR Article 3 started with the case of *Soering v. UK* [(1989) 11 EHRR 439]. Jens Soering, a German national living in the United States, brutally killed his girlfriend's parents, who had been opposed to his relationship with her. Their throats were slashed, the father was stabbed 39 times and the mother 8 times. [David Reed: www.apnews-archive.com-25 June 1990]. Soering and his girlfriend, who was also involved in the murders, then fled to Britain, where they were arrested on charges of cheque fraud. Soon after this Soering was indicted with the capital murder of his girlfriend's parents. The United States requested Soering's extradition under the 1972 extradition treaty between the two countries and a warrant was duly issued under the Extradition Act 1870 to commit him to prison to await the Home Secretary's order to extradite him to the US. Soering's appeal to the House of Lords (then the highest law court) and his petition to the Home Secretary both failed. The case then went to the European Commission of Human Rights, which decided that extradition would not constitute inhuman or degrading treatment contrary to ECHR Article 3. However, the Strasbourg court itself ruled in favour of Soering on the ground that the "death row phenomenon" breached Article 3, the relevant factors being essentially the length of time he was likely to have to spend on "death row" prior to his execution, and the conditions on death row: "Having regard to the very long period of time spent on death row in such extreme conditions, with the ever present and mounting anguish of awaiting execution of the death penalty, and to the personal circumstances of the applicant, especially his age and mental state at the time of the offence, the applicant's extradition to the United States would expose him to a real risk of treatment going beyond the threshold set by Article 3." After obtaining assurances from the US that the state of Virginia would not seek the death penalty against Soering, the UK extradited Soering to Virginia. At his trial, his girlfriend, who had pleaded guilty, testified that Soering had committed the murders and that she had been an accessory. Soering was convicted on two counts of first degree murder and on 4 September 1990 was sentenced to two consecutive life terms. His repeated applications for early release, ending up in the US Supreme Court, have all been turned down. The same approach to ECHR Article 3 was applied by Strasbourg in *Chahal v. UK* [1996] ECHR 54, which has been followed on numerous occasions by the UK courts.

Main Objections

The main objections to this interpretation of ECHR Article 3 are:

a)   Why should the UK be responsible for the way a foreign country treats someone who is rightly being removed from the UK?

b)   In Soering's case, why should he have been given special privileges not enjoyed by other murderers in the state of Virginia?

c)   And Soering was only in the UK as a fugitive from justice in the US.

d)   Moreover, it is a complete misinterpretation of Article 3 to oblige country X to force country Y to adopt the standards of country X.

e)   And ECHR Article 1 makes it absolutely crystal clear that the obligations of the signatory states, including the UK, in regard to the ECHR apply only within their own jurisdictions. [See more on this below].

f)   Above all, the UK courts are not obliged to follow Strasbourg slavishly, as they tend to do. Section 2(1)(a) of the Human Rights Act only requires them to "take into account" judgments, decisions, declarations etc. of the Strasbourg court. [See Michael Arnheim, *The Problem with Human Rights Law,* Civitas, 2015].

Saadi v. Italy (2008):
the UK's brief moment of defiance

The most extreme example of this "politically correct" approach on the part of the Strasbourg court was reached in the case of Nassim Saadi against Italy, in which the UK actually had the gumption to intervene as a third party to try to persuade the Strasbourg court to give up their irrational approach. Saadi, a Tunisian national legally resident in Italy, was arrested as a terrorist suspect in 2002. After a lengthy process, involving several appeals, he was released in 2006. In the meantime he was convicted in Tunisia of terrorist offences and sentenced to 20 years' imprisonment. Saadi was then served by the Italian government with a deportation order. Saadi then played the "Torture Card", applying for political asylum in Italy on the ground that he would be at risk of torture if returned to Tunisia. His asylum application was denied on the grounds of national security and Italy received assurances from Tunisia that Saadi would not be tortured if deported to Tunisia.

The UK as an "intervener" actually put some cogent arguments backing up the Italian Government's attempt to deport the terrorist suspect. [*Saadi v. Italy* 37201/06, 28 February 2008]. The UK government's sensible and logical arguments included the following:

- The degree of danger posed by the applicant should be taken into account—contrary to a supposed principle laid down by the Strasbourg court in *Chahal v. UK* (1996) 23 EHRR 413.
- The "real risk of torture or ill-treatment" standard laid down in *Chahal* should be modified and clarified in two respects. First, the security risk posed by the applicant's

dangerousness should be weighed against the risk to the applicant in the receiving state.

- And secondly, the standard applicable to a terror suspect should be that he is "more likely than not" to be exposed to prohibited treatment rather than the lower "real risk" standard currently applied.

Although the Strasbourg court accepted the right of member states like the UK and Italy to control the entry, residence and expulsion of aliens and confirmed that there is no Convention right to political asylum, it reasserted its longstanding insistence on the absolute nature of Article 3.

A few years later, the Strasbourg court actually softened its position in a more reasonable direction in *Babar Ahmad and Abu Hamza Othman v. UK* [2012] ECHR 609: "The absolute nature of Article 3 does not mean that any form of ill treatment will act as a bar to removal from a Contracting State. ... this court has repeatedly stated that the convention does not purport to be a means of requiring the contracting states to impose convention standards on other states. ... This being so, treatment which might violate Article 3 because of an act or omission of a contracting state might not attain the minimum level of severity which is required for there to be a violation of Article 3 in an expulsion or extradition case" [at §177].

Algerian Terror Suspects

However, the English courts have not always been so flexible. In a "third-party" case finally decided in April 2016, six unnamed Algerian terror suspects with alleged links to al-Qaeda won a ten-year deportation battle against the British Government and were effectively granted the right to live in Britain. The Government admitted defeat and announced that they would not be appealing against this decision handed down by the Special Immigration Appeals Commission (SIAC). The trump card played by the six terror suspects was the "torture card", an allegation that if deported to Algeria they would be at risk of torture. The court agreed with the terror suspects, concluding: "It is not inconceivable that these Appellants, if returned to Algeria, would be subjected to ill-treatment infringing Article 3 [of the ECHR]. There is a real risk of such a breach." To protect the identity of the terror suspects, the case is reported only as *BB, PP, W, U, Y & Z v. Secretary of State for the Home Department* [SC/39/2005, 18 April 2016]. A Home Office spokesman made this lame comment: "We are extremely disappointed with SIAC's judgment. Our priority remains the safety and protection of the British public and we will continue to take every measure possible to remove foreign nationals who we deem a risk." [Robert Mendick, "Judges stop Theresa May deporting terror suspects". *The Telegraph*, 7 May 2016.]

This is a troubling decision—but by no means the only one of its kind. Here are some of the major issues raised by this decision:

- This decision was *not* made by any European court but by a domestic UK court.
- You may perhaps be thinking: "This decision does seem a bit over-the-top, but what harm can it do to be kind?" In fact, it *can* do a lot of harm—even to you personally. Having potentially dangerous people on the loose threatens your personal safety. If allowed to remain in Britain, such people may possibly be subjected to supposedly strict conditions—which however are never as secure as they are meant to be and which will be financed at great cost by the taxpayer.
- These applicants are protected by anonymity—why? It is only terror suspects and convicted criminals, including convicted killers, who can expect this kind of privilege— because that is what it is, not a right but a special privilege.
- But why should people who are a potential danger to society be accorded this privilege when their potential

victims—ordinary law-abiding citizens—would be laughed out of court if they tried to apply for the same protection?

- For that matter, how did these people get into Britain in the first place? It appears that they were given political asylum by the UK government—even though terror suspects are disqualified from applying for asylum under Article 1F or Article 33(2) of the Refugee Convention and Art 14(5) of the Qualification Directive. [See Home Office booklet: "Exclusion (Article 1F) and Article 33(2) of the Refugee Convention", version 6 1 July 2016].

- *Government's dereliction of duty:* The six terror suspects in this particular case came from Algeria, a non-EU country with no connection with the UK. Their entry into Britain can only be blamed on the UK Government's dismal failure over many years to control immigration from *outside* the EU.

But, all that aside, what is wrong with SIAC's decision to block their deportation back to Algeria?

- You just need to read the SIAC court ruling to see on what a flimsy and insubstantial legal foundation it rests: "It is not inconceivable that these Appellants, if returned to Algeria, would be subjected to ill-treatment infringing Article 3 [of the ECHR]. There is a real risk of such a breach." *"Not inconceivable"* and *"real risk"*? Is that all? What exactly is "a real risk" anyway? A 10% risk, a 25% risk, or what? It's *not* a 50% risk—as we know from the fact that the much fairer test of "more likely than not" proposed by the UK Government was dismissed out of hand by the Strasbourg court in *Saadi v. Italy* in 2008.

- Besides the use of the vague phrases "not inconceivable" and "real risk", SIAC does not even go so far as to say that there was a risk of *torture*, but only the much weaker risk of "ill-treatment infringing Article 3".

- In the forlorn hope of being able to persuade "politically correct" judges to allow it to deport terror suspects and convicted criminals—a right that belongs to any sovereign state—the British Government has systematically compiled elaborate documentation in support of a policy of *deportation with assurances* (DWA). This entailed obtaining assurances from the governments of countries to which the UK Government wished to order deportations. One of these countries was Algeria—and the British Government in fact received personal assurances about these individual cases from the Algerian President.

- But even this was not good enough for SIAC, who concluded: "The different means of verification of adherence advanced by the Respondent [the UK Government] do not, taken together, amount to a robust system of verification."

- But why should it be the UK Government's responsibility to provide "a robust system of verification"—or any system of verification—anyway?

- In short, why should Britain be responsible for what happens to someone who should not be in the UK in the first place?

- This is a complete misinterpretation of ECHR Article 3. All that ECHR Article 3 says is: *"No one shall be subjected to torture or to inhuman or degrading treatment or punishment."*

- The courts are keen to stress the "absolute" nature of this Article—the absence of any exceptions. But ALL the human rights of the ECHR are governed by ECHR Article 1, which reads: *"The High Contracting Parties shall secure to everyone within their jurisdiction the rights and freedoms defined in Section 1 of this Convention."* The term "the High Contracting Parties" refers to the governments of all signatories to the ECHR, including the UK Government. But the really significant phrase here is **"within their jurisdiction"**. What this means as far as ECHR Article 3 is concerned is that the UK's responsibility for protecting people against torture and inhuman treatment does not extend beyond the areas under UK Government control.

• In *Al-Skeini v. UK* [Application 55721/07], decided in 2011, 'the Strasbourg court itself, in its most extended interpretation of ECHR Article 1 to date, still restricted the UK's human rights responsibilities to areas directly controlled by the UK Government. The case involved six Iraqi civilians killed by British troops in Basrah, in Iraq. The complaint was not of any substantive breach of the right to life under ECHR Article 2, but only that the UK Government had not carried out an effective investigation into the killings. Between the removal of Sadam Hussain and the appointment of an interim Iraqi Government, the court held, "the United Kingdom (together with the United States) assumed in Iraq the exercise of some of the public powers normally to be exercised by a sovereign government. ... In these exceptional circumstances, the Court considers that the United Kingdom, through its soldiers engaged in security operations in Basrah during the period in question, exercised authority and control over individuals killed in the course of such security operations, so as to establish a jurisdictional link between the deceased and the United Kingdom for the purposes of Article 1 of the Convention." [§149]. So, even in these *"exceptional circumstances"* it was only because the UK *"exercised authority and control"* so as to establish *"a jurisdictional link"* that the UK was held by

Strasbourg to have had any human rights responsibilities.

- This only underlines just how wrong it is to make the UK Government responsible for what happens to terror suspects in Algeria—a country over which the UK exercises no control of any kind—to the point of preventing the UK Government from keeping its people safe, the prime duty of any government.

- It is important to note in regard to the Algerian terror-suspects case, that, while SIAC, a domestic UK court, has stuck to the old hard-line Strasbourg approach—which it did not have to do—Strasbourg itself has in the meantime softened its position in these "third-party" Article 3 cases. For example, in a case involving extradition from the UK to the USA of four applicants, whose attempt to use the "torture trump" card—amazingly—failed on this occasion. A unanimous Strasbourg court waved the four men off to their new American home without so much as a tear, holding that if the four men were extradited to the USA, "there would be no violation of Article 3 of the Convention as a result of the length of their possible sentences" or "as a result of conditions at ADX Florence [a maximum security US federal penitentiary in Colorado]." *(Babar Ahmad & Abu Hamza (Othman) v. UK* [2012] ECHR 609). "The absolute nature of Article 3 does not mean that any form of ill treatment will act as a bar to removal from a Contracting State. ... This court has repeatedly stated that the Convention does not purport to be a means of requiring the contracting states to impose convention standards on other states. ... This being so, treatment which might violate Article 3 because of an act or omission of a contracting state might not attain the minimum level of severity which is required for there to be a violation of Article 3 in an expulsion or extradition case."[§177].

What can be done to counter this kind of decision?

As I have already mentioned, Parliament can revoke any court decision by legislation. Most people, including many who really ought to know, do not know about this power. It is an integral part of the Sovereignty of Parliament, the bedrock principle of the UK constitution. It also ties in with the checks and balances which form an integral part of the doctrine of the separation of powers, which is negated if, as is the case at present, the other two branches of government, namely the legislature and the executive, abdicate their own responsibilities and kowtow to the judiciary.

The best example of Parliament's exercise of this power occurred in the case of *Burmah Oil v. Lord Advocate* [1965] AC 75, in which the House of Lords as the top court decided by a 3–2 majority that the British Government should compensate an oil company for destroying oil fields at the government's behest during World War II. The majority really went to town with extremely wordy opinions which purported to lay down some fundamental constitutional principles. But the House of Lords decision in Burmah Oil was soon reversed by the War Damage Act 1965, which was not only an act of Parliament but also one with retroactive effect. [See the chapter on "The Sovereignty of Parliament."]

Bejhaj v. Straw (2017)

The *Burmah Oil* court decision was not nearly as damaging to national security as some more recent court decisions, like, for example, the *BB* case itself and *Belhaj v. Straw* [2017] UKSC 3. This was a claim for compensation by a Libyan national, a political opponent of the Gaddafi regime, and his Moroccan wife. They fled from Libya to China intending to claim asylum in the UK, but when on a commercial flight bound for London via Bangkok, they were taken off the aircraft in Bangkok by Thai officials and delivered to agents of the United States. They were then flown to

Libya in a US-registered aircraft, where they were taken to Tajoura prison. The claimant's wife was released in June 2004 after being held there for more than three months. Abdul-Hakim Belhaj himself was held in Libyan prisons for six years before being released in March 2010. "It is alleged that they were tortured and subjected to other serious mistreatment by US officials in Bangkok and in the aircraft carrying them to Libya, and by Libyan officials in Libya. ... The present proceedings are brought in support of a claim for damages against a number of departments and officials of the British government who are said to have been complicit in what happened to them. ... It is not alleged that British officials were directly involved in the rendition, torture or mistreatment of the claimants. But it is said that they enabled it to happen, knowing of the risk that the defendants would be unlawfully detained, tortured and otherwise mistreated by the Americans and the Libyans. It is also alleged that British officials took advantage of Mr. Belhaj's detention in Libya by interrogating him there at least twice. The defendants, it is said, thereby incurred liability in tort." [*Belhaj v. Straw* [2017] UKSC 3, *per* Lord Sumption]. The UK's alleged involvement in the alleged torture, inhumane and degrading treatment was therefore extremely remote, if it occurred at all. No proof of these allegations was presented, and even the UK Supreme Court accepted the first instance judge's finding "that all the claims depend upon proof that torts such as those alleged existed under the laws of the places where they were allegedly committed. ..."

In a sensible and carefully argued judgment in the High Court, the judge, Simon J, struck out the claims against the UK for "unlawful rendition" on the basis that the doctrine of immunity attaching to an "act of state" is a total bar to such claims, regardless of their gravity. [*Belhaj v. Straw* [2013] EWHC 411 (QB). [See Rosalind English, "Rendition to Libya an 'act of state' and therefore non-justiciable". www.ukhumanrights.blog.com —14 January 2014].

The "Act of State" doctrine obliges every sovereign state to respect the independence of every other sovereign state, so that the courts of one state will not sit in judgment on the acts of another state's government. It was on this basis that the judge came to the conclusion that the UK government was right in submitting "that the case pleaded against them depends on the Court having to decide that the conduct of US officials acting outside the United States was unlawful, in circumstances where there are no clear and incontrovertible standards for doing so and where there is incontestable evidence that such an enquiry would be damaging to the national interest. The most recent and authoritative decision, *Rahmatullah*, makes clear ... that this is something that the domestic court should not do." [*Belhaj v. Straw* [2013] EWHC 411 (QB)].

This careful and sensible judgment was reversed by the Court of Appeal and, for different reasons, by the UK Supreme Court, where the justices took a different view of the meaning of "act of state" from the judge and even, to some extent, from one another. Four of the seven justices disagreed so fundamentally with the judge's opinion that, as the brief joint opinion of Lady Hale and Lord Clarke put it: "The defences of state immunity and foreign act of state do not apply at all in the two cases before us." [*Belhaj v. Straw* [2017] UKSC 3, para 174.] This case, in an area where the relevant law is unclear and which threatens national security, cries out for the intervention of Parliament., which, needless to say, has not occurred.

Prince Charles's Letters

Serious problems arise even in cases only involving statutory interpretation.

On 26 March 2015 the UK Supreme Court decided (by 5 votes to 2) a case involving the disclosure of correspondence dating from 2004 and 2005 between Charles, Prince of Wales, and government ministers, including the then Prime Minister,

Tony Blair. [*R. (on the application of Evans) v. Attorney General* [2015] UKSC 21.]

Section 53 of the Freedom of Information Act ("FOIA") 2000 gives a government minister the power to veto the release of information if he has "on reasonable grounds formed the opinion" that disclosure is not in the public interest. In this particular case, the Attorney General, Dominic Grieve, vetoed the disclosure of the correspondence on those grounds. However, the majority on the Supreme Court found against the government and ordered the correspondence to be disclosed.

The case ought not to have gone to the Supreme Court at all, because in 2010 a new specific exemption from disclosure was made covering government communications with the sovereign, the heir to the throne and even the second-in-line to the throne for 20 years after the date of the communication concerned. In the words of Deputy Information Commissioner Graham Smith, this 2010 rule is "an absolute exemption, so the public interest test doesn't apply". The 2010 rule does not have retrospective effect, so, strictly speaking, it could not apply to Prince Charles's correspondence from 2004 and 2005. But would it not have been more sensible— and more just—to have decided the issue of the 2004–5 correspondence at a much lower level and on the same basis as the 2010 rule?

The Rule of Law

This decision was really just another case in which the judiciary was showing the government who was boss—and it was not the government or even Parliament, contrary to the sacred doctrine of the Sovereignty of Parliament, which is supposed to form the bedrock of the British Constitution. Lord Hughes, who dissented on the main issue in the case, put his finger on this crucial point: "The rule of law is of the first importance. But it is an integral part of the rule of law that courts give effect to

Parliamentary intention. The rule of law is not the same as a rule that courts must always prevail, no matter what the statute says." [para 154.] He concluded "that the Attorney General gave sufficient rational reasons for his conclusion that the public interest lay in non-disclosure" [para 166.]

Lord Wilson in his dissenting opinion scored another bull's eye when he pointed out that in reaching its decision the Court of Appeal, followed by the majority on the Supreme Court, "did not in my view interpret section 53 of the FOIA. It re-wrote it. It invoked precious constitutional principles but among the most precious is that of parliamentary sovereignty, emblematic of our democracy" [para 168.]

The courage of these two brave judges to stand up against judicial activism is commendable, but the fact that they were in a minority and that such action was needed in the first place reveals only too clearly the ease with which the courts can ride roughshod over both the government and Parliament.

9

UNITED STATES
UMPIRES OR EMPIRE BUILDERS?

"State courts are courts of law," it has been said: "federal courts are courts of policy." There is more than a grain of truth in this remark. By "policy" is meant judicial policy, or judge-made law, as was discussed in the chapter on *The Snail in the Bottle*. And the reason federal courts are more prone than state courts to resort to judge-made law is simply that the stock-in-trade of federal courts, and particularly the US Supreme Court, is judicial review. State courts do have judicial review jurisdiction as well, but it plays a much smaller role in their activities.

Judge-made law is a common feature between English and American judicial review. In the section on The Four Corners in English Law, I quoted Lord Neuberger's proud boast that the judiciary has been "responsible" for "the very substantial growth in domestic judicial review." It would be a rare American judge who would ever admit, let alone claim credit for, such judicial activism. Chief Justice John Roberts's disclaimer during his confirmation hearing in 2005 is famous:

> "Judges and justices are servants of the law, not the other way around. Judges are like umpires. Umpires don't make the rules; they apply them. The role of an umpire and a judge is critical. They make sure everybody plays by the rules. But it is a limited role. Nobody ever went to a ball game to see the umpire."

Another of Roberts's remarks that has gained currency is his retort to President Trump's criticism of an "Obama judge." Roberts fired back: "We do not have Obama judges or Trump judges, Bush judges or Clinton judges. What we have is an extraordinary group of dedicated judges doing their level best to do equal right to those appearing before them." With apologies to Shakespeare: *Methinks the gentleman doth protest too much.* Roberts is of course right that a judge's philosophical outlook is not necessarily the same as that of the president who nominated him or her. But it is undeniable that judges, and especially Supreme Court justices, tend to have certain identifiable ideological or at least jurisprudential leanings. The label "activist " is used as a term of opprobrium and is not one that any American judge would normally want to hang around his own neck.

As Governor of New York in 1907 Charles Evans Hughes (Chief Justice 1930–1941) famously remarked: "We are under a Constitution, but the Constitution is what the judges say it is, and the judiciary is the safeguard of our liberty and of our property under the Constitution." This recognizes the power of judiciary to interpret the Constitution, without however suggesting that they have the right to rewrite it in their own image. As an Associate Justice of the Supreme Court between 1910 and 1916 Hughes aligned himself with Oliver Wendell Holmes Jr. In upholding state laws and the power of Congress to regulate interstate commerce under the Commerce Clause. As Chief Justice from 1930 to 1941, Hughes tended to be the "swing vote" between the conservative "Four Horsemen" and the liberal "Three Musketeers."

John Paul Stephens (Associate Justice, 1975–2010), who is often considered to have been a "liberal" (though he preferred to label himself a conservative), so rejected the idea of legislating from the bench that he wrote a book advocating the making of six amendments to the Constitution—not by judicial fiat but by the democratic legislative route prescribed by Article V of the Constitution. [Stevens, John Paul (2014).]

Chevron and judicial deference

While the English courts were closing in on executive discretion, a unanimous US Supreme Court ruled that courts must generally defer to a government agency's own interpretation of legislation which that agency administers. In the words of Justice Stevens, writing for the Court:

"When a court reviews an agency's construction of the statute which it administers, it is confronted with two questions. First, always, is the question whether Congress has directly spoken to the precise question at issue. If the intent of Congress is clear, that is the end of the matter; for the court, as well as the agency, must give effect to the unambiguously expressed intent of Congress. If, however, the court determines Congress has not directly addressed the precise question at issue, the court does not simply impose its own construction on the statute, as would be necessary in the absence of an administrative interpretation. Rather, if the statute is silent or ambiguous with respect to the specific issue, the question for the court is whether the agency's answer is based on a permissible construction of the statute. … [T]he principle of deference to administrative interpretations has been consistently followed by this Court whenever decision as to the meaning or reach of a statute has involved reconciling conflicting policies, and a full understanding of the force of the statutory policy in the given situation has depended upon more than ordinary knowledge respecting the matters subjected to agency regulations." He concluded: "When a challenge to an agency construction of a statutory provision, fairly conceptualized, really centers on the wisdom of the agency's policy, rather than whether it is a reasonable choice within a gap left open by Congress, the challenge must fail. In such a case, federal judges—who have no constituency—have a duty to respect legitimate policy choices made by those who do. The responsibilities for assessing the wisdom of such policy choices and resolving the struggle between competing views of the public interest are

not judicial ones: 'Our Constitution vests such responsibilities
in the political branches." *TVA v. Hill*, 437 US 153, 195
(1978).'" [*Chevron USA Inc v. Natural Resources Defense Council
Inc.*, 467 US 837 (1984).]

Chevron is the most cited US administrative law case, and the
term "Chevron deference" has entered the language. [See: Miles,
Thomas J. & Sunstein, Cass R. (2006).]

In *Arlington v. FCC*, decided in 2013, Justice Scalia, writing
for a bipartisan majority made up of Justices Thomas, Ginsburg,
Sotomayor and Kagan, essentially reaffirmed Chevron. He
identified the issue before the court as follows: "We consider
whether an agency's interpretation of a statutory ambiguity that
concerns the scope of its regulatory authority (that is, its
jurisdiction) is entitled to deference under Chevron." He
concluded: "Those who assert that applying Chevron to
'jurisdictional' interpretations 'leaves the fox in charge of the
henhouse' overlook the reality that a separate category of
'jurisdictional' interpretations does not exist. ... If the agency's
answer is based on a permissible construction of the statute, that
is the end of the matter." [*Arlington v. FCC*, 569 US 290, 133 S.
Ct. 1863 (2013).] Interestingly enough, in *Arlington*, dissent
came from a "conservative" threesome made up of Chief Justice
Roberts joined by Justices Kennedy and Alito. The Chief Justice's
employed unusually strong language: "My disagreement with the
Court is fundamental. It is also easily expressed. A court should
not defer to an agency until the court decides, on its own, that
the agency is entitled to deference." Roberts then quoted the
lapidary words of Chief Justice John Marshall in *Marbury v.
Madison:* "It is emphatically the province and duty of the judicial
department to say what the law is." Adding: "The rise of the
modern administrative state has not changed that duty. Indeed,
the Administrative Procedure Act, governing judicial review of
most agency action, instructs reviewing courts to decide 'all
relevant questions of law.'"

After the death of President Franklin Roosevelt in 1945, there was a backlash against the "imperial presidency" with its multifarious agencies that had been set up as part of the New Deal. The Administrative Procedure Act (APA), enacted in 1946, emerged as a compromise between pro-New Deal and anti-New Deal forces. The APA provides that a court cannot set aside a regulation made by an agency unless it finds that regulation "arbitrary and capricious, an abuse of discretion, or otherwise not in accordance with the law." [It is worth comparing these criteria with those of *Wednesbury* and subsequent cases in England, as discussed in the previous chapter.]

What lies at the heart of this dispute is the separation of powers. Does that make Roberts, Kennedy and Alito judicial activists? Hardly. There is no attempt to legislate from the bench. Notice how both sides on the Supreme Court appeal to authority. In the original *Chevron* case, Stevens grounded the case for deference in long-established precedent, and in *Arlington* Roberts appealed to the APA and to *Marbury*.

Two kinds of activists

"Activism" is a label that is frequently bandied about, never as a compliment. In reality, activism has been engaged in by judges on both sides of the divide. The biggest activist of them all, who set the ball rolling in *Marbury v. Madison*, was John Marshall himself, a Federalist Party adherent and essentially a conservative. His successor, Roger Taney (Chief Justice 1836–1864), best known for the *Dred Scott* case, was another conservative activist. And so were the so-called "Four Horsemen" [of the Apocalypse], who fought tooth and nail against FDR's New Deal program in the 1930s. The first concerted liberal activist push came during the Warren court, which lasted from 1953 to 1969. Since then the Supreme Court has mostly been roughly split between two opposing camps, with a "swing vote" in the center, first Sandra Day O'Connor

(Associate Justice 1981–2005), who was jocularly described as "a majority of one," and then Anthony Kennedy (Associate Justice 1988–2018). At this writing, Chief Justice Roberts himself seems to be positioning himself as a swing vote.

Let us now take a look at some US Supreme Court decisions that are commonly regarded as examples of judicial activism, to see whether that is in fact a correct characterization.

Marbury v. Madison, as I argue in Chapter 2, "United States: A Despotic Branch," was probably wrongly decided. Thomas Jefferson, a distant cousin, was taken in neither by Marshall's bonhomie nor by his "twistifications." Yet, *Marbury's* iconic status remains undimmed.

The end of "separate but equal"

Brown v. Board of Education was the next decision of the Supreme Court after *Marbury* to be carved in stone. In a unanimous opinion authored by Chief Justice Earl Warren, the court overruled *Plessy v. Ferguson*, 163 US 537 (1896), which had stood unchallenged for more than half a century. In *Plessy* the Court ruled in favor of a Louisiana law requiring racial segregation on the railroad. The Court held that this did not violate the Equal Protection Clause of the Fourteenth Amendment. The Louisiana law, it held, satisfied the test of reasonableness and was based on "the established usages, customs and traditions of the people." In *Brown* the Court outlawed racial segregation in public schools throughout the United States. In so doing, the Court not only overruled its own ruling in *Plessy* but also declared 17 state laws unconstitutional, including some from northern states, that had also approved the "separate but equal" formula. Speaking through Earl Warren, the Court ruled: "We conclude that in the field of public education the doctrine of 'separate but equal' has no place. Separate educational facilities are inherently unequal."

President John F. Kennedy issued an Executive Order (which is not supposed to change the law) requiring government employers to "take affirmative action" in selecting applicants for government posts. This marked the beginning of widespread affirmative action, especially in education. In 1971, the US Supreme Court ordered the integration of all 105 schools in Charlotte-Mecklenburg, North Carolina, by busing students to different schools. The intention was to achieve the same white-to-blacks ratio in the schools as in the area as whole. The Supreme Court based its unanimous decision specifically on the Equal Protection Clause of the Fourteenth Amendment. [*Swann v. Charlotte-Mecklenburg Board of Education*, 402 USD 1 (1971).] The Supreme Court believed that forced integration would lead to greater equality in the education offered to members of the different ethnic groups—and to an improvement in the educational levels attained by minority students. Yet a 1992 Harvard University study led by Professor Gary Orfield found that black and Hispanic students lacked "even modest overall improvement" as a result of busing. Here are some other alleged long-term effects of busing:

- Some students were spending as much as three hours a day on the bus. As a result, less time was available for sports and other extracurricular activities.
- Busing sometimes transported children to dangerous neighborhoods.
- Children were sometimes bused from integrated schools to less integrated schools.
- There was "white flight" to the suburbs, a huge increase in the number of white children in private and parochial schools.
- The result was and a serious decline in the standards of the predominantly black inner city schools.
- Inner city public schools became largely made up of minorities—exactly the opposite of the intention behind busing. Today Boston public schools are 75% African

America and Hispanic, even though Boston's black and Hispanic populations together represent less than 40% of the city's total population. Similar examples abound. Private schools sprang up in Pasadena, California—48 at the last count—resulting in the fact that white children now make up only 15% of the public school population.

The *Bakke* case (1978)

Since 1971 the US Supreme Court has gradually pulled away from the extreme interpretation of the Equal Protection Clause that led to forced busing. In *Milliken v. Bradley*, 418 US 717 (1974), the Supreme Court banned forced busing across district lines unless a number of school districts had engaged in deliberate segregation. In *Regents of the University of California v. Bakke*, 438 US 265 (1978), a plurality on the Supreme Court found the quota system operated by the University's Medical School unconstitutional, while still allowing race to be taken into account in admissions. In an internal memo to his fellow justices dated April 13, 1978, Justice Thurgood Marshall, the only black member of the court, who was opposed to Bakke's application, wrote: "[T]he decision in this case depends on whether you consider the action of the Regents as *admitting* certain students or *excluding* certain other students."

"Stop discriminating on the basis of race"

In *Board of Education of Oklahoma City v. Dowell*, 498 US 237 (1991), the Supreme Court recognized that the existence of single race schools did not necessarily amount to a violation of the Equal Protection Clause. Then, in two cases decided together in 2007, the Supreme Court finally almost reversed its 1971 interpretation of the Equal Protection Clause. The two cases in question were *Parents Involved in Community Schools v. Seattle School District No. 1*, 551 US 701 (2007), known as *"PICS,"* and

Meredith v. Jefferson County Board of Education, 547 US 1178 (2007). The Court rejected the use of race as the sole basis for assigning students to schools. This turned the 1971 interpretation of the Equal Protection Clause on its head. Chief Justice Roberts famously concluded his plurality opinion with the words: "The way to stop discrimination on the basis of race is to stop discriminating on the basis of race"—an important recognition that affirmative action is racial discrimination, nevertheless. Or, as Justice Clarence Thomas puts it, the Constitution is "color-blind." He has placed a 15 cent discount sticker on his own diploma from Yale to show how little he thinks it is worth. "I'd graduated from one of America's top law schools," he explains, "but racial preference had robbed my achievement of its true value." It is a frank recognition by Clarence Thomas that he owed his admission to Yale to his color and that he had probably taken the place of a white student with better grades. In other words, he had benefited from a form of privilege to which he was not entitled.

"Disguised quota"

Does the Equal Protection Clause really support affirmative action? In *Grutter v. Bollinger*, 539 US 306 (2003), heard in 2003, the US Supreme Court upheld the University of Michigan Law School's affirmative action admissions policy. The case was brought by Barbara Grutter, a 43-year-old white Michigan resident who had been denied admission to the Law School in favor of minority students. Her surprise turned to "dismay" when she read a Detroit newspaper article indicating that minorities admitted to the university had lower test scores and grades than admitted whites. Justice Sandra Day O'Connor, writing for the majority, held that the US Constitution "does not prohibit the law school's narrowly tailored use of race in admissions decisions to further a compelling interest in obtaining the educational benefits that flow from a diverse student body." The policy carefully avoided using any quotas, and all applicants were given the same "individualized" and "holistic" review. She concluded: "We expect that 25 years from now, the use of racial preferences will no longer be necessary to further the interest approved today." Chief Justice Rehnquist, joined by Justices Scalia, Kennedy, and Thomas, dissented, claiming that the Law School's admissions policy was actually a "disguised quota" system, which was unconstitutional because the Court had condemned quotas in the well-known *Bakke* case in 1978. Justice Scalia likewise called the policy "a sham to cover a scheme of racially proportionate admissions." Adding: "The Constitution proscribes government discrimination on the basis of race, and state-provided education is no exception."

"Camouflage, winks, nods, and disguises"

By contrast with *Grutter*, in *Gratz v. Bollinger*, 539 US 244 (2003) decided on the same day, a 6–3 majority on the Supreme Court struck down as unconstitutional the University of Michigan points-based *undergraduate* admissions policy, under which minority ethnic groups were given an automatic 20-point bonus, with 100 points needed for admission. This, according to Chief Justice Rehnquist, writing for the majority, "operated as the functional equivalent of a quota running afoul" of the condemnation of quotas in *Bakke*. How different was this system from the more carefully crafted admissions policy applied in the law school? Two of the justices who approved the admissions policy for freshman undergraduates as well as the one for the law school made a surprising concession. These were Justice David Souter and Justice Ruth Bader Ginsburg, who were in the majority in *Grutter* and in the minority in *Gratz*. Souter admitted that the undergraduate "college simply does by a numbered scale what the law school accomplishes in its 'holistic' review." Ginsburg made a similar admission, writing that "institutions of higher education may resort to camouflage" and to "winks, nods and disguises." But, instead of making these two liberal justices reject both the naked quota system and the disguised quota system, this admission had the opposite effect of making them approve of both, on the assumption that they were in some sense fairer than a color-blind, pure merit-based system.

Scalia draws "gasps"

These two Michigan cases are not the most recent High Court decisions on affirmative action, but at this writing they are still the gold standard against which such issues are measured. Since then we have seen the playing out of the long saga of *Fisher v. University of Texas,* which had two incarnations before the US Supreme Court, *Fisher I,* 570 US ___ (2013) and *Fisher II,* 579 US ___ (2016). During oral arguments in Fisher II, Justice Scalia reportedly "drew gasps" from the audience when he said, citing an amicus brief: "There are those who contend that it does not benefit African Americans to get them into the University of Texas where they do not do well, as opposed to having them go to a less-advanced school, a less—a slower-track school where they do well." Before the final decision was handed down Scalia died. As Justice Kagan recused herself because of her earlier involvement with the case as solicitor general, the case was eventually decided by only seven justices: three liberals, three conservatives, and Justice Anthony Kennedy, who sided with the liberals and wrote the majority opinion, which held that: "The race-conscious admissions program in use at the time of [Abigail Fisher's] application is lawful under the Equal Protection Clause." It found the university's admissions policy similar to that approved in *Grutter.*

Negative quotas?

At this writing, the debate on affirmative action is still ongoing and shows no sign of abating. The old issue of racial quotas has now raised its head once more. This time it is about negative quotas, which are arguably even worse than positive quotas. Both are discriminatory and are disallowed under *Gratz*. The latest issue concerns allegations of the use of racial quotas to reduce the number of Asian-American students. A coalition of 64 Asian-American groups filed a complaint against Harvard University with the US Departments of Education and Justice in 2015, alleging that "for Asian-American students to gain admission, they have to have SAT scores 140 points higher than white students, 270 points higher than Hispanic students, and 450 points higher than African-American students." A non-profit organization known as Students for Fair Admissions (SFFA) has filed a lawsuit on the same basis against Harvard. In August 2017, at President Trump's prompting, it was revealed that the Department of Justice was seeking lawyers to work on "investigations and possible litigation related to intentional race-based discrimination in college and university admissions."

Affirmative Action and Diversity

One of the main arguments in favor of affirmative action is to promote "diversity". "Educators know that all students, and not just our students of color, benefit from diverse and inclusive classrooms", wrote Lily Eskelsen Garcia, president of the National Education Association, in a 2018 statement. By contrast, Clarence Thomas remarked in connection with his opposition to mandatory desegregation that "you [viz. a black student] don't need to sit next to a white person to learn how to read and write" (Clarence Thomas, *My Grandfather's Son*, New York: Harper Collins, 2008).

Advocates of affirmative action tend to assume that, despite discriminating against whites, affirmative action at least has the desired effect of advancing blacks and Hispanics. But even this may not be true. As mentioned above, a 1992 study led by Gary Orfield, a Harvard professor *and a supporter of desegregation busing,* concluded that black and Hispanic students lacked "even modest overall improvement" as a result of busing. Busing was not even popular with African Americans. A Gallup Poll published in *The New York Times* on September 19, 1973 revealed:

> "A majority of Americans continue to favor pubic school integration, but few people—black or white—think that busing is the best way to achieve that goal. Five per cent of the people in a recent survey by the organization—9% of the blacks and 4% of the whites—chose busing children from one district to another rather than several other alternatives.... Another part of the survey indicated that much of the opposition to busing was not based on racial animosity. Other reasons for the opposition, according to survey findings, are the belief that busing is an infringement of personal liberties, worry about busing children to schools in different neighborhoods and concern that busing will increase local school taxes."

But what about the benefits of affirmative action generally? Detailed recent research by a UCLA law professor concluded:

> "Mismatch largely explains why, even though blacks are more likely to enter college than are whites with similar backgrounds, they will usually get much lower grades, rank toward the bottom of the class, and far more often drop out; why there are so few blacks and Hispanics with science and engineering degrees or with doctorates in any field; and why black law graduates fail bar exams at four times the white rate." But what is the definition of "mismatch"? "It is not lack of talent or innate ability that drives these students to drop out of school, flee rigorous courses, or abandon aspirations to be scientists or scholars; it is, rather, an unintended side effect of large racial preferences,which systematically put minority students in academic environments where they feel overwhelmed."
> [Sander, Richard & Stuart Taylor, Jr. (2012), p. 4.]

This ties in with the remark quoted above that Justice Antonin Scalia made during oral arguments in *Fisher II* about "slower-track schools" for African Americans.

HCBUs

Needless to say, this proposition is hotly contested by the supporters of affirmative action. But there is some support for Scalia's point in the South. There are 105 "historically black colleges and universities" (HBCUs) in the US as a whole, the overwhelming majority of which are in the South and a number of which enjoy high reputations. Of these 105 HBCUs there are six Historically Black Law Schools that are accredited by the American Bar Association. Four of these law schools are in the South. In 2015 the Bipartisan HBCU Caucus was established to serve as an advocate for HBCUs on Capitol Hill. In September 2017 there were 62 elected federal lawmakers who were members of the caucus.

The *Schuette* case

The greatest victory against affirmative action to date has come in *Schuette v. Coalition to Defend Affirmative Action*, 572 US 291 (2014), in which the US Supreme Court by a plurality upheld a Michigan initiative supported by 58% of voters, which amended the state constitution by banning affirmative action "in the operation of public employment, public education, or public contracting (with the exception of actions mandated by federal law or where federal funding is needed)." The plurality opinion was written by Justice Anthony Kennedy, joined by Chief Justice Roberts and Justice Alito, and with the concurrence of Justices Scalia and Thomas. The opinion is somewhat puzzling, because, as Kennedy stressed, the ruling was "not about the constitutionality, or the merits, of race-conscious admissions policies in higher education. ... The question here concerns not the permissibility of race-conscious admissions policies under the Constitution but whether, and in what manner, voters in the States may choose to prohibit the consideration of racial preferences in governmental decisions, in particular with respect to school admissions." He concluded: "This case is not about how the debate about racial preferences should be resolved. It is about who may resolve it. There is no authority in the Constitution of the United States or in this Court's precedents for the Judiciary to set aside Michigan laws that commit this policy determination to the voters." For "Michigan laws" one may read "the laws of any state", as there is nothing in this decision that is not equally applicable to any other state. Justices Scalia and Thomas in their concurring opinion were more hard-hitting, reiterating Justice Harlan's oft-quoted dissenting opinion in *Plessy v. Ferguson* (1896): "Our Constitution is color-blind, and neither knows nor tolerates classes among citizens."

Schuette: **Three Principles**

The ruling in *Schuette* therefore combines three fundamental principles: the ideal of a color-blind Constitution, the right of every state to pursue that ideal, and the democratic right of the citizens of every state to implement it.

After *Schuette*, opponents of affirmative action lost no time in calling on other states to follow Michigan's example by banning affirmative action. None have done so, although seven states besides Michigan had already banned affirmative action. Florida's ban, which has been in place since 1999, was enacted not by popular vote but by an executive order of Governor Jeb Bush. It covers affirmative action not only in admissions to public universities but also in state hiring and contracting. Race-based university admissions have been replaced with the "talented twenty program", which grants automatic admission to students in the top 20% of their graduating high school class. The order has also increased financial aid to college students in need. Would this eminently fair order pass muster under the *Schuette* test if it were to face a challenge in the US Supreme Court? Almost certainly, yes.

Schuette a Blip

The *Schuette* decision allowing states to ban affirmative action is really a blip. It occurred only because a state had already taken the bull by the horns by banning affirmative action. Anthony Kennedy, the swing vote on the Court, wrote the winning opinions in both *Schuette* and *Fisher II*—the former allowing a ban on affirmative action and the latter upholding affirmative action. But this is not as ironic as it may seem. For, in allowing the ban *Schuette* was not passing judgment on the desirability or even the constitutionality of affirmative action, only on the legality and constitutionality of a state's democratic decision to ban it.

The *Schuette* solution remains open to the 42 states that have not yet availed themselves of it. But, unless or until they do embrace the safe haven of *Schuette,* those states are still subject to the vagaries of the law on affirmative action. It cannot be emphasized enough that a state that does not opt for the protection of *Schuette* is likely to find itself in the choppy and treacherous seas of the *Bakke-Grutter-Fisher* succession of cases.

Racial Discrimination & Affirmative Action: Conclusion

Running right through all the cases that we have considered, from *Brown* to *Fisher II,* is the Equal Protection Clause of the Fourteenth Amendment, reading: "nor shall any State ... deny to any person within its jurisdiction the equal protection of the laws." When *Brown v. Board of Education* first came before the US Supreme Court in 1953, the justices were far from united on whether racially segregated public schools violated the Equal Protection Clause. While four members of the court were minded to overrule the "separate but equal" standard in *Plessy v. Ferguson*, Tom Clark wrote, "we had led the states on to think segregation is OK and we should let them work it out;" Stanley Reed actually believed that segregation benefited the African-American; while Chief Justice Vinson noted that Congress had never enacted any desegregation legislation. Even Felix Frankfurter and Robert H. Jackson, who disapproved of segregation, were also committed to judicial restraint. [Sunstein, Cass R. (2004).]

But then Vinson died unexpectedly, which Felix Frankfurter reputedly greeted with delight as the only evidence he had ever had for the existence of God. The new Chief Justice, Earl Warren, made it his business to unite the Court's support behind a unanimous opinion written by himself, which, while citing very little law, rested squarely on the Equal Protection Clause.

But was that a correct interpretation of that Clause? The Fourteenth Amendment came into existence in a particularly turbulent period of American history. A long and bloody civil war had just ended and there was a major rift between Lincoln's successor, Andrew Johnson, a Tennessee Democrat, and the Republican-controlled Congress. In 1865 Congress passed what would become the Civil Rights Act of 1866 guaranteeing citizenship to all regardless of race, color or previous condition of slavery. President Andrew Johnson vetoed it on the ground that it gave citizenship to the former slaves at a time when 11 of the 36 states were still unrepresented in Congress and that it discriminated in favor of these freedmen and against whites. The President's veto was soon overridden by Congress and the Civil Rights Act became law. But the Republican Congress felt the need for an ironclad guarantee and so incorporated the provisions of the Civil Rights Act, plus more, in a proposed amendment to the Constitution, which would become the Fourteenth Amendment, ratified in 1868. Here is how Representative James F. Wilson, a "Radical" Republican, introduced the Civil Rights Act in the House of Representatives:

"It provides for the equality of citizens of the United States in the enjoyment of "civil rights and immunities." What do these terms mean? Do they mean that in all things civil, social, political, all citizens, without distinction of race or color, shall be equal? By no means can they be so construed. ....Nor do they mean that all citizens shall sit on the juries, or that their children shall attend the same schools." [Congressional Globe, House of Representatives, 39th Congress, 1st Session., p. 117 (March 1, 1866).]

This specific denial about schooling is interesting, especially coming from a "Radical" Republican as it does.

In a hard-hitting attack on *Brown v. Board of Education* titled "Usurpation by the Court," James F. Byrnes, who had himself served as an Associate Justice of the Supreme Court from 1941 to 1942 and would later become US Secretary of State and Governor of South Carolina, wrote: "The Court did not interpret the Constitution—the Court amended it." [Byrnes, James F. (1956). "The Court must be curbed," *United States News & World Report.*] Byrnes's point was, of course, that the Court had not only overruled its own 1896 decision in *Plessy v. Ferguson* and invalidated numerous state laws but had also essentially rewritten the Equal Protection Clause—something that could only be done by the elaborate process of constitutional amendment as laid down in Article V of the Constitution.

It was precisely the fear of overstepping the mark in this way that made Justices Felix Frankfurter and Robert H. Jackson initially hesitate to support *Brown.* So, is *Brown* an example of judicial activism? Probably, though Earl Warren was undoubtedly correct in asserting that "in the field of public education the doctrine of 'separate but equal' has no place. Separate educational facilities are inherently unequal."

Citizens United v. FEC

Brown was the first of a long list of "liberal" activist decisions taken by the Warren Court. This was why President Eisenhower, who had appointed Earl Warren as Chief Justice, reputedly remarked that that appointment was "the biggest damned-fool mistake I ever made." But, as mentioned above, judicial activism is not confined to "liberals."

One of the most important cases decided by the US Supreme Court by a "conservative" majority was *Citizens United v. Federal Election Commission*, 558 US 310 (2010). This highly controversial case is important for two reason: first, because of its effect on elections, and secondly, because it struck down a major bipartisan Act of Congress, which had been essentially upheld by the Supreme Court itself.

The conservative non-profit organization Citizens United wanted to run TV commercials to promote its film *Hillary: The Movie* in the run-up to the 2008 Democratic presidential primaries. This would have been illegal under the Bipartisan Campaign Reform Act, generally known as the McCain-Feingold Act of 2002, which prohibited the broadcast of "electioneering communications" paid for by corporations in the 30 days before a presidential primary and in the 60 days before a general election.

In the Supreme Court, Justice Kennedy wrote the majority opinion in favor of Citizens United, striking down the prohibition in McCain-Feingold of independent expenditure by corporations and labor unions as a violation of the First Amendment's protection of free speech. Kennedy wrote: "If the First Amendment has any force, it prohibits Congress from fining or jailing citizens, or associations of citizens, for simply engaging in political speech." The majority opinion also overruled provisions in earlier Supreme Court decisions which allowed restrictions on corporate spending on election campaigns, including *Austin v. Michigan Chamber of Commerce*,494 US 652 (1990) and *McConnell v. FEC*, 540 US 93 (2003).

In a strong dissenting opinion, Justice John Paul Stevens, joined by liberal Justices Ginsburg, Breyer, and Sotomayor, argued that the majority ruling "threatens to undermine the integrity of elected institutions across the Nation. ... A democracy cannot function effectively when its constituent members believe laws are being bought and sold." He concluded: "While American democracy is imperfect, few outside the majority of this Court would have thought its laws included a dearth of corporate money in politics." This ties in with Senator McCain's remark in his 2002 book with the curious title *Worth the Fighting For*: "Money does buy access in Washington, and access increases influence that often results in benefiting the few at the expense of the many."

The most worrying perceived result of the Citizens United decision was the rise of "super PACs," or "political action committees," which do not themselves contribute to political candidates or parties but can accept unlimited contributions from individuals, corporations, and labor unions. In fact, it was the decision by the US Court of Appeals for the District of Columbia in *SpeechNOW.org v. FEC*, 599 F.3d 686 (DC Cir 2010) that allowed the creation of super PACs. In a 9–0 decision, the DC Circuit Court held that on the basis of *Citizens United*, a non-profit like SpeechNOW, which itself made only "independent expenditures," could not be subject to any contribution limits. "Independent expenditure" means money spent advocating for the election of a particular candidate but without consultation, cooperation, or any "material" involvement with that candidate.

Citizens United also means that the laws of 24 states prohibiting or limiting "independent expenditures" by corporations and labor unions are under threat. And in *McCutcheon v. FEC*, 572 US 185 (2014), the US Supreme Court swept away the previous prohibition on individuals contributing more than $48,600 combined to all federal candidates and more than $74,600 combined to all parties and super PACs. But an individual's contributions to an individual politician's campaign are still capped at $2,700 per election. In the words of Chief Justice Roberts, for the majority: "The government may no more restrict how many candidates or causes a donor may support than it may tell a newspaper how many candidates it may endorse." Justice Breyer, writing for the dissenting minority, argued that the decision "creates a loophole that will allow a single individual to contribute millions of dollars to a political party or to a candidate's campaign." Whoever is right, election campaigns are now more awash with money than ever before.

The whole new approach to campaign finance rests on the definition of contributions to political campaigns as protected speech under the First Amendment. Though Chief Justice Roberts was one of the protagonists of this approach, he was also concerned about the way *Citizens United* struck down much of the McCain-Feingold Act and overruled some recent Supreme Court decisions to boot—in contradiction of Roberts's stated commitment to judicial restraint and *stare decisis*, or fidelity to precedent. So the Chief Justice, joined by Justice Alito, wrote a separate concurrence to address this important problem. "There is a difference between judicial restraint and judicial abdication," wrote Roberts. He quoted Justice Oliver Wendell Holmes, Jr., in remarking that "Judging the constitutionality of an Act of Congress is the gravest and most delicate duty that this Court is called upon to perform." But he did not really justify the complete redefinition of "political speech" in *Citizens United*. His justification of the majority's departure from precedent was more persuasive. If stare decisis were an "inexorable command," he explained, "segregation would be legal, minimum wage laws would be unconstitutional, and the Government could wiretap ordinary criminal suspects without first obtaining warrants."

The meaning of "the"

How would James Madison, the drafter of the First Amendment, feel about *Citizens United's* extended definition of freedom of speech? It is important to realize that the Amendment does not purport to be according Americans any more freedom of speech than they already enjoyed. This is revealed by the key word "the": "Congress shall make no law....prohibiting *the* freedom of speech, or of the press." (Emphasis added). In 1791, when the Bill of Rights including the First Amendment was adopted, a good deal of freedom of speech was already enjoyed under English common law. So, what the Amendment is doing is merely protecting that right against encroachment. It does not prevent the scope of freedom of speech from being expanded, but it also does not protect any such expansion. That at least is my take on freedom of speech. If that is right, then the definition of "protected speech" adopted by the majority in *Citizens United* is *not* actually protected by the First Amendment but is legislation from the bench in a direction which, for the reasons mentioned by the dissenting minority, should probably not have occurred.

Expressive Flag-Burning

The same applies, in my opinion, to the extension of the definition of protected speech to flag-burning in *Texas v. Johnson*, 491 US 397 (1989) and *US v. Eichman*, 496 US 310 (1990). The *Johnson* case arose out of a political demonstration at the 1984 Republican National Convention in Dallas, during which "Joey" Johnson, a self-described revolutionary communist, poured kerosene on the American flag stolen from a flagpole and set it alight while other demonstrators shouted anti-American slogans. Johnson was convicted under a Texas law, but his conviction was quashed by the Texas Court of Criminal Appeals on the ground that flag-burning was protected by the First

Amendment as symbolic speech and did not cause or threaten a breach of the peace. The state of Texas took the case to the US Supreme Court, where there was an unusual line-up, with a majority made up of a combination of liberals and conservatives. The majority held that Johnson's burning of the flag "constituted expressive conduct, permitting him to invoke the First Amendment." In a concurring opinion, Justice Kennedy wrote: "[W]e are presented with a clear and simple statute to be judged against a pure command of the Constitution...The hard fact is that sometimes we must make decisions we do not like." He concluded: "It is poignant but fundamental that the flag protects those who hold it in contempt."

Chief Justice Rehnquist stressed that "The flag is not simply another 'idea' or 'point of view' competing for recognition in the marketplace of ideas."

Justice Stevens, generally considered a liberal, put in a spirited dissent. He made the emphatic point that "The statutory prohibition of flag desecration does not prescribe what shall be orthodox in politics, nationalism, religion, or other matters of opinion. ... The Court is therefore quite wrong in blandly asserting that respondent (Johnson) 'was prosecuted for his expression of dissatisfaction with the policies of this country. Respondent was prosecuted because of the method he chose to express his dissatisfaction with those policies. Had he chosen to spray paint ... his message of dissatisfaction on the façade of the Lincoln Memorial, there would be no question about the power of the Government to prohibit his means of expression."

The decision in *Johnson* struck down laws in force in 48 of the 50 states and evidence from public opinion polls show a majority against the legalization of flag-burning. In response to the Supreme Court's ruling in *Johnson*, in 1989 Congress passed the Flag Protection Act (an amended version of the Flag Protection Act of 1968), which provides for a fine or imprisonment for not more than a year for burning or otherwise defacing the flag. However, the Act was struck down by the US Supreme Court in *US v. Eichman* (1990).

In *Eichman* there was the same line-up of justices as in Johnson. Justice Brennan with his motley band of supporters simply insisted that the Flag Protection Act was invalidated by the First Amendment. Justice Stevens' dissent was even feistier than before: "The Court's opinion ends where proper analysis of the issue should begin. Of course 'the Government may not prohibit the expression of an idea simply because society finds the idea itself offensive or disagreeable.' None of us disagrees with that proposition. But it is equally well settled that certain methods of expression may be prohibited…"

What is the state of the law now? The only way to overturn *Johnson* and *Eichman* would be by means of a constitutional amendment. A Flag Desecration Amendment has passed the House of Representatives on several occasions, but it has never garnered enough votes in the Senate to be sent to the states for ratification.

In the meantime, in June 2019, Joey Johnson received a settlement of $225,000 from the City of Cleveland for being arrested in violation of his First Amendment rights. [www.cleveland.com.]

An aspect of the flag-burning cases that has never received any attention is that burning the national flag is not an appropriate way of showing hostility to the President of the day, because it insults the United States as a nation. And the same applies to "taking a knee" during the playing of the national anthem. For more on this see Chapter 17, "A Parade of Paradoxes."

Umpires or Empire Builders?
Roundup

In our wide-ranging trawl we have encountered a certain amount of judicial activism on both sides of the Atlantic. In the US this is largely confined to federal courts, and in particular, the US Supreme Court, whereas in England it is more general.

Ironically, perhaps, belief in judicial self-restraint and deference to the other branches of government is much more prevalent in America than in England. The title of this section comes from a much-quoted remark made by US Chief Justice John Roberts during his confirmation hearings in 2005, claiming that judges, like umpires in baseball, "don't make the rules; they apply them." It could easily be dismissed as mere pretence, posturing or dissimulation—and Roberts has sometimes been accused of indulging in judicial activism in certain of his opinions. But the very fact that John Roberts felt the need to parade such strong judicial restraint credentials at his confirmation hearing shows his recognition of the importance attached to that by his interlocutors in the senate and the wider American public. It echoed commitments made by President George W. Bush, who promised to appoint judges who "will strictly apply the Constitution and laws, not legislate from the bench." And: "Every judge I appoint will be a person who clearly understands the role of a judge is to interpret the law, not to legislate from the bench. [Peabody, Bruce G. (2007), p. 193.]

"Jus dicere, non jus dare"

Although Roberts's declaration was painted in such memorably vivid and colorful tones, it does not differ materially from statements made by many other Supreme Court nominees, including some who would generally be characterized as "liberal." Here for example is an extract from the opening statement made by Elena Kagan at her confirmation hearing for the US Supreme Court before the Senate Judiciary Committee

[June 28–July 1, 2010–Serial No. J-111-98.] Not only is Justice Kagan a member of the "liberal" wing of the court, but the president by whom she was nominated was a Democrat, and the Senate by which she was confirmed was under Democratic Party control. Yet her statement stresses the "conservative" values of respect for precedent and judicial restraint:

> "Respect for precedent and judicial restraint more generally are necessary for the reason ... that the courts themselves have not been elected by anybody. There is no political accountability from the American citizenry. And there are precious few ways in which the legislature and the President can or should interfere with their function. They ought to be independent. But that places on them a responsibility which is also to be restrained."

Why are the same values of respect for precedent and judicial restraint not expressed by English judges? Respect for parliamentary sovereignty, the bedrock principle of the UK Constitution, should be enough to deter the judiciary from "legislating from the bench." As long ago as 1625 Lord Chancellor Francis Bacon left this matter in no doubt: "Judges ought to remember, that their office is *jus dicere*, and not *jus dare*; to interpret the law, and not to make law, or give law." [Bacon, Francis (1625). *Essays Civil & Moral.* [See Chapter 1 on The Sovereignty of Parliament.]

Yet, what we find in England is the exact opposite. Here for example is Lord Woolf threatening in 1995 to retaliate if Parliament enacted an "unthinkable" law. The courts, he said, would be very reluctant to declare any Act of Parliament invalid, but then went on: "However, if Parliament did the unthinkable, then I would say that the courts would also be required to act in a manner which would be without precedent. ... Ultimately there are even limits on the supremacy of Parliament, which it is the courts' inalienable responsibility to identify and uphold. They are limits of the most modest dimensions, which I believe any democrat would accept. They are no more than are necessary to enable the rule of law to be preserved." [Woolf, Harry (1995). *Public Law* p. 68f.]

What exactly did Woolf mean by an "unthinkable" Act of Parliament? Chiefly, it seems, an Act removing or reducing the courts' power of judicial review.

In a speech given to the Administrative Law Bar Association in 1995, Lord of Lairg (Lord Chancellor 1997–2003) tore into Lord Woolf's exorbitant claims together with similar claims made by two High Court judges, stressing that there was a "Constitutional imperative of judicial self-restraint," for which he gave three reasons, the most important of which being "the democratic imperative," under which judges, who are unelected, unaccountable and cannot be dismissed, must respect the democratic mandate of the other two branches of government. [Irvine, Derry (1996).]

Lord Irvine was simply reasserting the classic constitutional position as set out by Lord Reid in *Madzimbamuto v. Lardner-Burke* [1969] 1 AC 645 at 723: "It is often said that it would be unconstitutional for the United Kingdom Parliament to do certain things, meaning that the moral, political and other reasons against doing them are so strong that most people would regard it as highly improper if Parliament did these things. But that does not mean that it is beyond the power of Parliament to do such things. If Parliament chose to do any of them the courts would not hold the Act of Parliament invalid."

Lord Neuberger has repeatedly stressed the centrality of parliamentary sovereignty, yet has no compunction in congratulating the English judiciary on the exponential growth of judicial review, without however citing any decided cases or the benefits supposedly flowing from them. [See Chapter 8 on "The constitutional imperative of judicial self-restraint."]

The Ghosts of *Wednesbury*

The history of English judicial review, human rights law and public law generally is a history of judicial activism, without any legal justification. In the *GCHQ* case in 1984 and in *M v. Home Office* in 1992, as we have seen, the English judiciary simply arrogated to itself greatly expanded powers, riding roughshod over the government and Parliament alike. The expansion of human rights law since the coming into force of the Human Rights Act in 2000 is often attributed to the European Court of Human Rights (the Strasbourg Court). That court has indeed greatly expanded the scope of a number of Articles of the ECHR. But there was no need for the English courts simply to follow suit. That they so often did so was the result of a mistaken interpretation of §2(1) of the Human Rights Act, which only requires the UK courts to take Strasbourg decisions "into account," not to follow them slavishly, as Lord Bingham *in R (Ullah) v. Special Adjudicator* [2004] 2 AC 323 wrongly enjoined them to do. Lord Irvine, the architect of the Human Rights Act, has strongly condemned this "mirror principle," as he called it. [Irvine, Derry (2011). "A British Interpretation of Convention Rights," Bingham Centre for the Rule of Law.]

Why should it matter whether the judges act with judicial self-restraint or whether they strike out on their own? This appears to be Lord Neuberger's position: judge-made law is to be judged by its results. The trouble is that on the whole its results are not good—except for the special interest groups who tend to benefit from it, including gays, transgender people, racial minorities, asylum seekers, illegal immigrants, terrorist suspects and even convicted killers. The mass of ordinary law-abiding citizens are not only not beneficiaries of the system but are quite likely to be victims, because the rights of the special interest groups are not just rights but special privileges, which detract from the rights of the law-abiding majority.

From *Brown* to *Schuette*

Is American judicial review and civil rights law any better than its British counterpart? *Brown v. Board of Education I* and *II*, together with Lyndon Johnson's Civil Rights Act of 1964 and Voting Rights Act of 1965, did not succeed in achieving their goals. So resort was had to mandatory busing and affirmative action, which, contrary to its declared objective of equal rights, actually accords special privileges to groups perceived as discriminated against. But privilege is itself a form of discrimination. Fortunately, this was recognized by the US Supreme Court, which since *Bakke* in 1978 has set its face against quotas, which are just another form of privilege. And in *Schuette* (2014) it allowed individual states to ban affirmative action in public education.

Illegal Immigrants' Rights

An important area of judicial activism on the part of the US Supreme Court is immigration. In a 5–4 decision in *Plyler v. Doe,* 457 US 202 (1982) the Court ruled that the term "person" in the equal protection clause of the Fourteenth Amendment extended to include illegal aliens, thus giving them the right to free public education. [See Levin, Mark R. (2006), chapter 7.] In so doing, the majority, under the leadership of Justice Brennan, struck down a state statute and widened the scope of the equal protection clause. The majority rejected the claim by Texas officials that illegal aliens were not "within the jurisdiction" of the state and holding that "no plausible distinction with respect to the Fourteenth Amendment" could be drawn between lawful and unlawful immigrants. Surprisingly, perhaps, the dissenting minority agreed that illegal immigrants are indeed physically "within the jurisdiction" of the state, but claimed somewhat lamely that the distinction drawn by the Texas law between legal and illegal immigrants should nevertheless be upheld. The ruling in *Plyler* has in practice been restricted to K–12 schooling (i.e. from kindergarten to 12th grade.) This decision looks like a "liberal" vs. "conservative" one, but the majority did have some valid arguments for their ruling. The real problem with the Fourteenth Amendment is that, produced as it was by "B-Team" draftsmen—compared to James Madison and the Framers of the original parts of the Constitution and the Bill of Rights—its wording is less than pellucid. But there are sufficient constitutional and logical underpinnings in the *Plyler* ruling to acquit it of being a purely arbitrary decision—unlike some UK decisions.

Two contrasting models

The English courts, as we have seen, have paid scant attention to their constitutional duty of self-restraint. In *GCHQ* the Court gave the judiciary greatly expanded powers over the government—which was simply judge-made law flying in the face of parliamentary sovereignty. And in *M. v. Home Office* they just flouted a direct prohibition of the Crown Proceedings Act 1947, which of course they had no right to invalidate. Then, in regard to human rights, they have all too often misinterpreted the ECHR to the benefit of the special interest groups identified above.

The US Supreme Court has over the years struck down numerous Acts of Congress as unconstitutional, but they do have the right to do so in accordance with *Marbury v. Madison,* because, though that case was probably wrongly decided, it has never been overruled and probably never will be. This is very different from the way the House of Lords simply ignored the Crown Proceedings Act.

In the US, as in the English courts, there is a good deal of disagreement among the judges. But in England, as we saw in regard to "irrationality" and also in regard to the misinterpretation of Article 1, ECHR, there tends to be a great deal of arbitrary flailing around without any legal or logical underpinning. In the US, on the other hand, such disagreements and even errors are never arbitrary.

A good example is the meaning of "freedom of speech" in the First Amendment. In an interview, Justice Scalia admitted that if he were king he would have no compunction in throwing flag-burners into prison. Yet he joined the liberal Justice Brennan's majority opinion in both *Johnson* and *Eichman* holding that flag burning was protected speech under the First Amendment. But he also had no trouble finding, with Anthony Kennedy in *Citizens United*, that the First Amendment threw open the floodgates to "political speech" in the form of campaign donations—and in the process striking down the McCain-Feingold Act as unconstitutional and overruling a couple of Supreme Court decisions into the bargain. Both the flag-burning cases and *Citizens United* were probably wrongly decided. The definition of "political speech" adopted by *Citizens United* is just too broad and has made elections a saleable commodity. As for flag burning, is it really imaginable that the Framers of the Constitution would have encompassed that activity within "protected speech"? Moreover, if you do not happen to like the government of the day, you are obviously entitled to express your opposition. But burning the national flag is a rejection not just of the government of the day but of the state, the United States of America, which is a very different thing from "political speech." Finally, there is the question of the word "the." The First Amendment does not confer any new rights: it prohibits Congress from making any law "abridging (i.e. reducing) the freedom of speech" that already existed—which most certainly did not include flag burning. How come Scalia as an originalist and textualist did not realize this? His alignment with the "liberals" in the flag burning cases is obviously not attributable to his political conservatism, but to a genuine error born out of an unduly pedantic reading of the text of the Constitution.

10

PRIVACY
A STRANGE ROYAL CASE
AND AN UNCOMMONLY SILLY LAW

What is a court to do when faced with an unprecedented but meritorious claim? In the famous case of *Donoghue v. Stevenson*, the choice was between applying the settled principles of the law (as Lords Buckmaster and Tomlin urged) and creating a whole new "principle"—as of course was done by Lord Atkin, resulting in the state of disarray in which English tort law still languishes today. [See Chapter 6, "United Kingdom: The Snail in the Bottle."]

Privacy is another area which placed the law of both England and America in a quandary. In the absence of an existing "breach of privacy" cause of action, the obvious solution was legislation. However, the UK Parliament has steadfastly refused to respond to earnest judicial entreaties to enact the necessary legislation. There has been an attempt to fill the resulting vacuum by extending a very different cause of action, namely that of "breach of confidence," while at the same time extending the scope of Article 8 of the European Convention on Human Rights (ECHR), the "right to respect for private and family life." Neither of these extensions, either separately or together, succeeds in filling the vacuum created by the lack of an actual "breach of privacy" cause of action. As a result, there is still no real protection of privacy under English law.

The American position is quite different. There is protection of privacy under the US Constitution plus a good deal of state legislation, not to mention the authoritative Restatement (Second) of Torts § 652.

A Strange Royal Case

The story on both sides of the Atlantic begins with the same strange case, but with very different results! The case is called *Prince Albert v. Strange* (1849) 41 ER 1171, 47 ER 1302. Prince Albert, Queen Victoria's husband, made etchings of a number of his drawings, including portraits of their favorite dogs. A set of 63 prints made from the etchings got into the hands of a journalist, who, intending to put them on show, produced a descriptive catalogue of them, copies of which he stupidly sent to the royal couple. This only spurred Prince Albert into action, who went to court to obtain an injunction to prohibit the exhibition or publication of the etchings. Not surprisingly, perhaps, the Prince succeeded, both at first instance and on appeal before the Lord Chancellor, Lord Cottenham, who declared that "privacy is the right invaded"—separate from and additional to any property rights that the Prince might have had in the etchings.

"A Gross Intrusion"

In January 1990 Gorden Kaye, a well-known British television actor, was driving along in London during a gale when a piece of wood that had become dislodged from an advertisement hoarding smashed through his car's windshield and hit him on the head, causing severe injuries to his head and brain. After surgery, he spent three days on a life support machine and a further six days in intensive care. He was recuperating in a private ward in the hospital when a reporter and a photographer from the *Sunday Sport* (a light-hearted tabloid newspaper), dressed as medical staff, suddenly burst in and proceeded to interview and photograph him. He was in no fit state to be interviewed or to give informed consent to be interviewed, and his head was swathed in bandages.

Gorden Kaye's lawyers initially obtained a court injunction preventing the paper from publishing the material, but on appeal this decision was reversed by the Court of Appeal, so that the paper was permitted to publish the purported interview and the pictures, with the minor proviso that they were prohibited from giving the impression that Gorden Kaye had "voluntarily permitted" the newspaper to photograph or interview him. [*Gorden Kaye v. Drew Robertson* [1990] EWCA Civ. 21.]

All three judges in the Court of Appeal lamented the absence of legal protection of privacy under English law. Lord Justice Glidewell put it like this: "It is well known that in English law there is no right to privacy, and accordingly there is no right of action for breach of a person's privacy." He went on to implore Parliament to fill the void with legislation: "The facts of the present case are a graphic illustration of the desirability of Parliament considering whether and in what circumstances statutory provision can be made to protect the privacy of individuals."

Lord Justice Bingham (as he then was) sounded a slightly more optimistic note: "This case ... highlights, yet again, the failure of both the common law of England and statute to protect in an effective way the personal privacy of individual citizens. This has been the subject of much comment over the years. ... The problems of defining and limiting a tort of privacy are formidable, but the present case strengthens my hope that the review now in progress may prove fruitful." In fact, however, the "review" never bore any fruit.

Lord Justice Leggatt contrasted the position in England unfavorably with that obtaining in the United States. He identified the need for a right to privacy as a necessary counterblast to abuse of freedom of the press: "We do not need a

First Amendment to preserve the freedom of the press, but the abuse of that freedom can be ensured only by the legislature. Especially since there is available in the United States a wealth of experience of the enforcement of this right both at common law and also under statute, it is to be hoped that the making good of this signal shortcoming in our law will not be long delayed." The appeal to Parliament fell on deaf ears, and the pious hopes expressed by the three Court of Appeal judges have still not been realized thirty years later.

"Gross intrusion"

David Eady, a leading libel barrister who was later to become the so-called "privacy law judge," was shocked by the outcome of Gorden Kaye's case, in which he was not involved. He believed, as he put it, that there was "a serious gap in the jurisprudence of any civilized society, if such a gross intrusion could happen without redress."

Parliament's dereliction of duty in regard to privacy rights, particularly after being implored by the judges to act, is serious but not unique. The vacuum left by Parliament's inaction cried out to be filled by judge-made law—which only led, as it so often does, to greater confusion than ever, as we shall see.

The Court of Appeal in the *Gorden Kaye* case resisted the temptation to legislate from the bench, though there were some precedents that could have been used to fill the gap much more neatly than in the way it has actually been done. Had the Court of Appeal judges in Gorden Kaye's case been aware of *Prince Albert v. Strange*, would they have used it as a precedent for giving the beleaguered and beloved television star some well-deserved legal relief? It is hard to say. It is possible that the Prince's case may not have been found to be strictly in point— and there is little doubt that that decision itself was judge-made law without any proper underpinnings. So the Court of Appeal's caution coupled with a call for legislation was probably the right decision in the circumstances.

"A license coupled with a grant"

A decision that could have been prayed in aid but was not referred to in the *Kaye* case was *Hurst v. Picture Theatres Ltd* [1915] 1 KB 1. This case involved the ejection of a paying customer from a cinema seat. Having bought his ticket and duly taken his seat in the cinema, Mr. Hurst was approached by the manager, who was under the impression that Hurst had sneaked in without payment, and was told to leave, which he did. His claim for trespass to the person succeeded in a jury trial at first instance, which was affirmed by the Court of Appeal. The somewhat surprising basis of the decision was that Mr. Hurst's ticket gave him an interest in the real estate occupied by his cinema seat. The nature of this interest was "a licence coupled with a grant," which in law was irrevocable, at least for the duration of the show! This rather quirky decision has never been overruled and could easily have been applied to the *Kaye* case. For, if Hurst had an irrevocable interest in a theater seat, then *Gorden Kaye* must, *a fortiori*, have had a similar interest in his private room in the hospital, although this interest may have depended on whether he was a private fee-paying patient or whether he was being treated free of charge under the National Health Service. As the *Hurst* ruling was evidently not cited in *Kaye*, this question did not arise.

Falling Between Two Stools

The high-profile case of *Douglas v. Hello!* [2001] 2 All ER 289 is a good example of the way English law has tried to grapple with the lack of privacy protection. When Michael Douglas and Catherine Zeta-Jones tied the knot at the Plaza Hotel in New York in November 2000 they had already sold the exclusive rights to photograph their wedding to *OK!* Magazine for a fee of £1 million. Elaborate precautions were taken to protect *OK!'s* exclusive deal, including a ban on all cameras and recording devices at the reception. Despite this, *OK!'s* bitter rivals, *Hello!* magazine managed to get hold of pictures of the reception. Douglas and Zeta-Jones went to court to stop publication of these "unauthorized" pictures. Lord Justice Sedley in the Court of Appeal went so far as to suggest that "we have reached a point at which it can be said with confidence that the law recognizes and will appropriately protect a right of personal privacy." Sedley LJ also expressed the view that ECHR Article 8—and, balancing it, section 12 of the Human Rights Act—could be expanded to have horizontal effect, meaning that it could be used by one individual against another and not just by an individual against a public authority. The view that Article 8 now encompassed protection of privacy was not yet shared in the judiciary.

When the case went to trial, the judge, Lindsay J, gave a negative response to Sedley LJ's opinion, saying: "I am invited to hold that there is an existing law of privacy under which the claimants are entitled to relief. I decline that invitation for five reasons." The chief reason given was that the Douglases were adequately protected by "the law of confidence." However, Lindsay J. did at least recognize that, as he put it: "a judge should ... be chary of doing that which is better done by Parliament. That Parliament has failed so far to grasp the nettle does not prove that it will not have to be grasped in the future. A glance at a crystal ball of, so to speak, only a low wattage suggests that, if Parliament does not act soon, the less satisfactory course, of the Courts creating the law bit by bit at the expense of litigants and with inevitable delays and uncertainty, will be thrust upon the judiciary. But that will only happen when a case arises in which the existing law of confidence gives no or inadequate protection.; this case now before me is not such a case and there is therefore no need for me to attempt to construct a law of privacy and, that being so, it would be wrong of me to attempt to do so." Lindsay J.'s conclusion, therefore, was that Hello! magazine was liable to the Douglases and also to OK! Magazine "under the law as to confidence." [*Douglas v. Hello!* [2003] EWHC 786 (Ch).]

This decision was reversed by the Court of Appeal and then reversed back again—yo-yo like—by a 3:2 majority in the House of Lords. [*OBG v. Allan* [2007] UKHL 21] The majority agreed with Lindsay J and restored his finding of a breach of confidence by *Hello!*. Lord Hoffmann put it this way: "The photographer who took the 'unauthorized' pictures was subject to an obligation of confidence in respect of the pictures which he took. *Hello!* ... were subject to the same obligation." Really? How could the freelance photographer or *Hello!* have been bound by a confidentiality agreement to which they were not parties?

The leading case of the common law of breach of confidence is *Coco v. A.N. Clark* (*Engineers*) *Ltd* [1969] RPC 41, in which the judgment was delivered by Sir Robert Megarry, one of the most distinguished judges of the twentieth century.

The plaintiff designed a two-stroke engine for a moped and sought the cooperation of the defendant company in its manufacture. However, after Coco had disclosed all the details of his design and proposals for its manufacture, the parties fell out and the defendants manufactured their own engine based on a design closely resembling Coco's. The defendants denied that any confidential information had been supplied to them by Coco or used by them in their engine. In *Coco v. Clark* itself therefore no breach of confidence was found. Megarry J. identified the three essential ingredients of this cause of action:

    (a) "The information itself must have the necessary quality of confidence about it.

    (b) Secondly, that information must have been imparted in circumstances importing an obligation of confidence.

    (c) Thirdly, there must be an unauthorized use of that information to the detriment of the party communicating it."

Lindsay J. found all three conditions satisfied. The wedding photographs themselves supposedly constituted the confidential "information." But which wedding photographs? Hello! did not steal OK!'s pictures. The photographs that they published were different pictures altogether, purchased, as they claimed (without any proof to the contrary), from freelance paparazzi not commissioned by themselves. The second criterion is even more problematical. Because, in what sense could the "confidential information" be said to have been "imparted" to *Hello!* "in circumstances importing an obligation of confidence"? Hello! had no relationship with either the Douglases or OK!, and nothing was ever "imparted" to them by the Claimants in any circumstances whatsoever. As for the third criterion, although Hello!'s publication of their own wedding pictures undoubtedly caused OK! to suffer a loss, this was not through use of the "confidential information."

In *Douglas v. Hello!* it would be hard to find any of the three elements. There was no relationship or indeed contact of any kind between the parties; no confidential information was imparted by the Claimants to the Defendant, *Hello!* magazine; and *Hello!* made no use of any information obtained from either Douglas and Zeta-Jones or from *OK!* Did *Hello!* know that the Douglases had given an exclusive contract to their arch-rival magazine? Undoubtedly, but this was not information used by *Hello!* to compete with OK! Magazine. *Hello!* magazine used different photographs from the ones taken by OK! All that *Hello!* could really be said to have done wrong was to have trespassed on a wedding reception to which neither they nor the freelance photographer from whom they had bought their pictures had been invited. Trying to classify this case as one of breach of confidence is simply a stretch too far and amounts to judge-made law.

This attempt to extend the concept of confidence or confidentiality simply will not stand up to scrutiny. For an actual breach of confidence case, as set out in *Coco*, there has to be an existing relationship between the parties prior to any alleged breach. The two dissenting judges in the House of Lords were clearly right. Lord Nicholls flatly rejected OK!'s claim of confidentiality:

> "OK's claim is that Hello committed a breach of confidence by publishing a confidential secret. ... So the first step is to identify the 'secret'. The secret information cannot lie in the differences between the unapproved photographs and the approved photographs. The secret cannot lie there, because the six unapproved photographs contained nothing not included in the approved photographs...The expression of the bride in one wedding photograph compared with her expression in another is insufficiently significant to call for legal protection. ... Accordingly, once the approved pictures were published, albeit simultaneously, publication of the unapproved pictures was not a breach of confidence. ... For these reasons I am unable to accept OK's claim based on confidentiality."

Lord Walker, agreeing with Lord Nicholls, summed up his logical position in these words: "My Lords, my respectful dissent from the views of the majority arises not from any distaste for the modern celebrity world but from my perception (shared, no doubt, by all of us) of the need for consistent and rational development in the law of confidentiality." [*OBG v. Allan* [2007] UKHL 21].

If judge-made law was needed, why not just cut the Gordian knot?—as suggested by Lord Justice Sedley: "The law no longer needs to construct an artificial relationship of confidentiality between intruder and victim: it can recognise privacy itself as a legal principle drawn from the fundamental value of personal autonomy." [*Douglas v. Hello!* [2001] 2 WLR 992 (Court of Appeal).]

As we have seen, Sir John Lindsay, the first instance judge in *Douglas v. Hello!*, refused to accept this invitation. But he accepted the law of confidence as a protection of privacy, apparently without realizing just how artificial it was when used in that way, as in *Douglas v. Hello!* itself. At the same time he was optimistic that Parliament would grasp the nettle of providing a statutory remedy for breach of privacy. He cited the European Court of Human Rights case of *Peck v. United Kingdom* as showing "that, in circumstances where the law of confidence did not operate, our domestic law has already been held to be inadequate. That inadequacy will have to be made good, and if Parliament does not step in, then the Courts will be obliged to."

Privacy in English law has fallen between two stools: breach of confidence on the one side and "respect for private life" under the European Convention of Human Rights on the other. Neither of these actually provides protection for privacy as such. To close the chasm between them, the courts have resorted to stretching both these remedies to breaking point, resulting in some very muddled, unjust and unpredictable decisions.

The Peck case is a good example of how stretching European human rights law to cover the privacy void is no more satisfactory than extending the scope of breach of confidence.

Privacy in a public place

Geoffrey Peck complained that his image, which was picked up on closed circuit television (CCTV), was widely disseminated by the media. Peck was filmed late one night holding a large knife in his hand in the center of Brentwood, a town in Essex, England, just after he had attempted to commit suicide by slashing his wrists. The CCTV operator, who worked for the local authority, called the police, who rushed to Peck's assistance, detained him briefly under the Mental Health Act 1983, and drove him home. In short, the presence of the CCTV camera and the efficient monitoring of the footage saved Geoffrey Peck's life. The problem began with press releases put out by Brentwood Borough Council to publicize the success of its CCTV system. Some of the footage was later broadcast on the BBC's Crimewatch program watched over 9 million viewers.

Peck's face was pixilated, but some of his friends and relations who saw the program claimed to be able to recognize him. After failing to obtain any relief under English law, he took his case to the European Court of Human Rights in Strasbourg, which unanimously found that the Article 8 "right to respect for his private life" had been infringed by Brentwood's disclosure of the CCTV footage. Geoffrey Peck freely admitted that the CCTV system may have saved his life. So what was the problem? It was, held the Strasbourg court, the disclosure of the CCTV record "to the public in a manner which he could never have foreseen which gave rise to such an interference." What particularly exercised the Strasbourg court was the fact that there was no effective remedy open to Geoffrey Peck under English law. [*Peck v. United Kingdom* (2003) 36 EHRR 41; [2003] ECHR 44.]

It is quite a stretch to suggest that publication of a photographic image of somebody in a public place can violate that person's "right to respect for his private life." The *Peck* problem would not have arisen in France or Germany, for example, both of which have precise legislation protecting privacy. So here is further evidence of the unsuitability of both types of law used in an attempt to bridge the yawning chasm where proper statutory privacy law should be.

"The Privacy Law Judge"

In the words of Lindsay J. in *Douglas v. Hello!*: "If Parliament does not step in, then the Courts will be obliged to." It had long been obvious that the possibility of legislation was a forlorn hope, and Lindsay J. ought to have recognized that his own approach to the issue of privacy was already an example of judge-made law.

But the "privacy law judge," as he was dubbed, *par excellence* was Mr. Justice David Eady, who was accused by the media of "creating a privacy law by the backdoor." What was particularly galling to newspaper editors was the fact that, prior to his elevation to the bench, Eady had been a leading libel barrister, mostly representing the "red-top" sensational tabloid press.

The background to his emergence as an activist creator of privacy law was the long continued press intrusion into the private lives even of ordinary citizens that was so prevalent and serious that in 1990 the British Home Office set up a "Committee on Privacy and Related Matters" under Sir David Calcutt, a prominent barrister and Master of Magdalene College, Cambridge. However, Calcutt's proposal of privacy legislation was blocked by the representatives of the press on the committee, which ended up instead just recommending the creation of a toothless and ill-fated voluntary body that came to be called the Press Complaints Commission (PCC). So frustrated was Calcutt himself by this outcome that he described the PCC as "a body set up by the industry, dominated by, and operating to a code of practice devised by the industry, and which is over-favourable to the industry." [*The Times*, August 17, 2004.] The later Leveson Inquiry of 2011–2012, under Lord Justice Leveson, which looked into allegations of press intrusion and phone-hacking and produced a 2,000-page report costing £5.4 million, was hardly more successful in curbing the worst excesses of press freedom. Leveson did at least recommend legislation, which, though sometimes characterized as "statutory regulation of the press," stopped well short of that position—and David Cameron's Government was too much in awe of the press to implement it anyway.

Against this background, enter David Eady, who, as mentioned above, was a leading libel barrister who acted chiefly for the press but who was only too well aware of the need to curb press intrusion. As a member of the Calcutt Committee on Privacy, Eady favored a privacy law enacted by Parliament. As he was to put it twenty years later: " It seemed that the appropriate mechanism for introducing a law of privacy would be through the legislature." [*The Independent*, December 4, 2010.]

As quoted above, Eady was shocked at the outcome of Gorden Kaye's case and commented that there was "a serious gap in the jurisprudence of any civilized society, if such a gross intrusion could happen without redress." So, when he was elevated to the High Court bench in 1997, he set about filling that gap.

To at least some of his erstwhile media clients he appeared to have become a poacher turned gamekeeper. In a 2008 lecture to a conference of press editors, Paul Dacre, editor of the tabloid *Daily Mail* newspaper, launched an out-and-out attack on him, accusing him of bringing in a privacy law "by the back door": "The British press is having a privacy law imposed on it, which is, I would argue, undermining the ability of mass circulation newspapers to sell newspapers in an ever more difficult market. The law is not coming from Parliament—no, that would smack of democracy—but from the arrogant and amoral judgements, words I use very deliberately, of one man Surely the greatest scandal is that while London boasts scores of eminent judges, one man is given a virtual monopoly of all cases against the media enabling him to bring in a privacy law by the back door." [*Press Gazette*, November 9, 2008.]

"Backdoor privacy law"

A non-Eady high-profile privacy case that ended up in the House of Lords was *Naomi Campbell v. Mirror Group Newspapers* [2004] UKHL 22. The case was brought by Naomi Campbell, a well-known fashion model, who sought damages for newspaper photographs showing her leaving a rehabilitation center. This turned out to be what I call a yo-yo case, with the first instance decision reversed on appeal and then reversed back again.

At first instance Naomi Campbell won and was awarded £2,500 in damages plus £1,000 in aggravated damages. A unanimous Court of Appeal held that there was no liability on the part of the newspaper. But Naomi Campbell finally won with a 3–2 majority in the House of Lords.

Totting up the judges on both sides, Piers Morgan, the editor of the losing *Daily Mirror*, commented bitterly: ""Five senior judges found for the *Mirror* throughout the various hearings in this case, four for Naomi Campbell, yet she wins. If ever there was a less deserving case for what is effectively a back door privacy law it would be Miss Campbell's. But that's showbiz." [Gibson, Owen (2004). "Campbell wins privacy case against Mirror." *The Guardian*, May 6, 2004.]

The House of Lords engaged in a "balancing test," asking first whether Naomi Campbell had a "reasonable expectation of privacy" (which supposedly created a duty of confidence and also supposedly engaged Article 8 ECHR), and, if so, whether this would interfere with freedom of expression (engaging Article 10 ECHR). The majority held that her right to privacy outweighed the newspaper's right to freedom of expression. Lord Hoffmann and Lord Nicholls, dissenting, pointed out that, as it was permissible for the newspaper to state that Naomi Campbell was a recovering drug addict, printing the photographs was within their "margin of appreciation."

"Reasonable expectation of privacy"

The judge-made law of breach of confidence reached its apogee in *Mosley v. News Group Newspapers* [2008] EWHC 1777 (QB). The *News of the World*, a mass-circulation Sunday newspaper, published a front-page story headed "F1 Boss has Sick Nazi Orgy with 5 Hookers". The article concerned Max Mosley, president of the Fédération Internationale de l'Automobile and son of Sir Oswald Mosley, leader of the British Union of Fascists during the 1930s. It had a subheading reading: "Son of Hitler-loving fascist in sex shame." The claim was not for defamation but for "breach of confidence and/or the unauthorized disclosure of personal information" infringing

Max Mosley's rights under ECHR Article 8. Max Mosley won the case and was awarded £60,000 in damages, which he claimed was far less than his legal costs.

It is important to note that Article 8 does not protect *privacy* as such, and the word "privacy" does not appear in Article 8, only the term "private life". Max Mosley's legal representatives sought to bridge this gap by arguing, as explained by the judge, "not only that the content of the published material was inherently private in nature, consisting as it did of the portrayal of sado-masochistic ('S and M') and some sexual activities, but that there had also been a pre-existing relationship of confidentiality between the participants. They had all known each other for some time and took part in such activities on the understanding that they would be private and that none of them would reveal what had taken place. I was told that there is a fairly tight-knit community of S and M activists on what is known as 'the scene' and that it is an unwritten rule that people are trusted not to reveal what has gone on. That is hardly surprising."

As the claim was against a newspaper group, not against other participants in the party, it is hard to see what relevance this "confidentiality" could possibly have had. There certainly was no relationship of confidence or confidentiality between Max Mosley and the Publishers of the *News of the World*.

But the judge, David Eady J., did not base his decision on the relationship of confidentiality that was alleged to exist between the participants in the party. Instead, he relied on a line of recent cases which had extended the law of "old-fashioned breach of confidence": "The law now affords protection to information in respect of which there is a reasonable expectation of privacy, even in circumstances where there is no pre-existing relationship giving rise of itself to an enforceable duty of confidence." Rejecting the allegations of a Nazi theme to the party and finding that there was no "public interest justification" for publication of the story, the judge concluded that Max Mosley "had a reasonable expectation of privacy in relation to sexual activities (albeit unconventional) carried on between consenting adults on private property".

After winning his case in the English High Court, Max Mosley filed an application with the European Court of Human Rights in Strasbourg claiming that his Article 8 rights "were violated by the UK's failure to impose a legal duty on the *News of the World* to notify him in advance in order to allow him the opportunity to seek an interim injunction and thus prevent publication of material which violated his right to respect for his private life". The Strasbourg court rejected Max Mosley's application, on the grounds of (a) "the limited scope under Article 10 for restriction on the freedom of the press to publish material which contributes to debate on matters of general public interest"; (b) "the chilling effect to which a pre-notification requirement risks giving rise", (c) "the significant doubts as to the effectiveness of any pre-notification requirement"; and (d) the wide margin of appreciation in this area". The Strasbourg court therefore was "of the view that Article 8 does not require a legally binding pre-notification requirement. Accordingly, the Court concludes that there has been no violation of Article 8 of the Convention by the absence of such a requirement in domestic law." [*Mosley v. UK* [2011] 53 EHRR 30].

"Public interest"

This case probably represents the high-water mark of all the English cases in which a hugely expanded "breach of confidence" meets a greatly extended ECHR Article 8 in order to fill the vacuum of a true law of privacy, which exists neither at common law nor in ECHR Article 8.

It was this dereliction of duty on the part of the Government and Parliament—possibly prompted by a fear of the press—that created a vacuum into which the courts stepped with their "backdoor" law of privacy. Besides amounting to judicial usurpation of the legislative function of Parliament, this judge-made law is unclear or even muddled, as is practically inevitable with any judge-made law.

In particular, what *are* the criteria for deciding whether a publication should be protected as being "in the public interest" or whether it breaches some actionable right which is entitled to legal protection? In *A v. B plc* [2002] EWCA Civ. 337, a leading British soccer player was granted an interim injunction to prevent a newspaper from publishing details of an extra-marital affair. Lord Woolf held:

> "Where an individual is a public figure he is entitled to have his privacy respected in the appropriate circumstances. A public figure is entitled to a private life. The individual, however, should recognize that because of his public position he must expect and accept that his actions will be more closely scrutinized in the media. Even trivial facts relating to a public figure can be of great interest to readers and other observers of the media. Conduct which in the case of a private individual would not be the appropriate subject of comment can be the proper subject of comment in the case of a public figure. ...The courts must not ignore the fact that if newspapers do not publish information which the public are interested in, there will be fewer newspapers published, which will not be in the public interest."

The argument in the quoted passage seems to be that as the public is interested in the peccadilloes of so-called celebrities there is a public interest in not suppressing publication of such material. This is a non-sequitur. And the point about the number of newspapers is equally strange. It is doubtless true that if a newspaper does not pander to the tastes of the public it may have to fold. But would that be such a bad thing? And why should the courts be concerned to protect the proliferation of newspapers on the basis of cheap intrusive sensationalist reporting?

There are no clear criteria for "the public interest", and it is not always even possible to test the courts' reasoning, because of the rise of the "super-injunction." This was defined in 2011 by the Neuberger Committee, set up to examine the law and practice of super-injunctions, as: "an interim injunction which restrains a person from (i) publishing information which concerns the applicant and is said to be confidential or private; and (ii) publicizing or informing others of the existence of the order and the proceedings (the 'super' element of the order)." Because of their secrecy, it is not even known how many super-injunctions have been issued, and, in keeping with Government supineness, no government department has kept track of these injunctions and no record is kept of them.

In May 2011 the *Daily Telegraph* estimated that 80 "gagging orders" had been issued in the previous six years. The beneficiaries of these orders included: "nine footballers, nine actors, four pop stars, six wealthy businessmen and women, a senior civil servant and a Member of Parliament." [www.telegraph.co.uk—May 18, 2011].

Privacy in English Law: Conclusion

The protection of privacy under English law is still, to put it mildly, in a highly unsatisfactory state. Rightly eschewing the creation of a judge-made law of privacy and commendably but unsuccessfully imploring Parliament to legislate, the courts have opted for two very different substitutes for a law of privacy, neither of which actually does the job:

- The law of confidence, which, in the words of Lord Justice Sedley in *Douglas v. Hello!*, constructs "an artificial relationship of confidentiality between intruder and victim."
- "The right to respect for [a person's] private and family life and correspondence" enshrined in ECHR Article 8, which, however, is restricted to vertical effect, or

protection against government intrusion, and does not normally extend to have horizontal effect, or protection of one private individual against the intrusions of another private individual. The UK Supreme Court has correctly declined to give Article 8 horizontal effect in a case about a private landlord's right to evict a tenant with an Assured Shorthold Tenancy under section 21(4) of the Housing Act 1988: *McDonald v. McDonald* [2016] UKSC 28. The fact that this straightforward case went all the way up to the UKSC is a measure of the uncertainty in which English law finds itself. Article 8 is specifically limited to vertical effect. And section 21(4) of the Housing Act 1988 was intended as a simple, automatic no-fault form of eviction applicable after the expiration of a fixed term.

Stretching both these substitute causes of action to a breaking point still leaves a huge gap, a yawning chasm, between them which ought to have been filled by legislation.

However, in an area of privacy law governed by legislation, namely the interception of communications, instead of respecting that legislation under the principle of the sovereignty of Parliament, what we find is judicial activism actually invalidating the legislation.

American Privacy Law

The American response to the privacy dilemma has been very different. Before dealing with federal law, I will deal with the multi-faceted incremental approach detectable at state level., ultimately resting on legislation and at least what might be called "pseudo-black letter law" in the shape of the ALI's Restatements.

Like love according to the old song, privacy is a many splendored thing. Some of its main facets are:

- Protection of private property;
- Inviolability of the human person, including protection against intrusion;
- Protection of personal information.

Prince Albert's American Offspring

The English case of *Prince Albert v. Strange*, which would have made a far better precedent for privacy rights than the artificial "breach of confidence," never made any ripples in English law. But it made a great impression on Samuel Warren and Louis Brandeis (the future US Supreme Court Justice) in the writing of their renowned 1890 article titled "The Right to Privacy." [*Harvard Law Review*, Vol. 4, No. 5, (1890), pp. 193–220.] From the Prince's case Warren and Brandeis concluded: "[T]he protection afforded to thoughts, sentiments, and emotions, expressed through the medium of writing or of the arts, so far as it consists in preventing publication, is merely an instance of the more general right of the individual to be let alone." The phrase "the right to be let alone," popularized by the Warren-Brandeis article, became the buzz-word for privacy rights.

"Litigation bordering upon the absurd"

The growth of photography and the increasing availability of cheap cameras in the late 19th century gave rise to a number of lawsuits involving the unauthorized publication of photographs. In *Robertson v. Rochester Folding Box Co.*, the plaintiff was secretly photographed by a flour company, which used her picture to illustrate an advertising poster, of which 25,000 copies were printed. The unwelcome publicity caused the plaintiff to be ridiculed and humiliated, resulting in her suffering from nervous shock. She sought an injunction to stop the defendants from printing, publishing or distributing the poster, and damages of

$15,000 for invading her right of privacy—a novel cause of action at the time.

Having won in the Appellate Division, the plaintiff lost 4–3 in the New York Court of Appeals. The majority opinion, written by Parker CJ, found against the plaintiff because of the lack of any precedent, the absence of any mention of such a right in Blackstone "or any other of the great commentators upon the law," and especially because of the evil consequences that were expected to attend upon the judicial establishment of such a right. In the words of the Chief Justice: "If such a principle be incorporated into the body of the law through the instrumentality of a court of equity, the attempts to logically apply the principle will necessarily result, not only in a vast amount of litigation, but in litigation bordering upon the absurd. ..." [*Robertson v. Rochester Folding Box Co.*, 171 N.Y. 538, 544.]

"The Starving Glutton"

In Gorden Kaye's case Lord Justice Leggatt cited an American case which was remarkably similar to that of the British television actor, which he could possibly have used to "legislate from the bench," had he been so inclined, though American cases do not have binding authority in England. The case involved a Mrs Dorothy Barber of Kansas City, not a public figure, who suffered (?) from a condition that made her eat huge amounts of food and yet lose weight. She checked herself into a hospital and her history showed that although she had eaten enough in the past year to feed a family of ten, she had lost 25 pounds. When interviewed by *Time* reporters in the hospital, she pointedly refused her consent for any publicity, but her picture was taken by one reporter while she was remonstrating with his colleague. She subsequently found herself the butt of humor in a *Time* magazine story illustrated with a photograph of herself in her hospital bed, under the headline "Starving Glutton": *Barber v. Time Inc.* 159 S.W. 2d 291 (Missouri, 1942).

She successfully sued *Time* for invasion of privacy, winning both
at first instance and before the Supreme Court of Missouri. The
jury actually awarded her $1,500 punitive or exemplary damages,
but this was disallowed by the Missouri Supreme Court, which
however affirmed the first instance judgment for the same
amount in compensatory damages.

Time magazine tried to wrap itself in the First Amendment's
protection of freedom of speech and of the press. But this
defense was dismissed by the court. In the words of Chief Justice
Laurance M. Hyde, writing for a unanimous Missouri Supreme
Court: "[W]hatever may be the right of the press, tabloids or
newsreel companies to take and use pictures of persons in public
places, certainly any right of privacy ought to protect a person
from publication of a picture taken without consent while ill in
bed for treatment and recuperation."

Were these Missouri judges "legislating from the bench"?
Not really. Chief Justice Hyde cited a section of the first
Restatement of Torts which was very much in point: "A person
who unreasonably and seriously interferes with another's
interest in not having his affairs known to others or his likeness
exhibited to the public is liable to the other." [4 Restatement of
Torts, 398, § 867.] The ALI's comment on this section drew a
parallel between this right of privacy and "the much more
strongly protected interest to have one's person free from
unwanted intentional physical contacts by others. In some
aspects it is similar to the interest in reputation, which is the
basis of an action for defamation, since both interests have
relation to the opinions of third persons. ..."

Chief Justice Hyde added: "Twelve states (also Alaska and
the District of Columbia) have recognized such a right on
common law principles; two states have established the right
by statute; six states have expressly refused to accept it by
judicial decision; and the remaining states have not decided
the question."

By World War II, therefore, the American right to privacy had clearly come of age, with a very respectable lineage. We find *inter alia* what we might call the pseudo-black letter law of the Restatement, drawing its origin from two very different sources: the inviolability of the person on the one hand, and, on the other, protection of reputation. Then a firm statutory basis in two states coupled with a refusal in a further six states to allow privacy to be brought in by the back door by judge-made law—respect for the concept of law as principle enacted by statute. And then twelve states plus Alaska (which was not yet a state) and DC, where the right to privacy was recognized "on common law principles."

Privacy Protection in State Constitutions

In 1972, as the result of a popular initiative, Alaska added a strong protection of privacy as Art. I, § 22 to its Constitution. The Constitutions of California, Louisiana, Montana and Hawaii also contain clauses protecting privacy rights, and the Constitution of Pennsylvania specifically protects the right to informational privacy.

Limitations on Privacy

The expansion of the right of privacy inevitably leads to the need to keep it within bounds. Examples of this include the obligation of anyone who is HIV positive to warn their sexual partners: E.g. *Doe v. Johnson*, 817 F. Supp. 1382, 1393 (W.D. Mich. 1993). This is based on the principle enunciated in the Restatement (Third) of Torts: Liability for Physical & Emotional Harm § 18(a) (2010):

"A defendant whose conduct creates a risk of physical or emotional harm can fail to exercise reasonable care by failing to warn of the danger if: (1) the defendant knows or has reason to know: (a) of that risk; and (b) that those

encountering the risk will be unaware of it; and (2) a warning
might be effective in reducing the risk of harm."

The Sad Tale of the Sheep That Were Washed Overboard

An interesting case in this regard is the federal lawsuit
decided by the US Court of Appeals, Seventh Circuit, *Shadday v.
Omni Hotels Management Corp.* 477 F.3d 511. (S.D. Ind. Mar. 13
2006). The opinion of the court, upholding that of the District
Judge, was delivered by the irrepressible Judge Richard Posner.
Ms. Shadday was raped by another hotel guest in an elevator in
the upscale Shoreham Hotel in Washington DC. She sued the
hotel claiming that it had failed to discharge its duty of
reasonable care to its guests. The court expressly applied the
Hand formula, named for Judge Learned Hand (1872–1961):
"The practical question (and law should try to be practical) is
whether the defendant knows or should know that the risk is
great enough, in relation to the cost of averting it, to warrant the
defendant's incurring the cost." It also suggested that continuous
surveillance might be an undue intrusion on "privacy": "The
hotel cannot keep [guests] under continuous surveillance—they
would be unwilling to surrender their privacy so completely."
But the case had solid legal underpinnings, as can be seen from
Judge Posner's further remarks: "The hotel would probably not
be liable even if the plaintiff had proved that, had it not been for
the defendant's failure to exercise due care, she would not have
been injured. The injury must be of the kind that the duty of care
was intended to prevent." He cited the Restatement (Second) of
Torts § 281 comment f (1965). And then comes the *pièce de
résistance:* the sad old English case of *Gorris v. Scott*, 9 LR Ex. 125
(1874), in which the owner of sheep lost when washed
overboard in a storm filed suit against the shipowner for failing
to hold the sheep in pens as required by the Contagious Diseases
(Animals) Act 1869. Had the sheep been penned in, they would
not have drowned. "But," as Posner put it, "the statute's purpose

was merely to prevent infection, not to save the animals from a watery death. So the plaintiff lost." He applied this to *Shadday* as follows: "In the present case, similarly, in deciding how many precautions to take against intruders the hotel would hardly be thinking about the incremental value of those precautions to guests endangered by other guests, since guest-on-guest crime at a hotel like the Shoreham appears to be vanishingly rare.

"Negligent supervision"

A different limit on privacy was put in place in the Maine case of *Napieralski v. Unity Church of Greater Portland*, 802 A.2d 391 (Me. 2002). Maria Napieralski alleged that she had been sexually assaulted by a minister in a church-provided home. However, her meeting with him was not for church business or counseling. The plaintiff argued that the church was negligent in supervising its employee, but the Maine Supreme Judicial Court rejected this: "Where an employer does provide a residence for employees, it is very different from the employer's premises as addressed in the Restatement (Second) of Torts § 317. The employee retains rights of privacy and quiet enjoyment in the residence that are not subject to close supervision or domination by the employer."

Psychotherapist-Patient Privilege

It is commonly assumed that physician-patient privilege is carved in stone. In fact this is not so, and it is not recognized in the US Federal Rules of Evidence, though it is recognized by most states, including California. Justice Mathew Tobriner, one of California's most activist judges, carried the majority of the California Supreme Court with him in creating an exception to that privilege in certain circumstances in regard to mental health professionals in: *Tarasoff v. Regents of the University of California* 551 P.2d 334 (Cal. 1976). Tatiana Tarasoff was murdered by

Prosenjit Poddar, a former mental patient with whom she had been in a relationship. Poddar had confided his intention to kill Tarasoff to his psychotherapist, Dr. Moore, who requested that the Berkeley campus police detain Poddar as a dangerous paranoid schizophrenic. He was detained briefly but then released, and Dr. Moore's superior, Dr. Powelson, directed that Poddar should not be detained any further. No warning of Poddar's threat was ever conveyed to Tarasoff or her parents. After her murder, Tarasoff's parents sued Dr. Moore and other university employees. Writing for the majority on the California Supreme Court, Justice Tobriner wrote: "We conclude that the public policy favoring protection of the confidential character of patient-psychotherapist communications must yield to the extent to which disclosure is essential to avert danger to others. The protective privilege ends where the public peril begins." In support of his, he cited an interpretation of the Restatement (Second) of Torts § 315 and also the California Evidence Code § 1014 and 1024. Justice Clark, in a strong dissent, cited the comprehensive statute on mental health passed by the California Legislature with effect from July 1, 1969, which "establishes the therapist's duty to Not disclose." § 5328. It also provides that: "All information and records obtained in the course of providing services under Division 5 ... shall be confidential.

Psychiatrists have duty to warn a person when psychiatrist learns that a patient poses a threat to that person."

Regardless of the rights and wrongs of the 1976 decision, *Tarasoff* is now placed on a firm legislative footing. By 2012 a duty on the part of mental health professionals to warn or protect was codified in legislative statutes in no fewer than 23 states, it was recognized in the common law of a further 10 states, while 11 states have a permissive duty. [Johnson, Rebecca; Persad, Govind; Sisti, Dominic (2014), 469.]

US Federal Privacy Law

"Reasonable expectation of privacy"

The concept of "a reasonable expectation of privacy," a somewhat strained interpretation of which we have encountered in certain English cases, was also tackled head-on in America, A leading privacy-related case that came before the US Supreme Court was *Katz v. United States*, 389 US 347 (1967). Charles Katz placed illegal gambling bets by means of long-distance calls made from a public pay-phone. Katz was convicted on the basis of recordings of his calls made by the FBI (without a warrant) by means of an electronic eavesdropping device attached to the outside of the phone booth. Katz challenged his conviction on the basis that the recordings amounted to "unreasonable searches and seizures" prohibited by the Fourth Amendment. Following the earlier US Supreme Court ruling in *Olmstead v. United States*, 277 US 438 (1928), the Ninth Circuit Court of Appeals found in favor of the FBI, because there was no physical intrusion into the phone booth itself. But, by 7–1, the Supreme Court ruled in favor of Katz, on the basis that he had a "reasonable expectation of privacy." As Justice Potter Stewart put it, writing for the majority: Once someone has entered a phone booth, shut the door behind him, and paid the toll to place his call, he is "surely entitled to assume that the words he utters into the mouthpiece will not be broadcast to the world."

"Stark departure from precedent"

Scroll forward half a century and we come to *Timothy Ivory Carpenter v. US* [No. 16-402, 585 US (2018).] Timothy Ivory Carpenter was found guilty by a jury of aiding and abetting a robbery that affected interstate commerce and also of aiding and abetting use or carriage of a firearm during a federal crime of violence. He was sentenced to 116.25 years in federal prison. The evidence on which he was convicted was his cell phone provider's records showing that Carpenter's cell phone had communicated with cell phone towers at the time of major robberies of cell phones from RadioShack and T-Mobile stores in Michigan and Ohio. The evidence indicated that Carpenter was within a two-mile radius of four robberies while they were in progress. Carpenter unsuccessfully appealed his conviction and sentence to the US Court of Appeals for the Sixth Circuit as a violation of his Fourth Amendment protection from "unreasonable searches." But the Court held that there was no "search" within the Fourth Amendment, as the information had been obtained not from Carpenter or from Carpenter's phone but from his phone provider's records. Further, in keeping with the US Supreme Court ruling *in Smith v. Maryland*, 442 US 735 (1979), the Appeals Court held that only the content of a cell phone user's communication was protected by the Fourth Amendment. This decision was reversed by the US Supreme Court, which ruled 5–4 in favor of Carpenter. Writing for the majority, Chief Justice John Roberts held that the technology used by the FBI to arrest Carpenter was "a powerful new tool" which "risks Government encroachment of the sort the Framers … drafted the Fourth Amendment to prevent."

Justice Anthony Kennedy, who more usually exercised the swing vote and wrote the majority opinion, on this occasion sounded a strong dissent: "[T]he Court's stark departure from relevant Fourth Amendment precedents and principles is, in my submission, unnecessary and incorrect, requiring this respectful dissent. The new rule the Court seems to formulate puts needed, reasonable, accepted, lawful, and congressionally authorized criminal investigations at serious risk in serious cases, often when law enforcement seeks to prevent the threat of violent crimes."

In his dissenting opinion Justice Alito attacked the reasoning of the majority: "The Court's reasoning fractures two fundamental pillars of Fourth Amendment law. … First, the Court ignores the basic distinction between an actual search (dispatching law enforcement officers to enter private premises and root through private papers and effects) and an order merely requiring a party to look through its own records and produce specified documents. The former, which intrudes on personal privacy far more deeply, requires probable cause; the latter does not." Treating an order to produce like an actual search, as today's decision does, is revolutionary. It violates both the original understanding of the Fourth Amendment and more than a century of Supreme Court precedent. Unless it is somehow restricted to the particular situation in the present case, the Court's move swill cause upheaval. ... Second, the Court allows a defendant to object to the search of a third party's property. This also is revolutionary. The Fourth Amendment protects '[t]he right of the people to be secure in their persons, houses, papers, and effects.' (emphasis added), not the persons, houses, papers, and effects of others. ... By departing dramatically from these fundamental principles, the Court destabilizes long-established Fourth Amendment doctrine. We will be making repairs—or picking up the pieces—for a long time to come."

Justice Clarence Thomas went even further in his dissent, going so far as to reject the *Katz* "reasonable expectation of privacy" test itself: "The *Katz* test has no basis in the text or history of the Fourth Amendment. And, it invites courts to make judgments about policy, not law. Until we confront the problems with this test, *Katz* will continue to distort Fourth Amendment jurisprudence."

"Knock and announce"

In an earlier privacy case Clarence Thomas had the unusual role of writing for a unanimous Supreme Court: *Wilson v. Arkansas*, 514 US 927 (1995). His thoroughly researched opinion showed that the law in this area ultimately rested on a 700-year-old English codified statute! Arkansas State Police, armed with a search warrant, entered Wilson's residence through an unlocked screen door. The police officers identified themselves and announced that they had a warrant. On conducting a search, they confiscated quantities of several different illegal drugs together with drug paraphernalia, a firearm, and ammunition. Wilson was arrested while in the process of flushing marijuana down the toilet. Wilson filed a pre-trial motion to suppress the evidence found during the search, relying on *Miller v. United States*, 357 US 301 (1958), which she contended was based on a Fourth Amendment requirement that police officers "knock and announce" before entering premises to serve a warrant. Wilson's motion was denied, she was convicted of all charges by a jury, and was sentenced to 32 years' imprisonment. Her conviction, which had been upheld by the Arkansas Supreme Court, was reversed by a unanimous US Supreme Court. In the words of Clarence Thomas, writing for the Court: "Contrary to the decision below, we hold that in some circumstances an officer's unannounced entry into a home might be unreasonable under the Fourth Amendment. This is not to say, of course, that every entry must be preceded by an announcement." This rather begs the question of when "knock and announce" is mandated. Clarence Thomas continued, rather unhelpfully: "For now, we leave to the lower courts the task of determining the circumstances under which an unannounced entry is reasonable under the Fourth Amendment. We simply hold that although a search or seizure of a dwelling might be constitutionally defective if police officers enter without prior announcement, law enforcement interests may also establish the reasonableness of an unannounced entry." Whew! Justice Thomas traces the "knock and announce" rule back to *Semayne's Case*, 5 Co. Rep. 91a (King's Bench 1604). But in a footnote he recognizes that the "knock and announce" principle predates Semayne's Case by 330 years, deriving from Chapter XVII of the First Statute of Westminster of 1275, which has been described as a code of laws. Unlike any judicial decision, this legislation lays down very precise rules for the recovery by a Sheriff (or other officer of the

Crown) of "beasts" (that is, cattle) driven into the thieves' castle or fortress. The stolen cattle must be "solemnly demanded" by the Sheriff, and, only if this does not have the desired effect can the King "cause the said Castle or Fortress to be beaten down without Recovery." The requirement of a "solemn demand" is the origin of the "knock and announce" rule. Coke's gloss on this requirement of the 1275 statute is as follows: "That in all cases when the King is party, the sheriff (if the doors are not open) may break [into] the party's house, either to arrest him or to do other execution of the King's process, if otherwise he cannot enter. But before he breaks [into] it, he ought to signify the cause of his coming and to make request to open the doors." [*Semayne's Case*, 5 Co. Rep 91.]

This is an excellent example of the greater clarity and precision of statutory language over that of a court—even when the statute dates from 1275 and the court judgment from 1995!

"The tried and true counsel of judicial restraint"

Another unimpressive US Supreme Court decision on "searches" within the meaning of the Fourth Amendment was *Kyllo v. United States*, 533 US 27 (2001). Using a thermal imaging device, federal agents (without a warrant) detected an unusual amount of heat radiating from the roof and walls of Danny Lee Kyllo's home in Oregon, which aroused a suspicion of marijuana growing. Sure enough, federal agents armed with a search warrant found over 100 marijuana plants growing in the house. After vacillating several times, the US Court of Appeals for the Ninth Circuit allowed the evidence obtained from the thermal imaging to be admitted. But in a 5–4 decision the US Supreme Court held that Kyllo's constitutional right under the Fourth Amendment to be protected against "unreasonable searches" had been violated by the thermal imaging of his home, even though the device used in these "searches" could not penetrate walls or windows or pick up conversations, but could only detect heat radiated from the building. Justice Antonin Scalia, writing for a mixed majority of conservative and liberal justices, stressed that everyone has an "expectation of privacy" in their own homes, which is breached even by technology that does not enter the home. A strong dissent was registered by Justice John Paul Stevens, generally thought of as liberal, writing for a largely conservative coalition: "Since what was involved in this case was nothing more than drawing inferences from off-the-wall surveillance, rather than through any 'through-the-wall' surveillance, the officers' conduct did not amount to a search and was perfectly reasonable." He concluded by chiding the majority for failing "to heed the tried and true counsel of judicial restraint. Instead of concentrating on the rather mundane issue that is actually presented by the case before it, the Court has endeavored to craft an all-encompassing rule for the future. It would be far wiser to give legislators an unimpeded opportunity to grapple with these emerging issues rather than to shackle them with prematurely devised constitutional constraints."

"The blunt instrument of the Fourth Amendment"

Privacy law is now on a firmer footing as a result of the unanimous US Supreme Court decision in *Riley v. California,* which ruled that trawling though the digital contents of a cell phone without a warrant is unconstitutional as a violation of the Fourth Amendment. Chief Justice John Roberts waxed lyrical in defense of individual liberty in the digital age: "Modern cell phones are not just another technological convenience. With all they contain and all they may reveal, they hold for many Americans 'the privacies of life.' The fact that technology now allows an individual to carry such information in his hand does not make the information any less worthy of the protection for which the Founders fought."

Justice Alito, concurring, remarked that "the Court's broad holding favors information in digital form over information in hard-copy form. Suppose that two suspects are arrested. Suspect number one has in his pocket a monthly bill for his land-line phone, and the bill lists an incriminating call to a long-distance number. He also has in his wallet a few snapshots, and one of these is incriminating. Suspect number two has in his pocket a cell phone, the call log of which shows a call to the same incriminating number. In addition, a number of photos are stored in the memory of the cell-phone, and one of these is incriminating. Under established law, the police may seize and examine the phone bill and the snapshots in the wallet without obtaining a warrant, but under the Court's holding today, the information stored in the cell phone is out." He concluded: "[I]t would be very unfortunate if privacy protection in the 21st century were left primarily to the federal courts using the blunt instrument of the Fourth Amendment. Legislatures, elected by the people, are in a better position than we are to assess and respond to the changes that have already occurred and those that almost certainly will take place in the future." [See Arnheim (2018), p. 420.]

"The Fourth Amendment no longer exists"

In a 2014 NBC interview, Edward Snowden, a self-styled "whistle-blower," a former employee of an NSA contractor, leaked to the press thousands of classified NSA documents. Among these was a secret April 2013 order by the FISA Court (Foreign Intelligence Surveillance Court) requiring Verizon to provide the NSA with a daily feed of all call detail records, for domestic as well as foreign calls. In a 2014 NBC interview Snowden boasted that the Fourth Amendment "as it was written no longer exists. ... All of your private records, all of your private communications, all of your transactions, all of your associations, who you talk to, who you love, what you buy, what you read, all of these things can be

seized and then held by the government and then searched later
for any reason, without any real oversight, without any real
accountability for those who do wrong."

Snowden's quote paints a frightening picture of "Big
Brother" looking over your shoulder. But upon closer
examination, even this lurid description contains some
concessions. For example, the phrase "and then searched later" is
a tacit admission that what the government "seizes" and "holds"
is not data, only *metadata*—lists of numbers contacting one
another, together with the date, time, and duration of the calls,
but not the content of the conversations themselves. To be able
to read the content, the government needs a federal court order.
The same applies to the NSA's mass surveillance on the Internet,
which again produces not data but metadata. Metadata can be
defined as data about data. As an aid to identifying terrorists,
collecting metadata is only the first step. It cannot usually be
used in litigation.

"Almost Orwellian"

In *Klayman v. Obama* decided in December 2013, US District
Judge Richard Leon described the NSA's mass collection of
metadata as "almost Orwellian" and ruled that the program
"likely" violated the Fourth Amendment's prohibition of
"unreasonable searches and seizures." The judge granted the
request for an injunction to stop the NSA from collecting phone
metadata on the plaintiffs, but "in light of the significant national
security interest at stake and the novelty of the constitutional
issues, I will stay my order pending appeal."

Despite his opposition to the government program, the
judge quoted a declaration by NSA Director of Signals
Intelligence Directorate (SID), Teresa H. Shea, that if the Bulk
Telephony Metadata Program had been in placed before 9/11, it
"would have allowed the NSA to determine that a September 11

hijacker living in the United States had contacted a known al Qaeda safe house in Yemen."

"False choice between liberty and security"

The case of *ACLU v. Clapper* (SD NY, December 28, 2013), decided just ten days after *Klayman*, by the US District Court for the Southern District of New York, had a very different outcome. Judge William Pauley, a Clinton appointee, held that there was no infringement of Fourth Amendment rights. This was based squarely on *Smith v. Maryland* 442 US 735 (1979), the latest US Supreme Court decision in this area, which held that phone users have "no expectation of privacy" for information that they provide to phone companies, as all the metadata collected by the NSA is voluntarily revealed by users to the phone companies. Judge Pauley accepted the government's claim that the program had successfully blocked several planned terrorist attacks, and his judgment contained several interesting observations, including the following: "Fifteen different FISC judges have found the metadata collection program lawful a total of 35 times since May 2006."

And: "Like (sic) the 9/11 Commission observed: The choice between liberty and security is a false on, as nothing is more apt to imperil civil liberties than the success of a terrorist attack on American soil."

He concluded: "For all these reasons, the NSA's bulk telephony metadata collection program is lawful."

However, this eminently sensible and carefully reasoned decision was reversed on appeal by the Second US Circuit Court of Appeals in Manhattan, which on May 7, 2015, held that "the telephone metadata program exceeds the scope of what Congress has authorized and therefore violates [Section 215 of the Patriot Act]." The court did not rule on the constitutionality of the bulk surveillance and declined to halt the program. Noting the pending expiration of relevant parts of the Patriot Act, it was held that it would be "prudent" to give Congress a chance to decide the matter in view of the national interests at stake.

Parts of the Patriot Act, which had expired at midnight on May 31, 2015, were restored by the USA Freedom Act passed two days later. Section 215 of the Patriot Act was restored in amended form to stop the NSA from continuing its mass collection of phone metadata, which would now be retained by the phone companies, with the NSA needing to obtain a federal court order to obtain actual data about targeted individuals.

States' protection of personal information

As usual, state law is much more clear-cut than federal law. As of December 16, 2018, at least 31 states had passed laws regulating the secure destruction or disposal of personal information. At least 12 states had imposed broader security requirements. Some states, such as California and Indiana, require organizations to implement and maintain reasonable safeguards to protect personal information from unauthorized disclosure or use. In 2014 New York State Assembly passed A.10190: "An Act to in relation to the protection of personal information by businesses." And California has passed the Consumer Privacy Act of 2018. [See International Association of Privacy Professionals, https://iapp.org.]

"An Uncommonly Silly Law"

The story begins with the US Supreme Court ruling in *Griswold v. Connecticut*, 381 US 479 (1965). The question before the Court was the constitutionality of what Justice Potter Stewart called an "uncommonly silly law" banning contraceptives. The Court held that this state law was unconstitutional. Justice William O. Douglas, writing for the majority, held that, though the law in question did not exactly breach any express right in the Bill of Rights, it offended against a right of privacy. Justice Hugo Black, in a strenuous dissent, argued that even if the Supreme Court believed that certain laws were "unreasonable, unwise, arbitrary, capricious or irrational," the Court should not assume such broad authority as to strike down such laws. Otherwise the Court would have too much power, which would "jeopardize the separation of governmental powers that the Framers set up and ... threaten to take away much of the power of the States to govern themselves." Douglas's reasoning for the majority is far from persuasive, based as it was on lurking "penumbras" and "emanations" of other apparently unrelated constitutional protections, such as the Fifth Amendment privilege against self-incrimination and even the right of free association guaranteed by the First Amendment. The concurring opinions had a different and equally unconvincing legal basis. Justices Byron White and John Marshall Harlan II based their concurrence on a new-style Fourteenth Amendment "substantive due process" doctrine, while Justice Arthur Goldberg rooted his concurrence on the Ninth Amendment. [Arnheim (2018), p. 250.]

"Nascent democratic movement"

This flimsy foundation formed the basis of the landmark 7–2 ruling in *Roe v. Wade*, 410 US 113 (1973), which quickly became the litmus test for confirmation to the US Supreme Court. [See Arnheim (2018), p. 345.] The majority in *Roe* held that the right to privacy gave a pregnant woman the right to choose to have an abortion (at least, within the first trimester). Two strong dissents were sounded, by Justices Byron White and William Rehnquist. Labeling the majority opinion "an exercise of raw judicial power," White wrote: "I find nothing in the language or history of the Constitution to support the Court's judgment." In his dissent, Rehnquist (who would later become Chief Justice) stressed the fact that the right "found" by the majority within the scope of the Fourteenth Amendment "was apparently completely unknown to the drafters of the Amendment." From which he concluded that the drafters of the Amendment did not intend to deprive the States of the power to legislate on this issue, especially as 36 states had anti-abortion measures in force at the time, 21 of which were still on the books in 1973. By regarding the right of abortion as part of privacy, the majority implicitly treated the foetus as part of the woman's body, rejecting the rights of the unborn child and of the father.

Justice Ruth Bader Ginsburg, a staunch advocate for abortion rights, herself recognized that for the Court to have made abortion a constitutional issue could actually have harmed the pro-choice cause. Long before she took her seat on the Court she commented: The Court's ruling terminated "a nascent democratic movement to liberalize abortion law." And: "heavy-handed judicial intervention was difficult to justify and appears to have provoked, not resolved, conflict." Had abortion been legalized in the US by legislation rather than by the Supreme Court, it would, as Bader Ginsburg realized, have been much less controversial, because it would have had the democratic credentials which it currently lacks.

At the time of this writing there is a new onslaught in several states against *Roe v. Wade.* In 2019 alone no fewer than 11 states have passed laws restricting abortion, some more extreme than others. Alabama's law makes it illegal to perform an abortion, with no exceptions for rape or incest. The laws passed by Georgia, Kentucky, Mississippi, Ohio, and (with some exceptions) Louisiana, ban abortion once a fetal heartbeat is detected, which can apparently be as early as five weeks into pregnancy, before some women even know that they are pregnant. The law makes no exceptions for pregnancies resulting from rape or incest. The Kentucky and Mississippi laws and the Utah law banning abortion after 18 weeks (with some exceptions) have been blocked by federal courts. [*The Guardian*, April 12, 2019 and qz.com (May 30, 2019).] The whole question of abortion is clearly eventually going to be heading back to the US Supreme Court.

British Abortion Law

The right of abortion is one of the few areas of the law where the British approach is superior to the American—precisely because it was achieved by legislation and not by judicial fiat. As a result, abortion has been comparatively uncontroversial in Britain.

In 1966 David Steel (now Lord Steel), a backbench Liberal Party member of the UK Parliament, introduced a private member's bill, which, unusually for such bills, obtained a majority in both houses of Parliament and, on receiving the Royal Assent, became the Abortion Act 1967. In a 2017 interview Lord Steel explained how his bill got through, with unofficial Government support. "[I] was just lucky to benefit from a quirk of British politics in which names are drawn at random and the Members of Parliament selected have the chance to put forward a member's bill. After six previous attempts at reform all having failed because of lack of time, I was drawn third and able to introduce it again." [*Independent*, October 26, 2017].

The Abortion Act 1967, which is still in force in Great Britain (but not in Northern Ireland, where abortion has remained illegal) legalized abortion up to 28 weeks. The Act was amended by the Human Fertilisation and Embryology Act 1990, which lowered the time limit to 24 weeks for most cases. The Act amended all previous anti-abortion legislation going back to 1861 so that an abortion carried out in accordance with the Act by a registered medical practitioner was no longer a crime.

Section 4(1) of the Act allows a right of conscientious objection, providing that "no person shall be under any duty, whether by contract or by any statutory or other legal requirement, to participate in any treatment authorised by this

Act to which he has a conscientious objection," unless, according to section 4(2), it is "necessary to save the life or prevent grave permanent injury to the physical or mental health of a pregnant woman."

Although there was a flurry of debate over the legislation, including over additional laws that failed to gain enough traction in Parliament, the fact that the question of abortion was dealt with by means of legislation by an elected legislature has prevented it from becoming a polarizing issue in either politics or law.

One of the few British lawsuits about abortion was a case that ended up before the UK Supreme Court in 2014 called *Greater Glasgow Health Board v. Doogan & Wood* [2014] UKSC 68. Miss Doogan and Mrs Wood were two practicing Roman Catholic midwives who argued "that they have the right to object to any involvement with patients in connection with the termination of pregnancy to which they personally have a conscientious objection. ... In their case, as practising Roman Catholics, their objections extend to receiving and dealing with the initial telephone call booking the patient into the Labour Ward, to the admission of the patient, to assigning the midwife to look after the patient, to the supervision of the staff looking after the patient, both before and after the procedure, as well as to the direct provision of any care for those patients, apart from that which they are required to perform under section 4(2)."

Not surprisingly, the employing hospital objected that this was far broader than the ambit of the rights of "conscientious objection" contained in section 4(1) of the Act. Doogan and Wood challenged this decision in court, which turned into one of the many British yo-yo cases, my term for a case which is decided one way at first instance, is reversed on appeal, and finally reversed back again. The claimants lost at first instance, then succeeded on an initial appeal in the Scottish courts, but lost again finally before the UK Supreme Court, which adopted a narrow construction of the relevant words of the statute. In the words of Lady Hale, speaking for a unanimous Court: "It will immediately be apparent that the question in this case, and the only question, is the meaning of the words [in section 2(1) of the Act] 'to participate in any treatment authorised by this Act to which he has a conscientious objection.'" And again, characterizing the case as "a pure question of statutory construction." Lady Hale concluded: "In my view, the narrow meaning [of section 4(1)] is more likely to have been in the contemplation of Parliament when the Act was passed."

One can only imagine what a huge uproar this Doogan & Wood case would have caused if, instead of having to interpret the precisely drafted words of a statute, the court had had to grapple with a vague and rambling ruling of a court. Even so, the matter turned into a yo-yo case, because no legislation, however carefully drafted, is ever completely proof against divergent interpretations. The UK Supreme Court was undoubtedly right to adopt a narrow interpretation of the statutory words, and the result was a neat and fair solution.

The beauty of British abortion law is that it does not try to base itself on privacy, or any other farfetched right—simply because it does not have to. The British Parliament can pass any law it likes. [See Chapter 1, "United Kingdom: The Sovereignty of Parliament."] If England made such a good job of abortion law, you may well ask, why is so much of the rest of English law in such a state of disarray? The answer is that, as was explained by its sponsor, David Steel, as quoted above, the Abortion Act 1967, started out as a private member's bill that only came to be passed—after six previous attempts—as a result of a rare quirk of fate. It stands out as an exemplary exercise in legislative law-making and as a rebuke to the thoroughly unsatisfactory result achieved on the same issue in the US by judicial fiat. Unfortunately, the lesson of the Abortion Act proved abortive (no pun intended) and was lost on the British Government and Parliament, as is shown in Part V: "Problems and Solutions."

GDPR

A very different aspect of privacy is covered by the Data Protection Act 2018, implementing the EU General Data Protection Regulation known as GDPR (EU 2016/679). Non-compliant businesses can suffer heavy fines. As well as placing new obligations on companies and organizations collecting personal data, GDPR gives individuals more power to access information held about them, chiefly by means of a Subject Access Request (SAR). Individuals also have the right to have their personal data erased in certain circumstances. Under GDPR, individuals have to give explicit permission for businesses to keep emailing them, but fraudsters have already started to take advantage of this by deceiving people into disclosing their account details, phone numbers and pins.

Privacy: Conclusion

Parliament's dereliction of duty in simply ignoring the earnest entreaties of the judges in the *Gorden Kaye* case for a law of privacy explains why the judges felt impelled to fill the vacuum themselves. But it does not justify the way in which this was done, by extending the concept of breach of confidence and ECHR Article 8 to breaking point and still leaving a yawning chasm.

One area in which English law is less problematical than US law is abortion, for the very simple reason that, thanks to a persistent backbencher, abortion was put on a proper legislative footing—something that Justice Ruth Bader Ginsburg regretted did not happen in America. The UK's Data Protection Act 2018, implementing the EU's GDPR, is another legislative protection for privacy. But the UK still lacks any general legislative or common law protection of privacy rights.

11

DEFAMATION

"Chilling Effect on Freedom of Expression"

It is perhaps fitting to close this Part with some reflections on an area of law in which England and America have effectively come to blows—the law of Defamation. English defamation judgments, seen as not sufficiently protective of US First Amendment rights to freedom of speech, have often been described as having a "chilling effect on freedom of expression."

SPEECH Act

In 2010 the US Congress passed legislation, known as the SPEECH Act, signed into law by President Obama, which denies recognition to "foreign defamation judgments" that fail to provide defendants with as much protection of free speech as the US First Amendment. The law makes such judgments unenforceable in the US. The foreign defamation judgments targeted were primarily those from England, whose defamation law had a reputation of tending to favor claimants (plaintiffs), thereby inadvertently allowing "libel tourism" to flourish. [The full title of the SPEECH Act is Public Law 111-223, titled Securing the Protection of our Enduring and Established Constitutional Heritage Act (spelling S-P-E-E-C-H Act), passed by Congress on August 10, 2010.]

It was unprecedented for the US to go to such lengths against English court judgments. It was contrary to the doctrine of the "comity of nations", or "the recognition which one nation allows within its territory to the legislative, executive or judicial acts of another nation" (*Hilton v. Guyot*, 159 US 13 (1895) – US Supreme Court.]

English Defamation Legislation

Why then was this extreme action taken by the United States? Unlike so many areas of English law where Parliament has remained deaf to pleas for legislation, defamation has received more than its fair share of parliamentary attention over the years. Despite that, the law of this comparatively compact area has not only *not* been codified; it has not even been consolidated into a single Act of Parliament. *All* the following Acts of Parliament are still in force to greater or lesser extent—in addition to the English common law of defamation:

- Law of Libel Amendment Act 1888
- Defamation Act 1952
- Defamation Act 1996
- Defamation Act 2013

"Libel Tourism"

What triggered the SPEECH Act was the English lawsuit against Dr. Rachel Ehrenfeld, the American author of a book titled *Funding Evil,* in which she named a particular wealthy Saudi businessman as, in the words of Mr. Justice Eady, "one of the main sponsors of Al Qaeda and other terrorist organizations." The Saudi businessman sued her in the English High Court, even though the book had not been published in the UK and Dr. Ehrenfeld did not live in the UK and had never lived there. [*Mahfouz v. Ehrenfeld* [2005] EWHC 1156 (QB).]

Was this a case of "libel tourism," as Dr. Ehrenfeld maintained? The trial judge, Eady J., took a different view:

"In December 2003 it came to the claimants' attention that the book was being published in England and Wales containing defamatory allegations about them. The book was being sold

> through online retailers such as Amazon.co.uk,
> Blackwells.co.uk and Amazon.com. ... The claimants also
> discovered that the first chapter of the book was separately
> available on the ABC News website." [Ibid, para 14.]

Was this really enough to amount to publication in England,
giving the English court jurisdiction to hear the case? Or was it a
case of long-arm overreach? Apparently only 23 copies of the
book had been sold in the UK at the time of the original trial in
2004. [David Pallister (2007), "US author mounts 'libel tourism'
challenge," *Guardian*, November 15, 2007.] If that is true, the
claim that the book was published in England rings a bit hollow.

Under English law, a claimant wishing to serve a defendant
in the US needs to show that:

- His claim has a real prospect of success;
- There is a "good arguable case" that the claim falls within
  one or more of the "jurisdictional gateways"—in this case
  the "tort gateway" —set out in Practice Direction 6B of
  the Civil Procedure Rules; and
- England is the appropriate forum to bring the claim.

Did the Mahfouz claim really clear all these hurdles? It is hard to
say, as Rachel Ehrenfeld refused to acknowledge the jurisdiction
of the English court and was not represented in the case. The
English court heard the undefended claim anyway. Default
judgment was entered against her, with an award of damages
against her of £30,000 plus costs of £80,000, and an order to
publish a correction and an apology.

Dr. Ehrenfeld's book was far from being the only one
attacked by Khalid bin Mahfouz in the English courts. In an
interesting article by Nick Cohen in *The Guardian* on February 7,
2010, we read: "As well as going for Ehrenfeld, the Saudi
billionaire used the English law to stop us reading *Alms for Jihad:
Charity and Terrorism in the Islamic World,* by J. Millard Burr and
Robert O. Collins, Matthew Carr's *Unknown Soldiers*, Michael
Griffin's *Reaping the Whirlwind* and Craig Unger's *House of Bush,*

House of Saud. Their editors could not fight the cases because, as Simon Master of Unger's Random House explained, the cost was 'vastly more than the publisher could hope to earn from the book.'" [Cohen, Nick (2010). "Libel tourists will love the tales of Lord Hoffmann," *The Guardian*, February 7, 2010.] It is also perhaps worth mentioning that, in a report submitted to the United Nations Security Council in 2002, seven Saudis, including Khalid bin Mahfouz, are dubbed "the main individual sponsors of terrorism." [Mowbray, Joel (2002). "Saudis Behaving Badley," *National Review Online*, December 20, 2002. http:/www.nationalreview.com/mowbray122002.asp.] The report was prepared by the French international consultant and expert on terrorism Jean-Charles Brisard, who compiled an exhaustive report on the financial network of the Bin Laden organization, titled "The economic environment of Osama Bin Laden," which was written for the French intelligence community and published by the French national assembly. [*Wikipedia* article on Jean-Charles Brisard.]

"Rachel's Law"

But, I divert. Instead of complying with the judgment of the English High Court, Dr. Ehrenfeld filed a counter-suit in the US District Court for the Southern District of New York, asserting, among other things, that the English litigation violated her First Amendment rights. Her suit eventually ended up before a six-judge New York Court of Appeals, the highest court in that state, which, like the federal courts, declined jurisdiction on the basis that they lacked personal jurisdiction over Mahfouz.

SPEECH Act

But that was not, of course, the end of the story. The New York State Legislature took the matter up and unanimously passed legislation, which was signed into law by Governor David

Paterson on April 29. 2008. Commonly known as "Rachel's Law," the official title of the law says it all: the Libel Terrorism Protection Act. In the next two years six other states passed similar laws: Illinois, Florida, California, Tennessee, Maryland, and Utah.

And it was then that Congress picked up the ball and ran with it, unanimously passing, as mentioned above, the SPEECH Act, that was signed into law by President Obama in August 2010. Besides declaring foreign libel judgments unenforceable unless they conformed to the First Amendment's protection of freedom of speech, the Act even allows a counter-suit seeking damages against the foreign libel plaintiff.

The succession of Acts of Parliament amending the English law of defamation is indicative of the continuing concern about it—and the recognition that it still remained a problem. The 1952 Act was passed to implement recommendations made by a Committee on Defamation headed up by a law lord, Lord Porter, whose report, published in 1948, listed the general criticisms of the law of defamation at the time as "complication, cost, uncertainty, stifling of public discussion, undue severity upon unintentional defamation and bias in favour of 'gold-digging' plaintiffs." [Lloyd, Selwyn (1948). "Libel and Slander," *The Spectator*, October 29, 1948.]

"Laughing stock"

More than half a century later, these same problems (with the possible exception of unintentional defamation) still persisted. In 2010, Nick Clegg, Deputy Prime Minister in David Cameron's Coalition Government, committed the government to introducing legislation that would turn "English libel laws from an international laughing stock to an international blueprint." He stressed that: "Libel tourism is making a mockery of British justice." [Press Gazette, Jan 18, 2010,] Other promises made by Nick Clegg included: "A review of libel laws to protect freedom of speech" and "to end the libel farce." "This Government wants to restore our international reputation for free speech. ... We believe claimants should not be able to threaten claims on what are essentially trivial grounds. We are going to tackle libel tourism. ... "Separately, we are also going to address the high costs of defamation proceedings." [Clegg, Nick (2011). "Full transcript, Nick Clegg Speech on civil liberties, London January 7, 2011, New Statesman, January 7, 2011.]

End of "libel farce"?

Nick Clegg's wide-ranging critique of the English law of defamation and his promised reforms materialized in the shape of the 2013 Act. But has this finally succeeded in ending "the libel farce" that had already been the target of the 1888, 1952, and 1996 Defamation Acts? Let us take a look at some of the main problem areas:

- **Bias in favor of plaintiffs**: The main reason for this serious problem is the rule that in defamation, unlike other areas of the law, the burden of proof rests not on the claimant but on the defendant. Yet that is still the rule after the 2013 Act.

- **"Serious harm"**: The 2013 Act introduced a major new requirement intended to deter trivial or frivolous claims and thereby stop the law of defamation from continuing to have the effect of "chilling free speech": "A statement is not defamatory unless its publication has caused or is likely to cause serious ham to the reputation of the claimant." [Section 1(1).] The precise meaning of this provision was the subject of a major wrangle between the High Court, the Court of Appeal and the UK Supreme Court in the case of *Lachaux v. Independent Print Ltd.* [2019] UKSC 27. The trial judge held that the degree of seriousness of harm could only be determined "by reference to the facts about its impact and not just to the meaning of the words." The Court of Appeal took the opposite position, and the UK Supreme Court reverted to the judge's view.

- **Common Law:** Defamation law is bedeviled by the fact that the statutes of 1888, 1952, 1996 and 2013 all just *amend* the common law—which itself is far from certain—without replacing it. By contrast, *codifying* the law of defamation would have swept away the common law cobwebs and placed this branch of the law on a secure new footing.

- **Costs:** The trial judge's approach to the question of "serious harm," endorsed by the UK Supreme Court, would necessarily entail deciding that question as a "preliminary issue," thus escalating costs. The high cost of defamation litigation was already identified as a problem in 1948 (see above), and was still a problem flagged up by Nick Clegg in 2010 (see above). The availability of "no win, no fee" for defamation in certain very limited circumstances has not solved the costs problem.

- **Jury trial:** Defamation was one of the few areas spared the wholesale axing of jury trials in English civil litigation in 1933. But the 2013 Act has now effectively ended jury trial for defamation as well. In any event, however, the role of a defamation jury in England was always more restricted than in America. In England it was always for the judge to determine the meaning of an allegedly defamatory statement. In America this is left to the jury. The savings in costs (if any) in abolishing defamation jury trials are more than offset by the damage to democracy. For, as random representatives of the community at large, juries are surely better qualified to decide issues of public reputation than any lawyer or judge.

- **Libel tourism:** The 2013 Act has at least stanched the running sore of libel tourism, which was what prompted its enactment in the first place. This has been achieved by the provision in section 9(2) restricting the jurisdiction of the English court to cases where "the court is satisfied that ... England and Wales is clearly the most appropriate place in which to bring an action in respect of the statement."

- **"Chilling free speech":** But what about the more fundamental problem of "chilling free speech"? The requirement of "serious harm" in section 1(1) of the 2013 Act was intended to stop the fear of trivial or frivolous defamation actions from paralyzing free expression. But, as we have seen, this has backfired as a result of the section's lack of clarity.

- **Libel and Slander:** The term "defamation" encompasses libel and slander, libel being a defamatory statement in written or permanently published form and slander an oral defamatory statement. Defamatory words broadcast by radio or television are classified as libel rather than slander. The distinction causes unnecessary complications. The Faulks Committee, chaired by a High Court judge, recommended merging the English law of libel and slander (as under Scots law), but this was never implemented.

American Libel Law

American defamation law started diverging from English law very early on. In the 1735 libel trial of the New York publisher John Peter Zenger his counsel successfully argued that truth is a defense against defamation—at a time when that was not yet accepted in English law. To this day there is still a presumption in English defamation law that an alleged defamatory statement is untrue—and it is for the defendant to prove that the statement is true. This seems to be a hangover from the Medieval offense of Scandalum Magnatum, or "slander of great men," covering insulting words spoken of a peer, a great officer of state, or a judge. It was extremely difficult to defend oneself against this charge. [See Lassiter, John C. (1974). *Scandalum Magnatum: The "Scandal of Magnates" in English Law, Society, and Politics.*]

Burden of Proof

Defamation law inevitably clashes with the right of freedom of speech. The English law of defamation, overly protective as it is of plaintiffs wishing to shield their reputation from attack, is inevitably at loggerheads with American law, which places a premium on freedom of speech. In the words of Professor Kyu Ho Youm of the University of Oregon: "In the United States, reputation is not one of the fundamental rights protected by the Fourteenth Amendment to the Constitution." [Youm, Kyu Ho (2008). *Liberalizing British Defamation Law: A Case of Importing the First Amendment?* 13 Comm. L. & Pol'y 415, 421 (2008).]

In English defamation law, as we have seen, the burden of proof rests on the defendant, thus setting English defamation law apart from other branches of English law as well as from American law of all kinds. This anomalous rule derives from the curious presumption that an alleged defamatory statement is untrue—which again is not shared by American law.

The criticism of this double anomaly in the Restatement (Second) of Torts § 613, comment j (1977), is instructive:

"Placing the burden on the party asserting the negative necessarily creates difficulties, and the problem is accentuated when the defamatory charge is not specific in its terms but quite general in nature. Suppose, for example, that a newspaper publishes a charge that a storekeeper short-changes his customers when he gets a chance. How is he expected to prove that he has not short-changed customers when no specific occasions are pointed to by the plaintiff?"

"No such thing as a false idea"

American law, federal and state alike, rejects any presumption of falsehood in an allegedly defamatory statement. Justice Powell put the American position like this, writing for the majority in the US Supreme Court case of *Gertz v. Robert Welch, Inc.*, 418 U.S. 323 (1974): "Under the First Amendment there is no such thing as a false idea. However pernicious an opinion may seem, we depend for its correction not on the conscience of judges and juries, but on the competition of other ideas. But there is no constitutional value in false statements of fact. ... The First Amendment requires that we protect some falsehood in order to protect speech that matters." As far as the States were concerned, he concluded: "We hold that, so long as they do not impose liability without fault, the States may define for themselves the appropriate standard of liability for a publisher or broadcaster of defamatory falsehood injurious to a private individual." This rejects the rule of the English common law of defamation with its doctrine of presumed falsehood, which "invites juries to punish unpopular opinion, rather than to compensate individuals for injury sustained by the publication of a false fact."

"Strict Liability Startling to Americans"

Professor Vincent R. Johnson of St Mary's University School of Law sums up this crucial difference between English and American defamation law: "[T]he idea of imposing strict liability for oral and written statements is startling to Americans because such liability would pose a serious threat to the principles of free speech and free press that are enshrined in the First Amendment to the United States Constitution." [Johnson, Vincent R. (2017). "Comparative Defamation: England and the United States," 24 *U. Miami Int'l & Comp. L. Rev.* 1.]

Three Categories

American defamation cases are divided into three categories:

- Lawsuits filed by public officials or public figures in regard to matters of public concern. In these cases the plaintiff must prove "actual malice" on the part of the defendant – meaning that the defendant published the allegedly defamatory statement knowing that it was false or with reckless disregard whether it was true or false. The leading authority on public officials is the US Supreme Court case of *New York Times v. Sullivan*, 376 U.S. 254 (1964). For public figures see *Curtis Publishing Co. v. Butts*, 388 U.S. 130 (1967).
- Lawsuits filed by private persons suing in regard to matters of public concern. Here US federal law requires at least proof of negligence on the part of the defendant of the falsity of the impugned statement: *Gertz v. Robert Welch, Inc.* (see above). The constitutional requirement that a defamation plaintiff prove actual malice or negligence has placed the burden of proof on the plaintiff to prove the falsity of the offending statement – exactly the opposite of the rule under English law even after the 2013 Act.
- Defamation actions relating to matters of purely private concern. The leading authority here is the US Supreme Court case of *Dun & Bradstreet v. Greenmoss Builders, Inc.*, 472 U.S. 749 (1985), which held that a credit rating agency could be held liable in defamation for carelessly reporting that a company had declared bankruptcy, when in fact it had not done so. The US Supreme Court

affirmed the decision of the Vermont Supreme Court that damages for defamation could be awarded even without proof of special fault. Justice Powell, writing for the leading plurality, held: "In contrast [to speech concerning public affairs], speech on matters of purely private concern is of less First Amendment concern. As a number of state courts. ... have recognized, the role of the Constitution in regulating state libel law is far more limited when the concerns that activated *New York Times* and *Gertz* are absent." This ruling has left states free to determine the level of fault required in such cases. Most states require proof that the defendant was negligent in regard to the falsity of the defamatory statement.

English "public interest" defense

While eschewing the classification of defamation cases under categories, the English Defamation Act 2013, in section 4, makes it a defense to an action for defamation "for the defendant to show that—(a) the statement complained of was, or formed part of, a statement on a matter of public interest; and (b) the defendant reasonably believed that publishing the statement complained of was in the public interest." This defense can be relied upon for statements of fact and opinion alike. It replaces the *Reynolds* defense, named for the House of Lords decision in *Reynolds v. Times Newspapers Ltd.* [2001] 2 AC 127, in which a former Taoiseach (Prime Minister) of Ireland successfully sued a newspaper for publishing articles wrongly accusing him of duplicity. The newspaper's defense of qualified privilege was rejected. So, though referred to as a defense, it was not accepted as such in the *Reynolds* case itself. In *Doyle v. Smith* [2018] EWHC 2935 (QB) a blogger/community newspaper publisher was sued for falsely accusing a property developer of being involved in what was described as "a £10 million fraud." The blogger's public interest defense failed, largely on the ground that the offending articles were not sufficiently "on matters of public interest." By contrast, a public interest defense on behalf of a "citizen journalist" was allowed in *Economou v. de Freitas* [2016] EWHC 1853 (1853); [2018] EWCA Civ 2591. It is too early to tell what effect, if any, the section 4 "public interest" defense will have on the English law of defamation.

The main problem it has is that the term "public interest" is not defined in the Act and is therefore left to judicial interpretation, leading inevitably to uncertainty. In addition, the test in section 4(1)(b) is purely subjective: "(b) the defendant reasonably believed that publishing the statement complained of was in the public interest." Subjective tests like this are notoriously difficult to prove. But, above all, as Professor Vincent R. Johnson points out, "the standard articulated by subsection (1)(b) misses the mark. Whether a statement contributes to the discussion of public issues depends on whether it is true or false, not on whether the defendant reasonably believed that publishing it was in the public interest. The stated test fails to focus on this important reality." He concludes: "Thus, with respect to matters of public interest. ... In England, non-culpability must relate to whether the matter was in the public interest; in the United States, culpability must relate to the falsity of the defamatory statement. ... To that extent, English law is less protective of free expression than American law." [Johnson, Vincent R. (2017). "Comparative Defamation: England and the United States," 24 U. *Miami Int'l & Comp. L. Rev.* 1.]

Website Operators

When it comes to the liability for defamation of website operators, English and American law diverge again. In England, the 2013 Act creates two defenses that protect website operators from liability for certain statements posted on their sites. But these defenses are narrower than the broad immunities embodied in section 230 of the the American Communications

Decency Act of 1996: "No provider or user of an interactive computer service shall be treated as the publisher or speaker of any information provided by another information content provider"—which effectively immunizes defamation and other claims against internet website operators. Vincent R. Johnson's conclusion is again inescapable: "In summary, the American Communications Decency Act broadly insulates website operators from liability, and is essentially pro-defendant. In contrast, England law confers limited immunities on website operators, and to that extent is pro-plaintiff." [Ibid.]

Definition of Defamation

None of the four English Defamation Acts provides an actual definition of defamation. This is painfully obvious, among others, in the case of *Sim v. Stretch* [1936] All ER 1237, in which, after winning at trial and by 2–1 in the Court of Apeal, the plaintiff's claim was dismissed by a unanimous 3–0 decision in the House of Lords on the basis that, as Lord Atkin put it, "the words complained of are incapable of a defamatory meaning." So there were three judges on either side. It was a remarkably simple case, based purely on a 22-word telegram about a housemaid addressed by her employer to a previous temporary employer, reading as follows: "Edith has resumed her service with us today. Please send her possessions and the money you borrowed, also her wages to Old Barton." The Statement of Claim alleged: "By the said words the defendant meant and was understood to mean that the plaintiff was in pecuniary difficulties, that by reason thereof he had been compelled to borrow and had in fact borrowed money from the said housemaid, that he had failed to repay the sad housemaid her wages and that he was a person to whom no one ought to give any credit." The House of Lords decision was not based on the truth or falsehood of any of the allegations made in the telegram but purely on whether the words of the telegram could directly or by innuendo bear a defamatory meaning.

Lord Atkin (not for the first time) proposed a new test for defamation, which is still considered authoritative, subject to the requirement of "serious harm" imported by section 1(1) of the 2013 Act, discussed above. Here is Lord Atkin's formulation in *Sim v. Stretch*: "Judges and textbook writers alike have found difficulty in defining with precision the word 'defamatory.' The conventional phrase exposing the plaintiff to hatred, ridicule and contempt is probably too narrow. ... I do not intend to ask your Lordships to lay down a formal definition, but after collating the opinions of many authorities I propose in the present case the test: would the words tend to lower the plaintiff in the estimation of right-thinking members of society generally?"

Is this really a legal test? What exactly is the meaning of "right-thinking members of society generally"? It is not only vague but also purely subjective. And who is to decide which members of society are "right-thinking" and which not?

American Standard

The American standard is more objective, as explained by Justice Oliver Wendell Holmes, Jr., in the amusing US Supreme Court case of *Peck v. Tribune Co.*, 214 U.S. 185 (1909). The case concerned a newspaper advertisement for pure malt whiskey recommended by a nurse called Mrs. A. Schumann "as the very best tonic and stimulant for all local and run-down conditions." Accompanying this claim was a photograph of the plaintiff, who was not Mrs. Schumann, was not a nurse, and was "a total abstainer from whisky and all spirituous liquors." The Circuit Court of Appeals of the Seventh Circuit had held that the publication was not defamatory. This judgment was reversed by the Supreme Court. The law of defamation, held Justice Holmes, "should be governed by the general principles of tort. If the advertisement obviously would hurt the plaintiff in the estimation of an important and respectable part of the community, liability is not a a question of a majority vote. ... We know of no decision in which this matter is discussed upon principle. But obviously an unprivileged falsehood need not entail universal hatred to constitute a cause of action. No falsehood is thought about or even known by all the world. No conduct is hated by all. That it will be known by a large number, and will lead an appreciable fraction of that number to regard the plaintiff with contempt, is enough to do her practical harm."

Fact vs. Opinion

One of the greatest threats to freedom of speech in English law is the possibility of being sued for defamatory opinions as well as for untrue facts. But what exactly makes an opinion defamatory? In *Thornton v. Telegraph Media Group Ltd.*, which was largely about opinion, the trial judge stressed the importance of distinguishing between fact and comment: "Much learning has grown up around the distinction between fact and comment. For present purposes it is sufficient to note that a statement may be one or the other, depending on the context. Ferguson J. gave a simple example in the New South Wales case of *Myerson v. Smith's Weekly* (1923) 24 SR (NSW) 20 at 26: "To say that a man's conduct was dishonourable is not comment, it is a statement of fact. To say that he did certain specific things and that his conduct was dishonourable is a statement of fact coupled with a comment." This is unhelpful. Why should "dishonourable" be a factual statement when it stands alone and a comment when coupled with specific instances? Whether supported by detailed examples or not, "dishonourable" is surely always a subjective opinion. What is "dishonourable" conduct in one person's opinion may be regarded as perfectly proper or even commendable according to a different set of criteria.

Does it matter in English law whether an alleged defamatory statement is a fact or an opinion? It certainly does. If a factual statement is alleged to be defamatory, the defense under section 2 of the 2013 Act is "to show that the imputation conveyed by the statement complained of is substantially true"—which replaces the old common law defense of "justification." But, if it is a statement of opinion that is impugned as defamatory, then the only defense is "honest opinion" under section 3 of the 2013 Act, which replaces the old common law defense of "fair comment." The practical effect of the distinction between fact and opinion or comment was clarified by Lord Templeman in *Telnikoff v. Matusevitch* [1992] 2 AC 343: "If the contents of the letter were fair comment, then the plaintiff cannot complain notwithstanding that they were defamatory." So, it is an advantage to the defendant if the words complained of are opinion and not fact. As Scott LJ explained in *Lyon v. Daily Telegraph* [1943] KB 746: "The reason why, once a plea of fair comment is established, there is no libel, is that it is in the public interest to have free discussion of matters of public interest."

"Repugnant to US Law"

However, when *Telnikoff v. Matusevitch* was referred back to a jury trial, the defense of fair comment was rejected and a verdict and judgment entered in the amount of £240,000 for the plaintiff, Vladimir Telnikoff. But he was sharply rebuffed when he tried to have this judgment enforced in the US. The original defendant, Matusevitch, filed a motion for summary judgment with the US District Court for the District of Columbia to preclude enforcement and collection of the English libel judgment as both an unrecognized and unrecognizable judgment. [*Matusevitch v. Telnikoff*, 877 F. Supp. 1 (DDC 1995).] The District Court refused to recognize the English judgment because it was repugnant to US law, as English defamation law did not provide First and Fourteenth Amendment protections to libel defendants. [See Korsower, Rachel B. (1995). "Matusevitch v. Telnikoff: the First

Amendment Travels Abroad, preventing Recognition of a British Libel Judgment," *Md. J.Int'l L.* 225 (1995).]

"Honest Opinion"

The new defense of "honest opinion" introduced in the 2013 Act was based on the UK Supreme Court decision in *Spiller v. Joseph* [2010] UKSC 53, where it was held that "the comment must explicitly or implicitly indicate, at least in general terms, the facts on which it is based." [Defamation Act 2013, Explanatory Note 22.] It was explained by Lord Walker in *Spiller* as requiring the defendant "to identify, at least in general terms, the nature of the factual basis supporting it." But Note 21 to the 2013 Act makes it clear that the new defense of "honest opinion" was not intended to change the law but rather "to reflect the current law [i.e. the law prior to 2013] and embraces the requirement established in *Cheng v. Tse Wai Chun Paul* (2000) 10 BHRC 525 that the statement must be recognizable as comment as distinct from an imputation of fact." [See also *Barron v. Collins* [2015] EWHC 1125 (QB), per Warby J.] It is hard to say, therefore whether English defamation judgments in opinion cases will be any more welcome in America than before 2013.

Section 3 of the 2013 Act sets up several hurdles that need to be cleared in order to establish the new defense of "honest opinon." First, the defendant has to prove that the offending statement was indeed a statement of opinion rather than a statement of fact—never an easy hurdle to clear. The second hurdle is to prove that the opinion was "honest" in accordance with section 3 of the 2013 Act. The contrast with US law could hardly be starker. For, as we have already seen:

> "Under the First Amendment there is no such thing as a false idea." [*Gertz v. Robert Welch, Inc.*, 418 U.S. 323 (1974), per Powell J. in the US Supreme Court.]

"Disproportionate to the legitimate aim of protecting reputation"

Another English libel judgment to come under fire, this time from the European Court of Human Rights, was *Aldington v. Tolstoy & Watts*, in which the plaintiff, Lord Aldington, was awarded record damages of £1.5 million for falsely being accused of complicity in war crimes during World War II. [QBD, Nov. 30, 1989, unreported.] The defendant, Count Tolstoy Miloslavsky, a distant relative of the famous Russian novelist, took the case to the European Court of Human Rights, which held that the award of £1.5 million violated Tolstoy's right of Freedom of Expression under Article 10 of the European Convention on Human Rights because it was "disproportionate to the legitimate aim of protecting Lord Aldington's reputation." [*Tolstoy v. UK* (1995) 20 EHRR 442.] This finding did not, however, disturb the judgment or the award of damages.

Injunctive Relief

Another feature of English law that is repugnant to US law is the possibility of obtaining an injunction to stop publication of a statement adjudged to be defamatory. Section 13 of the 2013 Act extends this remedy for use against a non-party, such as a website operator or publisher of a defamatory statement. In the US by contrast, injunctive relief relating to defamatory statements is available only in exceptional circumstances. And even then, websites cannot normally be ordered to remove posts held to be defamatory. [See Johnson, Vincent R. (2017).]

SPEECH Act

In sum, the 2013 Act does not appear to have made English law any more protective of freedom of expression than before. In the circumstances, it would be hard to disagree with Professor

Vincent R. Johnson's conclusion to his 2017 monograph, *Comparative Defamation Law: England and the United States*:

> "Despite the United Kingdom's passage of Defamation Act 2013, it is still the case that American defamation law is far more protective of free speech and free press than English law. Consequently, under the American SPEECH Act, United States courts should continue to refuse to enforce English libel judgments." [24 *U. Miami Int'l & Comp. L. Rev.*, p. 97.]

Super-Injunctions

Besides injunctive relief for defamatory statements, English tort law even allows pre-publication "super-injunctions" preventing publication of potentially embarrassing confidential or private information. [See the 76-page report of Lord Neuberger's Committee on "Super-Injunctions, Anonymized Injunctions and Open Justice."] As the very existence of any such injunction is kept secret, it is not even known how many have been issued. In addition, there have been many more "gagging orders" issued by the English courts, whose existence is known but whose contents are secret. In 2011 Kenneth Clarke, the then Justice Secretary, opined: "Every time I watch a football team I don't think I necessarily need to know about the sex lives of each of the players." He went on to say: "It is probably right to say that Parliament passing a privacy act might well be the best way of resolving it." [Robert Winnett & Christopher Hope, "Kenneth Clarke signals privacy law to ease fears over gagging orders," *Telegraph*, May 18, 2011.]

Freedom of Speech, Privacy & Defamation

Needless to say, no law of privacy materialized. English law has been crying out—quite literally—for legislation to protect privacy ever since the earnest entreaties of the Court of Appeal fell on deaf ears in the shocking invasion of privacy case of the popular TV actor Gorden Kaye in 1991. [See Chapter 10, "Privacy: A Strange Royal Case".] Not surprisingly, the judiciary took it upon themselves to fill this gaping void in the law. This was done by extending two other branches of the law: breach of confidence and ECHR Article 8 (right to respect for private and family life). But certainty remains elusive and there is still a gap in the law, as we saw in Chapter 10.

In English law, the precious right to freedom of expression, though enshrined in the Human Rights Act 1998, is squeezed between two far from clearcut areas of law: quasi-privacy law on the one side and defamation law on the other.

US law, by contrast, long ago nailed its colors to the mast of freedom of speech in the First Amendment, with privacy very much only a runner-up. Some of the examples of protected speech are surprising. In the words of Justice Clarence Thomas in *Masterpiece Cakeshop v. Colorado Civil Rights Commission*, 584 US (2018), examples of protected speech recognized by the US Supreme Court include: "The right of white supremacists to burn a 25-foot cross, *Virginia v. Black* (2003), conduct a rally on Matin Luther King Jr.'s birthday, *Forsyth County v. Nationalist Movement* (1992), or circulate a film featuring hooded Klan members who were brandishing weapons and threatening to "Bury the Niggers," *Brandenburg v. Ohio* (1969)—not to mention the Court's protection of flag-burning as symbolic speech in *Texas v. Johnson* (1989) and *United States v. Eichman* (1990).

PART IV

A FISTFUL OF FALLACIES

12

RIGHTS VS. RIGHTS

It is important to recognize that every human or civil rights case involves rights *on both sides*. [See Arnheim (2015).] This is all too often ignored or simply not understood. Here for example is Lord Steyn (Law Lord 1995–2005) welcoming the Human Rights Act 1998 when it came into force in 2000:

> "Constitutional adjudication needs to be approached generously in order to afford citizens the full measure of the protections of a Bill of Rights. By contrast, decisions taken day by day by commercial judges in respect of the meaning of, say, standard forms of letters of credit may sometimes employ relatively strict methods of construction." [Speech kindly provided to the author by Lord Steyn. See Arnheim (2004a), p. 64.]

If this is an exhortation to judges, as it appears to be, to favor those claiming rights against those resisting such claims, this would be unjust, for two reasons. First, because it goes clean counter to the fundamental principle of fairness: *audi alteram partem* ("hear the other side," or "listen to both sides.") And secondly, because it fails to recognize that there are rights involved on both sides. UK cases involving terrorism or national security, for example, are commonly described by the courts as requiring a balance to be struck between human rights and national security, or between the individual right to liberty and the public interest. Putting it like this is misleading. Abstract terms like "national security" or "the public interest" tend to pale into insignificance by comparison with "the rights of the individual." Yet, "national security" and "the public interest" actually refer to the *human rights* of thousands or even millions of *individuals*. Preventing the government from detaining or deporting potentially dangerous individuals may result in the violation of the individual rights to liberty or even to life of thousands of law-abiding citizens. And this needs to be spelled out in each and every relevant case.

There is an even more direct clash of rights against rights when two different rights are involved. The commonest example of this is the clash between privacy and freedom of speech, which was discussed in Chapter 10. A less common clash is one between the free exercise of religion and the rights of protected minorities such as gays or transgender people, though a number of cases of this kind have arisen in recent years.

"Gay Wedding Cake"

Conveniently for our purposes, there have recently been two strikingly similar cases involving a "gay wedding cake" considered by the US Supreme Court and the UK Supreme Court respectively. In both cases a Christian baker refused to make a "gay" wedding cake. [See Arnheim (2018b).]

In the UK case, a gay activist ordered a wedding cake iced with the slogan "Support Gay Marriage," and in the American case the order was for a wedding cake to celebrate an impending same-sex marriage, without any discussion of the design of the cake. In both cases the bakers rejected the order because same-sex marriage offended their deeply held religious convictions. And in both cases the attempted order was made in a jurisdiction in which same-sex marriage was not legal: Northern Ireland in the UK case, and, in the American case, in Colorado, although the cake was intended for a wedding due to be solemnized in Massachusetts, where gay marriage had already been legalized.

In both cases, the rebuffed customer had their cake baked elsewhere but raised a complaint with a government agency, which took up the cudgels on their behalf. In the UK case this was the Equality Commission of Northern Ireland and in the American case the Colorado Civil Rights Commission.

"Witches on Hallowe'en Cake"

In the Northern Ireland case, the final result was a tepid victory for the Christian bakers after two defeats in the Northern Ireland courts. The County Court held that the Christian bakers had discriminated against the prospective customer, Gareth Lee, "directly on grounds of sexual orientation" and "directly on grounds of religious belief or political opinion": *Lee v. Ashers Baking Co. Ltd* [2015] NICty 2. This decision was upheld by the Court of Appeal in Northern Ireland: *Gareth Lee v. Colin McArthur, Karen McArthur and Ashers Baking Company Ltd* [2016] NICA 29. Both Northern Ireland court judgments against the Christian bakers were based primarily on the Equality Act (Sexual Orientation) Regulations (NI) 2006 ("the 2006 Regulations") and on the Fair Employment and Treatment (NI) Order 1998. The relevant provisions of both these instruments prohibit discrimination on grounds of sexual orientation. In other words, they are concerned to guarantee equal treatment for people regardless of their sexual orientation.

In fact, however, far from upholding equal treatment the two Northern Ireland court judgments did exactly the opposite and championed a "politically correct" form of special privilege. According to those two court decisions, the Christian bakers were obliged to make a cake proclaiming "Support Gay Marriage", effectively promoting the prospective customer's right to freedom of speech while suppressing the bakers' own right to freedom of speech together with their right to freedom of religion as well as their commercial right as a business to accept or reject any order. In other words, the rights of the prospective customer, Gareth Lee, were held by the courts to trump the rights of the Christian bakers. That is not equal treatment but its opposite, special privilege.

It would seem obvious that baking a cake with the slogan "Support Gay Marriage" amounts to the bakers' approving, promoting or supporting gay marriage. Yet the Northern Ireland courts simply rejected this proposition out of hand. The Court of Appeal judgment went so far as to say: "The fact that a baker provides a cake for a particular team or portrays witches on a Halloween cake does not indicate any support for either." This is a textbook example of an argument by false analogy—a classic case of illogicality. Hallowe'en, a contraction of "All Hallows Eve", may well at one time have had religious connotations, but it is now a purely fun celebration associated more with fancy dress, pumpkins and "trick-or-treat". Nobody would take a Hallowe'en cake to be an inducement to adopt any particular belief, and the same applies to a cake for a sports team. The word "support" would be absent from such cakes anyway. But it was crucial to the cake ordered by Gareth Lee. "Support Gay Marriage" is a political slogan advocating a change in the law at a time when gay marriage was (as it still is) illegal in Northern Ireland. Instead of the false analogies suggested by the Northern Ireland court, a genuine analogy to "Support Gay Marriage" would be "Support the Legalization of Cocaine".

A unanimous UK Supreme Court reversed this decision, holding that the bakers had not discriminated against Gareth Lee on grounds either of sexual orientation or religious belief. In the words of Baroness Hale, who delivered the lead opinion: "The less favourable treatment was afforded to the message not to the man." [*Lee v. Ashers Baking Company,* [2018] UKSC 49.] Had the Christian bakers been held to have discriminated against Gareth Lee because of his sexual orientation rather than just against the proposed cake because of its slogan, the decision would have gone the other way.

"One of the most despicable pieces of rhetoric"

The Colorado case had a similar history: *Masterpiece Cakeshop v. Colorado Civil Rights commission,* 584 US (2018). The Colorado Civil Rights Commission and the Colorado courts ruled against Jack Phillips, the Christian baker, ordering him to "cease and desist from discrimination against ... same-sex couples by refusing to sell them wedding cakes or any product [they] would sell to heterosexual couples."

The Commission, affirming an administrative law judge, ordered Jack Phillips to "cease and desist from discrimination against ... same-sex couples by refusing to sell them wedding cakes or any product [they] would sell to heterosexual couples." The Commission made no secret of their feelings about the case. One commissioner went so far as to disparage the claim of freedom of religion in extreme language: "Freedom of religion and religion has been used to justify all kinds of discrimination throughout history, whether it be slavery, whether it be the holocaust.... we can list hundreds of situations where freedom of religion has been used to justify discrimination. And to me it is one of the most despicable pieces of rhetoric that people can use to—to use their religion to hurt others."

Justice Kennedy, writing for a 7–2 majority, quite rightly condemned these sentiments out of hand. He summarized the issue before the court as "the proper reconciliation of at least two principles": government protection of gay rights on the one hand, and, on the other, the First Amendment rights of freedom of speech and the free exercise of religion His conclusion was: "Given all these considerations, it is proper to hold that whatever the outcome of some future controversy involving facts similar to these, the Commission's actions here violated the Free Exercise Clause; and its order must be set aside."

This certainly was a victory for Jack Phillips, though not perhaps as complete a victory as might have been expected. The phrase "whatever the outcome of some future controversy involving facts similar to these," is puzzling to say the least, indicating that this decision was only tentative. Though the Commission's hostile attitude to religion is condemned, it appears that they may have won had they adopted a "neutral" attitude to religion instead of an overtly hostile one. In Kennedy's words: "[T]he Commission's consideration of this case was inconsistent with the State's obligation of religious neutrality." But the strangest feature of the judgment was the failure to address Jack Phillips's claim of violation of his freedom of speech.

The main reason for this was that the majority on the Court were not sure whether, in Clarence Thomas's words, Jack Phillips "refused to create a *custom* wedding cake for the individual respondents, or whether he refused to sell them *any* wedding cake (including a premade one)." If the former, then his objection would have been only to making the *cake*; but if the latter, he could be taken as discriminating against *gay people*. In his concurring opinion, in which he was joined by Justice Gorsuch, Justice Thomas made it clear that the Christian baker's objection was just to the cake, not to the people. Although (unlike in the UK case) there had been no discussion of the design of the cake, Jack Phillips prided himself on "creating" custom wedding cakes "to ensure that each cake reflects the couple who ordered it." Phillips' conduct, in creating and designing custom wedding cakes, was "expressive," meaning that it should be protected by the First Amendment. And, as Clarence Thomas put it: "Once a court concludes that conduct is expressive, the Constitution limits the government's authority to restrict or compel it. States cannot punish protected speech because some group finds it offensive, hurtful, stigmatic, unreasonable or undignified." He then quoted from the judgment in *Texas v. Johnson*, which found flag-burning to have the status of protected speech: "If there is a bedrock principle underlying the First Amendment, it is that the government may not prohibit the expression of an idea simply because society finds the idea itself offensive or disagreeable." A contrary rule would allow the government to stamp out virtually any speech at will."

Clarence Thomas continued his powerful concurring opinion: "Consider what Phillips actually said to the individual respondents in this case. After sitting down with them for a consultation, Phillips told the couple, 'I'll make your birthday cakes, shower cakes, sell you cookies and brownies, I just don't make cakes for same-sex weddings.' It is hard to see how this statement stigmatizes gays and lesbians more than blocking them from marching in a city parade, dismissing them from the Boy Scouts, or subjecting them to signs that say 'God Hates Fags'—all of which this Court has deemed protected by the First Amendment. ... Concerns about 'dignity' and 'stigma' did not carry the day when this Court affirmed the right of white supremacists to burn a 25-foot cross, *Virginia v. Black* (2003); conduct a rally on Martin Luther King Jr.'s birthday, Forsyth County v. Nationalist Movement (1992); or circulate a film featuring hooded Klan members who were brandishing weapons and threatening to 'Bury the niggers," *Brandenburg v. Ohio* (1969). Nor does the fact that this Court has now decided *Obergefell v. Hodges* (2015) somehow diminish Phillips' right to free speech. 'It is one thing. ... to conclude that the Constitution protects a right to same-sex marriage; it is something else to portray everyone who does not share [that view] as bigoted' and unentitled to express a different view. (Idem, Roberts, CJ, dissenting.)

Equal Rights or Special Privileges?

In the final decision in both the UK and the US, the overriding concern seems to have been about discrimination against gay people. In *Ashers* the Christian bakers won only because the UK Supreme Court was satisfied that their rejection of the specific wedding cake ordered did not mean that they would have refused to sell Gareth Lee any *other* products. Lady Hale pointed out that both Article 9 (freedom of religion) and

Article 10 (freedom of expression) of the European Convention of Human Rights are "qualified rights which may be limited or restricted in accordance with the law and insofar as this is necessary in a democratic society in pursuit of a legitimate aim. The bakery could not refuse to provide a cake—or any other of their products—to Mr. Lee because he was a gay man or because he supported gay marriage. But that important fact does not amount to a justification for something completely different— obliging them to supply a cake iced with a message with which they profoundly disagreed." [para 55.]

In *Masterpiece,* similarly, Justice Kennedy stressed "that these disputes must be resolved with tolerance, without undue disrespect to sincere religious beliefs, and without subjecting gay persons to indignities when they seek goods and services in an open market." This wording is not even-handed. According to this, it is in order for sincere religious belief to be treated with disrespect as long as it is not "*undue* disrespect" (whatever that means), while gay persons must not be "subjected to indignities."

"Live Free or Die"

Justice Thomas's arguments, supported by Justice Gorsuch, are an eloquent plea for the right to religious freedom and freedom of speech not to be sacrificed to special privileges. A case that gives further support to Justice Thomas's argument is *Wooley v. Maynard*, 430 US 705 (1977), a US Supreme Court decision which I discussed in an article on *Ashers* that I wrote before that case was heard by the UKSC and which is equally relevant to *Masterpiece.* George Maynard, a Jehovah's Witness living in New Hampshire, successfully objected to having to display the state motto, "Live Free or Die", on his motor car licence plate. "The slogan", explained George Maynard, "is directly at odds with my deeply held religious convictions. ... I also disagree with the motto on political grounds." The motto was a standard feature of license plates in that state, and state legislation made it obligatory to affix such license plates to all non-commercial motor vehicles registered in New Hampshire. The US Supreme Court held the state law in question unconstitutional because, in the words of Chief Justice Warren Burger, it effectively required individuals to "use their private property as a 'mobile billboard' for the State's ideological message." The slogan on a custom-made cake would be far more closely identified with the bakery that produced it than the motto on a mass-produced number plate attached to every car in New Hampshire would be identified with any particular resident of that state.

Hate Speech

Wooley v. Maynard combines a religious objection with one based on freedom of speech. And the same applies in the Northern Ireland gay wedding cake case. ECHR Article 9 guarantees "Freedom of thought, conscience and religion" and specifically protects everyone's right "to manifest his religion or belief, in worship, teaching, practice and observance." Obliging Christian bakers to make a cake enjoining "Support Gay Marriage" infringes their Article 9 rights by effectively making them *manifest* a belief which they reject as sinful and wrong, which is a form of forced speech. And it also infringes on their Article 10 rights by forcing them against their will to advocate a change in the law. Although in *Masterpiece* no slogan or writing of any kind was involved, Jack Phillips' wedding cakes were, as he put it, in his "voice," and, as Clarence Thomas remarked, wedding "guests often recognize his creations and seek his bakery out afterward." Making a cake for a same-sex wedding would have meant endorsing the concept of gay marriage, which he simply could not bring himself to do, so that when ordered by the Colorado Commission to "cease and desist" to discriminate against gay people, he chose rather to stop baking wedding cakes altogether, at great cost to his business.

Clarence Thomas's list of cases in which a variety of abhorrent messages were upheld by the US Supreme Court is instructive. The question remains: why is the First Amendment strong enough to support hate speech but not the simple negative example of expressive conduct manifested by Jack Phillips? And, similarly, as far as *Ashers* is concerned, why do the rights of gay people trump the right of free expression and the right to manifest one's religion under the ECHR? The answer would appear to be: privilege.

13

COOKING THE BOOKS

Sir Edward Coke (1552–1634) is one of most prominent judges in English History, and he lived during a period of great turbulence leading up to the English Civil War, which culminated in the execution of King Charles I in 1649. Coke, pronounced "Cook," had a brilliant if somewhat chequered career of public service, with shifting loyalties dictated by self-interest. Hence the title of this chapter.

So diametrically opposed to one another were Coke's positions in the three phases of his life that they are almost like three different personalities, which we can label Coke I, Coke II and Coke III. The Coke who was attorney general from 1594 to 1606 under Queen Elizabeth I and the early years of King James I was a fierce upholder of the royal prerogative and a savage prosecutor. This incarnation may be labeled as Coke I. His elevation to the bench as Chief Justice, first of Common Pleas and then of King's Bench, which together account for the period 1606 to 1616, turned him into a champion of judicial power against the Crown—Coke II. After championing judicial power over Parliament he was dismissed by King James I with an order to busy himself "expunging and retracting such novelties and errors and offensive conceits as are dispersed in his *Reports*." After an interval he emerged in 1621 as Coke III—a Member of Parliament vociferously championing Parliamentary supremacy against the Crown, including taking a leading role in drafting the Petition of Right of 1628, which is still in force today (officially designated as 1627 Chapter 1 3 Cha 1), prohibiting the Crown from imposing taxes or forced loans without an Act of Parliament.

Dr. Bonham's Case

Dr. Bonham's Case [8 Co. Rep 107; 77 ER 638 (1610)] is a leading case representing an abortive attempt on Coke's part to place judge-made law above parliamentary statute law. Thomas Bonham, a medical graduate of my Cambridge college, St John's, and subsequently of Oxford university as well, was debarred from practicing medicine in London by the College of Physicians, which had the right, granted by Letters Patent and two Acts of Parliament, to license all medical practitioners in London and to fine and even imprison indefinitely anyone practicing without such a license. Bonham's protracted dispute with the College of Physicians even saw him thrown into prison for contempt. After his release following a successful application to court for a writ of *habeas corpus*, the College of Physicians appealed to a high-powered committee of four senior judges, who found in favor of the College. Emboldened by this success, the College of Physicians then sued Bonham for practicing medicine without a license, and Bonham, who was again in prison, counterclaimed for wrongful imprisonment "against the law and custom of this kingdom of England." It was this lawsuit that was heard by Coke as Chief Justice of Common Pleas sitting with four other judges. Coke, delivering the majority opinion (3–2) in favor of Dr. Bonham, clearly relished the opportunity at one and the same time to assert judicial authority over Parliament and, as a loyal Cambridge alumnus, to champion the two ancient universities against the College of Physicians, which he saw as an upstart institution.

"The Common Law Can Adjudge an Act of Parliament to be Void"

Coke's argument was quite simple but completely wrong, and largely supported by misquoted or distorted precedents. His reasoning ran as follows: As a medical graduate of Cambridge and Oxford, Dr. Bonham was entitled to practice medicine wherever he liked. So the claim on the part of the College of Physicians to have authority to license Dr. Bonham was bogus. Coke launched into a paean of praise of the Universities, belittling by comparison the College of Physicians, which he describes as "that private college":

> "No comparison is to be made between that private college and the universities of Cambridge and Oxford, no more than between the father and his children or between the fountain and the small rivers which descend from it. The University is Alma Mater, from whose breast those of that private college have suck'd al their science and knowledge."

But how was Coke to counter the fact that the authority of the College of Physicians rested on two Acts of Parliament? He did so by enunciating a broad doctrine giving judges a wide-ranging right to set aside Acts of Parliament:

> And it appears in our Books, that in many Cases, the Common Law does control Acts of Parliament, and sometimes shall adjudge them to be void: for when an Act of Parliament is against Common right and reason, or repugnant, or impossible to be performed, the Common Law will control it, and adjudge such Act to be void.

The specific basis of Coke's attack on one of the Acts of Parliament relied upon by the College of Physicians was that it made the college "prosecutor, plaintiff, and judge in the dispute," because the college was entitled to half of any fine that it imposed. So, claimed Coke, the statute in question offended against the principle of natural justice that "no person may be a judge in his own cause." This is indeed a fundamental principle, but it is hard to see its relevance to Dr. Bonham's case. For, in fining and imprisoning delinquent medical practitioners the College of Physicians was acting as a disciplinary body rather than as a tribunal adjudicating between two other parties.

"The power and jurisdiction of Parliament is absolute"

After Coke II had effectively consigned two Acts of
Parliament to the shredder, Coke III went to the other extreme
and championed Parliament's power in extreme terms:

> "Of the power and jurisdiction of the Parliament for the
> making of laws in proceeding by bill, it is so transcendent and
> absolute, as it cannot be confined either for causes or persons
> within any bounds. Of this court it is truly said: *Si antiquitatem
> spectes, est vetustissima, si dignitatem, est honoratissima, si
> jurisdictionem, est capacissima.* ('If you look at its antiquity, it is
> the most venerable; if you consider its dignity, it is the most
> honorable; if you measure its jurisdiction, it is the most
> ample'—my translation)." [Co 4 Inst 36].

Here at last we have a full-throated enunciation of true
principle—the doctrine of the supremacy of Parliament. It is
worth noting that Coke here specifically describes Parliament as
a "court" imbued with authority and power second to none—a
doctrine completely incompatible with that espoused by Coke II,
which allowed judges to strike down Acts of Parliament.

No wonder some commentators have found it hard to
believe that Coke II really meant that the common-law courts
could declare an Act of Parliament void—an expression of
judicial activism, or even judicial supremacism. (See for example:
Williams, Ian (206).] But there can be little doubt that that *was*
the import of Coke II's doctrine. The Oxford English Dictionary
quotes legal documents going back as far as 1433 in which "void"
means "having no legal force; not binding in law; legally null,
invalid, or ineffectual." One example, from Sleidane's
Commentaries, dating from 1560, half a century before Dr.
Bonham's Case, is: "Whatsoever is there done to be voyde and of
none effect."

How, you might ask, could so *bona fide* a champion of the
rule of law as Sir Edward Coke possibly have swung 180 degrees

in his pronouncements on the subject? The answer is that throughout his three incarnations Coke steadfastly championed just one thing: the power and authority of Edward Coke.

That is why the doctrine enunciated by Coke II is so pernicious—because it allows unelected judges to ride roughshod over the elected legislature and to make up the law as they go along.

The doctrine of Coke II was superseded by that of Coke III,—which had in fact been there all along. Coke III's encomium on Parliament was supported by the highly authoritative *De Republica Anglorum: the Maner of Gouernement or Policie of the Realme of England, written between 1562 and 1565* by Sir Thomas Smith (1513–1577), which summarized the position of Parliament like this: "*The most high and absolute power of the realme of Englande, is in the Parliament.*" [For a fuller quotation from this work see Chapter 1 "United Kingdom: The Sovereignty of Parliament."] Here, therefore, early in the reign of Queen Elizabeth I (1558–1603) we already have the full-blown principle of the Sovereignty of Parliament, whose power is described as "most high and absolute." Surprisingly, perhaps, Smith emphasizes Parliament's all-encompassing representative function, at a time when only a small fraction of the nation had the right to vote. And, significantly, as in Coke III, Parliament is described as "the highest court," leaving no room for its enactments to be set aside by the judiciary.

14

THE ELUSIVE
BRITISH CONSTITUTION

The British Constitution is generally described as unwritten—
though there are in fact a number of statutes in force dealing
with constitutional matters. But the fact that the Constitution is
largely unwritten has resulted in a good deal of debate about
some of its most fundamental features.

The Role of the Monarch

- For an Act of Parliament to be valid it needs to be passed by
  the House of Commons and the House of Lords and receive
  the Royal Assent. In legal terms the Queen can choose
  whether to give or withhold her assent. But the last time that
  the royal assent to a bill passed by both Houses of Parliament
  was withheld was in 1708, when Queen Anne, on the advice
  of her ministers, refused to give her assent to the Scottish
  Militia Bill. There was a fear that the Scottish militia might
  prove disloyal, an understandable concern in the wake of the
  Acts of Union 1707 uniting England and Scotland into the
  new state of the United Kingdom of Great Britain.
- This power to withhold the royal assent to a bill was the
  origin of the US President's veto power under Article II of
  the US Constitution, which is still used regularly. The main
  difference is of course that the US president is elected, while
  the British monarch is not.

- Could the Queen withhold her assent to a bill? Yes, she
  could. And it would not only be *lawful* for her to do so, but

343

also perfectly in accordance with the British constitution. So, it would be "constitutional" as well—not a term which is ever used in English law. The point is that under the British constitution the royal assent is required for any bill to become a law. So, the Queen clearly has the right under the Constitution to decide whether to give or withhold her assent to a bill. [Cf. Bogdanor, Vernon (2019). *Beyond Brexit: Towards a British Constitution*, where it is suggested that it would be unconstitutional for the Queen to withhold her assent to a Bill.]

- Why then has the royal assent never been withheld for over 300 years? The answer is political, not legal or even constitutional. As executive power gradually shifted from the Monarch to his or her ministers, it became a *convention* for the Monarch to accept all laws passed by both Houses of Parliament, where the ministers of the Crown normally have a built-in majority. What would happen if the Queen decided to veto a bill? It would probably precipitate a political crisis for an unelected monarch to override the people's elected representatives., but there would be nothing "unconstitutional" about it.

- The tradition of giving the royal assent to all bills is only one of a number of *conventions* affecting the monarchy. Another important convention obliges the monarch to appoint as Prime Minister the leader of the majority party in the Commons. However, the legal and constitutional position is that the Crown can hire and fire Prime Ministers at will. The last time a Prime Minister was dismissed by the Crown occurred not in the United Kingdom but in Australia in 1975, when the Governor General—who exercises the functions of the Crown there—unexpectedly dismissed the Prime Minister, Gough Whitlam, who still had a majority in the House of Representatives, and invited the leader of the opposition, Malcolm Fraser, to form a government. This was completely contrary to convention, but perfectly lawful.

It caused a huge political storm, but Fraser handily won the ensuing election, and, though the Governor General, Sir John Kerr, resigned two years later, he was appointed Knight Grand Cross of the Royal Victorian Order (GCVO), an award within the personal gift of the Queen, specifically for his services as Governor General of Australia.

• The US is of course governed by a codified written constitution, so the role of convention is minimal. The Twenty-Second Amendment lays down the two-term rule for the President. But, until that Amendment was ratified in 1951, that rule was merely a convention—which was of course broken by Franklin Roosevelt, who was elected President four times. And this was precisely the reason why the Amendment was introduced—to prevent any future president from emulating Roosevelt. FDR's flouting of the convention certainly raised some eyebrows, to say the least, but it did not precipitate a crisis.

Dicey's account "out of place in the modern UK"

The bedrock principle of the British constitution is the sovereignty of Parliament. This is explained in Dicey's famous summary: "Parliament means, in the mouth of a lawyer (though the word has often a different sense in conversation) the King, the House of Lords, and the House of Commons: these three bodies acting together may aptly be described as the 'King in Parliament, and constitute Parliament. The principle of Parliamentary sovereignty means neither more nor less than this, namely that Parliament thus defined has, under the English constitution, the right to make or unmake any law whatever: and further, that no person or body is recognized by the law of England as having a right to override or set aside the legislation of Parliament." [A.V. Dicey, *Introduction to the Study of the Law of the Constitution*, 1885.]

As we saw in Chapter 1, "United Kingdom: The Sovereignty of Parliament," the fundamental principle of the sovereignty of Parliament can be traced back to the coronation oath of Edward II in 1307. Yet in recent years some law academics and even a few judges have questioned it. Here is Lord Steyn (Law Lord 1995–2005) in the case of *Jackson v. Attorney General* [2006] 1 AC 262:

> "The classic account given by Dicey of the doctrine of the supremacy of Parliament, pure and absolute as it was, can now be seen to be out of place in the modern United Kingdom. Nevertheless, the supremacy of Parliament is still the general principle of our constitution. It is a construct of the common law. The judges created this principle. If that is so, it is not unthinkable that circumstances could arise where the courts may have to qualify a principle established on a different hypothesis of constitutionalism. In exceptional circumstances involving an attempt to abolish judicial review or the ordinary role of the courts, the Appellate Committee of the House of Lords or a new Supreme Court may have to consider whether this is a constitutional fundamental which even a sovereign Parliament acting at the behest of a complaisant House of Commons cannot abolish."

These assertions fly in the face of 700 years of evidence. The correct time-honored position was put by Lord Bingham (Master of the Rolls 1992–1996, Lord Chief Justice 1996–2000, Senior Law Lord 2000–2008) in the same case: "The bedrock of the British constitution is, and in 1911 was, the supremacy of the Crown in Parliament. ... Then, as now, the Crown in Parliament was unconstrained by any entrenched or codified constitution. It could make or unmake any law it wished. Statutes, formally enacted as Acts of Parliament, properly interpreted, enjoyed the highest legal authority."

And again: "It has to my mind convincingly been shown that the principle of parliamentary sovereignty has been recognized as fundamental in this country not because the judges invented it but because it has for centuries been accepted as such by judges and others officially concerned in the operation of our constitutional system. The judges did not by themselves establish the principle and they cannot, by themselves, change it." [Lord Bingham quoted by Professor Adam Tomkins in his evidence to the European Scrutiny Committee of the House of Commons, "Divergent opinion on the scope of Parliamentary sovereignty," 2010—publications.parliament.uk.]

For more on this see Chapter 1, "United Kingdom: The Sovereignty of Parliament."

"The Human Rights Act 1998 has higher order legal status"

Shortly after the Human Rights Act 1998, incorporating (most of) the rights contained in the European Convention on Human Rights (ECHR) came into force in 2000, Lord Steyn asserted in a lecture that it had higher law status: "The Human Rights Act has a constitutional or higher legal order status," adding: "The fact that a right is entrenched in a Bill of Rights is compelling testimony that it is to be accorded a higher normative status than other rights." [From a lecture by Lord Steyn at a conference organized by Justice and Sweet & Maxwell, October 19, 2000. Paper kindly provided to the author by Lord Steyn.]

However, the concept of "higher law" or "entrenchment," however defined, has no place in a constitution based on the sovereignty of Parliament, which could repeal even the Human Rights Act if it chose. In the same lecture, Lord Steyn identified the practical effect of his classification of the Human Rights Act: "This will be particularly important in regard to the interpretation and application of the Convention and the Act. Constitutional adjudication needs to be approached generously in order to afford citizens the full measure of the protections of a Bill of Rights. By contrast, decisions taken day by day by commercial judges in respect of the meaning of, say, standard forms of letters of credit may sometimes employ relatively strict methods of construction."

If this means that courts should interpret Convention rights in a way that favors human rights claimants against defendants, this would be unjust. [See Arnheim (2004b), p. 64ff.] It is also important to realize that there are always human rights on both sides of any case. It is sometimes suggested that in cases involving terrorist suspects and the like, the courts have to strike a balance between human rights and national security, as if national security was just some impersonal and less valuable interest than human rights. In fact, of course, national security represents the human rights of thousands or even millions of law-abiding members of society which are imperilled by terrorism. [See Chapter 12, "Rights vs. Rights."]

A similar assertion to Lord Steyn's is made by those who claim that: "The Human Rights Act has brought the principle of the rule of law into the constitution." [Bogdanor, Vernon (2019).] As mentioned above, the Human Rights Act (HRA) 1998, which came into force in the year 2000, incorporated most of the articles of the European Convention on Human Rights (ECHR), to which the UK signed up in 1950 but which only became part of UK law in 2000. So, did the UK lack the rule of law until then?

The term "rule of law" goes back to the great Greek philosopher Aristotle (384–322 BCE), who, interestingly enough, drew a contrast between legislation and court-made law: "Laws are made after long deliberation, whereas decisions in the courts are given at short notice, which makes it hard for those who try the case to satisfy the claims of justice." [*Rhetoric* 1354b]

As far as England is concerned, "the rule of law" is a term that has been bandied about by many writers, politicians and judges for the past three hundred years, going back to the liberal philosopher John Locke, who advocated for government through "established standing Laws, promulgated and known to the People"—in other words, legislation, as against "extemporary Arbitrary Decrees." [Locke 1689: §§135-7.] The classic British statement on the rule of law was made by A.V. Dicey in his

Introduction to *The Study of the Law of the Constitution*, first published in 1885, in which the concept is narrowly defined: "[W]ith us no man is above the law [and] every man, whatever be his rank or condition, is subject to the ordinary law of the realm and amenable to the jurisdiction of the ordinary tribunals." [1885: 114.] In this statement Dicey was chiefly concerned to distinguish the situation in England, where the same law applied to everyone, from French *Droit Administratif*, under which government officials were accorded special privileges. However, Dicey's lodestar throughout was always the sovereignty of Parliament, which he famously declared to be "the dominant characteristic of our political institutions."

Lord Bingham, who wrote a book titled *The Rule of Law*, published in 2010, admitted that "There is not, after all, a standard of human rights universally agreed even among civilized nations. ... But within a given state there will ordinarily be a measure of agreement on where the lines are to be drawn, and in the last resort (subject in this country to statute) the courts are there to draw them." [Lecture, 2006, p. 19.] The bracketed clause is crucial—a recognition of the sovereignty of Parliament, a principle which Lord Bingham also enunciated much more forthrightly from the bench, as we saw above.

"What happens if there is a conflict between parliamentary sovereignty and the rule of law?" Under the British constitution there simply cannot be any conflict between the sovereignty of Parliament and the rule of law, as explained by Lord Reid (Law Lord 1948–1975): "It is often said that it would be unconstitutional for...Parliament to do certain things, meaning that the moral, political or other reasons against doing them are so strong that most people would regard it as highly improper. ... But that does not mean that it is beyond the power of Parliament to do such things. If Parliament chose to do any of them, the courts would not hold the Act of Parliament invalid." [*Madzimbamuto v. Lardner-Burke* [1979] 1 AC 645.]

Professor Anthony Bradley has remarked that the sovereignty of Parliament, or what he prefers to call Parliament's "legislative supremacy," is "subject to no legal limitations, and the courts have no power to review the validity of Acts of Parliament." But he then adds: "This doctrine is always considered to be subject to the limitation that Parliament is unable to bind its successors." [*Evidence* to the European Scrutiny Committee of the House of Commons, "Divergent opinion on the scope of Parliamentary sovereignty," 2010—publications.parliament.uk.]

Upon reflection, however, it will be realized that, far from being a limitation, this feature forms an integral part of the sovereignty of Parliament. If it was permissible for one Parliament to bind its successors and the Parliament of the year 2035 fixed the rate of income tax at, say, 35% "forever," the Parliament of 2040 would have no power to reduce it to, say, 28%, which would be a denial of the sovereignty of Parliament. Each new Parliament must be free to pass whatever legislation it wishes, which means that it cannot bind any subsequent Parliament. Without this supposed "limitation" the concept of the sovereignty of Parliament would have no meaning.

"Membership of the European Union abrogated the sovereignty of Parliament."

"The European Communities Act of 1972 abrogated the sovereignty of Parliament." (Bogdanor, Vernon (2019). This belief is shared by all too many British people and undoubtedly contributed to the impetus leading to "Brexit." The European Communities Act (ECA) 1972 was the instrument that took the UK into what came to be known as the European Union (EU). It is certainly true that prior to the UK's accession to the EU, the British courts could not strike down any Act of Parliament for any reason, but after accession they suddenly acquired the power to "disapply" any Act of Parliament that conflicted with EU law.

This power was not sought by the UK judges, who were taken completely by surprise when they suddenly discovered that they possessed it. So where did it come from? Strangely enough, indirectly from the ECA itself, a statute of the sovereign UK Parliament, section 2(1) of which provides that the treaties under which the UK became a member of what was to become the EU "are without further enactment to be given legal effect."

This vague wording does not in itself give EU law primacy over UK law, but the European Court of Justice had in the meantime built up its own precedents going back to 1964 giving European law primacy over the law of the individual member states. Neither the British Government nor the UK courts were aware of this development—until it hit them in the *Factortame* case.

The case involved a group of Spanish fishermen who took the British Government to court on the ground that they were discriminated against by the Merchant Shipping Act 1988 because they were not British. As Spain was a fellow member of the European Community (EC—as it was then known), they claimed that the offending part of the 1988 Act was contrary to EU law and—on the basis of the primacy of EC law over UK domestic law—should therefore be disapplied. Both the Court of Appeal and the House of Lords threw their hands up in horror at the thought of a UK court assuming rights "directly contrary to Parliament's sovereign will." The case was referred to the European Court of Justice (ECJ), which ruled that EC law overrode UK law in this case and that the domestic UK court had the power and indeed the duty to set aside the offending part of the 1988 Act. [*R* (*Factortame Ltd.*) *v. Secretary of State for Transport* [1990] UKHL 7.]

This ruling was duly implemented, with a good many spin-offs, causing a huge stir in legal and political circles in Britain, leading some commentators, like Sir William Wade, a law academic, to conclude that *Factortame* had actually altered the UK constitutional "rule of recognition"—a fancy way of saying that it had abrogated the sovereignty of Parliament. [Wade, William (1996), p. 574.]

How could the ECJ arrogate to itself powers that it is not accorded by any of the EC treaties? This question was evidently never asked by either the British Government nor by the UK courts. Lord Denning (Master of the Rolls 1962–1982) opined that if Parliament deliberately passed an Act "with the intention of repudiating the Treaty or any provision in it or intentionally acting inconsistently with it and says so in express terms, then I should have thought that it would be the duty of our courts to follow the statute of our Parliament." [*Macarthys v. Smith* [1980] EWCA Civ 7.] But Denning added: "I do not however envisage any such situation." And, sure enough, though Denning's dictum was expressed in 1979, Parliament with its usual lethargy failed to take the precaution that he suggested when it came to passing the Merchant Shipping Act 1988, even though there were rumblings at the time—prior to *Factortame*—that that legislation might fall foul of EC law. Had his suggestion been acted upon, the Merchant Shipping Act could possibly have been protected against EC intrusion—and *Factortame* might have had a very different outcome! Some other EU member states have been less hesitant to challenge the primacy of EU law—including Germany, France, Poland and Lithuania.

More than twenty years later, with the prospect of a "Brexit" referendum looming, the British Government and Parliament suddenly awoke to the need to reassert the sovereignty of Parliament, which of course had been there all the time. On October 6, 2010, the Government announced its intention to include a "sovereignty clause" in a new European Union Act "to underline that what a sovereign Parliament can do, a sovereign Parliament can always undo." A statement to this effect was tabled on the same day in the House of Lords, reading (in part) as follows:

"The Coalition Programme for Government said that the Government would examine the case for a United Kingdom Sovereignty Bill affirming that ultimate authority remains with Parliament. The common law is already clear on this. Parliament is sovereign. EU law has effect in the UK because —and solely because—Parliament wills that it should. Parliament chose to pass the European Communites Act 1972. That was the act of a sovereign Parliament. ... In the autumn, the Government will legislate to underline that what a sovereign Parliament can do, a sovereign Parliament can always undo. A clause to this effect will be included in the European Union Bill." [Foreign and Commonwealth Office, 6 October 2010.] The relevant clause was enacted as section 18 of what became the European Union Act 2011.

The true constitutional position was again echoed by Lord Chief Justice Thomas in the leading *Miller* case: "There is no superior form of law than primary legislation, save only where Parliament has itself made provision to allow this to happen. The ECA 1972, which confers precedence on EU laws, is the sole example of this. But even then Parliament remains sovereign and supreme, and has continuing power to remove the authority given to other law by earlier primary legislation. Put shortly, Parliament has power to repeal the ECA 1972 if it wishes." [*R (Miller) v. Secretary of State for Exiting the European Union* [2016] EWHC 2768 (Admin).]

Why some referendums are advisory, while others are legally binding.

"[I]t has not always been clear why some referendums have been advisory, while others have been legally binding." [Bogdanor, Vernon (2019.] The whole question of the status of a referendum bedevilled the whole "Brexit" crisis.

In fact, there is a very simple reason why not all referendums are binding—namely, once again, the sovereignty of Parliament.

So far, besides several regional referendums, there have been only three national referendums in the UK, the first being the 1975 referendum on whether the country should continue to be a member of the EC—which it had already joined in 1973 pursuant to the European Communities Act 1972 passed by Parliament in the usual way with royal assent. On the basis of the bedrock constitutional principle of the sovereignty of Parliament, no Parliament can bind a future Parliament, as discussed above.

Those against holding a people's confirmatory vote on the outcome of the "Brexit" negotiations argued that Parliament delegated to the people the decision on Brexit in the 2016 referendum and that it would be anti-democratic to go back on that. The truth is that whether or not to implement the (very narrow) outcome of the 2016 referendum—including holding a confirmatory vote—could only be a matter for Parliament.

Shortly after the Brexit referendum of 2016, an open letter to then Prime Minister David Cameron signed by 1,054 barristers made the point that the referendum result had no binding force in law but was purely advisory. This is undoubtedly correct. But the letter went on to explain that the reason for this was the fact that there had been no "threshold" quota of "yes" votes needed to take the UK out of the EU. This "explanation" was completely wrong. And the letter made no mention at all of the sovereignty of Parliament—the real reason why the referendum result was not binding! [See Arnheim (2016), an article of mine on in the *Huffington Post*.]

Would it be possible to set up a referendum that *was* legally binding? Yes, it would. In fact, the now practically forgotten Scottish devolution referendum of 1979 would have been binding if it had succeeded, because *before* the referendum was held an Act of Parliament was passed establishing a Scottish

Parliament, so that, had the requisite number of "yes" votes been cast, this devolved institution would automatically have come into existence. The reason the Scottish referendum of 1979 (not to be confused with that of 1997) failed *was* indeed because of a threshold: a requirement not only of a 50%+ "yes" vote by those actually voting but also a stipulation that the "yes" votes should amount to over 40% of those *entitled* to vote—a threshold that was not reached. The failure to reach the threshold was the reason why the referendum failed—but it was *not* the reason why the result would have been binding if it *had* been reached. The reason for *that* was simply, as I have said, the passing of an Act of Parliament beforehand, setting up a Scottish Parliament. (That legislation had to be repealed when the referendum failed to secure the requisite number of "yes" votes.) But the outcome of the referendum would have been equally binding without a threshold—provided the legislation creating a Scottish Parliament was in place before the referendum.

"What the UK needs is a written or codified constitution."

There has long been support, especially among academics, for a written or codified constitution for the UK. Here is Vernon Bogdanor: "Sovereignty is an absolute concept. Like virginity, once it is lost, it cannot be regained. Perhaps, then, the problems raised by Brexit can only be resolved by further limiting the sovereignty of Parliament. ... [T]he constitutional problems likely to result can only be resolved by radically rethinking our constitutional arrangements and moving towards a written or codified constitution." [Bogdanor, Vernon (2019), p. 2].

Sovereignty, like virginity, is an absolute concept? Really? But the passage then refers to "*further* limiting the sovereignty of Parliament." Yet, if sovereignty is absolute, how can there be degrees of sovereignty, which is what "further" limitation must mean? As we have seen, Parliament is as sovereign today as ever.

Among its supporters the idea of a written constitution tends to be associated with democracy, the "rule of law" (whatever that means), limited government, and, above all, human rights or civil rights.

Justice Antonin Scalia's opening statement in his testimony on "The role of judges under the US Constitution" before the Senate Judiciary Committee on October 5, 2011, is relevant here:

"I speak to law students from the best law schools. ... I ask them, 'What do you think is the reason that America is such a free country?' 'What is it in our Constitution that makes us what we are?' And I guarantee you that the response I will get—and you swill get this from almost any American. ... The answer would be: freedom of speech, freedom of the press, no unreasonable searches and seizures, no quartering of troops in homes—those marvelous provisions of the Bill of Rights.

But then I tell them, if you think that a bill of rights is what sets us apart, you're crazy. Every banana republic in the world has a bill of rights. Every President for life has a bill of rights. The bill of rights of the former 'Evil Empire,' the Union of Soviet Socialist Republics, was much better than ours. I mean it, literally. It was much better. We guaratee freedom of speech and of the press—big deal. They guaranteed freedom of speech, of the press, of street demonstrations and protests; and anyone who is caught trying to suppress criticism of the government will be called to account. Whoa, that is wonderful stuff!

Of course—just words on paper, what our Framers would have called a parchment guarantee. And the reason is, that the real Constitution of the Soviet Union. ... did not prevent the centralization of power, in one person or in one party. And when that happens the game is over; the Bill of Rights is just what our Framers would call a parchment guarantee.

So, the real key to the distinctiveness of America is the structure of our government. One part of it, of course, is the independence of the judiciary; but there's a lot more. There are very few countries in the world, for example, that have a bicameral legislature. ... Very few countries have two separate bodies in the legislature equally powerful. Very few countries have a separately elected chief executive.

And the Europeans look at this system and they say, 'Ah, it is gridlock.' [in faux foreign accent of indistinct origin.] And I hear Americans saying this nowadays, and there's a lot of it going around. They talk about a 'dysfunctional government' because there's disagreement. And the Framers would have said, yes, that's exactly the way se set it up. We wanted this to be power contradicting power.

So, unless Americans can appreciate that and learn to love the separation of powers, which means learning to love the gridlock, which the Framers believed would be the main protection of minorities—the main protection. ... So, Americans should appreciate that and thry should learn to love the gridlock. It's therefore a reason—so that the legislation that gets out will be good legislation."

Scalia was here being characteristically witty, original, and challenging of conventional wisdom. He was of course absolutely right about "parchment guarantees" of civil or human rights that are found in constitution after constitution all around the world. But, if the bill of rights in a particular constitution is just "words on paper," what is there to stop the provisions for separation of powers and checks and balances in that same constitution from being equally ignored? That is a question that Scalia did not address, because it goes to the heart of the justification not just for a bill of rights but for a written constitution altogether—the need for which he does not seem ever to have questioned. Ultimately, the success of a system of governance comes down to *trust*.

The most immediate post-Brexit wrangle is not about a written constitution for the UK but, more narrowly, about protection of fundamental human rights. The Charter of Fundamental Rights of the European Union, which came into force in 2009, ceased to have any effect in the UK after Brexit, though the UK (together with Poland) supposedly already had an "opt-out" from it, the status of which was never clear. The Charter is not to be confused with the European Convention on Human Rights (ECHR), which has fewer protections of human rights than the Charter and comes not from the EU at all but from a completely different and separate European institution known as the Council of Europe. Brexit has no effect on the UK's membership of that body, nor on the incorporation of the ECHR into UK law by the Human Rights Act 1998, which also remains unaffected by Brexit. The problem with the ECHR as incorporated into the Human Rights Act is not with its actual wording but with the extended "politically correct" interpretation that it has tended to be accorded, both in Strasbourg and also by some domestic UK courts. That kind of interpretation of the Convention rights tends to provide only "parchment guarantees" for the majority of law-abiding citizens while favoring special interest groups, including suspected terrorists, asylum seekers, illegal immigrants and even convicted killers. The ECHR and the Human Rights Act are of course written down, but, as the problem is with interpretation, a written or codified UK constitution will not solve it. [See Arnheim (2015).]

15

DEMOCRATIC DEFICIT
THE ELECTORAL COLLEGE?

The Electoral College, the bulwark of federalism, is under attack. Straightforward abolition of the Electoral College would require a constitutional amendment, which is most unlikely to be passed in the foreseeable future. But, abolition of the Electoral College would not solve the problem anyway—which is the democratic deficit allowing a presidential candidate to win the White House with a minority of the popular vote. The true culprit for this is not the Electoral College but the winner-take-all voting system which is generally combined with it but which is not necessarily so linked and, above all, unlike the Electoral College, is not mandated by the U.S. Constitution.

Winner-take-all is also responsible for the two-party system that—for good or ill—exists in both the U.S. and the U.K. The emphasis on "one person, one vote" and on ensuring that all votes count, and count equally, leaves open the much more fundamental question: What is democracy? Is democracy just a method of electing a government, or does it have some more precise content? And if so, what? On both sides of the Atlantic there is a widening gulf opening up between two models of democracy: "liberal" democracy and populism.

What the Constitution Says

Article II, Section 1 of the Constitution stipulates that the president is to be elected by "electors" chosen by the states, the number of electors for each state being the number of congressional representatives plus the number of senators from that state. At present, for example, California has 55 electors (53 + 2), Florida 29 (27 + 2), Georgia 16 (14 + 2), and Arkansas 6 (4 + 2), The Constitution does not say how these electors are to be chosen, but leaves that up to each individual state to decide. The Constitution does stipulate that the winning presidential candidate needs a majority (in other words, over 50%) of the total of electoral votes. The total number of electoral votes currently stands at 538, so a candidate needs 270 electoral votes to move into the White House. It is these 538 electors who form the "Electoral College," a term that does not actually appear in the Constitution and which is slightly misleading, as the electors from all the different states never actually meet together. The Constitution does not concern itself with the popular vote, only with the electoral vote, but the way the electors are chosen is left entirely to the individual states.

Framers not Party Animals

Though there was no shortage of disagreements between the Framers of the U.S. Constitution, these disagreements had not yet crystallized into a fully-fledged party political system. So the Constitution completely ignores parties altogether. You will find the original arrangements for presidential elections in the unamended text of Article II, Section 1 of the Constitution. The arrangements were as follows:

- Each state appointed as many electors for that state as there were senators plus representatives from that state combined. A state with, say, 12 representatives in the

House of Representatives would also of course have had
two senators (because every state is entitled to two
senators). So, the total number of electors for that state
would have been 14. It is important to note that these
electors were not elected but *appointed* by the state
legislature.

- The electors of each state met separately.
- Each elector had two votes without differentiating
  between President and Vice President.
- The candidate with the most electoral votes (provided
  they amounted to over 50% of the total) was declared
  elected as President and the runner-up as Vice
  President.
- If no candidate obtained more than 50% of the votes, the
  presidential election was thrown into the House of
  Representatives, and the Senate picked the Vice
  President.

These rules omitted all mention of political parties. The
whole arrangement was undemocratic, because the Framers did
not trust the people (or even the small proportion of them who
had the right to vote) to pick the President. Their naïve idea was
that the electors, who were good, solid pillars of the
establishment, would choose the best man to be the President
and the second-best man to be Vice President.

1796: Opposing Candidates Harnessed Together

Not surprisingly, this whole arrangement came unstuck as
soon as it was put to the test in the first genuinely contested
presidential election in 1796. John Adams and Thomas Jefferson,
the two main contenders for President, ended up as President
and Vice President respectively. It is just as if Hillary Clinton had
become Donald Trump's Vice President in 2016! John Adams, a
Federalist, got 71 electoral votes—just above the 50% required

for election—and Thomas Jefferson, a Republican or Democratic-Republican, was the runner-up with 68 votes. Although Jefferson and Adams did not see eye-to-eye politically, Jefferson was sworn in as Adams's Vice President. What a mess! But worse was to come.

1800: Tying and Vying with your Running Mate

The 1800 election was a rematch between Adams and his own Vice President, Jefferson. To avoid a repetition of the fiasco of 1796, the political parties each nominated two candidates, one intended as their presidential candidate and the other as their vice-presidential candidate. The Federalist ticket of John Adams and Charles Pinckney was confronted by the Democratic-Republican ticket of Thomas Jefferson and Aaron Burr.

Jefferson and Burr won, with 72 electoral votes each. It was well understood that Jefferson was his party's lead candidate, but the Constitution drew no distinction between him and Burr. Each elector just had two equal votes.

As neither Jefferson nor Burr had a majority, the choice of President was thrown into the House of Representatives, where each state had just one vote. Here the contest was no longer between Jefferson and Adams but between Jefferson and his own running-mate, Aaron Burr. After 36 ballots and a lot of horse-trading, Jefferson was declared elected as President, with Burr as Vice President.

Twelfth Amendment

This chaotic election made an amendment to the Constitution a pressing necessity, and the Twelfth Amendment was duly ratified on June 15, 1804, less than five months before the next presidential election.

The Twelfth Amendment has stood the test of time, although it still does not mention political parties. It indirectly recognizes the existence of parties by providing that electors cast a separate vote for President and Vice President. So it is no longer a problem if a presidential candidate gets the same number of electoral votes as his or her running-mate—which indeed is what normally happens.

The Twelfth Amendment was a very narrow fix. Why, you may well ask, did the Framers not take a bolder step, sweep away the whole electoral college concept altogether, and replace it with direct popular election?

Democracy or Republic?

The short answer is that what the Framers wanted to establish was not a democracy, but a republic, a very different political animal. Not only did they not want to establish a democracy: they were actually afraid of doing so. John Adams attacked the proposals of the radical Thomas Paine as "so democratical, without any restraint or even an attempt at equilibrium or counterpoise, that it must produce confusion and every evil work."

James Madison, the "Father of the Constitution" and the future fourth president, was no fan of democracy either. Indeed, he outdid Adams in attacking democracy: "Democracy is the most vile form of government ... democracies have ever been spectacles of turbulence and contention, have ever been found incompatible with personal security or the rights of property, and have in general been as short in their lives as they have been violent in their deaths."

By contrast, here is how Adams described a republic: "A government, in which all men, rich and poor, magistrates and subjects, officers and people, masters and servants, the first citizen and the last, are equally subject to the laws."

As you start reading this definition, you may well get the impression that it is going to be egalitarian—based on the equality of all people. But the final phrase gives the game away.

Republicanism, according to this definition, is not about any power that the people *have* but about a power that they are *under*. In a republic, says Adams, everybody is equally under the law. This ties in with Adams's expressed goal, which he incorporated into the Massachusetts state constitution: "A government of laws and not of men."

Adams's ideal was not one of people power at all. Rather, his ideal was one in which the people were subservient to laws made by an elite group (of which he and the other Founding Fathers were prominent members)—with the last word on the interpretation of those laws going to judges drawn from the same elite group.

The Democratic Deficit

Democracy does not figure in the U.S. Constitution at all—but republicanism certainly does. Article IV, Section 4 provides: *"The United States shall guarantee to every State in this Union a Republican form of Government."* There is no precise definition of "Republican," but Adams's views on the subject are a reflection of the Framers' thinking. (In fact, Adams himself did not attend the Constitutional Convention, as he was serving as U.S. ambassador to the Court of St. James [the U.K.] at the time.)

Fast forward 230 years and the U.S. prides itself on being a democracy, but the electoral system is lamentably deficient. There have been five presidential elections in which the winner lost the popular vote: those of 1824, 1876, 1888, 2000—and 2016. In 2016 Donald Trump's conclusive victory of 304 electoral votes to Hillary Clinton's 227 was not matched by his popular vote, in which Trump polled 2.8 million *fewer* votes than Clinton nationwide—the biggest democratic deficit of any winning presidential candidate in history.

The election of a president without a popular mandate would not have bothered the Framers of the Constitution. They did not trust the voters, as we have seen, and "democracy" was a dirty word back in 1787. Today, however, America prides itself on being a democracy, which is defined in terms of the popular vote.

Culprit: The Electoral College?

There is no shortage of objections to the Electoral College, and most polls since 1967 have shown a majority in favor of replacing the Electoral College with a nationwide popular vote in presidential elections, though there have been sharp fluctuations depending on party affiliation. So, for example, according to a Pew Research poll of March 1918, switching to a popular vote system was supported by 55% of those polled, made up of 75% of Democrats and 32% of Republicans. ["The Electoral College, Congress and representation," Pew Research Center, April 26, 2018.]

The main objection to the Electoral College is that it is a denial of the democratic principle of one person, one vote—inevitably, as there is a built-in weighting in favor of the smaller states in the way that electoral votes are allocated. On the eve of the 2012 election, Donald Trump himself called the Electoral College "a disaster for a democracy" in a Twitter post. Needless to say, his attitude changed after the 2016 election!

Most of the criticisms of the Electoral College could not be addressed without abolishing the whole federal structure of the U.S. system of government, which would require an amendment of the Constitution but would be unthinkable anyway, as federalism is one of the cornerstones of the United States.

So I will concentrate on those attacks on the Electoral College that are based on misunderstandings. An example of this is a 2016 article by a political science academic called Robert Speel. The article is titled, "Three common arguments for preserving the Electoral College—and why they're wrong," published on November 15, 2016, in an online journal called *The Conversation*, whose watchword is "Academic rigour, journalistic flair."

Right at the beginning of the article, the Electoral College is mis-defined as "the 18th-century, state-by-state, winner-take-all system for selecting the president." This definition is seriously wrong, because it lumps together two completely different and distinct systems: the Electoral College on the one hand, and, on the other, the winner-take-all system. The Electoral College system is mandated by the U.S. Constitution, but winner-take-all is not.

Alternatives to Winner-Take-All

The two systems do often coexist, but that is by no means automatic, and there are several alternatives to the winner-take-all mechanism which can be used together with the Electoral College system. These include the so-called "congressional district" method used by Nebraska and Maine, the National Popular Vote Interstate Compact (NPVIC)—and a proportional system, which has hardly been mooted but which, I believe, is by far the simplest, fairest and most democratic of all. I discuss these alternatives later in this chapter.

The Constitution does not concern itself with the popular vote, only with the electoral vote, but, as already mentioned, the way the electors are chosen is left entirely to the individual states.

"Pregnant Chads"

Although there are several alternative mechanisms that can be combined with the Electoral College system, all but two of the states use the fundamentally unfair winner-take-all mechanism to choose their electors. This means that whichever candidate gets the most popular votes in a particular state—even if they win by just one vote—automatically receives ALL the electoral votes of that state. This problem came to a head in Florida in the presidential race of the year 2000. The result of the ballot in that state, then accounting for 25 of the 538 electoral votes, was very close and highly disputed, largely because of the use of punched cards for voting in several precincts. The problem was that the "chad," or bit of paper punched out, was often not completely detached, resulting in "hanging," "dimpled," or "pregnant" chads, which could either be counted as valid or invalid votes. After much toing and froing between the courts, the case was eventually decided by a 5–4 majority in the U.S. Supreme Court, which declared George W. Bush the winner of Florida by just 537 votes (a margin of 0.09%), giving him a one-vote victory in the electoral college—while his rival, Al Gore, polled over half a million more popular votes in the country at large. Winner-take-all meant that whoever won Florida—by even the slenderest of margins—would not only get all 25 of Florida's electoral votes but would also win the whole election, which of course is what happened. Bush ended up with 271 electoral votes and Gore with 266—a knife-edge result culminating in several knife-edge results. This thoroughly unsatisfactory situation was not the fault of the Electoral College but of the winner-take-all system.

NPVIC

How can this kind of problem be prevented from recurring? The latest proposal is the so-called National Popular Vote Interstate Compact (NPVIC), an agreement by a number of states and the District of Columbia to award all their respective electoral votes to the presidential candidate who wins the popular vote nationwide. This formula, which is designed to ensure the victory of the candidate polling the most popular votes nationally, would go into effect only once that result could be guaranteed, which would be when the participating states had a combined total of over 50% of the electoral votes (currently totaling 538). At present the NPVIC has been signed up to by 15 states with a total of 189 electoral votes, 81 short of the 270 needed to give the compact legal force.

The NPVIC encountered strong Republican opposition from the start. In 2011 all but one of the voting members of the

Republican National Committee voted against it. Governors
Arnold Schwarzenegger of California and Linda Lingle of
Hawaii, both Republicans, vetoed NPVIC legislation on the
sensible ground that it could throw all their states' electoral votes
to a candidate who was not supported by a majority of their own
voters and thereby effectively disfranchise that majority. Both
these states have since signed up to the NPVIC under
Democratic governors. Advocates of the NPVIC are adamant
that implementation of the compact would not require a
constitutional amendment, but this is by no means certain,
because it effectively abolishes the Electoral College while
pretending not to do so. It is even less certain that the NPVIC
would not need Congressional approval. If it ever gets enough
support to be implemented, it will inevitably be caught up in
legal wrangles for years and its fate will ultimately have to be
decided by the U.S. Supreme Court. But the danger of the
NPVIC is that it is being sold on the false basis that it is a more
democratic way than winner-take-all to deliver an Electoral
College majority. What is kept hidden is that it can only do so at
the expense of federalism, the bedrock of the U.S. Constitution.

"Congressional District" Method

A harmless but not entirely satisfactory alternative to the
winner-take-all arrangement is the so-called "congressional
district method" (or simply the "district method") used by
Nebraska and Maine, which dispenses with winner-take-all but
retains the Electoral College, which is why it did not need a
constitutional amendment to be implemented. Under this
system, two electors in each participating state are chosen by a
state-wide popular vote and the remaining electors on the basis
of the popular vote in each congressional district. This is more
democratic than the winner-take-all system in force in all the
remaining states, but only marginally so. For example, in the
2016 election Maine's four electoral votes were shared, with

three going to Hillary Clinton and one to Donald Trump. The fact that there was any sharing at all is significant, because it shows that the Electoral College system is not a problem in itself. But it also shows that the district method is not the solution, as Trump's share of the electoral vote, one out of four, or 25%, fell far short of his 44.87% of the state-wide popular vote.

Proportional Solution

The solution that I favor is much simpler than either the NPVIC or the district method. It really *is* a solution to the democratic deficit and, if adopted by all states, would ensure that all future presidential elections are truly democratic—while keeping the Electoral College firmly in place. Surprisingly perhaps, it is not a formula that has been seriously advocated before, although it is not only simple but would also not require a constitutional amendment. It would dump the winner-take-all system while retaining the Electoral College.

Too good to be true? No. Here is how it would work. The Electoral College remains in place with the same allocation of electors to the states as at present. In each state the number of electoral votes is shared between the candidates in proportion to their popular vote. So, for example, if this system had been in force in Texas in the 2016 election, that state's 36 electoral votes would have been split, with 19 going to Donald Trump (for his 52.23% of the popular vote), 16 to Hillary Clinton (for her 43.24%) and one to the Libertarian candidate, Gary Johnson (for his 3.16%). The shares will almost always have to be rounded up or down. For example, Clinton's 43.24% of the vote should translate to 15.57 electoral votes, but splitting an elector would be tantamount to murder! Pedantic critics of this model have suggested multiplying the number of electoral votes by a factor of 10 or even 100 in order to ensure a whole number for each candidate's share. However, that would require a constitutional amendment. Moreover, the minor margin of error in calculating the proportional split pales into insignificance against the wholesale unfairness built into the existing system, under which Hillary Clinton's 43.24% of the popular vote in Texas earned her not 16 nor even 15 but zero electoral votes.

Calculating the election result in this proportional model is child's play. As in the present system, the winner in each state is the candidate with the most electoral votes, but that candidate will now automatically have the biggest share of the popular vote in that state as well. Any state can opt for this system at any time. The more states that do so, the better. But it could coexist in some states side by side with other winner-take-all states, just as the district method already does.

So where does that leave us? Here is a roundup of the election models available:

- The present system, which is simply not fit for purpose because of its propensity to elect a president lacking a nationwide popular majority.
- The radical and controversial NPVIC, which effectively abolishes the Electoral College and threatens federalism while pretending not to do so;
- The district method currently in force in Nebraska and Maine, which is just tinkering around the edges of the present system.
- My simple proportional model, which abolishes winner-take-all but retains the Electoral College and therefore protects federalism and does not need a constitutional amendment. This will guarantee that the winning candidate in each participating state combines a majority of the electoral vote with a majority of the popular vote in that state, and that, if adopted by all states, a president will be elected with a majority not only of the Electoral College but also of the popular vote nationwide.

Two-Party System

Winner-take-all state by state in presidential elections naturally resulted in a two-party system. First it was Democratic-Republicans vs. Federalists, then Democrats vs. Whigs, and since 1854, Democrats vs. Republicans. There is no shortage of other parties, but most voters perceive a vote for a third party as a wasted vote and prefer to hold their nose while voting for one of the two main parties. As a result, the smaller parties never get a look-in. The closest third-party showing occurred in the famous "Bull Moose" election of 1912, in which, after retiring and handing over to his hand-picked successor, William Howard Taft, ex-President Theodore Roosevelt regretted his decision and contested the election as a "Progressive"—or "Bull Moose." Roosevelt beat Taft into third place, splitting the Republican Party and putting Democratic candidate Woodrow Wilson into the White House. Wilson garnered 41.8% of the popular vote, as against 27.4% for Roosevelt and 23.2% for Taft. So the combined popular vote for Roosevelt and Taft was 50.6%. The only other third party candidate with any hope of winning was Ross Perot, who polled 18.9% of the popular vote, but no electoral votes, as he carried no states. However, it is quite possible that he cost incumbent President George H.W. Bush the election, as Perot's supporters were more likely to have voted for Bush than for Clinton had Perot not been running.

To win election to the U.S. House of Representatives or the Senate a candidate does not need to obtain an absolute majority (over 50%) of the votes. The winning candidate only needs to poll more votes than any other candidate. But winner-take-all nevertheless exerts an insidious influence on these elections as well. That is because, though electing only one representative or senator at a time, voters are well aware of the importance of which party is in *control* of each branch of the legislature, where every decision requires at least a majority, and sometimes even a "super-majority."

The voting system for U.S. Congressional elections was imported from Britain, where it is used in elections to the House of Commons (though not in regional elections, many of which employ some form of proportional representation). It is commonly referred to as "first-past-the-post" (FPTP), on the analogy of a horse-race, because a candidate only needs to get ahead of the rest of the field in order to win. As in American Congressional elections, the vote in each voting district, or constituency, is counted in isolation to the rest. So, it is possible for a particular political party to poll, say, 40% in every constituency in the country and still win no seats at all. That is an extreme hypothetical example, but this voting system has a natural tendency to favor the larger parties at the expense of the smaller ones. So, for example, in the General Election of 2015, the United Kingdom Independence Party (UKIP), though obtaining 12.6% of the popular vote, won only one seat out of 650. In a more typical example, in the General Election of 2017, the Liberal Democrats polled 7.4% of the popular vote but won only 12 seats out of 650, amounting to 1.8% of the total number of seats. The reason for this, again, is the reluctance of voters to "throw away" their votes, as many see it, by voting for a smaller party.

In the U.K. the importance of which party controls the House of Commons is even greater than the equivalent question in the U.S. Because, whichever party has a majority in the House of Commons gets to form the Government. That is built into the system. Legally, the Queen can call on anyone she likes to be Prime Minister, but she is constrained by longstanding convention to pick the leader of the party commanding a majority in the House of Commons (if there is one). It took a long time before the Monarch learnt this political lesson. In 1834, for example, King William IV (reigned 1830–1837), Queen Victoria's uncle and predecessor, dismissed the Whig government of Lord Melbourne, a prominent member of which was Lord John Russell, whom the King called "a dangerous little Radical," and appointed as Prime Minister the Tory leader, Sir Robert Peel, who did not have a majority in the House of Commons and, as a result, suffered a series of parliamentary defeats. Six times Peel tendered his resignation to the King, who refused to accept it each time. The press, who did not know about these behind-the-scenes meetings, misunderstood Peel's apparent reluctance to resign, and wrote that Peel had all the qualities of a statesman except the quality of resignation! The King was eventually forced to recall Melbourne to office. That was the last time that any British Monarch refused to follow the will of the electorate in choosing a Prime Minister.

Ranked Choice Voting

Winner-take-all or first-past-the-post is criticized on both sides of the Atlantic as not being truly democratic. Instead, an assortment of proportional systems are put forward. In the U.S., a non-profit organization calling itself FairVote.org strongly advocates for Ranked Choice Voting (RCV), coupled in certain circumstances with "Instant Runoff." Under "Our Mission" on their website we read: "American democracy today is not working. Our national government is trapped in gridlock, leading to historic levels of dissatisfaction and lower turnout every year. ...."

Justice Antonin Scalia famously said Americans should "love the gridlock," which he believed was a deliberate part of the system of separation of powers and checks and balances set up by the Framers in the U.S. Constitution. But, that aside, how would RCV work in, say, an election to the U.S. Congress?

- Let us assume there are four candidates, Red, Blue, Green and Yellow.
- Only one of these can be elected, and 50% is needed to win.

- Our hypothetical voter, Jane Doe, ranks as many of these candidates as she likes by placing numbers against the names of the candidates.
- Jane Doe marks her ballot like this: Red–4, Blue–2, Green–1, Yellow–3. Green is her first choice.
- Let us assume that there are 1,000 voters, and the distribution of first choices is as follows: Red–250, Blue–400, Green–200, Yellow–150.
- On a straightforward winner-take-all system, Blue would win, even though he/she has only 40% of the votes, and 60% of the voters prefer one of the other candidates.
- We now operate RCV instead. Under RCV the winning candidate needs to have over 50% of the votes. As none of the candidates has enough to win, the lowest-scoring candidate is eliminated and their first-preference votes are redistributed according to the second choices indicated on those ballots.
- The lowest-scoring candidate on first choices is Yellow, who is therefore eliminated and his/her 150 ballots redistributed according to their second choices.
- Yellow's first-choice ballots reveal the following second choices: Red–75, Blue–50, Green–25.
- When added to the existing first-preference votes, this is what we get: Red – 250 + 75 = 325, Blue – 400 + 50 = 450, Green – 200 + 25 = 225.
- There is still no candidate with over 50% of the votes, so we now eliminate the current lowest-scoring candidate, Green, and redistribute his/her votes.
- This gives us the following totals: Red – 325 + 185 = 510, Blue – 450 + 40 = 490.
- Red therefore wins, instead of Blue, who would have won on the basis of winner-take-all.

Note: In November 2016, the voters of Maine approved a ballot initiative to introduce a state-wide system of Ranked Choice Voting. This was implemented in the 2018 General Election for Maine's 2nd Congressional District, which resulted, (after several visits to the US District of Maine Court) in the defeat of the incumbent Republican Bruce Poliquin by the Democrat Jared Golden. [See https://ballotpedia.org.]

Advantages and disadvantages of RCV

- The winning candidate has received support from more than 50% of the voters—but this includes second and even third choices. Is it really fair to count second and third choices as equal to a first-preference vote?

- No votes are wasted. On the normal winner-take-all system, Blue's votes alone count; the rest are discarded. But, for a voter like Jane Doe who particularly wanted to elect Green, how much of a consolation is it that her vote helped to elect Red, her lowest choice, rather than Blue, her second choice?

- Unlike winner-take-all, RCV does not discriminate against smaller parties. A small party, which by definition has gleaned only a small number of first-preference votes, may possibly pick up enough second- and third-preference votes to win. The prospect of this kind of outcome may embolden smaller parties, which will then be likely to proliferate, resulting in no party having control of the legislative body concerned. This is not purely hypothetical. Forty European countries use some form of PR. As a result of the fragmentation of political parties, countries that use PR to elect their legislatures often have to resort to coalition government on a regular basis, which does not provide a stable basis for government. We have recently had the spectacle of countries such as Austria, Belgium and Italy emerging from a general election with a hung parliament and then going for many months without an elected government.

Two Models of Democracy

All the emphasis on "one person, one vote" and on ensuring that all votes count, and count equally, leaves open the much more fundamental question: What is democracy? Is democracy just a method of electing a government, or does it have some more precise content?

At the time of this writing, there appears to be a widening gap on both sides of the Atlantic between "liberal democracy" on the one hand and, on the other, what is variously labelled "illiberal democracy," "majoritarianism," or "populism." These three terms cover a fairly wide spectrum of concepts and beliefs, including some but not necessarily all of the following:

- A belief in "the people" as against elites and pluralism. President Richard Nixon's "silent majority" typifies this attitude. President Donald Trump's promise to "drain the swamp" (of Washington D.C.) is another example. Similarly, Nigel Farage, one of the leading "Brexiteer" politicians in Britain: "Brexit was the first brick that was knocked out of the establishment wall." And again: "Either you support the existing global elite, or you want real change and believe in nation-state democracy."

- Patriotism, even nationalism. Trump's "Make America Great Again" is a good example, as is the British Brexiteers' goal of "Taking Back Control" (supposedly, from Brussels). Trump: "You know they have a word, it sort of became old-fashioned, it's called nationalist. And I say 'really, we're not supposed to use that word? Do you know what I am? I'm a nationalist." [23 October 2018, *Business Insider*]. Here is Farage: "I'm just a middle-class boy from Kent who likes cricket and who happened to have a strong view about a supernational government from Brussels."

- Opposition to immigration, or at least a desire to control migration. Trump: "I am proud to shut down the government for border security, Chuck. "[UPI, December 12, 2018.] Farage: "[O]nly by leaving the European Union can we control the numbers coming to our country."
- Opposition to protection of gays, trans people and other minorities. Examples of this abound, but there are many variations. In Europe, Russia, Poland and Hungary probably qualify, and in Asia we can probably include China, the Philippines, Iran and Saudi Arabia.
- Opposition to "political correctness."

Populists identify as democrats, sometimes even as the only "true democrats." [Albertazzi and McDonnell, 2008.] It would be hard to disagree with Mudde and Kaltwasser's remark that "populism is essentially democratic, but at odds with *liberal* democracy." Not surprisingly, therefore, supporters of "liberal democracy" deny that populists are democrats and generally regard themselves as the only true democrats. "Liberal" democracy is usually defined by its adherents in terms of a number of "shared values," including protection of minorities, pluralism, the rule of law, freedom of speech, and "equality" (of one sort or another). Populists may share some of these values but will define them differently. This applies particularly to the rule of law, freedom of speech, and equality—all of which impinge heavily on the law. For more on this, see the section in Chapter 17 titled The Rule of Law: or of Lawyers?

PART V

PROBLEMS AND SOLUTIONS

16

CRACKING THE CODE

"I could wish that, when time shall serve, the superfluous and tedious statutes were brought into one sum together, and made more plain and short, to the intent that men might better understand them, which thing shall most help to advance the health of the Commonwealth."

King Edward VI (1537–1553)
[Cited in: Thomas Erskine Holland (1870),
Essays Upon the Form of the Law, Butterworths, p. 63.]

The main *difference* between British and American law is codification—the prevalence of codification in US law and its almost total absence from UK law. Codified US law includes the following:

- **The US Constitution**—The United States federal constitution. [See Arnheim (2018).]
- **The United States Code (USC)**—The official codified compilation of the general and permanent federal statutes of the United States, covering all "public laws," or laws chiefly governing relationships between individuals and the government, but excluding "private laws" that apply only to a limited number of people or for a short period. Whenever a Bill passed by Congress is signed into law by the President, it is slotted into its appropriate place in the USC, which is divided into 53 Titles, each covering a different subject area. The first 6 of these deal with constitutional topics such as "The Congress" (Title 2), "The President" (Title 3), and "Domestic Security" (Title 6). The remaining Titles,

which are arranged alphabetically, include: "Aliens and Nationality" (Title 8), "Bankruptcy" (Title 11), and "Voting and Elections" (Title 52). Annotated versions of the USC for the use of legal practitioners are produced by several publishing companies. "Positive law codification" is a process in which the Office of the Raw Revision Counsel is required by law to revise and restate all general and permanent Federal statutory law. Without changing the law in any way, this process enacts existing law as a "positive law" title, tidying it up and improving its organization in the process. About half the titles have now gone through this process.

- **The Code of Federal Regulations (CFR)**—The official codified compilation of the general and permanent administrative law rules and regulations published in the Federal Register (the official journal of the US federal government) by the executive departments and agencies of the federal government. The CFR is divided into 50 Titles, most of which are arranged in alphabetical order. E.g. "The President" (Title 3), "Foreign Relations" (Title 22), "Indians" (Title 25), and "Public Welfare" (Title 45).

- **Federal Rules of Civil Procedure**—These rules govern civil procedure in US district courts and have also been adopted, with some variations, by 35 states.

- **State Constitutions**—Every one of the 50 sovereign states making up the United States has its own codified constitution. Though often modeled on the federal constitution, all are longer and more detailed than the US Constitution. In eighteen states it is possible for the constitution to be amended by ballot initiative, i.e. a referendum on a particular issue by the voters of that state, a form of direct democracy.

- **State Statutory Codes**—All but one of the 50 states have legal codes comprising their general statutory law. (At the time of this writing, the remaining sate, Pennsylvania, was still in the process of completing this process.) The codes are labelled variously, usually as "Codes," "Laws," or "Revised Statutes," arranged under thematic headings. In most states, contract, torts and certain other aspects of common law are not included in the codes. However, the codified laws of California, Montana, North Dakota, South Dakota and Georgia are fully comprehensive.

- **Uniform Commercial Code (UCC)**—This is one of a number of Uniform Acts established as law with the intention of harmonizing the law in a particular subject area. They are drafted by the Uniform Law Commission (ULC) and approved by its parent body, the National Conference on Uniform State Laws (NCCUSL). Other Uniform Acts include the Uniform Probate Code, Uniform Trust Code, Uniform Partnership Act, Uniform Limited Liability Company Act, and Uniform Arbitration Act. The UCC itself, which was drafted in conjunction with the American Law Institute (ALI), covers the law of sales and other commercial transactions under 9 Articles, ranging from Sales to Leases to Negotiable Instruments to Investment Securities. It has been adopted by all 50 states, though there are a few variations from one to another. Once adopted by a state, the UCC is enacted as law and slotted into the state's code of statutes.

- **Uniform Computer Information Transactions Act (UCITA)**—A controversial model law drafted by the NCCUSL and designed by the proprietary software developers. It has so far been passed in only two states, Virginia and Maryland.

- **Model Penal Code (MPC),** a uniform act developed by the ALI, seeking to harmonize state criminal law statutes.
- **Restatements**—These are essentially codifications of the common law published by the American Law Institute (ALI), whose aim is "to distill the 'black letter law' from cases," and in essence "restate existing common law into a series of principles or rules." [Kribble, Meg (2017).] At the launch of the ALI Justice Each Restatement is divided into a large number of Sections, each of which provides a "black letter" principle followed by comments, illustrations and detailed discussion. At the time of writing there have been three editions of Restatements, with a Fourth Restatement in its early stages. Described at the launch of the ALI in 1923 by the future US Supreme Court Justice Benjamin Cardozo as "something less than a code and something more than a treatise," a Restatement has persuasive but not binding authority in litigation. Topics covered include Contract, Agency, Torts, Restitution & Unjust Enrichment, Employment, Property, and Unfair Competition. The Restatements are generally treated as authoritative by state courts, where they are extensively cited. [Cf. Criticism by legal academics: Adams, Kristen (2007).]

These sources provide US law, federal and state alike, with a really solid underpinning of principle encapsulated in codified legislation—even including the Restatements, which I would characterize as "pseudo-black letter" law. As we have seen repeatedly, the legal culture of the United States is very much against judge-made law or "legislating from the bench." Of course, that does not mean that those things never occur, but that judges, especially state court judges, have to be extra-careful before breaking with long-established principle. This applies even where the principle in question is patently wrong.

Contributory Negligence

A good example of this is the unfair traditional principle of contributory negligence, which bars a plaintiff from any recovery if their own negligence has contributed to even the smallest extent to their own injury. Under this harsh rule, for example, a defendant whose negligence was 99% responsible for the plaintiff's injury wins the case if the plaintiff's own negligence accounts for the other 1%. This rule, which originated with the old English case of *Butterfield v. Forrester*, 103 English Reports 926 (1809), became part of the law of most US states as a result of a "reception statute," under which pre-existing English common law was automatically adopted as part of the law of the US state concerned—"subject to such alterations and provisions as the legislature shall from time to time make concerning the same." This proviso was cited by Alexander Hamilton in The Federalist No. 84, published in 1788, to emphasize that any such "reception" of English common law is always subject to control by the legislature. Adding: "They are therefore at any moment liable to repeal by the ordinary legislative power, and of course have no constitutional sanction." It is important to note that this is just part of the general principle of the superiority of the legislative to the judicial power, which applies in every state (as distinct from the vaunted but incorrect doctrine of "three coequal branches of government" at federal level).

But what if a state court wants to set aside an unjust principle—like that of contributory negligence—that the legislature has simply allowed to remain in place? This is what happened in the case of *Li v. Yellow Cab Co.*, 532 P.2d 1226

(1975), when a majority on the California Supreme Court set aside the traditional contributory negligence rule, which had become § 1714 of the California Civil Code, and replaced it with comparative negligence, meaning that if a plaintiff's negligence was, say, 25% responsible for their injury, they would no longer lose the case but only be deprived of one fourth of their damages. The old rule, unjust though it was, did not go down without a fight, as the judges on both sides were keenly aware of the deference that is normally expected of the judiciary towards the legislature. [See the full discussion of this case in Chapter 7, "United States:The Exploding Parcel."]

"The Rule which you ought to Walk by"

American codification started early, with The Laws and Liberties of Massachusetts, enacted in 1648, which was a compilation of laws, which "we have reduced under several heads in an alphabetical method, that so they might the more readily be found ... wherein (upon every occasion) you might readily see the rule which you ought to walke by."

The Official Code of Georgia, the original form of which dates from 1851, was actually the earliest comprehensive codification of substantive common law to be enacted anywhere in the US, being drafted quite independently of David Field (see below) by the Confederate lawyer Thomas Reade Rootes Cobb (1823–1862), who was killed during the Civil War in the Battle of Fredericksburg.

Field Code

However, the real pioneer of American codification was David Dudley Field II (1805–1894), a New York-based lawyer, politician and inveterate campaigner for codification. In 1850 the New York state legislature enacted a Code of Civil Procedure drafted by Field, as a result of which it came to be known as the

"Field Code," which, with some amendments, was eventually adopted by 24 states. As chairman of a New York state commission for the systematic codification of all substantive New York state law, Field personally drafted almost the whole of the civil codes, while the penal code was drafted by his colleague William Curtis Noyes.

Though New York rejected Field's civil code, it was one of 18 states that enacted the penal code. His civil code was later largely adopted by a number of states, including Idaho, Montana, North Dakota, South Dakota and, above all, California, where, thanks to the influence of Field's brother Stephen, who was Chief Justice of California and subsequently a member of the US Supreme Court, a whole raft of Field's codes were adopted and, with legislative amendments, are still in place today as the basis of the 29 current California Codes.

Field's interest in codification was evidently first sparked by the writings of that unrelenting British advocate of law reform, Jeremy Bentham (1747–1832), by whom the word "codify" was actually coined. In a letter to President James Madison written in 1811, Bentham even offered to draft a comprehensive legal code for the United States, and, when rebuffed, approached the governors of each of the states with the same offer. Another of the many (mostly abortive) terms that Bentham coined was "pannomion," (from the Greek for "all laws"), to describe a comprehensive code of laws replacing all existing laws of the country concerned. His proposed code was to be not only complete but also "rationalized," by which he meant that every law within it was to be accompanied by reasons justifying its enactment. Bentham's passion for codification was born out of his general "utilitarian" philosophy, the "fundamental axiom" of which was that the measure of right and wrong is "the greatest happiness of the greatest number." Existing law, he believed, was unnecessarily complex, cumbersome and illogical, and benefited only the lawyers rather than the general populace. Hence his description of English law as the "Demon of Chicane." By contrast, he believed, his proposed all-inclusive code of laws would be self-explanatory and enable ordinary people to represent themselves in court without a lawyer. [Bentham, Jeremy (1998).]

Bentham vs. Blackstone

At the age of 16, Bentham attended Sir William Blackstone's lectures on English law in Oxford, and he was far from impressed. Indeed, his earliest published work was 'A Comment on the Commentaries," an out-and-out attack on Blackstone's *Commentaries on the Laws of England.*

Bentham and his bête noire, Blackstone, may not appear to have had much in common. Blackstone, a High Court judge and an Oxford professor, looks at first sight like a pillar of the establishment, while Bentham, with his wild hair, straw hat and radical ideas, was obviously a maverick. Yet both in their different ways were advocates of codification—Bentham quite openly and extravagantly, and Blackstone subtly and almost imperceptibly. Blackstone never used the terms "codify" or "codification"—not surprisingly, as they were yet to be coined by Bentham. But, as a student of Roman Law—the only kind of law then taught at either Oxford or Cambridge—he would obviously have been very familiar with the chief compilations of Roman Law: Justinian's *Digest, Code* and *Institutes.* And his four-volume treatise, modestly titled *Commentaries on the Laws of England,* was in reality nothing less than a systematic and comprehensive exposition of what he termed the "primary rules and fundamental principles" of English law consciously modelled on Justinian's *Institutes.* Note the words "rules" and "principles."

But there was one crucial difference between Blackstone and Justinian. In the words of Blackstone's opposite number in Cambridge, Professor Samuel Hallifax: "The *Commentaries* of Mr. Justice Blackstone, excellent as they are, are still but the work of a private man, and without the stamp of public authority."

[Hallifax, Samuel (1774). An Analysis of the Civil Law, Preface.] Blackstone's lectures—the first ever delivered on English law at either Oxford or Cambridge—and his *Commentaries* turned out to be a sensation and a great financial success, enabling him to move to a grand residence in Lincoln's Inn Fields. But his fame across the Atlantic greatly outstripped his reputation at home. American lawyers are all still introduced at law school to Blackstone's *Commentaries,* which have often been cited as authoritative even in the US Supreme Court. In Britain, by contrast, Blackstone's name and writings are no longer familiar to many members of the legal profession.

"No essential change"

In America, as we have seen, codification got under way in the second half of the nineteenth century and quickly spread to all the states, while in Britain it never took off at all. In 1870 the Oxford jurist Sir Thomas Erskine Holland (1835–1926), referring to codification, lamented: "Although many a commission has debated the subject from his (Francis Bacon's) time to the present day, and although of late certain preliminary steps have been taken towards improvement, it is literally true that no essential change has yet been effected in the form of English law. Indeed, a solemn conference of the two Houses of Parliament came to the conclusion in 1816 that even a consolidation of the statutes was impractical." [Holland, Thomas Erskine (1870), p. 63.]

If Lord Bingham was right in a 1998 speech advocating for a criminal code, some at least of those parliamentarians must have had second thoughts, because in 1818, only two years later, both Houses of Parliament petitioned the Crown, then occupied by the rotund figure of the Prince Regent, soon to ascend the throne as George IV, for the establishment of a Law Commission to consolidate English statute law. [Bingham, Tom (1998).]

Needless to say, nothing came of this—or indeed of any of the subsequent recommendations, reports, or even actual draft codes, like the draft criminal code of over 550 clauses recommended for adoption by a Royal Commission in 1879. Lord Bingham remarked: "Between 1844 and 1882 Lord Brougham and others made no fewer than eight separate parliamentary attempts to secure enactment of such a code. All ended in failure."

Then complete torpor set in for another 83 years, until 1965, when suddenly a Law Commission was set up by Act of Parliament and charged to review the law of England and Wales (there was a separate one for Scotland) "with a view to its systematic development and reform, including in particular the codification of such law ... and generally the simplification and modernization of the law." But this was yet another false start. A Criminal Code was actually published in 1985 and revised in 1989, but was never enacted. The explanation given for this by Lord Bingham was "lack of parliamentary time"—a feeble excuse indeed.

Seven hundred years of codified law

From this sorry saga it is hard to avoid the conclusion that English law has a marked aversion to codification, or even, for that matter, to consolidation. Yet, as was shown in Chapter 3, for the first 700 years of its existence—from the Laws of King Ethelbert published in about the year 600 until the Second Statute of Westminster, issued in 1285—English law was based on statutory codes. And the next period of 600+ years after that, until the year of the snail, 1932, was what I call "The Era of Principle," when English common law developed based on Forms of Action issued by the Chancery and supported by principles encapsulated in Legal Maxims, and side by side with the common law, Equity, with its own set of Maxims—and largely free of judge-made law.

Codification for the Colonies

While the British authorities have eschewed codification of the law of their homeland, they have not had the same qualms about codification of law intended for subject populations in the British Empire. So, for example, the Indian Penal Code, a comprehensive code covering the whole of substantive criminal law, which was drafted by a law commission headed up by the historian Thomas Babington Macaulay and came into force in 1862, after most of India had come under British rule. It was subsequently adopted by the British colonial authorities in Burma (now called Myanmar), Ceylon (now called Sri Lanka), the Straits Settlements (now part of Malaysia), Singapore, Brunei, and even Nigeria, and it still forms the basis of criminal law in all those countries as well as in India, Pakistan and Bangladesh. This British-drafted code is widely acknowledged to have stood the test of time without major amendments, partly at least because it was drafted in language broad enough to accommodate crimes involving technology, ideas and activities unknown in 1862.

A similar example is the Indian Civil Wrongs Bill, covering all Torts, drafted in 1886 at the request of the Government of India (under British rule) by the Oxford law academic Sir Frederick Pollock (1845–1937). Though it was never actually brought into force, it is significant that it was drafted at the Government's specific instruction. This remarkable compilation contains several practical "Illustrations" after each section and also an "Explanation" after certain sections. Pollock added it as an Appendix to his *Law of Torts*, first published in 1887.

We are still left with the conundrum of why English law tends to shun codification. An examination of two judicial attitudes to codification may help: a 1967 article by Sir Leslie Scarman, the first chairman of the Law Commission; and that of Lord Bingham in his 1998 speech cited above.

English common law: "A maze and not a motorway"

In 1967, Sir Leslie Scarman, a High Court judge and the first Chairman of the newly created Law Commission for England and Wales, (Law Lord 1977–1986), published an article in the Indiana Law Journal titled "Codification and Judge-Made Law: A Problem of Coexistence." [Scarman, Leslie (1967.] At the outset he welcomed the Law Commissions Act 1965 setting up the Law Commissions as "a milestone in the development of our law." As evidence of the need to "simplify and modernize" the law, which the Law Commission is charged to do, he quoted Lord Justice Diplock (as he then was) as agreeing with the conclusion reached by Lord Denning in a particular case, but by a different route—with the comment: "After all, that is the beauty of the common law; it is a maze and not as motorway." [*Morris v. Martin* [1966] 1 QB 716, 730.] "How," asks Scarman, "can we 'simplify and modernize' the law, as the act requires, and yet allow judge-made law to remain, if in fact it is a maze?"

These words already make it obvious why the vaunted "milestone," as Scarman characterized it, turned out to be just another false start. Not only did he laugh off as a tongue-in-cheek remark Diplock's description of English common law as a "maze," but he even "corrected" Diplock's reference to "the common law" to mean "judge-made law." And of course "judge-made law" is prominently displayed in the title of his article.

"For these reasons," the article concludes, "I expect that, as the codification of our law proceeds, the judge's role will change, but hardly diminish in importance." And: "If one is weighing up the advantages and disadvantages of judge-made and codified law, are there not great advantages in the slow, maturely considered advance of the law, case by case, which is within the gift of the judges, and the judges alone?"

So, was Lord Scarman, the first chairman of the organization entrusted with the task of codification, in favor of codification at all?

- **Piecemeal codification:** He was certainly opposed to the production of a comprehensive code but was prepared to countenance piecemeal codification, as he explained: "Indeed, a close look at the wording of section 3(1) of the Act reveals that it is the law in need of reform which may have to be codified, that is to say, not necessarily all the law but only such law as needs systematizing or reforming." This is a strained, not to say incorrect, interpretation of the section, the relevant part of which reads as follows: "It shall be the duty of each of the Commissions to take and keep under review *all the law* with which they are respectively concerned with a view to its systematic development and reform, including *in particular* the codification of *such* law..."(Emphasis added). It is hard to know what this could mean other than that the two Law Commissions (English and Scottish) were to codify the whole law of their particular jurisdiction. But, be that as it may, piecemeal codification is almost an oxymoron, a contradiction in terms, because there is no necessary harmonization between the little islands of purported "codification" and the surrounding sea of related law. So it is not really codification at all.

- **French Civil Code:** Article 5 of the French Civil Code, which has retained the exact same wording since being incorporated into the original version of the *Code Napoleon* in 1803, reads as follows: ""The judges are forbidden to pronounce, by way of general and legislative determination, on the cases submitted to them." Scarman tries his best to show that, despite this very restrictive language, "judicial power" was still alive and well in France.

- **"Studiously repulsive":** Yet, despite his ambivalence towards codification, Scarman quotes, with apparent approval, a remark by Sir James Fitzjames Stephens describing English law as "studiously repulsive," and a comment by Maitland charging English law with being out of step with modernity and likening it to a "blunderbuss, apt to go off at the wrong end." In response to these strictures, Scarman concludes his article like this: "The law is on its way to modernity."

- **The sovereignty of Parliament:** Lord Scarman was plainly conscious of the need for parliamentary consent to any codification that might be proposed by the Law Commission. Any codification of UK law could be achieved only by parliamentary legislation. Yet there is no sign of recognition in Scarman's article that his beloved "judge-made law" flew slap in the face of the sovereignty of Parliament, the bedrock principle of the British constitution. Codification and judge-made law are plainly mutually incompatible. No wonder therefore that the purported initiation in 1965 of an era of codified law turned out to be just another in a long line of false starts.

Fast forward 21 years and we come upon yet another ambivalent judicial attitude toward codification:

"Codification would bring clarity, accessibility, coherence, consistency and certainty to the criminal law"

In his 1998 speech to an audience of judges, Lord Chief Justice Bingham (Senior Law Lord 2000–2008) made no secret of his "general disbelief in codes," yet the theme of his address is the desirability of a Criminal Code! [Bingham, Tom (1998).] He provides three arguments in favor of codification (*printed in italics*):

- *"First, it [viz, codification] would bring clarity and accessibility to the law."* I could not agree more. And, as mentioned above, this is the very reason that attracted Bentham to codification. But why should this apply to Criminal law any more than to any other branch of law?
- *"Secondly, a code would bring coherence to this branch of the law (viz. criminal law)."* Bingham went on to quote Professor Sir John Smith (1922–2003) of Nottingham, an authority on criminal law, as saying: *"The criminal law is entirely different. It is incoherent and inconsistent."* That codification would bring coherence is undeniable—but, again, is it only criminal law that is incoherent and inconsistent? We have found similar features in other areas of English law examined in this book, notably tort, judicial review and privacy. So, are these areas not crying out for codification as well?
- *"Thirdly, a code would bring greater certainty to the law, and in this of all fields (viz. criminal law) the law should be so far as possible certain. The arguments for incremental development of the law, persuasive elsewhere, have no application here."* To this latest acknowledgment by Bingham that codification would bring greater certainty to the law must be added his earlier admissions that it would bring coherence, consistency, clarity and accessibility. This makes quite a tidy lineup of attributes—which are needed just as much in fields such as tort, judicial review and privacy as in criminal law. As for the "persuasive" arguments for "incremental development of the law," in other words, for judge-made law, he does not say what those arguments are. But we saw in the chapter on The Snail in the Bottle that those arguments are not at all persuasive. Without the five qualities of certainty, coherence, consistency, clarity and accessibility there can be no justice and no

rule of law. So the inescapable conclusion must be that codification is needed—and it is needed across the board.

The Dormant English Criminal Code Awakens?

In April 2009 the Law Commission (yes, it was still in existence!) announced in its Newsletter: "We are revisiting Part 1 of the draft Criminal Code that we published in 1989, in particular the following topics:

- Conspiracy and attempts—we plan to publish a report and draft Bill by the end of 2009;
- Intoxication—we published a report and draft Bill on 15/01/09."

When is a Conspiracy not a Conspiracy?

In 2018 two 15-year-old boys, Thomas Wyllie and Alex Bolland, were convicted of a conspiracy (when aged 14) to murder teachers and pupils at their own school by shooting them in a re-enactment of the Columbine school massacre in Colorado in 1999. In fact, however, the "conspiracy" never got beyond the planning stage, if that. It was more of a fantasy. The boys never got hold of any firearms or assembled a single explosive device. And there was also no evidence that either of them had ever handled a firearm. Yet they were sentenced to 12 and 10 years' imprisonment respectively! [*R v. Wyllie & Bolland*, Leeds Crown Court July 20, 2018.]

In short, therefore, the evidence of the existence of a conspiracy between the boys was thin, as I pointed out in an article in the *New Law Journal.* [Arnheim (2018b)]. The problem lies in the state of English law on conspiracy. The essential ingredient of a conspiracy under section 1(1) of the Criminal Law Act 1977 is an "agreement" between two or more people to pursue a course of conduct "which, if the agreement is carried out in accordance with their intentions" will (unless factually impossible) "necessarily amount to or involve the commission of any offence or offences by one or more of the parties to the agreement." In *R v. Anderson* [1986] AC 27 (HL) Lord Bridge held: "But, beyond the mere fact of agreement, the necessary *mens rea* of the crime is, in my opinion, established if, and only if, it is shown that the accused, when he entered into the agreement, intended to play some part in the agreed course of conduct."

What overt act in furtherance of the conspiracy agreement did Wyllie and Bolland, or either of them, actually undertake? Answer: None. The "conspiracy" never got off the ground. But that does not matter under the current English law of conspiracy, which contains no such requirement.

Many other jurisdictions *do* require some practical step or "overt act" to be taken for a conspiracy conviction. This step goes by different names in different jurisdictions. In US Federal law, for example, this practical step is referred to as "any act to effect the object of the conspiracy" [18 US Code § 371]. The act in question does not have to be criminal in itself. So, in the present case the examples of obtaining a firearm or making a bomb would be valid acts for this purpose.

The advantage of a requirement of an overt act is that it *simplifies* the law of conspiracy and makes it more *certain* and *objective*, all of which must surely be considered desirable qualities in a law. Yet English law is moving in the opposite direction. The current statutory offence of conspiracy, which abolishes the previous common law offence, was created in response to a recommendation contained in an earlier Law Commission report [Law Com No. 76, 1976]. The interpretation of the law soon became problematical, and the Law Commission was asked by the Government to "review" the offence of statutory conspiracy. The Law Commission obliged, publishing first a Consultation Paper in 2007 and then, in 2009, a very full report plus a Draft Bill [Law Com No. 318, 2009].

Alas, the Draft Bill contains no recommendation of the requirement of an "overt act". It is peppered instead with subjective terms, such as *intention, recklessness* and *reasonableness,* which would only make the law more uncertain than ever. Fortunately, this Bill has not yet received government approval and will probably never see the light of day.

Combination of two extremes

The Commission's draft Criminal Law (Intoxication) Bill has not fared any better. In fact, it was specifically rejected by the Government as "unnecessarily complex," as indeed was an earlier version of it drafted in 1995. And the Commission itself accepted that their previous version "might legitimately be regarded as unduly complex." [www.lawcom.gov.uk.] The 2009 Bill combines two extremes—but not in a good way. On the one hand it is extremely detailed, but at the same time it deliberately avoids defining the word "intoxicant." As a result, if it were ever to become law it would be left to the courts to determine what substances were to be regarded as intoxicants—making the law more uncertain than ever.

US: Intoxication Defense

The main question here is whether self-induced intoxication can be used as a defense in criminal law on the basis that the defendant "could not form the mental intent" to commit the crime concerned. In the US, federal law in this area is governed by an Act of Congress passed in 1984, which provides that it is a defense for the accused to prove that at the time when the crime was committed he could not appreciate:

- The nature and quality of his action; or
- The wrongfulness of his action

Due to severe mental disease or defect, including intoxication. [18 USC § 17(a).]

At state level, every state has its own Criminal Code, and in addition there is the Model Penal Code (MPC), which, like the

Restatements of Law, is published by the American Law Institute (ALI). It was first issued in 1962 and was last updated in 1981, with some periodic updates since then. The MPC does not have the force of law unless specifically adopted by the legislature of a state. Some states, such as New York, New Jersey and Oregon have adopted the MPC almost in its entirety, and the criminal codes of more than half the states are heavily modelled on it, while it is cited by courts even in states that have not adopted any part of it.

UK: Forfeiting Forfeiture?

In a report published in 2006 the Law Commission recommended the abolition of forfeiture of a lease or tenancy on the ground that the tenant has not complied with their obligations. The Law Commission proposed replacing forfeiture with "a modern statutory scheme for the termination of tenancies on the ground of tenant default that would balance the interests of all parties affected and promote more proportionate outcomes"—another highly complex proposal. In March 2019 a Ministry of Housing report into leasehold reform recommended that the Commission's proposals should be implemented. However, by the time of this writing, nothing had happened.

I discussed forfeiture in the chapter titled "Maxims or Mimims?" I pointed out there that forfeiture is completely contrary to a Maxim of Equity and how this problem has been overcome in the US.

The Defense of Illegality

An area in which the Law Commission was asked by the judiciary to get involved is the issue of the defense of illegality, which the Law Commission itself described as an area of law that "has been criticized for being complex, uncertain, arbitrary and occasionally unjust." But the Commission's response was less than helpful. Except where a trust has been set up, they recommended that nothing should be done: "We think that the law should be left to develop through the case law." [www.lawcom.gov.uk/project/ illegality/.] The result, as we have seen, has been highly unsatisfactory, and all the more so considering the longstanding principle involved, which in the UK, by contrast with the US, has been honored more in the breach than in the observance. [See Chapter 5, "Maxims or Minims?"]

UK: Privacy

And there is of course the prime example of Parliament's shrugging off its responsibility to legislate in the face of earnest entreaties by the Court of Appeal in the *Gorden Kaye* case: Privacy. To fill this void, the courts have resorted to extending two very different causes of action: breach of confidence and the ECHR Article 8 "right to respect for private and family life, home and correspondence." But, alas, even with these two extensions drawn to breaking point, a yawning chasm still opens up between them for proper privacy protection. [See Chapter 10, "Privacy: A Strange Royal Case."]

UK: Dangerous Codification

To say that codification in the UK is going at a snail's pace we would have to be thinking of the semi-decomposed snail that Mrs Donoghue found in her ginger beer. But one type of codification that might just grow legs is the creation of a written or codified Constitution. It is a favorite hobbyhorse among "politically correct" law and political science academics and even among some judges. But, as Justice Scalia famously pointed out, every banana republic has a Bill of Rights, and the Constitution of the old Soviet Union contained very elaborate civil rights—yet these were just "parchment guarantees," or words on paper. In fact, the UK already has a bill of rights in the form of the

European Convention on Human Rights, as (largely) incorporated into the Human Rights Act 1998 (ECHR). As we have already had occasion to see, the problem with the ECHR is what may be termed "mission creep" coupled with "judicial overreach," namely a tendency to interpret the Convention in a "politically correct" way, extending the protections contained in it to favour certain "special interest groups," including asylum seekers, illegal migrants, terror suspects, and even convicted killers. As the ECHR is already in place, how would it differ if it were to become an official Bill of Rights with special "entrenched" constitutional status, making it impossible, or virtually impossible to repeal it? In the 1990s some judges believed that the ECHR already enjoyed this status, but of course they had no authority to invest it with that status. If Parliament were ever to delegate its sovereignty to an "entrenched" constitution or Bill of Rights, the next step would inevitably be to give the UK Supreme Court, or a specialist Constitutional Court with the power to set aside Acts of Parliament, a power which no court enjoys under the present "unwritten" constitution. What, you may ask, could possibly be wrong with that? It would, after all, bring the UK into line with most other Western nations. True, but, as the judiciary is already in practice dominant over the executive and the legislature alike, such a move would only give it a stranglehold over the government as a whole, which would be undemocratic, or even anti-democratic.

UK: Consolidation

In the absence of codification, is there at least consolidation?—uniting a number of existing statutes on the same subject into one comprehensive Act of Parliament. There has been some consolidation, though not perhaps as much as might have been expected.

- Companies Act 2006—Containing 1,300 sections plus 16 schedules and running to nearly 700 pages. This is the latest Companies Act, superseding the 1929, 1948, 1967 and 1985 Acts, though parts of the 1985 Act still survive. Why could there not have been just a single consolidation Act with amendments and deletions to that single Act as and when they were needed?

- Marine Insurance Act 1906—This classic Act, compiled by the master-draftsman Sir Mackenzie Chalmers, is still in force. It is sometimes described as a codifying Act, because it united many years of court decisions. But in fact it is now not even a consolidating Act, because two new statutes have been passed—namely the Consumer Insurance (Disclosure and Representations) Act 2012 and the Insurance Act 2015—which amend the 1906 Act without however being consolidated with it to form a single insurance statute.

- Sale of Goods Act 1979—This was a consolidated version of the Sale of Goods Act 1893, also drafted by Sir Mackenzie Chalmers. The Consumer Rights Act 2015 replaced some parts of it that dealt with consumer contracts, but it still remains the main statute for non-consumer contracts.

- Equality Act 2010—This really is a consolidation Act, combining as it does the numerous prior anti-discrimination statutes on the books, including the Equal Pay Act 1970, the Sex Discrimination Act 1975, the Race Relations Act 1976, the Disability Discrimination Act 1995, and a number of other enactments. It also served to implement four major EU Equal Treatment Directives. Sections 104–105 allow political parties to create all-women shortlists (at least until the year 2030), which has been acted upon already. This provision, which had been declared unlawful by an Employment Tribunal, has been dubbed by Anne

Widdecombe MEP as an example not of equal rights but of "special privileges." It effectively creates a quota, which, it is worth noting, is not allowed under US law under the *Bakke* principle. The opening section of the Act was described by a Minister in the Labour Government sponsoring it as "Socialism in one clause." It obliges public authorities, when making strategic decisions, to have "due regard to the desirability of exercising [its functions] in a way that is designed to reduce the inequalities of outcome which result from socio-economic disadvantage." Having put this legislation through and obtaining the royal assent for it on April 8, 2010, Gordon Brown's Labour Government lost the general election held on May 6, 2010.

- Even the brief Law Commission Act 2009 itself, which could and should have been consolidated with the 1965 Act, was enacted as a stand-alone statute—though that was probably not the Commission's fault. It requires the Government to give reasons for not implementing any Law Commission proposal, or, in Lord Kingsland's phrase, "to put up or shut up about Law Commission proposals."

- In November 2018 the Commission published a Sentencing Code. By the time of this writing it had not yet received Government approval.

- According to the 2017–2018 Annual Report of the Law Commission, the only "Reports Implemented" in that year were the following:

  - Digital Economy Act 2017—"This project focused on private property rights between landowners and electronic communications operators. It did not consider planning law." (page 29).

  - Intellectual Property (Unjustified Threats) Act 2017— This Act "creates a framework within which parties can negotiate fairly over intellectual property disputes, but will protect those who can be most harmed by unjustified threats to sue for infringement."

- Late Payment of Insurance Claims—"We recommended that there should be an implied term in every insurance contract requiring the insurer to pay valid claims within a reasonable time. ... We said that breach of that term should give rise to contractual remedies, including damages, but that insurers should not be liable for delays caused by genuine disputes. Our draft clauses were included in the Enterprise Act 2016, and now form part of the Insurance Act 2015."

None of the Law Commission's work in these three areas could remotely qualify as "consolidation."

"Welsh Law Beginning to Diverge from English Law"

The Law Commission's Chairman's introduction to the Annual Report 2017–2018 contains this puzzling little gem: "Welsh law is beginning to diverge in a variety of areas from English law." (p. 2.) Is that not exactly the opposite tendency from what the Commission should be trying to achieve? Yet there is no explanation for this development, let alone a word of concern or criticism. [The Law Commission—Annual Report 2017–2018 (Law Com N. 379) HC 1308.] The UK is made up of three separate jurisdictions: England & Wales, Scotland, and Northern Ireland. Wales is not a separate jurisdiction but is an integral part of the jurisdiction of England & Wales. There is therefore no reason for Welsh law to diverge from English law, and any such movement should be viewed with concern.

The US of course has 52 jurisdictions—the 50 states, federal and Washington DC, but the Restatements, the Model Penal Code, the Uniform Commercial Code and other Uniform Acts, tend in practice to harmonize the laws of the different jurisdictions to some extent, while leaving each jurisdiction free to decide how much harmonization, if any, it wishes to embrace. However, the UK does not even have any overarching jurisdiction equivalent to that of US federal law.

UK: When is a knife not an offensive weapon?

Though the UK has doggedly set its face against codification, and even the amount of consolidation has been far less than expected, the UK Parliament has been churning out legislation at fever pitch—but these have been stand-alone statutes, sometimes overlapping or tripping over one another.

Parliament is constantly agitated about the increasing incidence of knife crime, but the law on knife crime is far from clear. Under section 1 of the Prevention of Crime Act 1953 it is a criminal offence for anyone to have with them "without lawful authority or reasonable excuse. ... any offensive weapon" in any public place. On summary conviction (i.e. in a magistrates' court) the penalty is imprisonment not exceeding six months or a fine, or both, and on conviction on indictment (i.e. before a judge and jury in the Crown Court) imprisonment for four years or a fine, or both.

A completely separate criminal offense of having in a public place "any article which has a blade or is sharply pointed" (except a folding pocketknife with a blade of 3 inches or less in length) is created by section 139 of the Criminal Justice Act 1988. Here it is a defense if the defendant can prove "that he had good reason or lawful authority for having the article with him in a public place." The penalty for this crime is again imprisonment for not more than six months on summary conviction, and on conviction on indictment imprisonment for not more than four years, with the possibility of a fine instead of imprisonment or in addition to it.

At the time of this writing yet a third overlapping Act of Parliament has just been enacted under the title of Offensive

Weapons Act 2019, which is concerned chiefly with the purchase of offensive weapons but also, in section 25, even makes possession *in private* of certain offensive weapons a crime.

All this overlapping legislation causes confusion and injustice. English criminal practice allows a person to be charged under one of these statutes—only to find on the day of the trial the charge has been changed to another statute. For example, it is a defense under the 1953 Act if a defendant caught in possession of a knife can prove that it was not an "offensive weapon." The term "offensive weapon" is defined in section 1(4) of the 1953 Act as "any article made or adapted for use for causing injury to the person, or intended by the person having it with him for such use by him or by some other person." On this definition a small kitchen knife might possibly escape classification as an "offensive weapon." But if the charge is suddenly switched to possession of a "bladed article" under the 1988 Act, that defense can no longer be used.

This is far from being the only example of overlapping legislation. The UK statute book is littered with Acts of Parliament with similar or even the same name. For example:

- There have been no fewer than 14 Acts of Parliament dealing with terrorism passed since 2000, eleven of which have the word "Terrorism" or "Anti-Terrorism" in their title.
- Six Acts with the words "Criminal Justice" in their title have been passed since 1967.
- Nine Acts with the word "Employment" in their title have been passed since 1980, notably the Employment Rights Act 1996 (plus a few other Employment Rights Acts), the Employment Relations Act 1999 (plus a few other similarly named Acts), not to mention a whole raft of other laws containing employment-related provisions, such as the National Minimum Wage Act 1998, the Work & Families Act 2006, the Pensions Act

2008, and the Equality Act 2010. At least all trade union legislation has been consolidated in the Trade Union & Labour Relations (Consolidation) Act 1992—but why such a narrow consolidation?

The result is messy, confusing and a source of injustice. In this computer age there is no excuse for having so many overlapping stand-alone laws. In 2010 a useful UK Government website called www.legislation.gov.uk was set up to serve as the "official home of UK legislation." It includes all legislation enacted since 1267, showing statutes in their original as well as in their amended state, with notes giving details of each amendment. But it does not get over the problem of overlapping statutes like the knife laws mentioned above that have not been amended.

UK: Yet another knife law

There is yet a further Act of Parliament impinging on the possession of knives, the Restriction of Offensive Weapons Act 1959, which is chiefly concerned to prohibit the manufacture, sale or hire of flick knives, but also makes it an offence to "offer" such a knife for sale or hire. Interesting, it also extends to lending or giving a flick knife to another person, regardless of possession or use.

This law came under attack over the display of a flick knife in a shop window with a ticket reading "Ejector knife—4 shillings" in a case called *Fisher v. Bell* [1961] 1 QB 394. The store owner was prosecuted under the 1959 Act for "offering" a flick knife for sale. It was held that displaying an article, even with a marked price, did not constitute a contractual offer but only an "invitation to treat." This meant that the contractual offer would come from the customer, leaving it up to the store to accept or reject it—a somewhat strained interpretation of the practicalities of shopping. The 1959 law was quickly amended by making it an offense not only if anyone "sells or hires or offers for sale or hire" any flick knife but also if anyone "exposes or has in his possession" such a knife " for the purpose of sale or hire."

UK: Offer and Acceptance

A related problem arose in connection with self-service stores, which were a novelty in England in the early 1950s. When Boots the Chemists changed to self-service stores, with the goods, including non-prescription medicines, arranged on open shelves with marked prices, they came under fire from their regulator, the Pharmaceutical Society, who claimed that self-service was unlawful because the law required the sale of all pharmaceutical drugs to take place under the supervision of a qualified pharmacist. Both the High Court and the Court of Appeal upheld Boots's contention that the display of goods was merely an "invitation to treat" and not a contractual offer. There was no contractual "offer" until a customer brought an item to the till intending to pay for it. The contract was only concluded when the cashier "accepted" the customer's "offer" and payment was made at the till under the watchful eye of a qualified pharmacist, thus complying with the law: *Pharmaceutical Society of Great Britain v. Boots Cash Chemists* [1953] 1 QB 401.

This analysis remains the law in England in regard to *all* self-service transactions, making the offer come from the customer and the acceptance from the merchant—a somewhat artificial interpretation of the commercial realities. When a customer comes up to the till with a shopping cart full of groceries, for example, can the cashier refuse to allow her to purchase them? Yes, of course. This particular customer may possibly have been banned by the store for some reason or may be suspected of hiding undisclosed items in her shopping bag or clothing, or may for some other reason be *persona non grata,* but such cases are in practice extremely rare. In normal circumstances it does not really matter whether the contractual offer comes from the customer or from the store, nor at what particular point in the shopping ritual a contract is concluded.

Exploding soda bottles: three scenarios

In the English legal analysis of the self-service shopping experience there is no concluded contract until goods and money are exchanged at the till. But what is the contractual relationship between the parties if, say, a soda bottle explodes after the customer has taken it off the shelf but before she has paid for it? Britain seems to have been mercifully spared such incidents, preferring mice or snails in ginger beer bottles instead. But exploding soda bottles are surprisingly common in the pages of the American law reports. There are essentially three alternative legal analyses of the contractual situation when the customer has selected the bottle and put it in her shopping cart but has not yet paid for it:

- According to English law, the customer is in limbo and nothing that happens to her during this period can give her a contractual cause of action;
- According to one American model, by displaying the goods with prices the store is making a contractual offer, which is accepted by the customer only when she pays the cashier. Until she does so, the customer is in limbo in this scenario too as far as contract law is concerned. [See the 1946 Massachusetts case *Lasky v. Economy Grocery Stores* 319 Mass. 224 (Mass. 1946). [ALI Restatement: Contracts, § 58.]
- According to a different American model, which is more widely followed, the retailer's act of placing priced goods on open shelves constitutes an offer, acceptance of which occurs as soon as a customer removes an item from the shelf—even though title to the item only passes when payment is made. By taking possession of

the item from the shelf, the customer is deemed to have made a promise to pay at check-out, and this promise amounts to sufficient consideration to support a contract. What if a customer selects an item and then changes her mind and puts that item back on the shelf? That flexibility is built into the model, say its adherents. [See the beautifully argued judgment of the Court of Special Appeals of Maryland in *Sheeskin v. Giant Food Inc.* 20 Md App. 611 (1974). This decision was followed, among others, by the Georgia Court of Appeals in *Fender v. Colonial Stores Inc.*, 138 Ga. App. 31, 225 S.E. 2d 691 (1976), and by the Oklahoma Supreme Court in *Barker v. Allied Supermarket*, 596 P.2d 870 (1979).]

By finding that there was a contract between a customer and the store as soon as the customer selected an item from the shelf and placed it in her shopping cart (even though it had not yet been paid for), the third alternative allows a customer injured by an exploding soda bottle to claim against the seller for breach of an implied warranty of merchantability. This legal analysis is fairer to the customer than either of the other two analyses, and also offers a more realistic explanation of the practicalities of self-service shopping.

Crucially, this third analysis rests squarely on a finding that a contract is entered into the moment the customer takes possession of an item by lifting it off the shelf and placing it in her shopping basket. The *Sheeskin* Court in Maryland, one of the 49 states that have adopted some version of Article 2 of the Uniform Commercial Code, based their decision on the wording of Code (1957), Art 95B, § 2-206: "Unless otherwise unambiguously indicated by the language or circumstances (a) An offer to make a contract shall be construed as inviting acceptance in any manner and by any medium reasonable in the circumstances …" The Official Comment 1 to this section states; "Any reasonable manner of acceptance is intended to be regarded as available unless the offeror has made quite clear that it will not be acceptable." The *Sheeskin* court held: "In our view the manner by which acceptance was to be accomplished in the transaction herein involved was not indicated by either language or circumstances. The seller did not make it clear that acceptance could not be accomplished by a promise rather than an act. Thus it is equally reasonable under the terms of the specific offer that acceptance could be accomplished in any of three ways: (1) by the act of delivering the goods to the check-out counter and paying for them; (2) by the promise to pay for the goods as evidenced by their physical delivery to the check-out counter; and (3) by the promise to deliver the goods to the check-out counter and to pay for them there as evidenced by taking physical possession of the goods by their removal from the shelf." In the *Sheeskin* case itself it was, of course this third method of acceptance that was held to have taken place. On this basis the court held that the plaintiff customer had made out a prima facie case of the defendant seller's breach of warranty of merchantability and that this breach was the cause of the plaintiff's injury from the exploding bottle. Having made this prima facie showing, [plaintiff] was entitled to have the jury pass upon the questions of whether the warranty was breached, and if so, whether the breach caused his injury." [This was in addition to finding that the plaintiff had a prima facie case against the retailer in terms of the tort doctrine of *res ipsa loquitur.*]

It is particularly important to note that what we may call the "English rule" is purely judge-made, while the two American rules are based on black-letter law, either the Restatement (Second) of Contracts, Section 58, or, in the most widely accepted analysis, the UCC and a state code.

17

A PARADE OF PARADOXES

This chapter is a brief survey of a number of paradoxes between British and American law, starting with some constitutional paradoxes. One of the most remarkable paradoxes of all is that, though the British Constitution has at its heart the fundamental principle of the sovereignty of Parliament, while the US Constitution merely accords Congress the legislative power without elevating it above the executive or the judiciary, yet greater deference is paid by the judiciary to the legislature in the US than in the UK.

"A Republic, if you can keep it."

A fun paradox is the fact that Britain is a monarchy, yet the US President has far more power than the UK King or Queen. The Declaration of Independence of 1776, drafted by Thomas Jefferson, the future third president of the US, blames King George III personally for establishing "an absolute Tyranny over these States." In fact, the power of the British monarchy had already been greatly eroded by this time, largely being exercised in the name of the King by his Ministers. Because of this misunderstanding of the royal power, the first American constitution, known as the Articles of Confederation, which came into force in 1781, contained no executive at all, only a legislature. It was when this system proved unworkable that the Constitution that is still in force today (with amendments) was hammered out in debate by a Constitutional Convention held in Philadelphia and eventually came into force in 1789. When

Benjamin Franklin (1706–1790), who had attended the Convention as a delegate from Pennsylvania, emerged from its final deliberations, he was accosted by a Philadelphia matron and asked what sort of government had been created. "A republic," he is reputed to have said, "if you can keep it." The choice in the mind of his interlocutor was presumably between a republic and a monarchy. Franklin's answer presumably implied that vigilance on the part of the citizenry was needed to prevent the government from being dominated by one man. There was much debate in the early days on how the first President, George Washington, should be addressed. John Adams (the first Vice President who would become the second President), favored the title of "Your Highness" or even "Your Majesty" for the President, and other suggestions included "Your Electoral Highness" and "Your Excellency," but in the end George Washington's much less pretentious preferred form of address of "Mr. President" was adopted and is still in use today (probably with "Madam President" in the event of a female president.)

In his *Commentaries* Sir William Blackstone (1723–1780) described the Executive power of the government as vested in the King. However, as the executive power drifted imperceptibly to the Prime Minister and other ministers, a distinction grew up between the role of Head of State (occupied by the King or Queen) and that of Head of Government (occupied by the Prime Minister). This has worked well, especially when reinforced by the convention that the Monarch should remain politically neutral. One advantage of this dichotomy is that hostility towards the government of the day should not entail disloyalty to the State.

The US Constitution gives the President the executive power in the government and also makes him Commander in Chief. No mention is made of the position of head of state, but the President does of course occupy that position as well. The distinction between loyalty to the United States as a country and support for the President and government of the day could be used to good effect—provided this distinction is made by Congress and the courts. The national flag and the national anthem should command respect from everyone, whether they support or oppose the President of the day. So "taking a knee" during the playing of the national anthem should be punishable as showing disrespect to the United States. Similarly, flag-burning, which is now recognized by the US Supreme Court as protected speech under the First Amendment, should be viewed instead as amounting to disloyalty and disrespect to the United States. There are plenty of other ways of showing opposition to the President and government.

The Sovereignty of Parliament

As we have seen, the sovereignty of Parliament goes back well before there was a United Kingdom. It can be traced back at least to the coronation of Edward II in 1307. [See Chapter 1.] And it remains the bedrock principle of the UK constitution today. One of the best recent statements of this principle can be found in a 2019 BBC radio lecture given by Lord Sumption, (Justice of UKSC 2012–2018), who described the British constitution like this: "[T]here is only one truly fundamental constitutional rule, which is that Parliament is sovereign. There is no legal limit to what it can do, the limits are political. Since the House of Commons, as the dominant element in Parliament, is an assembly of elected representatives, the sovereignty of Parliament really is the foundation of our democracy." [The Reith Lectures 2019: Law & the Decline of Politics, Lecture 5: Shifting the Foundations, June 18, 2019.]

"Elective dictatorship"

Though Parliament is sovereign, in practice Parliament is normally dominated by the executive government of the day This is what Lord Hailsham (Lord Chancellor 1979–1987)

termed an "elective dictatorship." Under the UK's electoral
system of "first-past-the-post," the candidate with the most votes
in each constituency or voting district wins that seat, regardless
whether that candidate has obtained a majority of over 50% of
the votes or just a plurality, beating the next highest competitor.
This system generally favors the bigger parties at the expense of
the smaller parties, which normally gives one party a healthy
majority in the House of Commons. And, by convention, the
King or Queen is obliged to call on the leader of the majority
party to become Prime Minister and form a government.
Government ministers are in practice drawn from among
Members of Parliament and members of the House of Lords. In
these circumstances, most legislation originates with the
government in the form of Bills, which are almost invariably
passed by Parliament. Once a Bill has passed both Houses of
Parliament, it goes to the Monarch for the royal assent, which by
convention (since 1708) is always given, which turns the Bill
into an Act of Parliament with the force of law. The control
exercised by the executive over Parliament is of course loosened
to the point of non-existence in the event of a minority
government. But in normal circumstances it enables the
government and Parliament to work harmoniously together—
which makes it all the more paradoxical that Parliament gave up
its power of enacting legislative codes more than 700 years ago.
The explanation is, that, with the stability of the government-
controlled system of forms of action underpinned by a raft of
principles n the form of maxims of law and maxims of equity,
there did not appear to be a need any longer for statutory codes.
That did not of course mean that the volume of legislation
waned. On the contrary, in 2010 alone, for example, no fewer
than 700 new criminal offences were created, largely by statute,
These were all stand-alone offences, the creation of which was
the very opposite of codification, or even of consolidation, and
therefore detracted not only from the clarity of the law but also
ultimately from justice.

Well-oiled machine?

The British system of government, with the Government and Parliament generally united, ought to work smoothly as a well-oiled machine in exercising parliamentary sovereignty, not least by using the power of revocation to cancel any court decisions that it does not like. Parliament does not have to give any reason for exercising this power. Indeed, when it was used to revoke the House of Lords decision in *Burmah Oil v. Lord Advocate* (1965) by passing the War Damage Act 1965, that Act was never questioned even though it combined revocation of a House of Lords judicial decision with retroactive effect. And the purpose of this serious but perfectly valid blow to the judiciary was simply to save the government money. The Law Lords (by 3 votes to 2) had ruled that the Government had to compensate an oil company for carrying out the government's own scorched earth policy by destroying oilfields in Burma to prevent them from falling into the hands of the advancing Japanese forces. Not surprisingly, the Government did not welcome this judicial decision, and simply revoked it. But there are many more recent judicial decisions which are crying out for revocation, like for example the judicial decisions preventing the British Government from deporting terror suspects who claim to be likely to be tortured if sent back to their own countries. These decisions are based on a misinterpretation of ECHR Article 3 coupled with Article 1, as we saw in Chapter 8. Yet, instead of revoking these decisions—as Parliament is fully entitled to do—it has become paralyzed by them and in so doing has been guilty of a dereliction of its duty to protect the overwhelming law-abiding majority of society. In a sense, the power of revocation can be regarded as potentially the opposite of the American model of judicial review. In the US, judicial review gives the courts power over Congress and the President: in the UK, revocation potentially gives Parliament power to control the worst excesses of the courts—but the emphasis is on the word "potentially," as

Parliament lacks the guts to exercise this important power which forms an integral part of parliamentary sovereignty.

Three-horse team

The US system of separation of powers is much stricter than its British counterpart. [See Chapter 2.] In particular, for example, no member of Congress is permitted to serve in the President's Cabinet, whereas in the UK Cabinet Ministers (with a few very brief exceptions) have to be members of one or other House of Parliament. Conflict between the President and Congress is not at all uncommon, with the President having a veto-power over Bills passed by both Houses of Congress, and of course Congress has the ultimate weapon against the President in the shape of impeachment. President Franklin Roosevelt famously referred to the American form of government as a "three-horse team" in a Radio "fireside chat" in March 1937 in which he appealed to the people to support his "court-packing" scheme in order to stop the majority on the US Supreme Court from striking down one after another of the legislative planks of his New Deal. The three horses were of course the Congress, the President and the courts. As FDR put it: "Two of the horses, the Congress and the executive, are pulling in unison today, the third is not." As he had won two landslide victories in a row, Roosevelt was understandably peeved. Roosevelt's plan was unpopular even with some of his own supporters in Congress, but the day was saved by the defection to the President's side of Justice Owen Roberts—"the switch in time that saved nine" (the Supreme Court, then as now, was made up of nine justices). The New Deal enjoyed plain sailing after that. But spats between the President and the Supreme Court are certainly not unknown in more recent times. For example, in his State of the Union address in 2013 President Obama launched a diatribe against the Court for its *Citizens United* (2010) decision as reversing a century of law "to open the floodgates for special interests—

including foreign companies—to spend without limit in our elections." Justice Samuel Alito's mouthed rejoinder of "not true" as the President was speaking was unprecedented. But no American president has allowed the court to thwart a major administration policy in the way that the British government regularly does.

"No Obama judges or Trump judges ..."

After President Trump disparagingly characterized a judge who had ruled against him as an "Obama judge," Chief Justice Roberts angrily retorted: "We do not have Obama judges or Trump judges, Bush judges or Clinton judges. What we have is an extraordinary group of dedicated judges doing their level best to do equal right to those appearing before them" The second half of this remark is very likely true. But the more memorable first sentence is somewhat disingenuous. Federal judges, who serve for life, are appointed by the President subject to confirmation by the Senate. This fits neatly into the American pattern of separation of powers qualified by checks and balances. The Senate hearings for Supreme Court nominees arouse great public interest, sometimes rising to fever pitch, as occurred notably in the hearings of Robert Bork, Clarence Thomas and Brett Kavanaugh. State court judges are chosen in a variety of ways, with no fewer than 39 states using some form of election for courts at some level. What the federal and state processes have in common is that they are essentially democratic, whether directly or indirectly, and largely transparent.

"Self-perpetuating oligarchy"

In Britain, by contrast, all judges are appointed in a process that is neither democratic nor transparent. Most judicial appointments for England and Wales are handled by a body known as the Judicial Appointments Commission (JAC), which

is described on its website as "an executive non-departmental public body sponsored by the Ministry of Justice." [www.judicialappointments.gov.uk.] It was set up under the Constitutional Reform Act 2005 (CRA) to make recommendations for judicial appointments. According to the JAC website: "Under the CRA, the JCA's statutory duties are to:
- select applicants solely on merit
- select only those of good character
- encourage a diverse range of applicants."
"The JAC is also required to set specific, measurable equality objectives, and publish reports on our performance against these goals." This is under the Equality Act 2010. After an elaborate highly "politically correct" process of selection, JAC Commissioners sitting as the "Selection and Character Committee ... will then recommend candidates to the Appropriate Authority (Lord Chancellor, Lord Chief Justice or Senior President of Tribunals) for appointment. The role of the Lord Chancellor, a Government minister (doubling as Secretary of State for Justice), and that of the other two "appropriate authorities," who are judges, is restricted to deciding whether to accept or reject JAC recommendations. The names of the 15 members of the JAC are published. Twelve are appointed through "open competition"— exactly how is not clear—and the other three selected by the Judges' Council or the Tribunal Judges' Council. Five of the 15 JAC members must themselves be judges. Appointment to the UK Supreme Court (UKSC) are made by a "selection commission" made up of the President and Deputy President of the UKSC itself plus a member each of the JAB and its counterparts for Scotland and Northern Ireland. Only one name is then put before the Lord Chancellor, who can only either accept or reject it, or ask for the selection to be reconsidered. If the selected person is approved by the Lord Chancellor, the Prime Minister (who apparently has no say in the matter} must recommend that person to the Queen for appointment. [CRA §§ 25–31.] There has been some criticism of this appointments system. In a 2012 article, Joshua Rozenberg

quoted from a report prepared by Chris Paterson of the think-tank CentreForum and Professor Alan Paterson of Strathclyde University: "In the UK, the appointment of a Supreme Court judge requires the direct input of up to 26 individuals, 21 of whom are judges themselves. This, say the authors, shows the 'potential danger for this branch of government to become a self-perpetuating oligarchy.'" According to Joshua Rozenberg, the report quotes Lord Justice Etherton (Master of the Rolls since 2016) "as arguing that the dominant extent to which the senior judiciary is involved in the selection of the senior judiciary is 'quite unacceptable ... for constitutional legitimacy.'" [Joshua Rozenberg (2012). "Current judicial appointments system is 'not fit for purpose', says report" Guardian, March 26, 2012.].

This whole system was set up under the CRA, which essentially represented a capitulation of the executive to the judiciary. All in all, it is a "politically correct" and less than transparent system, with strong judicial input, and no element of democracy. Quite a contrast with the various American systems of judicial selection, which generally combine transparency with democratic accountability.

The Constitutional Reform Act 2005 (CRA)

The UK's CRA opens with this cryptic provision in section 1: "This Act does not adversely affect—(a) the existing constitutional principle of the rule of law, or (b) the Lord Chancellor's existing constitutional role in relation to that principle." The meaning of § 1(a) is (deliberately?) vague. See the discussion on "the rule of law" below. As for § 1(b), it is slightly ironic, considering that the original Bill introducing this legislation into the House of Lords actually proposed abolishing the office of Lord Chancellor altogether. This provision was dropped when it was realized that it would necessitate amending literally thousands of statutes. So, the position of Lord

Chancellor was subsequently merged with that of Secretary of State for Justice, with its holder in the House of Commons.

Some of the later provisions are more worrying. § 3(1) reads as follows: "The Lord Chancellor, other Ministers of the Crown and all with responsibility for matters relating to the judiciary or otherwise to the administration of justice must uphold the continued independence of the judiciary." This provision is picked up in § 17, with a remarkable oath to be taken by the Lord Chancellor: "I, ..., do swear that in the office of Lord High Chancellor of Great Britain I will respect the rule of law, defend the independence of the judiciary and discharge my duty to ensure the provision of resources for the efficient and effective support of the courts for which I am responsible. So help me God." The key to § 3(1) is the word "must": the executive "must uphold the continued independence of the judiciary." Independence from whom? Presumably from the government itself. And the oath in § 17 reaffirms this duty. The government therefore has to swear not to encroach on the preserve of the judiciary. But, should the judges not have to take a reciprocal oath not to encroach on the proper preserve of Parliament and the executive and Parliament? That would be only fair and in keeping with the doctrine of the separation of powers. But, no such reciprocal oath exists. The only oath that judges have to take is the one laid down by the Promissory Oaths Act 1868, which reads as follows: "I, ..., do swear that I will well and truly serve our Sovereign Lady Queen Victoria in the office of, and I will do right to all manner of people after the laws and usages of this realm, without fear or favour, affection or ill will, So help me God."

This capitulation by the executive to the judiciary is undemocratic, or even anti-democratic. For, although the executive is not directly elected, it emerges from the elected House of Commons. This Act makes no attempt to challenge the sovereignty of Parliament, nor could it, nor does it try to prevent Parliament from revoking judicial decisions, which it also could not do, as that power is an integral part of the sovereignty of

Parliament. The paradox of course is that, though armed with these formidable powers, in practice the UK Parliament has failed to exercise them and in that respect has been guilty of a long-continued dereliction of duty.

The Rule of Law: Or of Lawyers?

The idea of the rule of law goes back to ancient times, though its meaning is by no means certain. The great Greek philosopher Aristotle (384–322 BCE) opined: "It is more proper that law should govern than any one of the citizens." Entrusting power to a human ruler "gives it to a wild beast, for such his appetites sometimes make him; for passion influences those who are in power, even the very best of men: therefore, law is reason without desire." [Aristotle, *Politics* 3:16.] The rule of law is therefore seen as an alternative to arbitrary power.

John Adams (1735–1826), the second president of the US, while excoriating democracy as "the most vile form of government" and "incompatible with personal security or the rights of property," championed republicanism: "A government in which all men, rich and poor, magistrates and subjects, officers and people, masters and servants, the first citizen and the last, are equally subject to the laws." He even managed to insert into the Massachusetts Constitution of 1780 his slogan, "a government of laws, and not of men" (adapted from the phrase, "Empire of laws, not of men," coined by the English political theorist James Harrington (1611–1677).] Although Harrington, was a personal friend of King Charles I's and is even reputed to have been with the King on the scaffold during Charles's execution in 1649, he was an ardent advocate of republicanism and was particularly concerned to avoid arbitrary power. In his utopian republic as described in minute detail in his book titled *The Commonwealth of Oceana* (1656) there are frequent elections at every level of government and a whole system of legislation.

To John Adams's cry of "A government of laws, and not of men," or more euphoniously, "A government not of men but of laws," an early wag retorted: "A government not of laws but of lawyers." This cynical riposte has an obvious immediate appeal. After all, a law is just words on paper, so how can it rule? Its meaning is subject to interpretation by judges, which means that it is the judges and not the law that rules.

This issue was confronted head-on by Chief Justice Charles Evans Hughes (1862–1948), to whose oft-quoted remark made as Governor of New York in 1908 I have referred previously: "We are under a Constitution, but the Constitution is what the judges say it is, and the judiciary is the safeguard of our liberty and of our property under the Constitution." The fact that the meaning of the Constitution depends on the court's interpretation clearly did not bother Hughes at all—perhaps he foresaw his future role in that capacity!

"The great object should be certainty"

The term "the rule of law" is not much in evidence in the US, but has assumed great importance in Britain. In his book titled *The Rule of Law*, published in 2010, Lord Bingham identified eight "principles" of the rule of law, the first two of which are:
- "The law must be accessible and so far as possible intelligible, clear and predictable;" and
- "Questions of legal right and liability should ordinarily be resolved by application of the law and not the exercise of discretion."

By these criteria the UK's current legal system would be unlikely to pass muster. The disarray and lack of principle, lack of clarity and lack of predictability characteristic of the law of tort which was admitted by Lord Neuberger as cited in Chapter 6, go clean against Lord Bingham's first principle. And the same applies to the law in the areas of public law and privacy as discussed in Chapters 8 and 10 respectively.

Bingham's first array of criteria necessary for the rule of law boils down to certainty, and he quotes Lord Mansfield in *Vallejo v. Wheeler* (1774) 1 Cowp 143, 153: "[I]n all mercantile transactions the great object should be certainty: ... it is of more consequence that a rule should be certain than whether the rule is established one way rather than the other." [Cited Bingham p. 38.] Without certainty, justice is at risk. The number of "yo-yo" cases is one factor militating against justice—that is, cases decided one way at first instance, reversed on appeal and then reversed back again on final appeal. The reason for the surprisingly high number of such cases is precisely the uncertainty of the law, which makes it unpredictable.

What about Lord Bingham's second principle for the rule of law, which opposes "law" to "discretion"? The term "discretion," it is important to note, applies equally to judicial discretion as to discretion exercised by the executive or anyone else. Lord Bingham quotes a picturesque illustration of this point by Lord Shaw of Dunfermline: "To remit the maintenance of constitutional right to the region of judicial discretion is to shift the foundations of freedom from the rock to the sand." [*Scott v. Scott* [1913] AC 417, 477.] If we substitute principle vs. policy for Bingham's not very dissimilar law vs. discretion, we will immediately see that those same areas of law, namely tort, public law and privacy, fail again in terms of the rule of law. [See Chapters 6, 8 and 10.]

"Parliament can legislate as it wishes"

Is there a conflict between the principle of the sovereignty of Parliament and the rule of law? In discussing this in Chapter 14, "The Elusive British Constitution," we encountered those who opined not only that there is such a conflict but also that, if not resolved, it "could generate a constitutional crisis." [Bogdanor

(2006). "The Sovereignty of Parliament or the Rule of Law?", Magna Carta Lecture, 15 June 2006, p. 20.)] [Quoted Bingham p 161] This is simply incorrect. The sovereignty of Parliament means that Parliament can pass any laws it likes, subject to no constraints of morality, human rights, or the rule of law, however defined. I have cited Lord Reid in *Madzimbamuto v. Lardner-Burke* (1969) to this effect. And I was pleased to see that Lord Bingham, after carefully examining several arguments to the effect that the sovereignty of Parliament is no more, came to this eminently sensible conclusion: "Thus, for those who have followed me this far, we reach these conclusions. We live in a society dedicated to the rule of law; in which Parliament has power, subject to limited, self-imposed restraints, to legislate as it wishes; in which Parliament may therefore legislate in a way which infringes the rule of law; and in which the judges, consistently with their constitutional duty to administer justice according to the laws and usages of the realm, cannot fail to give effect to such legislation if it is clearly and unambiguously expressed." (p. 168).

"Unjust, oppressive or pernicious laws"

As mentioned above, the term "rule of law" is not often encountered in the US, but we do come across some sentiments relevant to it. For example, James Wilson, a leading delegate to the Constitutional Convention in 1787 and a subsequent Associate Justice of the US Supreme Court, is on record as saying: "Laws may be unjust, may be unwise, may be dangerous, may be destructive; and yet not be so unconstitutional as to justify the judges in refusing to give them effect." Another prominent delegate to the Convention, George Mason, similarly remarked that, unless a law was unconstitutional, a court could not strike it down even if it was "unjust, oppressive or pernicious." Mason was one of the only three delegates who refused to sign the Constitution, but he was the chief draftsman of the Virginia Declaration of Rights, on which the United States Bill of Rights was modeled. His attitude to slavery was likewise ambivalent. He was a big slave owner who opposed the African slave trade but (unsuccessfully) proposed a measure in the Virginia House of Delegates requiring freed slaves to leave the state within a year or be sold at auction. [Wallenstein, Peter (1994). "Flawed Keepers of the Flame: The Interpreters of George Mason." *The Virginia Magazine of History and Biography*, 102. Virginia Historical Society. pp. 229–260.] The reason for Mason's stand on "unjust, oppressive or pernicious" laws may possibly have been his desire to protect slavery, which is implicitly sanctioned by the Constitution.

The American Founding Fathers and Framers of the Constitution were generally imbued with the ideas of natural law and natural rights, as can be seen reflected in the Declaration of Independence. But, once the US Constitution was ensconced, its authority superseded that of natural law. This is in a sense parallel to the principle of the sovereignty of Parliament in English law, under which no court can challenge any Act of Parliament, however repugnant or even unreasonable it may be.

18

ROUNDUP

This chapter is a bird's-eye view of the main conclusions contained in this book.

- **UK: Sovereignty of Parliament**—The fundamental bedrock principle of the UK Constitution is the sovereignty of Parliament, or, strictly speaking, of the Crown-in Parliament, or Queen-in-Parliament. What this means is that a law passed by the House of Commons and the House of Lords, with the consent of the monarch, becomes an Act of Parliament, which is the highest form of law known to the UK Constitution. In the famous words of A.V. Dicey: "The principle of Parliamentary sovereignty means neither more nor less than this, namely that Parliament thus defined has, under the English Constitution, the right to make or unmake any law whatever, and further, that no person or body is recognized by the law of England as having a right to override or set aside the legislation of Parliament." This has been the position for at least 700 years and is still the law today. [Chapter 1, "The Sovereignty of Parliament."]

- **UK: Revocation**—As an integral part of the sovereignty of Parliament, Parliament can by statute revoke, i.e. cancel, the decision of any court for any reason—or none. The best-known use of this nuclear power was the passing of the War Damage Act 1965 to revoke the judicial decision of the House of Lords in *Burmah Oil v. Lord Advocate* (1965). [Chapter 1, "United Kingdom: The Sovereignty of Parliament."]

- **UK: Separation of Powers**—"It is a feature of the peculiarly British conception of the separation of powers that Parliament, the executive and the courts have each their distinct and largely exclusive domain. Parliament has a legally unchallengeable right to make whatever laws it likes. The executive carries on the administration of the country in accordance with the powers conferred on it by law. The courts interpret the laws, and see to it that they are obeyed." (Lord Mustill). In practice, however, the courts have increasingly encroached on the domain of the executive and even of Parliament. In the 1990s some judges took it upon themselves to claim that the courts could declare an Act of Parliament void in certain circumstances. This is completely contrary to the fundamental constitutional principle of the sovereignty of Parliament. In response, the future Lord Chancellor, Lord Irvine of Lairg, in 1995 asserted the correct principle of the "constitutional imperative of judicial self-restraint" based on "the democratic imperative" under which the judges must respect the democratic mandate of the other two branches of government. [Chapter 1, "United Kingdom: The Sovereignty of Parliament."]

- **US: Separation of Powers**—The US Constitution allocates power between the three branches of government: the legislature (Congress), the executive (the President) and the judiciary (the law courts). It is commonly believed that in the US these institutions constitute three coequal branches of government. The US Constitution certainly did set up a system of separation of powers, coupled with checks and balances between the three branches. But nowhere does it say that the three branches are equal. In practice, at federal level, the power of the US Supreme Court has come to surpass that of either the legislature (Congress) or the executive (the President). This has been achieved largely through *judicial review*, which enables the Supreme Court (and all other federal courts) to set aside Acts of Congress and executive decisions alike that it deems to be unconstitutional. Some such decisions of the US Supreme Court have been criticized as constituting "judicial activism," and the different schools of thought among the justices have different criteria for interpreting the Constitution and other legislation, but it would be hard to find an example where a member of the US Supreme Court wrote a completely arbitrary opinion. The important American doctrine of *Chevron* deference to the decisions of executive agencies has no parallel in the UK. [Chapter 2, "United States: A Despotic Branch," & Part I, "Supreme Law: Conclusion."]

- **Early English Codification**—Contrary to widespread belief, common law did not develop out of "judge-made law," but out of legislation and indeed out of statutory codes. Legislation is prior to the common law both in time and status. The earliest Anglo-Saxon statutory codes date from around the year 600 and continued for about 700 years. [Chapter 3, "From Codified Statutes to Common Law."]

- **The Era of Principle in English Law**—The period from 1285 to 1932 was one dominated by the "forms of action," particularly "trespass on the case" or "action on the case," for negligence, and "assumpsit" for breach of contract. The medieval principle protecting professionals and skilled tradesmen acting conscientiously even if they caused injury in the process has survived in some respects down to the present day. Concurrent liability is another issue that is still with us, which has been more successfully tackled in

America than in Britain. [Chapter 4, "The Era of Principle in English Law."]

• **Maxims or Minims?**—Bolstering up the array of "forms of action" writs and pleadings was an impressive assemblage of principles encapsulated in pithy Legal Maxims, some of which still survive today and are discussed in a modern context as well. Equity, which had its own Maxims, was a further stabilizing factor of English law prior to 1932. [Chapter 5, "Maxims or Minims?"]

• **The Snail in the Bottle**—*Donoghue v. Stevenson* (1932), the well-known case of the snail in the bottle, marked a departure from some 1300 years of codified and principled English law and opened the floodgates of judge-made law. Lord Neuberger (Head of the UK Supreme Court 2012–2017) recently described UK tort cases as appearing "to demonstrate a notable degree of disarray and a marked lack of reliable principle." Yet he concluded that "in some areas at least, it my be more helpful to abandon principle and to take a stand on policy." "Policy" here refers essentially to judge-made law, which of course flies in the face of the bedrock constitutional principle of the sovereignty of Parliament. Lord Neuberger recognizes that principle embodies predictability, logical cohesion and clarity, which he admits "are vitally important ingredients of the rule of law." In these circumstances it is hard to see what justification there is for judicial policy-making, alias judge-made law. The vacuum created by Parliament's dereliction of duty in failing to legislate even in the face of earnest entreaties from the judiciary can explain judge-made law to some extent. But Parliament's torpor is certainly not a sufficient justification of the rise of judicial policy-making at the expense of principle. [Chapter 6, "United Kingdom: The Snail in the Bottle".]

- **The Exploding Parcel**—By contrast with *Donoghue v. Stevenson*, which opened the floodgates to judge-made law in Britain, in the US neither *Palsgraf v. Long Island Railroad Co.* nor any other state court decision had the same effect. This chapter takes a comparative look at a number of British and American tort cases which illustrate this crucial difference. Even supposedly activist California judges like Roger Traynor and Mathew Tobriner turn out upon examination to have far more respect for principle, statute and pseudo-black letter law (i.e. the Restatements) than their English counterparts in the post-snail era. [Chapter 7, "United States: The Exploding Parcel."]

- **Judicial Review: UK**—A senior UK judge is quoted as taking great pride in the judges' achievement of "very substantial growth in domestic judicial review" with its "substantial macro-social and economic implications." However, he does not name any cases or the benefits that have supposedly flowed from them. On the contrary, legislating from the bench not only flies in the face of parliamentary sovereignty, but is also undemocratic or even anti-democratic. It also encroaches on the preserve of the executive, which again is undemocratic. And when judges announce new "rules" or "tests" for any legal issue, the wording tends to be woolly and imprecise. Moreover, court decisions in judicial review and also in human rights and public law generally have often been "politically correct" and have tended to favor certain special interest groups, including asylum seekers, illegal immigrants, terrorist suspects and even convicted killers. [Chapter 8, "United

Kingdom: The Constitutional Imperative of Judicial Self-Restraint."]

- **Judicial Review: US**—The important doctrine of "Chevron deference" to executive agencies enunciated by a unanimous US Supreme Court in 1984 contrasts markedly with the developments in the UK. The decision in the leading case of *Brown v. Board of Education* (1954) was probably an example of "liberal" judicial activism, while decisions such as *Citizens United v. FEC* (2010) may be regarded as examples of "conservative" judicial activism. But the conservative-liberal split is by no means invariable. For example, in the highly controversial decisions allowing flag-burning as an expression of protected speech, for example, there were "conservative" and "liberal" justices on both sides. Ironically, perhaps, belief in judicial self-restraint and deference to the other branches of government is much more prevalent in America than in Britain. [Chapter 9, "United States: Umpires or Empire-Builders?"]

- **Privacy**—When the UK Parliament failed to respond to the earnest judicial entreaties in the *Gorden Kaye* case in 1990 to enact statutory protection of privacy, the judiciary took it upon itself to fill the gap. This was done by a combination of two different mechanisms—by an extension of the ancient equitable cause of action of breach of confidence, and, on the other by an expansion of the scope of ECHR Article 8 providing a right to respect for "private and family life." However, neither of these extensions, either separately or together, succeeds in filling the vacuum left by the lack of an actual "breach of privacy" cause of action. As a result, there is still no real protection of privacy under English law. The American position is quite different. There is protection of privacy in federal law under the US Constitution, plus a good deal of state legislation, not to mention the authoritative Restatement (Second) of the Law of Torts § 652. [Chapter 10, "Privacy: A Strange Royal Case."]

- **Defamation**—In this area, the difference between English and American law is such that in 2010 the US Congress actually passed legislation, signed into law by President Obama, which prohibits domestic US courts from recognizing or enforcing English defamation judgments that are inconsistent with the First Amendment to the US Constitution. The title of this law says it all: the SPEECH Act, standing for the Securing the Protection of our Enduring and Established Constitutional Heritage Act. The Act was intended to counter "libel tourism" and the "chilling effect" of English defamation judgments on the freedom of speech protected by the First Amendment. The Defamation Act passed by the UK Parliament in 2013 has successfully addressed "libel tourism" but has failed to cure the "chilling effect" problem. (Chapter 11, "Defamation.")

- **Rights vs. Rights**—As is not sufficiently recognized, every human rights or civil rights case involves rights on both sides. Courts often say, for example, that they need to strike a balance between individual rights and national security, but it is important to realize that national security is not just some abstract term but actually represents the individual human rights of thousands or even millions of law-abiding citizens. There is an even more direct clash of rights against rights when two different rights are pitted against each other, such as the clash between privacy and freedom of speech, or the free exercise of religion and the rights of protected minorities such as gay and transgender people. Both the UK and the US have a problem upholding traditional fundamental rights such as freedom of speech and religion against protection of minorities such as gays, with the danger that the latter are being accorded not equal rights but special privileges. [Chapter 12, "Rights vs. Rights."]

- **The Three Cokes**—This is a fun chapter about Sir Edward Coke (1552–1634), the famous English judge, jurist and politician, who was a Marxist at heart—not Karl Marx but Groucho, whose slogan was: "These are my principles—and if you don't like them, I have others." Coke (pronounced "Cook") had three distinct incarnations with three very different sets of values: Coke I—a fierce upholder of the royal prerogative; Coke II—a champion of judicial power over the Crown and Parliament alike; and Coke III—a vociferous champion of Parliament against the Crown. One of Coke II's best-known decisions as a judge was *Dr. Bonham's Case* (1610), in which Coke arrogated to himself the right to set aside an Act of Parliament if it is "against common right and reason." This was not the law then—and never had been—and is also not the law now, When it shows sign of recrudescence from time to time, as it did in the UK in the 1990s, it is important to scotch it firmly, as, to their credit, was done by Lord Irvine of Lairg, Lord and Lord Keith of Kinkel, among others. Coke II must have been well aware all along of the true ancient bedrock principle of the sovereignty of Parliament, which he would espouse with a vengeance as Coke III. [Chapter 13, "Cooking the Books."]

Some fallacies about the British constitution— This chapter is devoted to countering some common (and uncommon) fallacies about the British Constitution. These include:

- The effect of a possible veto by the Queen of a Bill passed by both Houses of Parliament.
- Whether Dicey's account of the Constitution is still valid.
- Whether the Human Rights Act 1998 has "higher law status".
- Whether the sovereignty of Parliament was abrogated by the UK's membership of the European Union.
- Why some referendums are purely advisory while others are legally binding.

The common mistaken belief that the UK needs a written or codified constitution. [Chapter 14, "The Elusive British Constitution."]

- The Electoral College established by the US Constitution to elect the President is often blamed for being undemocratic. To win the presidency you have to have a majority of electoral votes, regardless of whether or not you win the popular vote. So the Electoral College is blamed when the successful candidate does not win a majority of the popular vote, as happened, for example, in the 2016 election. However, this is a fallacy. The true reason why it is possible to win the White House with a minority of the popular vote is not the Electoral College, but the winner-take-all system of voting—which is *not* mandated by the Constitution. An easy solution to the problem of the "democratic deficit"—which does not require a constitutional amendment—is to split the electoral vote proportionately with the popular vote in each state. So, in a state with, say, 20 electoral votes, if Candidate A polls three fourths of the popular vote and Candidate B polls one fourth, the electoral vote should be split 15–5 in favour of Candidate A, instead of the present system under which Candidate A gets all 20 electoral votes. [Chapter 15, "The Democratic Deficit: The Electoral College?"]

- Though statutory codes formed the lifeblood of English law
  for some 700 years starting from around the year 600, the
  Government subsequently set its face doggedly against
  codification. This remains the case today, though punctuated
  by periodic false starts. In 1998, while making no secret of
  his "general disbelief in codes," Lord Bingham nevertheless
  supported codification as bringing clarity, accessibility,
  coherence, consistency and certainty to criminal law. But, if
  codification has these major advantages for criminal law,
  why should it not be equally beneficial in other areas? The
  advantages of codification can be proved in two ways—
  negatively, by examining the state of disarray of such areas
  of UK law as tort, public law and privacy, which are sorely
  in need of help; and positively, by examining the vibrant
  effect of various forms of codification on US law. [Chapter
  16, "Cracking the Code."]

- Although the British Constitution has at its heart the
  fundamental principle of the sovereignty of Parliament,
  while the US Constitution merely accords Congress the
  legislative power without elevating it above the other two
  branches of government, yet greater deference is paid by the
  judiciary to the legislature in the US than in the UK. And the
  UK's Constitutional Reform Act 2005, in which the
  executive effectively capitulates to the judiciary, is essentially
  undemocratic, or even anti-democratic—for, although the
  executive is not directly elected, it emerges from the elected
  House of Commons. [Chapter 17, "A Parade of Paradoxes."]

19

CONCLUSION

The UK's Law Reform (Contributory Negligence) Act 1945 is a good example of the superiority of statute law over judge-made law. The Act replaced the all-or-nothing rule of contributory negligence with that of comparative negligence. Under the Act, where a defendant was mainly responsible for the plaintiff's injury but the plaintiff's negligence was partly responsible for his own injury as well, the plaintiff would only lose a proportion of his damages as assessed by the court. So, for example, a plaintiff might lose 25% of his damages for failing to wear a seatbelt, once that had become mandatory. However, under the old rule a plaintiff got no damages at all and lost the case if he was responsible for his own injury to even the slightest degree. This manifestly unfair rule is usually traced back to an old English case called *Butterfield v. Forrester* ER 926 (1809), which was probably not actually intending to establish a new rule at all, but, ironically, came across the Atlantic as part of a "reception statute" and became embedded in statutory codes like that of California. But, such is the respect accorded in the US to legislation, and especially to statutory codes, that for the California Supreme Court to abrogate the all-or-nothing rule and replace it with comparative negligence was a major production—even though 25 states had already switched by means of legislation. See my discussion of the relevant case, *Li v. Yellow Cab Co. of California* 13 Cal 3d 808 (1975), in Chapter 7.

Another rare example of a British statutory triumph over America is the Abortion Act 1967, which started life (no pun intended) as a private member's Bill introduced into the House of Commons by a determined David (now Lord) Steel. As a result of the democratic stamp of approval obtained in this way, abortion

439

has aroused very little controversy in Britain over the years (except in Northern Ireland, where the Abortion Act does not apply.) Justice Ruth Bader Ginsburg, a staunch advocate for abortion rights, herself recognizes the value of a democratic legislative solution. She commented that the highly controversial US Supreme Court decision in *Roe v. Wade*, 410 US 113 (1973), which made abortion rights a constitutional issue, terminated "a nascent democratic movement to liberalize abortion law." And: "heavy-handed judicial intervention was difficult to justify and appears to have provoked, not resolved, conflict." Had abortion been legalized in the US by legislation rather than by the Supreme Court, it would, as Bader Ginsburg realized, have been much less controversial, because it would have had the democratic credentials which it currently lacks. [See Chapter 10, "Privacy."]

These two British legislative triumphs are rare indeed, but they are isolated, stand-alone enactments. The UK Parliament regularly passes hundreds of stand-alone statutes every year but it has remained largely impervious to requests from the courts to legislate even on pressing matters, such as privacy and the so-called defense of illegality. The earnest entreaties of the Court of Appeal in *Gorden Kaye v. Robertson* [1990] EWCA Civ 21] for statutory protection for privacy fell on deaf ears, leading to a wholly unsatisfactory judge-made solution. [See Chapter 10, "Privacy."] As for the defense of illegality, the Law Commission specifically recommended that, except where a trust has been set up, nothing should be done: "We think that the law should be left to develop through the case law." [www.lawcom.gov.uk/project/illegality/.] The result has been far from satisfactory. [See Chapters 5 & 16.]

Above all, despite a long early history of statutory codes stretching from Ethelbert's Code from about the year 600 to the Second Statute of Westminster of 1285, in the reign of King Edward I, the British Parliament and Government has now long stubbornly resisted codification of the law, with occasional false starts. In 1998 Lord Bingham recognized the benefits of clarity, accessibility, coherence, consistency and certainty as flowing from the codification of the criminal law, and there is no reason why these same qualities should not inure to the codification of any other branch of law. In fact branches of English law such as tort, public law and privacy are probably in greater need of these qualities than criminal law.

The US has however taken to codification, at both state and federal level, with gusto. The main codified enactments are as follows:

- The US Constitution—The United States federal constitution. [See Arnheim (2018).]
- The United States Code (USC)
- The Code of Federal Regulations (CFR)
- Federal Rules of Civil Procedure—also adopted by 35 states
- State Constitutions
- State Statutory Codes
- Uniform Commercial Code (UCC)
- Model Penal Code (MPC)
- Restatements

These sources provide US law, federal and state alike, with a really solid underpinning of principle encapsulated in codified legislation—including the Restatements, which I would characterize as "pseudo-black letter" law. As we have seen repeatedly, the legal culture of the United States is very much against judge-made law or "legislating from the bench." Of course, that does not mean that those things never occur, but that judges, especially state court judges, have to be extra-careful before breaking with long-established principle encapsulated in legislation.

SELECT BIBLIOGRAPHY

This bibliography contains only those secondary sources actually mentioned in the text of the book.

Adams, Kristen David (2007). "Blaming the Mirror: The Restatements and the Common Law." *Indiana Law Review* 40 (2) 205–270.

Arnheim, Michael (1994). (editor) *The Common Law* (International Library of Essays in Law & Legal Theory), Dartmouth.

Arnheim, Michael (1994). (author) (1999). (with District Judge Christopher Tromans) *Civil Courts Practice & Procedure Handbook*, Butterworths.

_____. (2004a). *Handbook of Human Rights Law,* London, Kogan Page.

_____. (2004b). *Principles of the Common Law*, London, Gerald Duckworth.

_____. (2004c). The Human Right to Press Freedom, *"New Law Journal,* January 23, 2004.

_____. (2004d). The Rule of Law or the Rule of Lawyers? *"New Law Journal,* May 21, 2004.

_____. (2011). Five Centuries of Legal Thinking, *" The Eagle,* Cambridge, St. John's College, Cambridge.

_____. (2015). *The Problem with Human Rights Law*, London, Civitas.

_____. (2016). *Two Models of Government*, Exeter, Imprint Academic.

_____. (2017). *A Practical Guide to Your Human Rights & Civil Liberties*, London, Straightforward Publishing.

_____. (2018a). *US Constitution for Dummies*, 2ed, New York, John Wiley.

_____. (2018b). 'A Conspiracy Too Far? *"New Law Journal,* August 2018.

_____. (2018c). Lord Neuberger's Salutary Warning, *"New Law Journal,* November 2018.

_____. (2018d). The Gay Wedding Cake Saga, "*New Law Journal*, December 2018.

Baker, J.H. (1971), New Light on Slade's Case," *Cambridge Law Journal* Vol. 29 Issue 2, pp. 213–36.]

Baker, J.H. & Milsom, S.F.C. (B&M) (1986). *Sources of English Legal History: Private Law to 1750*, London, Butterworths.

Bede, the Venerable (731). *Ecclesiastical History of the English People,* ed. Judith McClure, Oxford's World Classics, 2008, Oxford, Oxford University Press.

Beever, Allan (2013). *The Law of Private Nuisance*, Oxford, Hart Publishing.

Bentham, Jeremy (1998). *"Legislator of the World": Writings on Codification, Law & Education,* eds. Philip Schofield & Jonathan Harris, Oxford, Clartendon Press.

Bingham, Tom (2010). *The Rule of Law,* London, Penguin Books.

Bingham. Tom (1998). Speech at Dinner for HM Judges, The Mansion House, London, July 22, 1998. www.judiciary.gov.uk/publications_-media/speeches/pre–2004/mnsion98.htm.

Blackstone, Sir William (1765–69). *Commentaries on the Laws of England, 4 vols,* (1979 reprint), Chicago, University of Chicago Press.

Bogdanor, Vernon (2019). *Beyond Brexit: Towards a British Constitution,* London, I.B. Tauris.

Broom, Herbert (1845). *A Selection of Legal Maxims,* Philadelphia, T. & J.W. Johnson.

Burnham (2006). *Introduction to the Law and Legal System of the United States,* 4th ed., St. Paul, Thomson West, 2006.

Cardi, W. Jonathan (2011). "The Hidden Legacy of Palsgraf: Modern Duty Law in Microcosm." *Boston University Law Review*, Vol. 91, 1873–1913.

Chapman, Matthew (2010). *The Snail and the Ginger Beer.* London, Wildy, Simmonds & Hill Publishing.

Coke, Sir Edward (1628–44). *Institutes of the Laws of England,* London, Society of Stationers.

Dicey, A.V. (1885). *The Study of the Law of theConstitution,* London, Macmillan.

English, Rosalind (2014). "Rendition to Libya an 'act of state' and therefore non-justiciable". ukhumanrightsblog.com – 14 January 2014.

Farnsworth, Ward (2016), "The Economic Loss Rule," 50 *Valparaiso University Law Review*, p. 545.

Federalist Papers (1788). By James Madison, Alexander Hamilton and John Jay, (online reprint) The Avalon Project, avalon.law.yale.edu/subject_menus/fed.asp.

Gewirtz, Paul (2005). "So who are the activists?" *The New York Times*, July 6, 2005.

Griffith, J.A.G. (1983). "Constitutional and administrative law," in P. Archer & A. Martin (eds.), *More Law Reform Now*, Chichester, B. Rose..

Griffith, J.A.G. (2000). "The Brave New World of Sir John Laws," *Modern Law Review*, Vol 63, Issue 2.

Griffith, J.A.G. (2001). "The common law and the political constitution," *Law Quarterly Review.*

Griffith, J.A.G. (2010). *The Politics of the Judiciary*, London, Fontana Press.

Hallifax, Samuel (1774). *An Analysis of the Civil Law,* Cambridge, University of Cambridge Press.

Holland, Thomas Erskine (1870). *Essays Upon the Form of the Law,* (2016 reprint), London, Palala Press.

Hough, Carole (2014*). "An Ald Reht":* Essays on Anglo-Saxon Law, Cambridge, Cambridge Scholars.

Ibbetson, David & D.J. (2001*). A Historical Introduction to the Law of Obligations*, Oxford, Oxford University Press.

Irvine of Lairg, Lord (1996). "Judges and decision makers: the theory and practice of Wednesbury review," [1996] *Public Law*, p. 1, reprinted as Chapter 9 of *Human Rights, Constitutional Law and the Development of the English Legal System*, Oxford, Hart Publishing, 2003, p. 135ff.

Irvine of Lairg, Lord (2003). *Human Rights, Constitutional Law and the Development of the English Legal System,* Oxford, Hart Publishing.

Irvine of Lairg, Lord (2011). "A British Interpretation of Convention Rights," Bingham Centre for the Rule of Law. London, British Institute of International & Comparative Law.

Johnson, Rebecca (2014). "The Tarasoff Rule: The Implications of Interstate Variation and Gaps in Professional Training," Journal of American Academy of Psychiatry and tge Law, 42(4): 469.

Lee, Maria (2003). "What is private nuisance?" *Law Quarterly Review* 119 (2) 298–325.

Levin, Mark R. (2006). *The Men in Black,* Washington DC, Regnery Publishing Inc.

Levin, Mark R. (2019). *Unfreedom of the Press,* New York, Threshold Editions.

Locke, John (1690). *Two Treatises of Government,* ed. Peter Laslett ed., Cambridge, Cambridge University Press 1988.

Lunney, M. & Oliphant, K. (2013). *Tort Law: Text & Materials,* Oxford, Oxford University Press.

Madison, James; Hamilton, Alexander; and Jay, John (1788). *The Federalist Papers,* (online reprint) The Avalon Project, avalon.law.yale. edu/subject_menus/fed.asp.

Maitland, Frederic (1909). *The Forms of Action at Common Law,* Cambridge, Cambridge University Press.

McBride, Nicholas & Bagshaw, Roderick (2012) *Tort Law,* 4ed, London, Pearson.

McCain, John (2002). *Worth the Fighting For,* New York, Random House.

Miles, Thomas J. & Sunstein, Cass R. (2006). "The Real Judicial Activists," *The American Prospect,* December 17, 2006.

Miles, Thomas J. & Sunstein, Cass R. (2006). "Do Judges Make Regulatory Policy? – An Empirical Investigation of Chevron," *73 University of Chicago Law Review,* 823.

Milsom, S.F.C. (1981). *Historical Foundations of the Common Law,* London, Lexis Law Publishing.

Milsom, S.F.C. (2003). *A Natural History of the Common Law,* New York, Columbia University Press.

Milsom, S.F.C. (2010). "Plucknett, Theodore Frank Thomas (1897–1965)," *Oxford Dictionary of National Biography,* Oxford, Oxford University Press.

Miles, Thomas J. & Sunstein, Cass R. (2006). "Do Judges Make Regulatory Policy? – An Empirical Investigation of Chevron," *73 University of Chicago Law Review,* 823.]

Montesquieu (1748). *The Spirit of the Laws,* Anne M. Cohler ed., Cambridge Univ. Press 1989.

Neuberger, David (2017). "Implications of Tort Law decisions," Address to Northern Ireland Personal Injury Bar's Inaugural Conference, County Down, www.supremecourt.uk/docs/speech-170513.pdf.

Oliver, Lisi (2002). *The Beginnings of English Law*, Toronto, University of Toronto Press.

Owen, David (2009), "Figuring Foreseeability", 44 *Wake Forest Law Review*, 1277.

Palmer, Robert C. (1993). *English Law in the Age of the Black Death: A Transformation of Governance and Law, 1348–81*, Chapel Hill & London, University of North Carolina Press.

Peabody, Bruce G. (2007). "Legislating from the Bench: A Definition and a Defense," *11 Lewis & Clark L. Rev.* 185.

Pollock, Frederick (1887). (2018 reprint), *Law of Torts*, London, Forgotten Books.

Posner, Richard A. (1993). *Cardozo: A Study in Reputation*, Chicago, University of Chicago Press.

Reynolds, Osborne M., Jr. (1992). "Of Time and Feedlots: The effect of Spur Industries on Nuisance Law," 41 *Washington University Journal of Urban & Contemporary Law*, 75.

Sander, Richard & Stuart Taylor, Jr. (2012). *Mismatch: How Affirmative Action Hurts Students It's Intended to Help, and Why Universities Won't Admit it*, New York, Basic Books.

St. Germain, Christopher (1530). (1874 reprint). *The Doctor and Student*, Lonang Institute, lonang.com/library/reference/stgermain-doctor-and-student/.

Scarman, Leslie (1967). "Codification and Judge-Made Law: A Problem of Coexistence," *Indiana Law Journal*, Vol. 42, Issue 3.

Simpson, A.W.B. (1987). *History of the Common Law of Contract*, Oxford, Clarendon Press.

Smith, Jeremiah (1895). "The Use of Maxims in Jurisprudence," *Harvard Law Review*, vol. 9, No. 1, pp. 13–26.

Smith, Sir Thomas (1562–65). *De Republica Anglorum*, (edited Mary Dewar, 2009), Cambridge, Cambridge University Press.

Stephen, Henry John (1824). *Treatise on Pleading in Civil Actions*, London, Joseph Butterworth & Son.

Stephen, Sir James Fitzjames (2010 reprint). *History of the Criminal Law of England*, London, Franklin Classics Trade Press.

Stevens, John Paul (2014). *Six Amendments: How and Why We Should Change the Constitution*, Boston, Little, Brown.

Stevens, Robert (2012). *Torts and Rights*, Oxford, Oxford University Press.

Stubbs, William (1874–78). *The Constitutional History of England, 3 vols,* Cambridge, Cambridge University Press.

Sugarman, Stephen (1996). "Assumption of Risk,: 31 *Val. U.L. Rev.*

Sunstein, Cass R. (2004). "Did Brown Matter? *The New Yorker,* May 3. 2004.

Townshend, John (1872). *A Treatise on the Wrongs Called Slander and Libel,* (2016 reprint), London, Wentworth Press.

Twerski, Aaron D. (2009). "Negligence per se and res ipsa loquitur: kissing cousins," *Wake Forest Law Review.*

Vile, M.J.C. (1998). *Constitutionalism and the Separation of Powers,* 2d ed., Indianapolis, Indiana, Liberty Fund Inc.

Waldron, Jeremy (2013). "Separation of Powers in Thought and Practice?" 54 *Boston College Law Review.*

Watt, Graeme (2017). "The Coronation Oath," *Ecclesiastical Law Journal,* September 2017, p. 325.

Williams, Ian (2006). "Dr. Bonham's Case and 'void' statutes," *Journal of Legal History,* vol. 27, 2006, 111–128.

Winfield, Percy (2000 reprint). *The Chief Sources of English Legal History,* London, Beard Books.

Woolf, Harry (1995). *Droit Public—*English Style, *"Public Law* p. 57.

Wormald, Patrick (1999). *The Making of English Law: King Alfred to the Twelfth Century, Vol I: Legislation and its Limits,* Oxford, Blackwell.

Wormald, Patrick (2005). *The First Code of English Law,* Canterbury, The Canterbury Commemoration Society.

INDEX

ABOUT THE AUTHOR

D r. Michael Arnheim is a practicing London Barrister and Sometime Fellow of St. John's College, Cambridge. He started life as a Classicist, and his Cambridge Ph.D. dissertation was published as a book by the Oxford University Press. He was then elected a Fellow of St. John's College, where he did a good deal of teaching as well as research. At the age of 31 he was invited to take up the position of full Professor and Head of the Department of Classics back at his old university in South Africa. He returned to Britain, where he was called to the Bar in 1988. He has combined his legal practice with teaching and writing, including the book *US Constitution for Dummies,* published by Wiley, which is now in its second edition. The present book is Dr. Arnheim's 21st published book. For more information see https://en.wikipedia.org/wiki/Michael_Arnheim.